"In the current debates over the authority of the Bible and the truth of the Christian faith, the historicity of Adam and the fall has taken a prominent role. These doctrines have been challenged by some scientific theories, and some theologians have (as often before) been caught up in an unseemly scramble to keep up with them. But if we abandon the Christian belief that we fell in Adam, by what right do we maintain that we are saved in Christ? These doctrines are 'threads in a seamless garment,' in the felicitous words of Madueme and Reeves, editors of *Adam, the Fall, and Original Sin*. They and the other authors of this book speak with real cogency about these matters, giving their readers a substantial basis for assurance that Adam really existed, that we fell in him, and that we can trust in Jesus to undo what Adam did."

—**John Frame**, Reformed Theological Seminary

"Both on the biblical surface and in the Christian tradition, the historical existence of Adam and the entry of sin into the world through him are taught or assumed. This volume demonstrates that these are not merely surface appearances and cannot simply be consigned to tradition. Aimed at a Protestant evangelical readership and those who would surrender these beliefs, the book persuasively argues that we should not demur from the traditional interpretation of Scripture. Whatever readers make of the detail of the arguments presented in this volume, they will come away sobered by the sense of what is at stake."

—**Stephen Williams**, Union Theological College, Belfast

"This is a welcome defense of classical doctrines of the historicity of Adam and the reality of original sin. It is occasioned by the increasing denials of both of these, even in evangelical circles. The authors of the book's essays marshal new and convincing arguments as they address the new challenges to these doctrines. I highly recommend this book."

—**David M. Howard Jr.**, Bethel University

ADAM,

THE FALL,

and ORIGINAL SIN

Theological, Biblical, and Scientific Perspectives

EDITED BY

HANS MADUEME *and* MICHAEL REEVES

Baker Academic
a division of Baker Publishing Group
Grand Rapids, Michigan

Published by Baker Academic
a division of Baker Publishing Group
P.O. Box 6287, Grand Rapids, MI 49516-6287
www.bakeracademic.com

Printed in the United States of America

Library of Congress Cataloging-in-Publication Data
Adam, the fall, and original sin : theological, biblical, and scientific perspectives / Hans Madueme and Michael Reeves, editors.
    pages cm
    Includes bibliographical references and index.
    ISBN 978-0-8010-3992-8 (pbk.)
    1. Sin, Original. 2. Adam (Biblical figure) 3. Fall of man. I. Madueme, Hans, 1975– editor.
BT720.A33 2014
233'.14—dc23   2014021973

14   15   16   17   18   19   20   7   6   5   4   3   2   1

Contents

Introduction

ADAM UNDER SIEGE

Setting the Stage

Hans Madueme and Michael Reeves

Adam seems today a figment of ancient imagination. His ghost still haunts the edifice of original sin, but the Augustinian structure is falling apart, crumbling, gone with the wind. Emil Brunner linked its underlying patristic picture of time and space with the centaur of mythology, something like a Brothers Grimm fairy tale; such notions, he wrote, have "irrevocably been swept away, even for the most orthodox people."[1] Affirming Adam's historicity in the twenty-first century is thus a quaint, but hopeless, attempt "to place the Augustinian 'Adam in Paradise' in a post-Copernican world." Of course, we can choose to defend the traditional Adamic narrative with the careful rhetoric of anxiety-ridden theological guardians, but all that noise is pathetically "quixotic and reactionary"—much ado about nothing.[2] So goes the diagnosis of Brunner, a faithful spokesperson for modern theology. After Darwin the doctrines of the fall and original sin have become simply incredible for many people today.

What is perhaps surprising is that even evangelicals are increasingly losing faith in these classical doctrines. They are looking for new ways to make sense of Adam in Scripture. In 2007 Francis Collins, now director of the National Institutes of Health, was awarded a large grant from the Templeton Foundation

---

1. Emil Brunner, *Christian Doctrine of Creation and Redemption*, trans. Olive Wyon (Philadelphia: Westminster Press, 1952), 48.
2. Ibid., 49.

to launch his new organization BioLogos.[3] Its mission is to address "the escalating culture war between science and faith" and to model a better way:
"the harmony of science and faith" (see www.biologos.org). BioLogos stands
on firm ground since this approach embodies a long tradition that stretches
back to the natural philosophy of the seventeenth and eighteenth centuries.
This ground has become slippery, however, and controversy soon followed
when BioLogos raised questions about the historical reality of Adam and Eve.[4]

Bruce Waltke, the noted evangelical Old Testament scholar, resigned from
Reformed Theological Seminary (RTS, Orlando) after recording an interview
explaining how he reconciled his belief in theistic evolution with his interpretation of Genesis 1–3. In an excerpt of the interview, published on the
BioLogos website on March 24, 2010, Waltke warned that evangelicals who
reject the overwhelming consensus for evolution are in danger of becoming
a "cult."[5] In Reformed circles and within broader conservative Protestant
theology, those were fighting words. Although Waltke eventually clarified his
unflinching commitment to Adam's historicity, the fallout led to his resigna-
tion from his position at RTS (however, he was soon hired as distinguished
professor of the Old Testament at Knox Theological Seminary).

Not long after, another interview surfaced, this one by evangelical Old
Testament professor Tremper Longman. In the video, he cautioned against a
"very highly literalistic" reading of Genesis 1–2. He was uncertain whether
"Adam" referred to an actual individual or to humankind as a whole; he also
suggested that the early chapters of Genesis "do not prohibit the idea that
there is an evolutionary process." The original interview by the Wilberforce
Fellowship was recorded in September 2009 and was posted online the following year.[6] Soon after, RTS released Longman from his adjunct teaching
responsibilities. The dominoes were falling.

Already in 2005 Peter Enns had invoked the incarnation to revitalize the
doctrine of inerrancy.[7] He accused the traditional evangelical doctrine of
Scripture of docetism and offered instead the *humanity* of the Bible as key to

3. On the origin of the term "BioLogos," see Francis Collins, *The Language of God: A Scientist Presents Evidence for Belief* (New York: Free Press, 2006), 203–10.
4. More recently, BioLogos has adopted a more inclusive approach that invites dialogue and collaboration among a wide range of theological and scientific perspectives, including those that affirm a historical Adam.
5. For a brief synopsis of the controversy, see "Why Must the Church Come to Accept Evolution?: An Update," *The BioLogos Forum*, April 2, 2010, http://biologos.org/blog/why-must-the-church-come-to-accept-evolution-an-update.
6. See Tremper Longman, "Is There a Historical Adam?," Wilberforce Fellowship Video, September 16, 2009, http://www.youtube.com/watch?v=I8Pk1vXL1WE.
7. Peter Enns, *Inspiration and Incarnation: Evangelicals and the Problem of the Old Testament* (Grand Rapids: Baker Academic, 2005).

understanding the nature of the Old Testament text. The book proved too hot to handle and, in 2008, he resigned under a dark cloud from Westminster Theological Seminary. He extended his thesis in a sequel volume, claiming that Christian theology can dispense with a historical Adam and Eve with no harm done.[8] The chips were down, the stakes were raised, and the wider controversy threatened to splinter the already frail bonds within the evangelical coalition.[9]

All this is just the tip of the iceberg. Shipwrecks litter the ocean. Other professors have lost tenured positions under similar circumstances. Some see impending doom, a new fundamentalist inquisition looming on the horizon— if not already knocking at the door. This family quarrel has even caught the attention of the secular media.[10] Are we, perhaps, witnessing another chapter in that unending polemical duel, the conflict between biblicists and evolutionists—creationists and theistic evolutionists facing off, pistols cocked, on opposite sides of the field? Well, surely some connections exist. For one, old-earth and young-earth creationists equally defend the historicity of Adam; demurring Christians are invariably theistic evolutionists.

But the reality is far more complex. So-called creationists agree on the historicity of Adam—yet they often disagree on the mode of his creation as well as the literary significance of the early chapters of Genesis.[11] And, of course, a theistic evolutionist *can* affirm a fall in history. One need look no further than early twentieth-century theistic evolutionists like James Orr, Pope Pius XII, and the Old Princeton theologians; they all insisted on Adam's supernatural creation and subsequent fall.[12]

The temptation in this debate is to think that Adam is simply one piece in a puzzle in which the fall and evolution are separate pieces that we can rearrange and shuffle around the board. But such a picture is misleading, too flat and one-dimensional. Adam and the fall do not float free in Scripture like rootless, atomistic, independent ideas. They are central nodes that hold together and are completely enmeshed in a much broader, organic, theological matrix. If we remove

8. Peter Enns, *The Evolution of Adam: What the Bible Does and Doesn't Say about Human Origins* (Grand Rapids: Baker Academic, 2012).

9. See Richard N. Ostling, "The Search for the Historical Adam," *Christianity Today*, June 2011, 23–27.

10. E.g., see Barbara Bradley Hagerty, "Evangelicals Question the Existence of Adam and Eve," NPR Morning Edition, August 9, 2011, http://www.npr.org/2011/08/09/138957812/evangelicals -question-the-existence-of-adam-and-eve.

11. E.g., see the book symposium, *Journal of Creation Theology and Science Series B: Life Sciences* 2 (2012): 27–47, between five young-earth creationists and C. John Collins, old-earth creationist, on his *Did Adam and Eve Really Exist? Who They Were and Why You Should Care* (Wheaton: Crossway, 2011).

12. E.g., see David Livingstone, *Darwin's Forgotten Defenders: The Encounter between Evangelical Theology and Evolutionary Thought* (Grand Rapids: Eerdmans, 1987).

Adam and the fall from the architecture of the faith, what will the repercussions be? Something mild, like tossing a pebble into a pond with the ripples absorbed back into the system? Or something more serious, like the great fall of Humpty Dumpty, where all the king's exegetes and all the king's theologians couldn't put the faith back together again? Christians need reliable answers to such questions.

Much of the debate circles around three key areas. The first concerns the epistemological status of natural science for theology. Some argue that traditional beliefs simply have to change, one way or another, before what they see as the assured results of science. Other Christians have become militantly *anti*-science because they sense a growing threat from emerging scientific theories. On the one hand we need to recognize that the noetic effects of sin infect all strata of scientific investigation.[13] Science should not usurp the authority of Scripture. Yet on the other hand there needs to be a due recognition that the empirical investigations of scientists can glorify God by helping us understand and relish his creation more deeply.

The second area is historical criticism of the Bible. Once we appropriately modify how we understand the nature of Scripture, the controversy loses its sharp teeth and largely vanishes. As Enns remarks, "We have to adjust our expectations of what the Bible can or cannot do; that is, we need to calibrate our genre expectations of Genesis in view of newer historical information."[14] A historical-critical reading calls into question the traditional assumption that Genesis 3 and Romans 5 require a historical Adam. The question that many religious scholars are asking is whether an infallibilist picture of the Bible has held the evangelical mind captive. Biblical scholars operating with historical-critical assumptions have long made their peace with an Adam-less world. But evangelicals have only recently begun wrestling with these questions in a constructive way.[15] The question remains whether evicting infallibilism from the house of evangelical theology will simply open the door to far more devastating historical-critical problems. Will the final condition of evangelical scholarship be worse than the first?[16]

13. See Thomas S. Kuhn, *The Structure of Scientific Revolutions*, 2nd ed. (Chicago: University of Chicago Press, 1970).

14. Enns, *Evolution of Adam*, 42.

15. See Christopher Hays and Stephen Lane Herring, "Adam and the Fall," in *Evangelical Faith and the Challenge of Historical Criticism*, ed. Christopher Hays and Christopher Ansberry (Grand Rapids: Baker Academic, 2013), 24–54. This book continues the conversation started in Mark Noll, *Between Faith and Criticism: Evangelicals, Scholarship, and the Bible in America*, 2nd ed. (Grand Rapids: Baker, 1991). See also Noll's related volume, *The Scandal of the Evangelical Mind* (Grand Rapids: Eerdmans, 1994).

16. That case is advanced in Robert Yarbrough, "Should Evangelicals Embrace Historical Criticism? The Hays-Ansberry Proposal," *Themelios* 39 (2014): 37–52. See also Paul Wells, "The

The final area of debate is church tradition, with Galileo as the poster boy. Geocentrism was widely accepted by the medieval church, a position rightly overturned by the heliocentric observations of Copernicus, Galileo, and Kepler. In the process, the church—both Protestant and Catholic—appeared defensive, reactionary, and woodenly literalistic in its reading of Scripture.[17] Are we today facing another Galileo moment? In defending Adam's historicity, are conservative evangelicals held captive by tradition? Even the Westminster Confession emphasizes the fallibility of tradition: "All synods or councils, since the apostles' times, whether general or particular, may err; *and many have erred.* Therefore they are not to be made the rule of faith, or practice; but to be used as a help in both."[18] Some have suggested that the evangelical intransigence is motivated by fear. To rethink the historicity of Adam would be to challenge a certain understanding of biblical authority and thereby threaten the group identity of conservative Protestants. As Enns writes, "For some Christians, therefore, evidence from natural science or archaeology, no matter how compelling, is simply inadmissible. *Too much is at stake.*"[19] In short, what is the positive epistemic and instructional role of church tradition in the dialogue between science and theology, and what can we learn from the older perspectives of the patristic and Reformation traditions?

The book that you hold in your hands speaks into this situation and, while certainly not the final word, offers a measured word that seeks not only to engage important questions for specialists but also casts a wider gaze to more integrating, large-picture concerns. That is, after all, where normal Christians actually live, where the dogmatic rubber meets the existential road. But some have suggested that genuine theological scholarship should avoid any discussion that draws the Christian faith into *apologetics*—for such a situation can distract us from the very particular theological priorities of the faith and can even distort the balanced shape of the gospel (e.g., Karl Barth famously argued along those lines). We heed those concerns gladly. And yet any theology worthy of the gospel cannot shy away from adopting an apologetic orientation whenever extrabiblical factors threaten the integrity of the apostolic tradition handed down to us. Gospel fidelity sometimes demands apologetic instincts.

Lasting Significance of Ernst Troeltsch's Critical Moment," *Westminster Theological Journal* 72 (2010): 199–217.

17. See Ernan McMullin, ed., *The Church and Galileo* (Notre Dame: University of Notre Dame Press, 2005) and Maurice A. Finocchiaro, "The Biblical Argument against Copernicanism and the Limitation of Biblical Authority: Ingoli, Foscarini, Galileo, Campanella," in *Nature and Scripture in the Abrahamic Religions: Up to 1700*, ed. Jitse M. van der Meer and Scott Mandelbrote (Leiden: Brill, 2008), 627–64.

18. Westminster Confession of Faith, 31.3, emphasis added.

19. Enns, *Evolution of Adam*, 146, emphasis added.

Indeed, if apologetics is a component of the *pastoral* function of theology—as we would argue—then it is precisely by engaging such contemporary questions that Christian theology can have a powerful existential and pastoral traction in the lives of believers.

There is no one chapter in this volume that can stand alone like Hercules and single-handedly rescue Adam from his rapidly diminishing theological, cultural, and scientific plausibility. However, when all the chapters are taken together as a unified voice, they offer "one long argument"[20] that engages these questions in a comprehensive way. Our basic thesis is that the traditional doctrine of original sin is not only orthodox but is also the most theologically cogent synthesis of the biblical witness.

The first part of this book begins with two chapters on the exegetical evidence for the historicity of Adam in the Old and New Testaments.[21] The third chapter, written by "William Stone," places Adam in conversation with crucial evidence from paleoanthropology. Stone is an academic paleontologist, and in his essay he has chosen for professional reasons to work under a pseudonym (neither his guild nor his colleagues will look kindly on what he has written here). We suggest that this curious, if not uncommon, situation is symptomatic of a debate that has become unhelpfully polarizing and politicized. The second part of the book includes four chapters that elaborate on the importance of original sin in patristic, Lutheran, Reformed, and Wesleyan traditions. Serving as a counterpoint, there is also a chapter on the waning prospects of the doctrine in modern theology. In the third part of the book, several chapters examine the doctrine of original sin in its rich biblical, theological, and pastoral dimensions. These important realities turn out to be remarkably resilient, bursting with life-giving theological energy, amid the massive scientific shifts that loom large in a post-Darwinian world. The final part of the book addresses some recurring challenges to the doctrines of the fall and original sin and demonstrates their continuing relevance and vitality.

Christian theology at its best will always be—can only be!—orthodox. Precisely for that reason it is also burdened to minister to the church in a way that always seeks to promote a functional and deep-rooted *confidence* in the great things of the gospel. It is that kind of theology that motivates this book. It is that kind of joyful theology that is worth living and dying for. With that intent we commend these chapters to the reader.

---

20. Darwin famously summarized his seminal volume as "one long argument" in *On the Origin of Species by Means of Natural Selection* (London: John Murray, 1859), 459.

21. See also Ardel Caneday and Matthew Barrett, eds., *Four Views on the Historical Adam* (Grand Rapids: Zondervan, 2013).

PART 1

Adam in the Bible and Science

1

ADAM AND EVE
IN THE OLD TESTAMENT

C. John Collins

Traditionally Christians, like the Jews from whom they arose, have read the story of Adam and Eve in the opening chapters of the Bible as describing the first human beings, from whom all other humans descend. They have also taken the account of the "disobedience" in Genesis 3 as narrating the origin of all human sin: that is, these readers have supposed that God first made humans morally innocent and that the events of Genesis 3 transformed the moral condition of Adam and Eve, and thus of all humankind after them.[1]

Many contemporary scholars have cast doubt on this traditional under-standing of the origins both of humans and of sin. For example, James Barr (1924–2006), a biblical scholar of considerable influence in the twentieth cen-tury, asserted that the conventional way of reading Genesis "derives essentially from St Paul," while a close reading of Genesis on its own terms will lead to

---

1. This essay draws on and develops material found in my "Adam and Eve in the Old Testa-ment," *Southern Baptist Journal of Theology* 15.1 (2011): 4–25, and *Did Adam and Eve Really Exist? Who They Were and Why You Should Care* (Wheaton, IL: Crossway, 2011), with those publishers' permission. In 2009 I participated in a forum on historical Adam and Eve at the annual meeting of the American Scientific Affiliation, with Daniel Harlow and John Schneider arguing that we should *not* take them as historical persons. Our revised papers were published in the journal *Perspectives on Science and Christian Faith* 62.3 (2010). In particular, my entry is "Adam and Eve as Historical People, and Why It Matters," 147–65; and I will refer to Harlow's here: "After Adam: Reading Genesis in an Age of Evolutionary Science," 179–95.

different conclusions.[2] Further, Claus Westermann (1909–2002), another influential scholar, insisted that Genesis 3 (taken as a "fall" story) is of minimal importance in the entire Old Testament: "It is nowhere cited or presumed in the Old Testament; its significance is limited to primeval events."[3] And Peter Enns, an Old Testament scholar with an evangelical background, has carried forward this notion that the Old Testament (as distinct from Paul) does not attribute human sinfulness to Adam's primal disobedience; indeed, it is a mistake to take Adam in Genesis as the actual first human being: "Paul's Adam is not a result of a 'straight' reading of the Old Testament."[4]

Several factors in the modern climate of thought make it attractive to reduce the importance of Adam and Eve. First, there is the perennial question of just *how* deeds done by someone else so long ago—even if that someone is my ancestor—can have such a major impact on life here and now.[5] Second, there are parallels between the stories in Genesis and the tales that come from other parts of the ancient Near East (most notably from Mesopotamia); perhaps Genesis is doing something similar to what these other tales do, and if we do not accord "historicity" to the other tales, why should we suppose that it matters for Genesis?[6] And third, many take current biological theories to imply that humans arose by way of an evolutionary, natural process rather than by the special action of God; these theories make it difficult to speak of the *first* members of a new species. I will address these climatic factors only in a very cursory way here and defer the larger discussion to another venue.

At first glance, it may seem that "Adam and Eve" do in fact play only a very small role in the whole Hebrew Bible (as distinct from the Apocrypha and New Testament). Victor Hamilton observed,

> Apart from its uses in Gen. 1–5, the only other unambiguous occurrence of the proper name "Adam" in the OT is 1 Chron. 1:1. It may occur in Deut. 32:8; Job

2. James Barr, *The Garden of Eden and the Hope of Immortality* (Minneapolis: Fortress, 1992), 4. Harlow, "After Adam," 187, follows Barr on this point. I have provided a critical review of Barr's book in appendix 3 of *Did Adam and Eve Really Exist?*

3. Claus Westermann, *Creation* (London: SPCK, 1974), 89, as cited with approval in W. Sibley Towner, "Interpretations and Reinterpretations of the Fall," in Francis A. Eigo, ed., *Modern Biblical Scholarship: Its Impact on Theology and Proclamation* (Villanova, PA: Villanova University Press, 1984), 72.

4. Peter Enns, *The Evolution of Adam: What the Bible Does and Doesn't Say about Human Origins* (Grand Rapids: Baker Academic, 2012), 80.

5. J. Matthew Ashley, "Original Sin, Biblical Hermeneutics, and the Science of Evolution," in Jitse van der Meer and Scott Mandelbrote, eds., *Nature and Scripture in the Abrahamic Religions*, 4 vols. (Leiden: Brill, 2008), 2:407–36, discusses this impulse in the "modern" period, which leads to a rejection of traditional notions of "original sin."

6. See, for example, Enns, *Evolution of Adam*, 37.

31:33; Hos. 6:7. This is surprising, given the fact that OT literature does not hesitate to recall early heroes of Israel's past such as Noah, Abraham, Jacob, and Moses, and thus link the past with the present in one corporate continuum. . . . Unlike the OT, intertestamental literature and the NT have numerous references to Adam. For the former, compare Sir. 17:1; 49:16; Tob. 8:6; Wis. 2:23; 9:2. For the latter, compare Luke 3:38; Rom. 5:12–21; 1 Cor. 11:12; 15:22, 45–49; 1 Tim. 2:13–14.[7]

If the citational statistics were all that there is to the discussion, it would indeed be hard to warrant the traditional Christian emphasis on Adam and Eve. But, as I hope to show, these statistics are potentially misleading, and should not control our discussion.

Here is what I intend to accomplish in this essay. Since the explicit references to Adam and Eve occur primarily in Genesis 1–5, I will first show how chapters 1–11 of Genesis have a clear literary unity in their current form (regardless of their compositional history). If the rest of the Bible treats this material as a whole, then echoes of one part may well be evoking the whole. Second, I will examine specific issues within Genesis 1–5 to see how the text portrays Adam and Eve and their significance. Third, I will consider how the rest of the Old Testament refers to, evokes, or presupposes the story of Adam and Eve. Finally, I will briefly sample Jewish writings from the Second Temple period (outside of the New Testament) that show that these authors, from the mainstream of Judaism, saw Adam and Eve in much the same way as I do. Throughout my discussion I will draw attention to how the whole Old Testament story presupposes the historical significance of Adam and Eve as the fountainhead of humanity and as the doorway by which sin came into God's world.

The Unity of Genesis 1–11

Scholars commonly assign the different pericopes in Genesis 1–11 to separate sources. In particular, we often read that Genesis 1–2 presents two *different*

---

7. Victor P. Hamilton, "'*dm* (no. 132)," in *New International Dictionary of Old Testament Theology and Exegesis*, ed. W. A. VanGemeren, 5 vols. (Grand Rapids: Zondervan, 1997), 1:264. Generally speaking, I agree with his assessment of the proper name, and am happy to consider the common *ben*/*bᵉnê 'adam* as properly "son of man"/"children of mankind," agreeing with the normal Septuagint rendering υἱὸς ἀνθρώπου/οἱ υἱοὶ τῶν ἀνθρώπων (except for Deut. 32:8, which renders *bᵉnê 'adam* as υἱοὶ Ἀδαμ; ESV "mankind"). Hamilton has probably overstated the situation with Noah, especially as compared with the many references to Abraham, Jacob, and Moses: outside of Gen. 5–10, Noah appears only in 1 Chron. 1:4; Isa. 54:9; Ezek. 14:14, 20; in the Apocrypha, see Tob. 4:12; Sir. 44:17–18; 4 Macc. 15:31: a situation comparable to that with Adam.

creation accounts (1:1–2:3 and 2:4–25), which may even be difficult to reconcile with each other.[8]

If we can establish that the current form of Genesis invites us to read Genesis 1–11 as a coherent whole, then we can say that any reading that fails to incorporate such coherence is inadequate—and that this is so regardless of what we think about the prehistory of the individual pericopes.

Its Setting in the Book of Genesis

The first line of argument is the fact that Genesis 1–11 is now part of the whole structure of Genesis. The organizing function of the *toledot* ("generations") in Genesis is well known: see Genesis 2:4; 5:1; 6:9; 10:1, 32; 11:10, 27; 25:12, 19; 36:1, 9; 37:2. According to the *toledot*, Genesis 1 (really 1:1–2:3) stands as a kind of preface to the whole book, while Genesis 2–4 (2:4–4:26) is the next section, and so on.[9]

I shall argue that Genesis 1–11 (1:1–11:26) has its own coherence, and we can see that it stretches over several sections marked by the *toledot*. At the same time, as R. W. L. Moberly has noted, there is no real grammatical break from Genesis 11 to Genesis 12.[10] The story as a whole progresses smoothly.

Now consider how Genesis 1:28 records God's "blessing" on the human couple, urging them to "be fruitful and multiply." These themes run throughout Genesis and beyond. In Genesis 9:1, Noah is a kind of "new Adam":[11] "And God *blessed* Noah and his sons and said to them, "*Be fruitful* and *multiply* and fill the earth.*" In Genesis 12:2–3, the Lord will *bless* Abram and make him a channel of *blessing* for his own descendants, and for the rest of the world. These promises are repeated to Abraham's heirs: to Ishmael (17:20), Isaac (26:3–4), and Jacob (28:3; 48:3–4). The book of Exodus opens by telling us, "But the people of Israel *were fruitful* and increased greatly; they *multiplied* and grew exceedingly strong, so that the land was filled with them." Deuteronomy promises that the people of Israel, when they are faithful, will continue to enjoy this blessing (30:16; see also 7:13):

8. See, for example, Enns, *Evolution of Adam*, 140; Daniel Harlow, "Creation according to Genesis: Literary Genre, Cultural Context, Theological Truth," *Christian Scholars Review* 37.2 (2008): 163–98.

9. See discussion in my *Genesis 1–4: A Linguistic, Literary, and Theological Commentary* (Phillipsburg, NJ: P&R, 2006), 229.

10. R. W. L. Moberly, *The Theology of the Book of Genesis*, Old Testament Theology series (Cambridge: Cambridge University Press, 2009), 121.

11. See, e.g., William Dumbrell, *Covenant and Creation: A Theology of the Old Testament Covenants* (1984; Carlisle, UK: Paternoster, 1997), 27; Tremper Longman III, *How to Read Genesis* (Downers Grove, IL: InterVarsity, 2005), 117–18; Bruce Waltke and Cathy J. Fredericks, *Genesis* (Grand Rapids: Zondervan, 2001), 127–28.

If you obey the commandments of the LORD your God that I command you today, by loving the LORD your God, by walking in his ways, and by keeping his commandments and his statutes and his rules, then you shall live and *multiply*, and the LORD your God will *bless* you in the land that you are entering to take possession of it.

All of this allows us to see that Genesis focuses on the ways in which God has made new starts after Adam and Eve—with Noah, and then with Abram and his offspring. Hence Noah, Abram, and Israel are "new Adams," which shows how fully Genesis 1–2 is integrated into the whole Pentateuch.

God's calling of Abraham is not simply for his own benefit but also for the rest of the world.[12] One of the chief themes of Old Testament messianic hope is the expectation that under the leadership of the Messiah, the people of God will succeed in bringing God's light to the gentile world. The shape of this biblical story assumes that all human beings have a common origin, a common predicament, and a common need to know God and have God's image restored in them; this assumption comes from including Genesis 1–11 in the story, with some version of the conventional reading of the "fall" of the whole human family.

Parallels between Genesis 1–11 and Ancient Near Eastern "Myths"

A second avenue for establishing that we should read Genesis 1–11 together comes from the parallels with materials from other ancient Near Eastern peoples, particularly from the Mesopotamians.[13]

12. Here I agree with, e.g., Christopher Wright, *The Mission of God: Unlocking the Bible's Grand Narrative* (Downers Grove, IL: InterVarsity, 2006), 194–221, as over against Moberly, *Theology of the Book of Genesis*, 141–61. Wright's position does better justice than Moberly's to: (1) the likely sense of the passive or reflexive verb in Gen. 12:3 ("all the families of the earth shall be blessed/shall find blessing for themselves," rather than "shall bless themselves"); (2) the context of Gen. 12:1–3 in Genesis, with its evocation of 1:28 and the other "blessing" texts addressed to Abraham's descendants; (3) the biblical themes of blessing coming to the gentiles by way of Abraham's family; and (4) the way that Ps. 72:17 echoes Gen. 22:18. On points (2) and (4), see further T. D. Alexander, "Further Observations on the Term 'Seed' in Genesis," *Tyndale Bulletin* 48.2 (1997): 363–67; my "Galatians 3:16: What Kind of Exegete Was Paul?" *Tyndale Bulletin* 54.1 (2003): 75–86. As for the sense of "*in* you," Moberly makes no place for covenant inclusion, but this seems to me to be the best explanation of the Hebrew term: people are "in" someone when they are members of the people that the someone represents. This general perspective plays no part in the argument of Enns, *Evolution of Adam*.

13. I have a much fuller discussion of this topic in appendix 1 of my *Did Adam and Eve Really Exist?* Enns, *Evolution of Adam*, 35, claims that the discovery of the relevant texts beginning in the nineteenth century has "for the first time—and irrevocably—placed Israelite religion in a larger context." This is actually incorrect: Second Temple Jewish and early Christian authors

I noted that we intuitively see a transition between Genesis 1–11 and the rest of Genesis. Even though there is no grammatical shift, nevertheless our intuition finds support in how the narrator slows down in the Abraham story: he has been covering large stretches of time in brief narratives, whereas now he is taking more narration time to cover less elapsed time in more detail.

These other stories from the ancient Near East further confirm our intuition. I see no reason to quarrel with the way in which specialists on the ancient Near East find the chief parallels with Genesis 1–11 to include the Sumerian King List, the Atrahasis Epic, and the Eridu Genesis/Sumerian Flood Tale.[14] (Another story, *Enuma Elish*, or the *Babylonian Epic of Creation*, once seemed a promising source for comparisons as well, and some biblical scholars still turn to it; Assyriologists, however, seem less willing than formerly to endorse much of a comparison.[15])

---

were aware of this context, although their sources were predominantly in Greek. For example, Theophilus of Antioch (whom Enns mentions in another context, 88) addressed questions about the relation of the Genesis flood story to what he took to be versions of the same story coming from pagan sources. See discussion in my "Noah, Deucalion, and the New Testament," *Biblica* 93.3 (2012): 403–26. The great contribution of the archaeologists has been to give us these texts in their ancient Near Eastern language forms.

14. See, for example, David T. Tsumura, "Genesis and Ancient Near Eastern Stories of Creation and Flood: An Introduction," in *I Studied Inscriptions from before the Flood: Ancient Near Eastern, Literary, and Linguistic Approaches to Genesis 1–11*, ed. Richard S. Hess and David T. Tsumura (Winona Lake, IN: Eisenbrauns, 1994), 27–57, esp. 44–57; Richard Averbeck, "The Sumerian Historiographic Tradition and its Implications for Genesis 1–11," in *Faith, Tradition, and History: Old Testament Historiography in Its Near Eastern Context*, ed. A. R. Millard, James K. Hoffmeier, and David W. Baker (Winona Lake, IN: Eisenbrauns, 1994), 79–102; Kenneth A. Kitchen, *On the Reliability of the Old Testament* (Grand Rapids: Eerdmans, 2003), 423–25; and Anne Drafkorn Kilmer, "The Mesopotamian Counterparts of the Biblical *Nephilim*," in *Perspectives on Language and Text*, ed. Edgar W. Conrad (Winona Lake, IN: Eisenbrauns, 1987), 39–43. Richard S. Hess, "The Genealogies of Genesis 1–11 and Comparative Literature," *Biblica* 70 (1989): 241–54 (reprinted in Hess and Tsumura, *I Studied Inscriptions*, 58–72), adds some helpful cautions about the differences between the biblical genealogies and the king lists. Tikva Frymer-Kensky, "The Atrahasis Epic and Its Significance for Our Understanding of Genesis 1–9," *Biblical Archaeologist* 40.4 (1977): 147–55, supports the parallel between the biblical flood story and Atrahasis over, say, Gilgamesh; at the same time, despite her helpful observations about the contrast between the biblical and Mesopotamian accounts, I do not find all of her specific exegetical points on Genesis to be compelling.

15. W. G. Lambert has argued for a reduced interest in *Enuma Elish*; see his article, "A New Look at the Babylonian Background of Genesis," *Journal of Theological Studies* n.s. 16.2 (1965): 287–300. He contends (291), "The first major conclusion is that the *Epic of Creation* is not a norm of Babylonian or Sumerian cosmology. It is a sectarian and aberrant combination of mythological threads woven into an unparalleled composition. In my opinion it is not earlier than 1100 B.C." See also Alan R. Millard, "A New Babylonian 'Genesis' Story," *Tyndale Bulletin* 18 (1967): 3–18, and Kitchen, *On the Reliability of the OT*, 425. A further argument that the notion of *Chaoskampf* (such as that found in *Enuma Elish*) is absent from Gen. 1 comes from Gordon H. Johnston, "Genesis 1 and Ancient Egyptian Creation Myths," *Bibliotheca Sacra* 165.658 (2008): 178–94; he contends that the Egyptian stories are a promising

There is much to say about the connections, and about the ways in which Genesis 1–11 is both similar and dissimilar to these other sources, which space forbids me to do here. The point of interest for now is that this overarching pattern from Mesopotamia provides a literary and ideological context into which Genesis 1–11 speaks: it is reasonable to conclude that Genesis 1–11 does so *as a whole*.

What does this parallel tell us about the function of Genesis 1–11? The Mesopotamian sources provide what Assyriologist William Hallo calls "prehistory"—the period of human existence before there are any secure written records—and "protohistory"—the earliest stages for which there are records.[16] Another way to put this is to recognize that these materials provide what we can call the front end of the official Mesopotamian worldview story. Further, it appears that the Mesopotamians aimed to accomplish their purpose by founding their stories on what they thought were actual events, albeit told with a great deal of imagery and symbolism. This means that those who think that a text is historically referential *only* if we can read it with a literalistic hermeneutic are making a fundamental mistake: not only are they failing to read the ancient text on its own terms, but they are actually ignoring the way that human communication works.

Thus it is reasonable to take Genesis 1–11 as providing the "official"— divinely approved—version by which God's people are to picture prehistory and protohistory, expecting similar attention to history without undue literalism.[17]

---

backdrop for Genesis. While I do not doubt the relevance of the Egyptian material, I find the pattern of the Mesopotamian material to provide the best overall parallel. Similarly, John H. Walton, "Creation in Genesis 1:1–2:3 and the Ancient Near East: Order out of Disorder after *Chaoskampf*," *Calvin Theological Journal* 43.1 (2008): 48–63, rejects both *Chaoskampf* and "theomachy" but goes on to argue that Genesis 1 is a "temple cosmology," as in his popular *The Lost World of Genesis One: Ancient Cosmology and the Origins Debate* (Downers Grove, IL: InterVarsity, 2009) and in his academic *Genesis 1 as Ancient Cosmology* (Winona Lake, IN: Eisenbrauns, 2011). Nevertheless, Bruce Waltke (see Waltke and Fredericks, *Genesis*, 23) still finds what he considers important parallels in *Enuma Elish*, as does Enns, *Evolution of Adam*, e.g., 38–43. The factors mentioned here seriously weaken both cases. See also the chapter by Noel Weeks in this volume.

16. William W. Hallo, "Part 1: Mesopotamia and the Asiatic Near East," in *The Ancient Near East: A History*, ed. William W. Hallo and William K. Simpson (Fort Worth: Harcourt Brace, 1998), 25.

17. I make this point more fully in "Adam and Eve as Historical People," 150–53, and even more fully in chapter 2 and appendix 1 of *Did Adam and Eve Really Exist?* Contrast Harlow, "After Adam," 185–87, who notices symbolic and pictorial elements in both Genesis and the Mesopotamian stories, and pronounces them both unhistorical. Enns, *Evolution of Adam*, makes a similar assumption throughout. These authors are conflating historicity with a literalistic scheme of interpretation, without argument.

Literary and Linguistic Links across Genesis 1–11

My third line of argument for the propriety of reading Genesis 1–11 as a unit comes from the literary and linguistic links between these pericopes.

Well-known links for the whole of Genesis 1–11 include those already noted between Adam and Noah, presenting Noah as a "new Adam." Further, there are clear links between Genesis 1 and Genesis 5, such as 1:26–27 and 5:1–5 (the life of Adam), and between Genesis 4 and 5, such as 4:25–26 and 5:3–11 (Seth and Enosh). There may be a link between the genealogy descended from Cain (4:17–22) and that from Seth (5:6–32), especially in the names Enoch, Methushael/Methuselah, and Lamech (see 4:18 with 5:18, 21, 25), although this is not entirely certain.[18]

Genesis 9–11 is coherent with the previous pericopes, since these chapters record the sequel to the great flood, with the descent of various peoples from the family of Noah (see 10:1), as linked by the genealogies (see 11:10, picking up the line of Shem), with 11:10–19 paralleling 10:21–25 (through Peleg), and 11:20–26 bringing the line down to Abram, Nahor, and Haran (who, with their descendants, will feature in the rest of Genesis).

Within Genesis 1–4 there are also clear linkages. First, Genesis 2–4 is commonly assigned to the J source, with a few redactions; the overall unity is not controversial.[19] Second (see below), Genesis 2:4–25 serves to elaborate the sixth "day" of Genesis 1. Third, the common assertion that the P creation story (Gen. 1) is free of anthropomorphisms is mistaken;[20] this story actually depends on an anthropomorphism, namely, the portrayal of God as one who goes through his work week and enjoys his Sabbath rest.[21] Genesis 2 contributes its own anthropomorphism to this pattern, depicting God as if he were a potter "forming" the first man (2:7), and a worker who "builds" the first woman (2:22). Finally, several verbal links show that, whatever separate origins the individual pericopes might have had, they have been edited in such a way as

18. See my *Genesis 1–4*, 201, where I suggest that maybe the contrast between the two families is prominent. Perhaps as well this indicates that the decline we see in Cain's family was not an inevitable outcome of being human; rather it flowed from the moral orientation of the members, which in turn was influenced by the orientation of the head member of the list. We might also suspect that the author saw the orientation of Cain's line as becoming dominant, and perhaps drawing Seth's descendants away from God, so that "the wickedness of man was great in the earth" (6:5).

19. See Richard Elliott Friedman, *The Bible with Sources Revealed: A New View into the Five Books of Moses* (New York: HarperCollins, 2003), and my discussion in *Genesis 1–4*, 227–28.

20. E.g., Friedman, *Bible with Sources Revealed*, 12; S. R. Driver, *The Book of Genesis*, Westminster Commentary (London: Methuen, 1904), xxv.

21. I have argued this in a number of places, e.g., in *Science and Faith: Friends or Foes?* (Wheaton: Crossway, 2003) and *Genesis 1–4*, 77.

to exhibit coherence. For example, in 1:28 we read, "And God *blessed* them. And God said to them, 'Be fruitful and *multiply*.'" In Genesis 3 the "blessing" (*brk*) has turned to "curse" (*'rr*), the proper antonym. And whereas the blessing was for them to *multiply* by having children, after the disobedience God says to the woman that he will "surely *multiply* your pain in childbearing"—the arena of blessing has turned into one of pain and danger. The genealogical chapter 5 (v. 29) also refers to God's "curse" on the ground (3:17): "and [Lamech] called his name Noah, saying, 'Out of the ground that the LORD has *cursed* [*'rr*] this one shall bring us relief from our work and from the *painful toil* [*'itstsâbôn*, see 3:16, 17] of our hands.'"

Further, three "enigmatic" first-person plurals, by which God addresses "us," appear through Genesis 1–11: 1:26; 3:22; and 11:7. Many suppose that these (or at least the first) are God addressing his angelic council, although I judge the best explanation to be a "plural of self-address."[22] The specific conclusion here does not matter for my purpose: the point is that this is a distinctive feature of this stretch of material, from supposedly separate sources. Once we recognize how Genesis 1–11 is integrated into the whole flow of the book of Genesis, and how these chapters parallel basic worldview-shaping materials from Mesopotamia, it is no surprise to find that whoever put these chapters together did so in such a way that they display their unity at the literary and linguistic level.

Do Genesis 1 and 2 Give Us Two Creation Accounts?

Now let us focus more narrowly on the two pericopes, Genesis 1:1–2:3 ˇ and 2:4–25. Do these passages not indeed foil every attempt to read them coherently?

As for whether they come from separate sources, the arguments for and against such sources will forever be indecisive, since none of these putative sources is actually known to exist. The only text that we have is the one that places these two passages together. Further, we have no reason to expect that whoever put these passages together was a blockhead (or a committee of blockheads), who could not recognize contradictions every bit as well as we can. As James Barr—who accepted the common critical breakup of Genesis into putative sources, and a late date for its final composition—points out, it

---

22. For relevant discussion, see Collins, *Genesis 1–4*, 59–61. More recently, Lyle Eslinger, "The Enigmatic Plurals like 'One of Us' (Genesis i 26, iii 22, and xi 7) in Hyperchronic Perspective," *Vetus Testamentum* 56.2 (2006): 171–84, argues that these plurals reflect a heightened focus on the divine-human difference. I am not convinced, and retain what I find to be a simpler, and more exegetically based, explanation.

is reasonable to expect an editor to have smoothed out genuine contradictions between his sources, and tensions that remained would have invited ancient audiences to seek ways to "recognize the truthfulness of *both* narratives."[23] (Barr himself did not explain how he thought this smoothing actually worked.) Therefore, if literary and linguistic studies point to a way to read the whole production coherently, we do well to pay heed.

My own literary and linguistic studies have led to just such coherence. I support a version of the traditional rabbinic opinion, namely that, far from finding two discordant accounts, we should see Genesis 1:1–2:3 as the overall account of God creating and preparing the earth as a suitable place for humans to live, and Genesis 2:4–25 as elaborating the events of the sixth day of Genesis 1.[24] This traditional reading lies behind, say, the way Haydn's oratorio *Die Schöpfung (The Creation)* weaves the two narratives together: on the sixth day, God created man in his "own image" (Gen. 1:27), and "breathed into his nostrils the breath of life" (Gen. 2:7).[25] More important, it also underlies the way that Jesus read the two passages together, in Matthew 19:3–9 (Mark 10:2–9), combining Genesis 1:27 with 2:24.[26] My work supplies a grammatical justification for this traditional approach by showing how Genesis 2:4–7 links the two stories. Further, the validity of this reading does not rest on any view of the authorship and date of Genesis.[27]

The purpose of Genesis 1:1–2:3 is to celebrate as a great achievement God's work of fashioning the world as a suitable place for humans to live. "The

23. James Barr, "One Man, or All Humanity? A Question in the Anthropology of Genesis 1," in *Recycling Biblical Figures: Papers Read at a NOSTER Colloquium in Amsterdam*, ed. Athalya Brenner and Jan Willem van Henten, May 12–13, 1997, Studies in Theology and Religion (Leiden: Deo, 1999), 6. Speaking frankly, as a traditional Christian I am wary of any exegetical gift that Barr might offer; see my critical discussion of his famous 1984 letter to David Watson in my *Science and Faith: Friends or Foes?*, 364–66. At the same time, Barr's contributions to linguistic rigor in biblical studies are substantial, and we ought to acknowledge his positions when he presents arguments to show their validity.

24. See my *Genesis 1–4*, 108–12, 121–22. For examples of the traditional Jewish opinion, see the Hebrew commentary of Yehudah Kiel, *Sefer Bereshit* (Genesis), Da'at Miqra' (Jerusalem: Mossad Harav Kook, 1997), page מב (citing "our sages of blessed memory," with n7 listing some of them).

25. Franz Joseph Haydn, *Die Schöpfung* (Hob. xxi:2), §§23–24. Observe in addition how Ps. 104, widely acknowledged to depend on Gen. 1, alludes as well in v. 14 to Gen. 2, with its mention of "cultivate" (Heb. 'bd, "work," in Gen. 2:5, 15; 3:23).

26. Harlow, "After Adam," 189, mistakenly asserts that Paul "is the only writer to appeal to the story of Adam, Eve, and the serpent," and he denies that the Gospels or Revelation appropriate the story. This is an astonishing claim, but addressing it is not within my scope here. Similarly, Enns, *Evolution of Adam*, misses the significance of these texts. I refer the reader to chap. 3 of my *Did Adam and Eve Really Exist?*

27. I argue that the material is substantially Mosaic in *Did Adam and Eve Really Exist?*, appendix 3.

exalted tone of the passage allows the reader to ponder this with a sense of awe, adoring the goodness, power, and creativity of the One who did all this."[28]

Then comes Genesis 2:4–7:

> These are the generations
>   of the heavens and the earth when they were created,
>   in the day that the LORD God made the earth and the heavens.
> When no bush of the field was yet in the land and no small plant of the field had yet sprung up—for the LORD God had not caused it to rain on the land, and there was no man to work the ground, and a mist was going up from the land and was watering the whole face of the ground—then the LORD God formed the man of dust from the ground and breathed into his nostrils the breath of life, and the man became a living creature.[29]

The chiastic structure of 2:4 (a *heavens* | b *earth* | c *when they were created* // c' *in the day that the* LORD *God made* | b' *earth* | c' *heavens*), looking back to the first pericope and forward to the second, invites us to read the two passages in union. The change in divine name, from "God" (*'elohîm*) in 1:1–2:3 to "the LORD God" (*YHWH 'elohîm*) in 2:4–3:24, functions rhetorically to identify the universal, majestic, transcendent Creator (God) with the covenant God of Israel (the Lord), which in turn grounds God's purpose for Israel to be a particular people called to be a vehicle of blessing to the whole world.

The action of Genesis 2:7 parallels that of 1:27. The ESV of 2:5–7 shows how verses 5–6 provide the setting for the event of verse 7: in a particular region ("the land," verse 5), at a particular time of year (at the end of the dry season, before it had begun to rain, when the rain clouds ["mist"] were beginning to rise)—that is when God formed the man. In other words, we read Genesis 1 and 2 together by taking 2:4–25 as filling out details of the "sixth day," amplifying 1:24–31.[30] Specifically, it explains how it was that God created humankind as

---

28. Collins, *Genesis 1–4*, 78–79. Moshe Weinfeld has declared that the passage is "liturgical" in its origin: see "Sabbath, Temple, and the Enthronement of the Lord—the Problem of the Sitz im Leben of Genesis 1:1–2:3," in *Mélanges Bibliques et Orientaux en l'Honneur de M. Henri Cazelles*, ed. A. Caquot and M. Delcor (AOAT 212; Neukirchen-Vluyn: Neukirchener, 1981), 501–12. While I do not agree with all that lies behind Weinfield's statement, I do think that it captures the celebratory tone of the passage.

29. The English Standard Version reflects the linguistic arguments given in my "Discourse Analysis and the Interpretation of Gen. 2:4–7," *Westminster Theological Journal* 61 (1999): 269–76. The Holman Christian Standard Bible is similar, except for the water source in v. 6; but see Max Rogland, "Interpreting אֵד in Genesis 2.5–6: Neglected Rabbinic and Intertextual Evidence," *Journal for the Study of the Old Testament* 34.4 (2010): 379–93, for strong support of the ESV.

30. On the specific question of Gen. 2:19 and the order of events, see my discourse-oriented grammatical study, "The Wayyiqtol as 'Pluperfect': When and Why," *Tyndale Bulletin* 46.1 (1995): 135–40. Harlow, "After Adam," 185, refers to the NIV (and by implication, the ESV)

male and female and equipped them to be fruitful and multiply. We can see this further from the way "it is not good that the man should be alone" in 2:18 jars with the "very good" of 1:31: this shows us that chapter 2 has not reached the point of 1:31 until the man and the woman have become one flesh. Once we get to 2:25, with the man and woman naked and not ashamed, we breathe a sigh of relief: we are now at the point where it is all "very good."

Hence we have every justification to read Genesis 1–11 as a connected narrative, with Genesis 2 serving as an elaboration of Genesis 1, and chapters 3–11 describing the events that followed the making of the world. Genesis 1–11 thus provides a coherent front end of the Bible's worldview story for the people of God.

Adam and Eve in Genesis 1–5

Adam and Eve as the First Human Pair

The figure named "Adam" appears unambiguously in Genesis 2–5. The proper name "Adam" transliterates the Hebrew word for "human being, humankind," *'adam*.[31] In Genesis 2:20, "the man" is first called "Adam."[32] Genesis 2:5 says "there was no *man* (*'adam*) to work the ground," and thus in 2:7 the Lord God formed "the man" using dust from the ground. In 2:18 "the man" is alone, and the Lord God sets out to make a helper fit for him. Throughout 2:4–4:26, whether he is called "the man" or "Adam," he is presented as one person. The man's one wife is simply called either "the woman" or "his wife" throughout—although once she receives her name Eve in 3:20, that name becomes another option (see also 4:1, where both are used together). The name Adam appears also in the genealogy of 5:1–5.

The divine plan to "make *man* in our image, after our likeness" (1:26) may refer to humankind in general (as most commentators think),[33] or it may refer

---

rendering with a pluperfect at Gen. 2:19 as "translational sleight of hand," but shows no awareness of the grammatical issues.

31. It is common to connect "man" (*'adam*) with the "ground" (*ᵃdamâ*, 2:7) from which he was formed. However, since the account goes on to say that the other animals were also formed from the ground (2:19), this wordplay seems less likely. The first-century Jewish writer Josephus (*Antiquities* 1.1.2, line 34) connected the word with the Hebrew for "red" (*'adôm*), which is as likely an explanation as any other (assuming that we have to find a wordplay).

32. The usual rule is that the form with the definite article, *ha-'adam*, is "the man," the newly formed human being of 2:7. In the received Hebrew text the form in 2:20 lacks the article, so it is rendered "Adam." Some prefer to insert the article at 2:20 (which would only be the change of a vowel, from *lᵉ'adam* to *la'adam*), thus deferring the first instance of the proper name to 3:17 (or even to 4:25).

33. See Richard Hess, "Splitting the Adam," in *Studies in the Pentateuch*, ed. J. A. Emerton (Leiden: Brill, 1991), 1.

to *the man* in particular (as Barr argues).[34] Whichever we prefer, we can see that 2:4–25 fills in the details of how humankind came to be composed of male and female members, both of whom are in God's image. Both the title "the human" ("the man") and the proper name Adam ("human") are fitted to someone whose actions are in some sense *representative* of all humankind.[35]

But he might "represent" humankind either as a personification, or as a particular member, or perhaps as both. Which sense fits here? Barr—rightly, I judge—argues the following in regard to 5:1–2: "This text, just here at the start of the genealogy, seems to me to make sense only if the writer intends one human pair, from whose descendants the world will gradually come to be populated."[36]

This reading, that Adam and Eve are presented as a particular pair, the first parents of all humanity, is widespread in the exegetical literature, both from writers who have some kind of traditionalist commitment to the Bible's truthfulness and from those who do not (such as Barr).[37] At the same time, this does not exclude Adam from being a *representative* in the sense of being a kind of paradigm through which we learn something about how temptation works.[38]

At any rate, the man who was once "alone" (2:18) now has a wife; these two disobey God and leave the garden of Eden. They have children, who also have children (chap. 4). The genealogy of Genesis 5 links this pair to subsequent people, leading up to Noah (5:32), from whom came Abraham (11:10–26), the forefather of Israel. It makes no difference for our purposes whether the flood is thought to have killed *all* humankind (outside of Noah and his family); nor does it matter how many generations the genealogies may or may not have skipped. The genealogies of Genesis 1–11 link Father Abraham, whom the people of Israel took to be historical, with Adam, who is otherwise hidden from the Israelites in the mists of antiquity.

34. Barr, "One Man, or All Humanity?," 9, based on the wording of 5:1–2. Harlow, "After Adam," 185, insists that Genesis 1 and 2 differ in this respect, without really interacting with any effort to read the two together.

35. See Hess, "Splitting the Adam," 12; see also Kiel, *Sefer Bereshit*, קב (at Gen. 4:1); and Dexter E. Callender Jr., *Adam in Myth and History: Ancient Israelite Perspectives on the Primal Human*, Harvard Semitic Studies (Winona Lake, IN: Eisenbrauns, 2000), 32: "There is an obvious and understandable awareness that Adam stands between God and humanity."

36. Barr, "One Man, or All Humanity?," 9.

37. See also Barr, "One Man, or All Humanity?," 5: "We no longer believe that all humanity originated in one single human pair. In respect of our beliefs about humanity the narrative of chapter 1 is closer to what we actually believe"—i.e., under the reading that "man" is just a collective for all humanity, which Barr proceeds to reject.

38. Harlow, "After Adam," 187, engages in an unnecessary contrast: "not reporting historical events but picturing paradigmatic ones." Why can it not do *both*?

I say "the mists of antiquity" to remind us that we are dealing with "prehistory" and "protohistory." As Kenneth Kitchen argues, in the nineteenth century BC, people "*knew already* that their world was old, very old";[39] thus "the mists of antiquity" represents the perspective of the ancients themselves. I have already indicated that Israel's narrative of prehistory bears a relationship with the narratives of prehistory found in Mesopotamia. This implies that, like those other stories, Genesis aims to tell the true story of origins, but it also implies that there are likely to be figurative elements and literary conventions that should make us wary of being too literalistic in our reading.[40] That is, the genre identification for Genesis 1–11, prehistory and protohistory, does *not* mean that the author had no concern for real events; far from it, it implies that real events form the backbone of his story.

At the same time, as is widely known, there are important contrasts between Genesis 1–11 and the Mesopotamian prehistories. The differing ways the stories are told convey very different stances toward the divine, the world, and man's calling.

Umberto Cassuto saw this clearly. After describing the similarities and differences between the other stories and those of Genesis, he observes the stress in Genesis on the unified origins of humankind: "In another respect, too, the Pentateuchal account differs from those given in the aforementioned texts, namely, in that it speaks of the creation of only one human pair, a fact that implies the brotherhood and equality of man, whereas the pagan texts refer to the mass creation of mankind as a whole."[41]

The ideology of the Genesis prehistory-protohistory is clear from its own literary context as the front end of the book of Genesis: that is, Genesis 1–11 is the backdrop of the Abraham-Isaac-Jacob story, which is the backdrop of the Exodus story. This prehistory grounds the call of Abraham by showing how all human beings are related, and therefore equally in need of God's blessing, and equally reachable with that blessing. Abraham is God's answer to this universal need (Gen. 12:1–3): he is to be the vehicle of blessing to "all the

---

39. Kitchen, *On the Reliability of the Old Testament*, 439.

40. Compare the remark of A. R. Millard on the topic of excessive literalism in general: "The writers were describing unusual riches in phrases that convey the thought clearly enough, *without demanding a literal interpretation.*" "Story, History, and Theology," in Millard, Hoffmeier, and Baker, eds., *Faith, Tradition, and History*, 49, emphasis added.

41. Umberto Cassuto, *From Adam to Noah: Genesis I–VI.8* (Jerusalem: Magnes, 1961 [1944]), 83. This remark has an extra poignancy when we recall that Cassuto was an Italian-born Jew who emigrated to Israel and wrote this commentary in Hebrew during the Holocaust. It is not entirely clear how Cassuto wanted to reconcile this insight with his general demurral from historical reading, except that he appears to have been looking for timeless lessons ("brotherhood and equality").

families of the earth" (12:3), starting the family through which all humankind, which is now estranged from God, will come to know the true God.

Once we recognize this, we also recognize that Genesis 1–11 is deliberately shaped with this purpose in mind. Many, for example, have noticed the way in which the garden of Eden becomes a pattern for describing the Israelite sanctuary, and even the land of Israel.[42] That is to say, the Old Testament views Eden as the first sanctuary, where God is present with his covenant partners (Adam and Eve); the tabernacle, and later the temple, reinstate this Edenic blessing. What makes the Promised Land special is that it too is to be like a reconstituted Eden, whose fruitfulness displays God's presence to the whole world.[43] There is every reason to expect that Genesis has portrayed Adam and Eden with goals like this in mind: that is, Adam is "like" an Israelite, and Eden is "like" Israel and the sanctuary, so that each member of God's people will see himself or herself as God's "renewed Adam" in the world. Hence the notion, put forward most recently by Enns, that "some elements of the [Genesis] story suggest that it is not about universal human origins but Israel's origin," has things exactly backward, because it takes no account of Israel's calling to be a vehicle of universal blessing and restoration of properly functioning humanity, nor does it account for the literary impact that calling would have on the Pentateuch's way of describing Eden and Adam.[44] (It also overlooks the way Genesis 1–11, in its current coherent form, presents Adam as the ancestor for a whole range of "families of the earth," not just for Israel.)

These considerations show why the author may well use such devices as "anachronism" if it serves his purpose; "historical verisimilitude" (aiming to get all the details of life exactly as the characters would have known them, even if the audience did not live that way) is not strongly claimed by the text itself.[45]

---

42. This is the thesis of, for example, Martin Emmrich, "The Temptation Narrative of Genesis 3:1–6: A Prelude to the Pentateuch and the History of Israel," *Evangelical Quarterly* 73.1 (2001): 3–20. Not all of his points are persuasive, but his suggestion that "the garden of Genesis 2–3 wants to be viewed as the archetype of the land of Israel" (5) is sound. Harlow, "After Adam," 185, notices this but then concludes that therefore Genesis is not historical. Again, he is confusing historicity with literalistic reading.

43. See, for example, Wright, *The Mission of God*, 334.

44. Enns, *Evolution of Adam*, 65.

45. Indeed, historical verisimilitude in literary compositions did not arise, at least in the West, until the modern period. This, by the way, is one of the arguments in favor of seeing ancient tradition, rather than free composition, behind the stories of the patriarchs (Gen. 12–50): their manners and customs reflect accurate recollections of the time in which the events occurred, not simply the time of whoever wrote the stories down. On this last point, see A. R. Millard, "Methods of Studying the Patriarchal Narratives as Ancient Texts," in *Essays on the Patriarchal Narratives*, ed. A. R. Millard and Donald J. Wiseman (Leicester, UK: Inter-Varsity, 1980), 43–58.

The marriage of Adam and Eve (Gen. 2:23–25) becomes the paradigm for any sound future marriage of human beings. The comment in 2:24 makes clear that this is programmatic for human life: "Therefore [because of the events of verses 21–23] a man [Hebrew *'ish*, any male human being] shall leave his father and mother and hold fast to his wife, and they shall become one flesh."

And what shall we make of the "death" that God threatens in Genesis 2:17? I maintain that the primary reference is "spiritual death" (alienation from God and one another) as exhibited in Genesis 3:8–13. But that is not all: it would appear that this is followed by their physical death as well (v. 19). For now I simply observe that we should be careful about letting the *distinction* between spiritual and physical death, which is proper, lead us to drive a wedge of *separation* between the two kinds of death: it looks like the author presents them as two aspects of one experience. In other words, physical death is not any more "natural" for human experience than spiritual death is.[46]

In Genesis 3:20 the woman receives a name, "Eve." This is connected in some way to the Hebrew word for "live," and the Septuagint renders it as *Zoë*, "life." The form of the Hebrew name, however—*Khawwâ*, from the root *kh-w-h*, "to live"—probably indicates a causative significance, i.e., "she who gives life," "life-giver" (see ESV footnote).[47] This supports the interpretation found in the ancient Jewish Aramaic translation called Targum Onkelos (no later than fourth century AD): "the mother of all the children of man"—that is, all humans descend from her.[48]

Good Literary Reading of Genesis 2–3

To be good readers of Genesis requires that we adapt ourselves to its literary conventions and style. I have already noted that the prehistory and protohistory genre leads us to certain stylistic expectations (namely in regard to both "history" and literalism). Further, since about 1980 there have been enormous advances in the study of narrative poetics for the Bible. The most important result for us is to realize that, in view of the features found in biblical narrative, we should expect that the authors will communicate their point of view by indirect and laconic means, especially emphasizing *showing* (displaying the heart by action and speech) over *telling* (explicitly evaluating

---

46. See further my *Genesis 1–4*, 116–19, 160–62. In contrast, Barr, *Garden of Eden*, chap. 2, claims that the Old Testament views death as "natural"; but, as I point out in my *Did Adam and Eve Really Exist?*, 162–63, this depends on an astounding equivocation on the word "natural."

47. See my *Genesis 1–4*, 154n22, drawing on Scott C. Layton, "Remarks on the Canaanite Origin of Eve," *Catholic Biblical Quarterly* 59.1 (1997): 22–32.

48. See Kiel, *Sefer Bereshit*, כ (on Gen. 3:20).

the characters and actions).[49] Readers must draw the right inferences from the words and actions recorded. To the extent that this literary methodology is valid, scholars who ignore these principles limit their ability to read Genesis for what it is.[50]

Consider the fact that the snake in Genesis 3 talks. The commentator Hermann Gunkel (1862–1932) finds this to be a feature of fairy tales and legends, where we expect to read of talking animals; oddly enough, he refers to Balaam's donkey in Numbers 22 as another of the "Hebrew legends."[51] This is odd because the narrator in Numbers 22:28 says that the Lord "opened the mouth of the donkey," which is what enabled it to speak. That is, the writer did *not* portray a world in which donkeys speak; he instead recounted what he thought was a *miracle*.[52] Hence, the only other example of a talking animal in a biblical narrative attributes that speech to some kind of interference with the animal's proper "nature." Besides, when we observe the serpent's knowledge of what God said in Genesis 2:17 (in 3:4 the serpent echoes the divine "surely die"), in addition to the evil that the serpent speaks (he urges disobedience to God's solemn command, calls God a liar, and insinuates that God's motives cannot be trusted), we perceive the firm footing of the Jewish and New Testament interpretive tradition that sees the Evil One ("Satan" or "the devil") as the agent who used this serpent as its mouthpiece (e.g., Wis. 1:13; 2:24; John 8:44; Rev. 12:9; 20:2).[53] In fact, to deny this by insisting that Genesis never *mentions* the Evil One is actually a poor reading, because it fails to appreciate "showing" over "telling." If we read the story thus poorly, we miss a crucial part of its import.[54]

We can also infer the function of the two trees, the "tree of the knowledge of good and evil" and the "tree of life."[55] The "knowledge of good and evil"

49. Helpful resources include Meir Sternberg, *The Poetics of Biblical Narrative: Ideological Literature and the Drama of Reading* (Bloomington: Indiana University Press, 1985); V. Philips Long, *The Reign and Rejection of King Saul: A Case for Literary and Theological Coherence* (Atlanta: Scholars, 1989), esp. his section on "Selected Features of Hebrew Narrative Style," 21–41.

50. Authors such as James Barr and Peter Enns, who embrace some level of what is called "historical criticism" (and claim to speak for the consensus of biblical scholars), ignore such questions entirely. I take encouragement from C. S. Lewis, "Modern Theology and Biblical Criticism," in *Christian Reflections*, ed. Walter Hooper (Grand Rapids: Eerdmans, 1967 [1959]), 152–66, who finds a lack of literary judgment to be a recurring feature of skeptical criticism.

51. Hermann Gunkel, *Genesis* (Macon, GA: Mercer University Press, 1997 [1910]), 15.

52. On this point see my discussion in *The God of Miracles: An Exegetical Examination of God's Action in the World* (Wheaton: Crossway, 2000), 96–97.

53. See further my *Genesis 1–4*, 171–72.

54. See ibid., 173n66, for another example of a leading commentator's (Westermann) failure to account for showing over telling.

55. See ibid., 115–16.

has received many competing interpretations; I hold that this tree is the means by which the humans were to acquire a knowledge of good and evil—if they stood the test, they would know good and evil from above, as those who have mastered temptation; sadly, they came to know good and evil from below, as those who have been mastered by temptation. This explanation fits well with the fact that God acknowledges that the humans have actually gained some knowledge (3:22); it also fits with the other uses of the expression, "to know good and evil" (and phrases like it), in the rest of the Hebrew Bible, to express the idea of discernment (which is often gained through maturation).

In fact, this interpretation also helps us to appreciate what is going on in the temptation. I have argued that the humans were created morally innocent ("innocence" is not naïveté or moral neutrality), but not necessarily "perfect." Their task was to mature through the exercise of their obedience, to become confirmed in moral goodness. We cannot say that they were *at this point* necessarily "immortal"; but the narrative does not dwell on what might have been. This, as it turns out, has some similarities to Irenaeus's reading of Genesis 1–3. By his understanding, the innocence of Genesis 2 was more like that of a child than of a full adult; God's goal for them was their maturity (a possible sense of "knowing good and evil," see Deut. 1:39). Their fall broke the process of growth.[56]

But what of the "tree of life"? Does it work "automatically," which is what most mean by calling it magical? Genesis says very little about it. What it does say (3:22, where God fears that the man might live forever if he takes of the tree of life) should be put together with the other passages that use the same idea. In Proverbs 3:18; 11:30; 13:12; 15:4, various blessings are likened to a tree of life: all of these blessings, according to Proverbs, are means to keep the faithful on the path to everlasting happiness. In Revelation 2:7; 22:2, 14, 19, the tree is a symbol of confirmation in holiness for the faithful. This warrants us in finding this tree to be some kind of "sacrament" that sustains or confirms someone in his moral condition: that is why God finds it so horrifying to think of the man eating of the tree in his current state. I call it a "sacrament" because I do not know how it is supposed to convey its effects, any more than I know how the biblical sacrifices, or the washing

56. See Anders-Christian Jacobsen, "The Importance of Genesis 1–3 in the Theology of Irenaeus," *Zeitschrift für antikes Christentum* 8.2 (2005), 302–3. It appears that Harlow, "After Adam," and Enns, *Evolution of Adam*, 88, in finding in Irenaeus an ally for their readings, have misunderstood Irenaeus's actual view of what happened. Further contra Harlow and Enns, I do not know that Western Christianity has uniformly held that Adam and Eve were created "spiritually mature," so much as morally innocent.

ceremonies, or baptism, or the Lord's Supper work. But they *do* work. Only in this sense may the tree be called "magic," but this sense has moved us away from folklore.[57]

Historical Consequences of Adam and Eve's "Fall"

The disobedience of Adam and Eve has historical import, as its consequences make clear. The hiding from God in Genesis 3:8; the fear and blame game of 3:10–13; the solemn sentences of 3:14–19; the evil deeds of chapter 4: all of these are in jarring discord with the idyllic scene of blessing and benevolent dominion (1:28–29) and innocent enjoyment (2:8–9, 18–25). Some have suggested that, because there are no words for "sin" or "rebellion" in Genesis 3, the text does not "teach" that Adam and Eve "sinned."[58] Of course, this is absurd: the question of 3:11 (have you done what I told you not to do?) is as good a paraphrase of disobedience as we can ask for. Some have also suggested that, since the text of Genesis does not *say* that humans "fell" by this disobedience, therefore Genesis does not "teach" such a thing.[59] But the jarring discord we have just noticed is instruction enough on that point. Again, our reading strategy should reckon with *showing* over *telling*.

The descendants of Adam and Eve (Gen. 4 and onward) exhibit sad and shameful behavior, which contrasts with the exuberant expectation of Genesis 1:26–31: the average Israelite's experience is probably more like Genesis 4 than it is like Genesis 1 or 2. This cries out for an explanation, and we need some version of the traditional reading of Genesis 3 to make sense of these facts. If that were not enough, the storyteller has actually pushed us in that direction: Genesis 5:29 deliberately evokes 3:16–17: "Out of the *ground* that the LORD has *cursed*, this one shall bring us relief from our work and from the *painful toil* ['*itstsâbôn*] of our hands."[60]

---

57. See C. S. Lewis, *Prayer: Letters to Malcolm* (London: Collins, 1966), 105. He describes the sacrament of communion as "big medicine and strong magic," and then defines his term: "I should define 'magic' in this sense as 'objective efficacy which cannot be further analysed.'"

58. E.g., James Barr, *The Garden of Eden*, 6. For more on this matter, see my *Genesis 1–4*, 155 and my *Did Adam and Eve Really Exist?*, 164–65.

59. See, for example, Harlow, "Creation according to Genesis": "Genesis itself, however, does not propound a doctrine of the fall or original sin" (189); also his "After Adam," 189. See also Towner, "Interpretations and Reinterpretations of the Fall," e.g., 59: "Nowhere is it said [in Genesis] that human nature was irrevocably altered in a fundamental way that afternoon in the garden. . . . That is all that the Biblical account says—it has never said any more than that."

60. Enns, *Evolution of Adam*, 84, asserts, "The Old Testament portrays humanity in general and Israel in particular as out of harmony with God, *but the root cause of this condition is nowhere laid at Adam's feet*" (emphasis added). His entire section of the book (84–88) exhibits the most wooden reading of the Genesis narrative.

I have heard people object that the disobedience of Genesis 3 is pretty tame in comparison with the violence of Genesis 4, therefore how can the one be the cause of the other? I would not put the relationship between the two sins as simply "cause" and "effect": I would rather say that the sin of Genesis 3, under the influence of a dark power that has the goal of ruining human life, has opened the door to all manner of evil in the world, and that evil has come rushing through. I might further query whether the disobedience of Genesis 3 is really all that "small": after all, it came after God had loaded the human beings with blessings and delights, and it resulted from yielding to a subtle and despicable assault on the character of the God who had shown himself so overflowing with goodness. Let Israel, and all who read this, take warning, and never underestimate the power of even the apparently smallest sins.

Does Genesis give us any clues—showing, if not telling—as to *how* sin was transmitted to Cain, to Lamech, and on to others? The details are sketchy; it is surely not enough to say that Adam and Eve set a bad example for their children. Probably the best answer is that of Paul, who uses the expression "in Adam," implying a way in which human beings are somehow "included" in Adam.

Conclusions

In sum, then, we have plenty of reasons from the text itself to be careful about reading it too literalistically, and at the same time we have reasons to accept a historical core. The genealogies of Genesis 5, 10, and 11, as well as those of 1 Chronicles 1:1 and Luke 3:38, assume that Adam was a real person. Similarly (although the style of telling the story may leave room for discussion on the exact details of the process by which God formed Adam's body and how long ago) we nevertheless can discern that the author intends us to see the disobedience of this couple as the reason for sin in the world. It explains why the Mosaic covenant will include provisions for the people's sins: Mosaic religion, and Christianity its proper offspring, is about redemption for sinners, enabling their forgiveness and moral transformation to restore the image of God in them. This story also explains why all humankind, and not just Israelites, need this redemptive, healing touch from God.

Adam, Eve, Eden, and the Fall in the Rest of the Old Testament

For an interpretation of Genesis 1–5 to be adequate, it must account for the details of the Hebrew narrative, the similarities and differences between that narrative and its possible parallels from elsewhere in the ancient Near

East, and the location of that narrative as the front end of the whole book of Genesis—indeed, of the whole Pentateuch, which therefore means of the whole Old Testament.[61] In this section I will show how the themes of Genesis 1–5 play out in the rest of the Hebrew Bible.

I have already mentioned Claus Westermann's claim that the story of Genesis 3 is "nowhere cited or presumed in the Old Testament." This claim suffers from several difficulties. For example, what exactly constitutes a citation, presumption, or echo? Further: does an allusion to any part of Genesis 1–5 count as one of these echoes? And there is still more: has this perceived rarity of allusion become part of a circular argument—that is, once we think that there are no allusions, do we then dismiss possible allusions because we "know" that such an allusion is unlikely since it is so rare? Finally, does not the presence or absence of allusions depend on the communicative intentions of the biblical writers and their perceptions of the needs of their audiences? That is, a later writer may or may not find an echo of this passage useful to what he is trying to do with his later text—which means that the (perceived) rarity of citation hardly implies that this story has no bearing on the rest of the Hebrew Bible.

Certainly the literary unity of the current text of Genesis 1–5 requires us to qualify any claim of rarity: after all, there are numerous references to creation (e.g., Pss. 8; 104) and to marriage (e.g., Mal. 2:15, using Gen. 2:24). Human rest on the Israelite Sabbath imitates God's rest after his work of creation (Exod. 20:11, echoing Gen. 2:2–3).[62]

Genesis 1–5 is well integrated into Genesis 1–11 and into the whole of Genesis. The genealogies of Genesis 5 and 11 connect the primal pair to subsequent generations, particularly to Abraham. Further, the connection with Mesopotamian stories of prehistory and protohistory comes from the pattern of creation, early generations of people, flood, further generations of people, leading to "modern times"; this makes the first five chapters an inherent part of this pattern, which includes *all* of Genesis 1–11.

We have seen that Genesis presents Noah to us as a new Adam, who receives God's covenant on behalf of his descendants and also of the animals (6:18–19;

---

61. In light of this, there are numerous proposed readings of this story, or parts of it, that I need not spend time assessing: for example, Lyn M. Bechtel, "Genesis 2.4b–3.24: A Myth about Human Maturation," *Journal for the Study of the Old Testament* 67 (1995): 3–26, finds here a myth about the process of growing up, but she has not taken account of the story's themes of obedience and disobedience, the meaning of the "curses," or of the sequel in Gen. 4, which depicts the increase of sin. Further, her reading does not fit into the rest of Genesis, nor does it explain what later biblical authors have found in the story. When Harlow, "After Adam," 189, says that "Genesis 2–3 can be read on a certain level as a coming-of-age story," he too is failing to take enough account of the details of the literary presentation in Genesis itself.

62. I discuss many such "reverberations" in my *Genesis 1–4*.

9:8–17). The call of Abraham is another fresh start on God's plan to bring his blessing to the human race. The "blessing" idea is explicit in 12:2–3 and is combined with being fruitful and multiplying in 17:20; 22:17–18; 26:3–4, 24; 28:3, 14: these echo God's blessing on the original human pair (1:28). Another theme that ties Genesis 1–5 with the rest of Genesis is the repeated word "seed" (best translated "offspring," as in the ESV): see, in Genesis 1–5, 3:15; 4:25; in the rest of Genesis, 13:15–16; 15:3, 5; 17:7–9, 19; 22:17–18; 26:3–4; 48:4. Especially pertinent is the apparently individual offspring referred to in 3:15; 22:17–18; 24:60—who, by the time of Psalm 72, is identified as the ultimate heir of David through whom God's blessing will finally come to the whole earth (Ps. 72:17, echoing Gen. 22:17–18).[63]

The call of Abraham to be the vehicle of blessing to the rest of the world presupposes that the other nations need the blessing of God's light. The story of Genesis 3, and the progression into further moral and spiritual darkness in Genesis 4–11, explains *why* the other nations are so needy.

I have also already observed that the garden of Eden is the pattern for the Israelite sanctuary. Gregory Beale has a book-length argument that this sanctuary in Genesis was intended to be the pattern for the whole earth as a sanctuary.[64] The expulsion of Adam and Eve from the garden interrupted the plan but did not deter God from carrying it out eventually. Israel's sanctuaries, the tabernacle and then the temple, were God's down payment on the accomplishment of his plan; the Christian church furthers it, and the description of the final state of the world (Rev. 21–22) is the completion. There are details in Beale's development that I might say another way, but his overall case is sound and persuasive. This means that the image of the sanctuary from Genesis 2–3, from which humans are exiled and to which they need to return—a return that God provides purely by his grace—is a controlling image for the entire Bible story.

Outside of Genesis 1–5, explicit references to Eden as a prototypical place of fruitfulness occur in Genesis 13:10; Isaiah 51:3; Joel 2:3; and Ezekiel 28:13; 31:8–9, 16, 18; 36:35. In particular, Ezekiel 28:11–19 portrays the king of Tyre as having once been in Eden, blameless, who nevertheless became

63. On the matter of the "offspring" in Genesis, see T. Desmond Alexander, "From Adam to Judah: The Significance of the Family Tree in Genesis," *Evangelical Quarterly* 61.1 (1989): 5–19; "Genealogies, Seed and the Compositional Unity of Genesis," *Tyndale Bulletin* 44.2 (1993): 255–70. On the individual offspring, see my "A Syntactical Note on Genesis 3:15: Is the Woman's Seed Singular or Plural?" *Tyndale Bulletin* 48.1 (1997): 141–48; Alexander's development in "Further Observations on the Term 'Seed' in Genesis," *Tyndale Bulletin* 48.2 (1997): 363–67; and further development from my "Galatians 3:16: What Kind of Exegete Was Paul?"

64. Gregory Beale, *The Temple and the Church's Mission: A Biblical Theology of the Dwelling Place of God,* New Studies in Biblical Theology (Downers Grove, IL: InterVarsity, 2004).

proud and violent. That is, Ezekiel has a "fall story" based on Genesis 3. I count it a mistake to call this *another version* of the Eden story; rather, we should think of it as a rhetorically powerful application of that story to the Phoenician king, or, better, to the city that he represented. That we are dealing here with personification becomes clear when we read the prophet's mention of "your trade" and "your midst" (Ezek. 28:16): "you," the king, personifies the city. And when the prophet says that his addressee was "an anointed guardian cherub," we can recognize that we are reading imagery here, not a literal description. The point is that "the extravagant pretensions of Tyre are graphically and poetically portrayed . . . along with the utter devastation inflicted upon Tyre as a consequence."[65] The rhetorical power derives from reading Genesis 3 as a fall story; there would be no such power in another reading.[66]

Another likely echo of Genesis-3-read-as-a-fall-story is Ecclesiastes 7:29: "See, this alone I found, that God made *man* [Hebrew *ha-'adam*, humankind] upright, but *they* [Hebrew *hémmâ*] have sought out many schemes."

As the Israeli commentator Yehudah Kiel suggests, this is best taken as an allusion to the foolish behavior of Adam in Genesis 3:10.[67] It is well to appreciate what this says: it gives a historical sequence, in which humankind was once (namely, at the time that God made them) "upright,"[68] but through their own "seeking out of many schemes" became other than upright—probably, in context, came to have the character described in verse 20: "Surely there is not a righteous man on earth who does good and never sins" (see 1 Kings 8:46; Prov. 20:9). It also makes good sense to read the notion "return to the dust" (Eccles. 3:20; 12:7) as a deliberate echo of Genesis 3:19 ("for you are dust, and to dust you shall return"). By the way, this also implies that sin is a disruptive intruder (see below).

65. David J. Reimer, note on Ezek. 28:11–19, in Lane Dennis et al., eds., *The ESV Study Bible* (Wheaton: Crossway, 2008), 1542. See also Moshe Greenberg, *Ezekiel 21–37*, Anchor Bible (New York: Doubleday, 1997), 590.

66. For a similar take, see Daniel Block, *Ezekiel 25–48*, New International Commentary on the Old Testament (Grand Rapids: Eerdmans, 1998), 105–6; A. B. Davidson, *Ezekiel*, Cambridge Bible for Schools and Colleges (Cambridge: Cambridge University Press, 1906), 205.

67. Kiel, *Sefer Bereshit*, עו (commenting on Gen. 3:10). Expounding Ecclesiastes in the same series (commentaries written by Israelis who are traditional Jews), Mordecai Zar-Kavod seems to agree, contrasting the *'adam* that God created, "in his image and after his likeness" (Zar-Kavod himself uses the terms from Gen. 1), to "the children of man" (plural *they*) who have gone astray: see Zar-Kavod, "Qohelet," in P. Meltzar et al., *Khamesh Mᵉgillot*, Da'at Miqra' (Jerusalem: Mossad Harav Kook, 1973), מז–מו.

68. As already noted, this need not be the same as "perfect in every way," though it does describe moral innocence.

Two other passages deserve our attention, but they are both highly disputed. The first is Hosea 6:7:

> But *like Adam* they transgressed the covenant;
> there they dealt faithlessly with me.[69]

Others prefer to interpret the words rendered *like Adam* in the ESV as "like any human beings," or even "at (the place called) Adam." The ESV, however, is the simplest interpretation of the Hebrew words, k^e*'adam*, as Vasholz summarizes:

> The hard issue is: to whom or to what does "Adam" refer? Many commentators suggest a geographical locality. The difficulty is that there is no record of covenant breaking at a place called Adam (Josh. 3:16), and it requires a questionable taking of the preposition "like" (Hb. *ke-*) to mean "at" or "in." "There" represents the act wherein Israel was unfaithful to the covenant (cf. Hos. 5:7; 6:10). "Mankind" is another suggestion for "Adam," but that would be a vague statement with no known event indicated, and therefore it would not clarify the sentence. It is best to understand "Adam" as the name of the first man; thus Israel is like Adam, who forgot his covenant obligation to love the Lord, breaking the covenant God made with him (Gen. 2:16–17; 3:17). This also implies that there was a "covenant" relationship between God and Adam, the terms of which were defined in God's words to Adam, though the actual word "covenant" is not used in Genesis 1–3.[70]

This reading makes sense in light of the way that Hosea stresses the abundant generosity of God, who had loaded Israel down with all manner of good things—and Israel had simply repudiated the giver (a running theme in Hosea; see 2:8–13; 7:15; 11:1–4; 13:4–6). That is, Israel's unfaithfulness toward the Lord was like Adam's primal disobedience in its ugliness and insanity.[71]

---

69. My former student Brian Habig has promised a full discussion of this passage defending this interpretation, but as his work has not yet appeared in print, I will say enough here to show why I think it is correct.

70. Robert I. Vasholz, note on Hosea 6:7 in Dennis et al., eds., *The ESV Study Bible*, 1631. For a fuller discussion see Thomas McComiskey, "Hosea," in *The Minor Prophets*, vol. 1, ed. Thomas Edward McComiskey (Grand Rapids: Baker, 1992), 95. Yehudah Kiel, "Hosea," in Kiel et al., *T^erê 'Asar*, Da'at Miqra' (Jerusalem: Mossad Harav Kook, 1990), נח, prefers the "like any human beings" interpretation, but notes that a number of esteemed Jewish interpreters ("our teachers of blessed memory") had taken the "like Adam" reading. Enns, *Evolution of Adam*, 83–84, insists that the place-name interpretation is "certainly correct," without really engaging the lexical and grammatical difficulties that arise.

71. As we will see in the following section, the much later author Ben Sira could use Eve's sin as a pattern that an "evil wife" conforms to, so it is at least not out of the question to find something similar here.

Another possible allusion to Adam as transgressor is Job 31:33:

> If I have concealed my transgressions *as others do* [margin: *as Adam did*],
> by hiding my iniquity in my bosom . . .

There is really no good way to decide between the interpretation of the text ("as others do") or the margin ("as Adam did"); the Hebrew, *ke'adam*, can go either way.[72] What we must not do is enforce circular reasoning, to the effect that since references to Adam are so rare, therefore one is unlikely here. We will instead leave this one as an open question.

Further, the Old Testament as a whole seems to assume that sin is an alien intruder; it disturbs God's good creation order.[73] This comes through in how the sacrifices in Leviticus deal with sin: they treat it as a defiling element, which ruins human existence and renders people unworthy to be in God's presence—and that is dangerous. Genesis makes sense, then, as providing the story of how this intruder came to be a part of human experience, and this also explains why Revelation would portray sin's banishment as a feature of the fulfillment of the world's story.[74]

Finally, we have seen that the tree of life receives further mention in the rest of the Bible (Prov. 3:18; 11:30; 13:12; 15:4; Rev. 2:7; 22:2, 14, 19).

Adam and Eve in Second Temple Jewish Literature

The Second Temple period, which technically began with the Jews building a new temple after their exile to Babylon (c. 516 BC) and ended when the Romans destroyed that temple (AD 70), was one of severe foment among Jews, as they sought to explain their situation in light of their understanding of

72. The "like Adam" option appears, e.g., in a grammatical-historical commentary by the Israeli Amos Hakham, *Sefer 'Iyyob*, Da'at Miqra' (Jerusalem: Mossad Harav Kook, 1984): "the first man, who sinned, and sought to cover over his sin and hid from before God." John Hartley, in a traditional Christian grammatical-historical commentary, *Job*, New International Commentary on the Old Testament (Grand Rapids: Eerdmans, 1988), notes another Jewish author (Robert Gordis) who agrees, while Hartley gives a linguistic reason (the mention of the "bosom") for "like a human being."

73. Barr, *Garden of Eden*, 92–93, asserts that the imperfections in Adam and Eve make their disobedience completely natural and expected. To Enns's credit, he does not suggest in his *Evolution of Adam* that the sin of humans was an inevitable consequence of their creation, but without an original transgression (and transgressors), he cannot explain the presence of sin *as an alien intruder*.

74. I have a brief discussion in *Did Adam and Eve Really Exist?*, 91–92. Enns, *Evolution of Adam*, 74, mentions the passage but does not allow it to affect his thinking about Genesis.

the covenants with Abraham, Moses, and David. There were still parts of the Hebrew Bible to be produced (such as Ezra and Nehemiah), and many other writings as well (some Christian churches include some of this other material in their canon, though no one includes it all). One must use great discretion in reading this other material since there is no one single form of Judaism, and many of these writings are from very sectarian groups (such as the Qumran community, who produced what we call the Dead Sea Scrolls). At the same time, if there is widespread consistency among these various writings, that will give us some idea both of how people read the Old Testament material they had and of what features of the Jewish world the New Testament writers faced. Of the Second Temple material available to us, the books we call the Apocrypha, together with the writings of Josephus, come the closest to being in the Jewish mainstream. It is therefore worthwhile to give them most of our attention.

A clear statement about Adam and Eve comes in the book of Tobit (from somewhere between 250 and 175 BC).[75] The character Tobias is taking Sarah to be his wife, and the angel Raphael has instructed him on how to protect himself and his wife from a demon that threatens harm. Following the angel's instructions, Tobias prays these words (8:6): "[O God of our fathers,] You made Adam and gave him Eve his wife as a helper and support. From them the race of mankind has sprung. You said, 'It is not good that the man should be alone; let us make a helper for him like himself.'"

As was common in Jewish prayers, Tobias begins with a historical recital of God's good deeds in the past as the basis for hope. This recital agrees with what I find in Genesis itself.

For a reference to the creation and fall of Adam and Eve, consider the Wisdom of Solomon (from some time after 200 BC and before the New Testament), whose aim was to relate Jewish faith to the higher elements of Hellenistic culture in Alexandria, Egypt. Alexandria was one of the most highly cultured cities in the Greco-Roman world, and the writer probably wanted to fortify Jews against assimilating and perhaps also to draw cultured gentiles to Jewish faith. After describing the schemes of wicked people against the "righteous" (faithful Jews), he tells us that the wicked are ignorant of God's secret purposes and do not discern the prize blameless souls receive; in 2:23–24 he says,

---

75. Ordinarily I use the dates suggested in David A. deSilva, *Introducing the Apocrypha: Message, Context, and Significance* (Grand Rapids: Baker Academic, 2002). I cannot say that I agree with all of his assessments, but this will do for our purposes. I cite the English of the Apocrypha from *The English Standard Version Bible with Apocrypha* (Oxford: Oxford University Press, 2009), though I have checked the original.

for God created mankind for incorruption,
and made him in the image of his own character,
but through the devil's envy death entered the world,
and those who belong to his party experience it.

Most readers suppose that the author is recounting the story of Genesis 3, seeing the serpent as "the devil's" mouthpiece.[76] He takes it as a historical event that shapes contemporary life (see also 1:13–14; 7:1; 10:1).[77]

Jesus Ben Sira was a wisdom teacher in Jerusalem who finished his book in Hebrew somewhere between 196 and 175 BC and whose grandson translated the book into Greek around 132 BC,[78] giving us the book called Ecclesiasticus (or Sirach, or Ben Sira).[79] This author mentions the creation of man, and the fall with its consequences, mostly in passing (Sir. 14:17; 15:14; 17:1; 33:10 [Heb. 36:10]; 40:1).

In one passage (25:16–26) he makes use of the "fall story" to explain a current malaise, namely the situation in which one's wife is evil. In 25:24 he says,

From a woman sin had its beginning,
and because of her we all die.

This sounds misogynistic, and it may be, but Ben Sira does go on to allow that a woman can be virtuous, and a blessing to her husband (26:1–4, 13–18), so we should take his words as portraying evil women as followers of Eve at her worst.[80] The simplest reading of this is that he took the event as historical.

Undoubtedly Ben Sira did take Adam as historical. In chapters 44–49 he recalls worthies from the history of Israel ("let us now praise famous men," 44:1), leading up to his contemporary Simon (II), son of Onias (high priest ca. 219–196 BC). He begins with Enoch and Noah as the first named "famous men," then goes on to Abraham and through biblical history. Just before his extended praise of Simon, he finishes with Nehemiah (49:13), then returns

---

76. Enns, *Evolution of Adam*, 99, says that in this book "death entered the world 'through the devil's envy,' not through Adam's disobedience," but he never explains why these are exclusive options. Why is it not *both*?

77. Thus the claim that Harlow makes in "After Adam," 189, that Paul and the church fathers are the earliest to talk about the fall and original sin, seriously needs some nuance.

78. As we learn from his translator's prologue to the Greek.

79. Parts of the Hebrew text have been discovered, but textual difficulties still remain.

80. Stanley Porter, "The Pauline Concept of Original Sin, in Light of Rabbinic Background," *Tyndale Bulletin* 41.1. (1990):3–30, denies that Ben Sira is referring to Eve, but his reading seems to me inadequate; see the Hebrew commentary of Moshe Segal, *Sefer Ben Sira Hashshalem* (Jerusalem: Mosad Bialik, 1958), קנח, for the connection.

to Genesis, naming Enoch and Joseph (49:14–15). He completes the run-up
to Simon in 49:16:

> Shem and Seth were honored among men,
> and Adam above every living being in the creation.

The way he mentions these men in this context indicates that he took them
all as historical figures.[81]

Two Jewish writers who are partly contemporary with the New Testament
are Philo of Alexandria (roughly 20 BC–AD 50) and Josephus. Philo, with
his interest in philosophical allegory, does not say clearly whether he thought
Adam to have been historical. In his discussion of Genesis 2:7, he seems to
distinguish the man of Genesis 1 from the man of Genesis 2: the heavenly and
the earthly man, he calls them.[82]

Josephus's way of writing is far more accessible to educated Westerners.
At times he is unduly literalistic, perhaps writing to connect the Genesis
account with the received world picture of the Greco-Roman world (since
he aimed to commend Judaism). He calls Adam "the first man, made from
the earth."[83] He also says that the gracious God of Israel is the one source
of happiness for all humankind,[84] which is connected to his view that all
people descend from Adam. This conviction of common humanity doubtless
underlies his notion that all people should worship the true God, and his
explanation for the admission of gentiles into Jewish worship.[85] Josephus is
more representative than Philo of the Judaism we find in the other Second
Temple sources.

Finally, from the Mishnah (compiled in Hebrew, ca. AD 220), we have the
same sentiment, in Sanhedrin 4:5:

---

81. There are other references, in 2 (or 3 or 4!) Ezra and 2 Baruch, all of which follow the
same lines. The book called 2 Esdras in the ESV is called 4 Ezra in the Latin Vulgate (where it
is an appendix), and 3 Esdras in the Slavonic Bible. It is thought to have been written originally
in Hebrew around the end of the first century AD, then translated into Greek, but neither the
Hebrew nor the Greek is extant. It has several passages about the fall of Adam as the means by
which sin and suffering came into the world, e.g., 3:4–11, 21–22; it is hardly a treatise on "original
sin," however. A translation and commentary are available in Michael E. Stone, *Fourth Ezra*,
Hermeneia (Minneapolis: Fortress, 1990); see 63–66 for an excursus on Adam's sin.

82. *Allegorical Interpretation*, 1.31. On the other hand, apparently Philo can deal with Gen.
1:27 as the creation of the first, earthly, man: see his *On the Creation*, 25, 69, etc. See Jarl Fos-
sum, "Colossians 1.15–18a in the Light of Jewish Mysticism and Gnosticism," *New Testament
Studies* 35.2 (April 1989): 187–88.

83. *Antiquities*, 1.2.3 (1:67).

84. Ibid., 4.8.2 (4:180).

85. *Against Apion*, 2.23, 37 (2:192, 261).

But a single man was created [first] . . . for the sake of peace among mankind, that none should say to his fellow, "My father was greater than your father." Again, [a single man was created] to proclaim the greatness of the Holy One, blessed is he; for man stamps many coins with the one seal and they are all like one another; but the King of kings, the Holy One, blessed is he, has stamped every man with the seal of the first man, yet not one of them is like his fellow.[86]

In the period that bridges the Old Testament and the New, the Jewish authors most representative of the mainstream consistently treat Adam and Eve as actual people, at the head of the human race.

Conclusion

There are at least four possible ways of taking the material in Genesis:

1. The author intended to relay "straight" history, with a minimum of figurative language.
2. The author was talking about what he thought were actual events, using rhetorical and literary techniques to shape the readers' attitudes toward those events.
3. The author intended to recount an imaginary history, using recognizable literary conventions to convey "timeless truths" about God and man.
4. The author told a story without caring whether the events were real or imagined; his main goal was to convey various theological and moral truths.

I conclude that option (2) best captures what we find in Genesis. There is an irony about option (1): it is held both by many traditional Christians, especially those who are called "young-earth creationists," and by many biblical scholars who embrace "historical criticism." The difference is that the young-earth creationists think that Genesis was telling the truth, and the critical scholars think that Genesis is largely incorrect in its history. Mind you, this does not mean that critical scholars find no value in Genesis; they will commonly resort to something like option (4).

These critical biblical scholars will often (though not always) deny that Adam and Eve were real people, though they agree that the author of Genesis *intended* to write of real people. Those who follow option (3) say that the author never intended for us to think of Adam and Eve as real, while those who

86. Cited from Herbert Danby, *The Mishnah* (Oxford: Oxford University Press, 1933), 388, with comparison of the Hebrew. In the Talmud, see Sanhedrin 38a.

follow option (4) say that it simply does not matter. When a particular scholar denies that Adam and Eve were historical, I cannot always tell which interpretive option he or she has followed; sometimes I wonder if the scholar knows!

When the New Testament authors, and Christian theologians following them, have based their arguments on the presupposition that the human race began with an actual Adam and Eve, and that God made this couple morally innocent, and that evil came into human experience by way of this couple's sin, they were basing themselves upon a good reading of the Old Testament: both as to the specific texts, and as to the logic of the story.

2

ADAM IN THE NEW TESTAMENT

Robert W. Yarbrough

Survey of Explicit New Testament References

Explicit references to Adam are sparse in the New Testament writings, with a total of just nine occurrences in seven different verses: Luke 3:38; Romans 5:14 (2x); 1 Corinthians 15:22, 45 (2x); 1 Timothy 2:13–14; Jude 14. A quick overview of these passages is in order at the outset. More thorough discussion will follow below.

Luke mentions Adam in the last verse of his genealogy (Luke 3:23–38). Unlike Matthew's genealogy (Matt. 1:2–16), which begins with Abraham and moves forward to "Joseph the husband of Mary, of whom Jesus was born, who is called Christ" (Matt. 1:16), Luke's works backward from Jesus (Luke 3:23), through generations of other Second Temple and then Old Testament Jews and Hebrews, to "the son of Enos, the son of Seth, the son of Adam, the son of God" (Luke 3:38). The figure whose name in many accounts is associated with (original) sin is here accorded the status of God's son.

Romans 5:14 is part of a passage (Rom. 5:12–21) so rich in significance for our topic that a whole essay (by Thomas R. Schreiner) is devoted to it later in this volume: "Yet death reigned from Adam to Moses, even over those whose sinning was not like the transgression of Adam, who was a type of the one who was to come." This verse echoes the Old Testament narrative in which

(1) sin's entrance into the world and universal permeation of humanity begin with Adam (in conjunction with Eve); (2) people after Adam sin in the same way (in that they too sin) yet differently from the way he did; and (3) Adam somehow foreshadows "one who was to come." In the larger context of Romans it is clear that the coming one turns out to be Christ.

This is in contrast to a slightly later Hellenistic Jewish document that also draws on the Genesis 1–3 passage. Fourth Ezra 7:46–50 agrees with Paul that "the human condition [is] already so conditioned by our descent from Adam that none of us begins with a blank slate, but with the evil tendency already firmly planted within us."[1] But unlike Paul, who in Romans often erupts in praise,[2] the writer of 4 Ezra is "burdened by the fate of the many, and unable to join in Paul's doxology."[3]

The three occurrences in 1 Corinthians accompany Paul's most extended discussion of Christ's resurrection and by extension the resurrection of those who are united with him by faith. "For as in Adam all die, so also in Christ shall all be made alive" (1 Cor. 15:22) relates human mortality to the first mortal, who, according to the Genesis account, suffered death in connection with his sinful action. Adam underwent physical death after a life span given as 930 years (Gen. 5:5). This can be seen as the physical counterpart to both real and proleptic death in the form of ruptured communion with God, who had warned him that "in the day you eat of it you shall surely die" (Gen. 2:17), "it" referring to the tree of the knowledge of good and evil. Immediately in the wake of his (and Eve's) transgression, they were banished from the garden and from pristine fellowship with God. In exchange came attenuated life, qualitatively speaking, under the terms of the curse (Gen. 3:14–19). Adam's death as the result of sin, Paul implies, had direct universal implications for all people after him. Correspondingly, "in Christ" Adam's lapse is offset in such a way that all "shall . . . be made alive."

The other Corinthian passage names Adam twice: "Thus it is written, 'The first man Adam became a living being'; the last Adam became a life-giving spirit" (1 Cor. 15:45).[4] Paul takes two slight liberties in his citation of what we know as Genesis 2:7. Both the Masoretic Text (MT) and the Septuagint read simply, "And the man became a living being" or "living creature." Paul inserts the proper name "Adam," and he adds the adjective "first." Neither liberty is excessive. Genesis 2:7 (MT) has "the man," the same word that in

---

1. M. E. Boring, K. Berger, and C. Colpe, eds., *Hellenistic Commentary to the New Testament* (Nashville: Abingdon, 1995), 360.

2. See Andy Naselli, *From Typology to Doxology* (Corvallis, OR: Pickwick, 2012).

3. Boring, Berger, and Colpe, *Hellenistic Commentary to the New Testament*, 361.

4. For parallels, but also decisive contrasts, in Qumran writings and in Philo, see ibid., 442–43.

later verses becomes "Adam." So Paul is simply supplying the proper name that is implicit in the generic word "man" ('*adam* in Hebrew). As for "first," this is factually true according to the Genesis narrative, and it sets up Paul's reference to Christ as "last" (*eschatos*) Adam at the end of the verse.[5]

Two more Pauline references occur in 1 Timothy 2:13–14: "For Adam was formed first, then Eve; and Adam was not deceived, but the woman was deceived and became a transgressor." As in 1 Corinthians, Paul draws on the narrative order of Genesis, which depicts Adam as being formed (2:7) and active (2:15–20) for some time before God creates his female counterpart (2:21–22). He also draws on narrative details in noting the sequence in which humanity's first parents succumbed to the tempter's wiles: Eve first, then Adam. The quintessentially Pauline nature of this is confirmed in 1 Corinthians 11:8–9 as well as 2 Corinthians 11:3. For Paul, God's act and order in creation, and the misdeeds of Adam and Eve in the fall, have left imprints still relevant to human nature and optimal ecclesial order.

The final New Testament reference to Adam is found in Jude 14–15:

> It was also about these that Enoch, the seventh from Adam, prophesied, saying, "Behold, the Lord comes with ten thousands of his holy ones, to execute judgment on all and to convict all the ungodly of all their deeds of ungodliness that they have committed in such an ungodly way, and of all the harsh things that ungodly sinners have spoken against him."

In Jude's flow of discourse, this passage helps summarize and epitomize the error of certain troublemakers in the church (see vv. 4–16) against whom Jude writes to stir up resistance (v. 3). These troublemakers, Jude maintains, bear resemblance to various persons or movements in Old Testament times—disobedient Israelites (v. 5); rebellious angels (v. 6); residents of Sodom and Gomorrah (v. 7); and an unholy trio consisting of Cain, Balaam, and Korah (v. 11). The passage cited above (vv. 14–15) that mentions Adam does not highlight him so much as use his name to locate the "Enoch" associated with the document Jude quotes (1 Enoch 1:9) in verses 14 and 15: he was seventh in line from Adam. G. Green has pointed out that "the 'seventh' position held particular significance for the Semitic mind," so that highlighting Enoch in the manner Jude does has the effect of asserting: "*no less than* the seventh from Adam spoke against these heretics!"[6]

---

5. For more extended discussion, see Roy Ciampa and Brian Rosner, "1 Corinthians," in *Commentary on the New Testament Use of the Old Testament*, ed. G. K. Beale and D. A. Carson (Grand Rapids: Baker Academic; Nottingham, UK: Apollos, 2007), 746–47.
6. Gene L. Green, *Jude and 2 Peter* (Grand Rapids: Baker Academic, 2008), 104.

Interpretive Options—Glimpses from the History of the Bible's Reception

Before a deeper exegetical examination of the New Testament passages listed above (and some others as well), a glance is warranted at a team of scholars' recent attempt to characterize reception of the Genesis Adam through various documents, movements, or historical periods. That is, with the beginning of the appearance of the projected thirty-volume *Encyclopedia of the Bible and Its Reception*,[7] fresh treatment of both Old and New Testament references to Adam from various perspectives is at hand.[8] Taking stock of observations made there will help focus our own exegetical investigations in subsequent sections below.

Regarding the Old Testament,[9] H. Wallace stresses etymology, the paucity of occurrences of "Adam" in Hebrew as a proper name, and the "unquestioning complicity" of Adam when compared to "the theologically probing nature of Eve." Wallace separates the Genesis 1:1–2:4a portion of the narrative from Genesis 2:4b–3:24, a distinction New Testament authors did not seem to recognize (just as they did not seem to find Eve more theologically astute than Adam). Wallace implies that those who think Eve is accorded a subordinate role in the narrative are in the minority. In a related article, he notes that recent Jewish Old Testament interpreters have challenged traditional Christian interpretation of the Adam passages in Genesis 2–3.[10] An effect of Wallace's summation is to call in question if not deconstruct readings of Adam reflected in the New Testament and Christian thought in many circles through the centuries.

Regarding Judaism (Second Temple, rabbinic, and medieval), S. Bunta calls attention to the divergence of understandings from early on: "There is little to no unity in the depiction of Adam in the Second Temple period."[11] He does suggest that there are "occasional agreements" when the Genesis narrative (as opposed to unfolding allegories and traditions using that narrative as a springboard) is the focus.[12] These agreements involve "Adam's sinfulness and purity, mortality and immortality, and his dominion over other creatures."[13] Still, divergence dominates, with Philo himself "not entirely consistent in his

7. *Encyclopedia of the Bible and Its Reception*, ed. Hans-Josef Klauck et al. (Berlin and New York: Walter de Gruyter, 2009), hereafter *EBR*.
8. See "Adam (Person)," *EBR* 1:300–33 and "Adam and Eve, Story of," *EBR* 1:341–64.
9. See "Adam (Person)," *EBR* 1:300.
10. "Adam and Eve, Story of," *EBR* 1:341–43.
11. "Adam (Person)," *EBR* 1:301.
12. Ibid.
13. Ibid.

thought on Adam."[14] Turning from Second Temple and Hellenistic to "classical rabbinic" Judaism, Bunta finds "a vast spectrum of ideologies" and no "consistent portrait of Adam."[15] Yet "most of the classical rabbinic literature reads *adam* of Genesis 1–4 as the person of Adam," and several psalms (e.g., 92 and 139) were seen as autobiographical statements traceable to Adam.[16] Medieval Judaism is still more fluid and varied, veering off eventually into hekhalot mysticism and kabbalistic speculation.[17] Jewish philosophers, like Maimonides (1138–1204), Judah ha-Levi (twelfth century), and Joseph Albo (fifteenth century), apply their respective philosophical and religious convictions to the Adam accounts.[18] This foreshadows Enlightenment interpretation, which likewise rejects historic (in this case Christian) understanding and simply incorporates Adam into reigning thought systems.

In looking at Adam in the New Testament, J. Dunn expounds on the nine explicit references to the person of Adam (cited in the previous section).[19] In addition, he finds allusions to "Adam theology" in several passages that draw on Psalm 8:4–6 (Heb. 2:6–8; 1 Cor. 15:25–27; see also Eph. 1:20, 22; Mark 12:36; 1 Pet. 3:22).[20] Dunn feels that Adam allusions (or the Genesis narratives containing Adam references) may also lie behind Romans 3:23; 7:7–13; 8:19–22; and other passages.[21] These exegetical proposals will receive further attention below.

With respect to Christianity (Greek patristic and Eastern Orthodox, Latin patristic and early medieval), G. Anderson stresses the fork in the road between Greek and Latin tendencies.[22] The Greek Fathers in their exegesis of Adam texts were concerned not so much with sin as with "the corruptibility of the body."[23] In their view Adam and Eve had angelic constitutions (see Matt. 22:30) prior to the fall. This correlates with the view that Adam and Eve's clothing with skin post-fall (Gen. 3:21) meant their demotion to mortal bodies. In the incarnation "Christ enters the world by assuming the post-lapsarian state of Adam,"[24] meaning the inglorious bodies of current human existence. But at

---

14. Ibid., 302.
15. Ibid., 303.
16. Ibid., 303.
17. Ibid., 304–6.
18. Ibid., 306.
19. Ibid., 306–8.
20. Ibid., 308–9.
21. Ibid., 309–10.
22. See also his treatments in "Adam and Eve," *Religion Past and Present*, ed. D. Brown et al. (Leiden and Boston: Brill, 2007), 1:49–50; "Adam," *The New Interpreter's Dictionary of the Bible*, ed. K. Sakenfeld (Nashville: Abingdon, 2006), 1:48–50.
23. "Adam (Person)," *EBR* 1:311.
24. Ibid., 312.

Christ's resurrection "he sheds this mortal body and assumes the bodily form that had been Adam's in the Garden."[25] Anderson succeeds at showing the substantial differences that a few key moves, or rather affirmations of Hellenistic convictions (like the essential inferiority of created matter), by Greek Fathers have made for one of the major Christian communions through the centuries. (As of 2010, Eastern Orthodoxy accounts for over 10 percent of the world's Christian population.)[26]

On the Latin side, Anderson affirms the standard view that the major figure was Augustine. While Augustine's earlier writings handled Genesis and Adam allegorically, his views matured to differ from Greek readings in two important respects. First, Augustine "put a decided emphasis on the problem of sin as opposed to that of death."[27] Second, "he saw a very tight relationship between the moment of sexual awakening and original sin."[28] Here Augustine's cue was Paul's statement in Romans 7:23 that there was war between his high theoretical ideals and "the law of sin that dwells in my members." Anderson argues that Augustine was not advancing "an inherently negative attitude toward the sexual organs" and "was not simply fixated on sex."[29] He rather saw in Genesis 3:7 that after the fall Adam and Eve "were ashamed of their genital members."[30] Prior to that, "their bodies and souls existed in perfect harmony,"[31] as Genesis 2:25 may be taken to imply: "And the man and his wife were both naked and were not ashamed." In sum, the major lesson of Adam is not (as for the Greek Fathers) about the loss of angelic bodily makeup but about the entrance of a sinister presence into human existence that had previously not been there and from which only God could deliver. Augustine highlighted humans' sin problem and God's exclusively sufficient solution.

Augustine, with his attempt to handle the Adam narrative in somewhat historical terms, furnishes a bridge to European and modern times, as D. Callender Jr. points out: "The assumption that Adam was an actual historical figure persisted largely unchallenged in the Christian West until the development of modern literary criticism and the rise of biological evolutionism."[32] On various grounds and for various reasons, thinkers ranging from Johann Gottfried Herder to Kant, Schleiermacher, Troeltsch, Brunner, and Barth opted for nonhistorical

25. Ibid.
26. Patrick Johnstone, *The Future of the Global Church* (Downers Grove, IL: InterVarsity, 2011), 65.
27. "Adam (Person)," *EBR* 1:313.
28. Ibid.
29. Ibid., 314.
30. Ibid.
31. Ibid., 313.
32. Ibid., 318.

or relatively dehistoricized treatments of Adam.[33] In broad terms this correlates with the Enlightenment's fundamental rejection of biblical authority and vigorous (and often anti-Semitic[34]) promotion of "a de-Judaized Christianity" in the wake of Kant,[35] who regarded the Jews as "aliens" and "degenerate."[36] Not scientific but ideological considerations (arguably legitimated by what we today term "racism") were the first to cast a pall over the Adam account's relevance to human existence and Christian theology in Western understanding.

This is far from all that might be said about Adam in the history of the Bible's reception, but it is sufficient to observe that contrasts (as well as similarities) between various readings in the Christian tradition (the subject of the bulk of this book) pale in comparison to the varied conceptualizations of Adam found outside that tradition. This suggests that exegesis of New Testament Adam texts, far from being yet another exercise in using those texts to support the certainties of systems foreign to them, might well provide a fresh glimpse of the relatively homogenous biblical testimony that has fed various Christian traditions over the centuries. For a good deal of Adam lore in circulation finds little in common with that testimony apart from the use of Adam's name. One finds dubious amplification of varied fragments of biblical accounts regarding his life, his actions, and their historic and eschatological ramifications. The New Testament accounts themselves share a much tighter and less speculative focus.

Adam in the New Testament: A Deeper Look

We will now consider eight of the New Testament's nine Adam passages (surveyed above) at greater length. (There is little additional to say about Jude 14.) These eight references occur in four passages: Luke 3:38; Romans 5:14; 1 Corinthians 15:22, 45; and 1 Timothy 2:13–14. We will also take stock of more oblique references to Adam found in passages where the actual word "Adam" does not appear.

Luke 3:38

This verse, the last in a chain beginning with "Jesus . . . the son . . . of Joseph" (3:23), refers to "Adam, the son of God." Overall, the genealogy has

33. Ibid., 318–19.
34. See Anders Gerdmar, *Roots of Theological Anti-Semitism: German Biblical Interpretation and the Jews from Herder and Semler to Kittel and Bultmann* (Leiden and Boston: Brill, 2009).
35. Gary Dorrien, *Kantian Reason and Hegelian Spirit: The Idealistic Logic of Modern Theology* (Chichester, UK: Wiley-Blackwell, 2012), 549.
36. Ibid., 547.

Jesus as its focus, not Adam.[37] But the latter is foundational to the former, in four different ways.

First, God stands at the head of all things human and indeed of humanity. Whatever else may be said of human nature and origin, the human story is inextricably bound to this God, who stands behind it all in creation, judgment, redemption, and final restoration. Human existence is inexplicable apart from God's foundational acts, providential oversight, and eschatological intentions.

Second, Adam is not an isolated figure in the redemptive account we call the Gospel of Luke. He is an integral component in the line that includes Enoch, Noah, Abraham, Isaac, Jacob, Judah, Boaz, Jesse, David, and all the others in Jesus's ancestry. One cannot properly call Adam Jewish or Hebrew, but neither can one conceive of God's judgment and redemption in the flood, in God's covenant with Abraham, in God's promise to the house of David, or in the son of David whom David called Lord (Luke 20:44) apart from Adam. In this respect, nothing that Luke writes about the world in which humanity is a factor can be separated from Adam, who humanly speaking gets things rolling and whose identity and behavior are definitive for the human race he fathered.

Third, redemptive mystery attends not only Adam's origin (given his direct rootage in God) but also his descendants' destiny, as Adam's lineage eventuates in someone "supposed" to be the son of Joseph (Luke 3:23)—but who was actually not. The word translated "supposed" (*nomizō*) is used frequently in Luke-Acts to refer to a mistaken assumption.[38] Jesus was not *really* Joseph's son, as Luke 1:26–38 makes clear. He was miraculously conceived. Adam's miraculous creation by God, implied when Luke terms him God's son, has its correlate in Jesus's supernatural origin. In this sense, details of Luke's genealogy foreshadow Paul's coinage of First Adam–Second Adam imagery. Both Adam and Jesus are in key aspects *sui generis* (in a class of their own), yet both have universal and paradigmatic significance for the human race.

Fourth, Adam is not mentioned at all in the Gospels and only once in Luke-Acts; this might be taken to imply his insignificance for those vital accounts of the person and work of Christ (the Gospels) and the rise of the early church (Acts). But another view is possible. Adam's integral importance is implicitly verified by the Jewishness of the Gospel and Acts accounts. As was indicated in the previous section, Second Temple and rabbinic thought about Adam contains substantial variation. But Adam receives widespread attention. He is, in Jewish thought, the starting point of humanity and key to the truth of

---

37. See J. Greene, *The Gospel of Luke*, New International Commentary on the New Testament (Grand Rapids: Eerdmans, 1997), 189.
38. See Luke 2:44; Acts 7:25; 8:20; 14:19; 16:27; 21:29.

human nature, whatever that turns out to be. Similarly, in all the Gospels as well as Acts, there is no doubt that the story of Jesus is the extension and indeed fulfilment of redemptive promises stretching back to primordial humanity (and to eternity prior to it) and primal sin. The hundreds of Old Testament citations, allusions, and echoes in the Gospels and Acts are inexplicable apart from the acceptance by New Testament writers of the Old Testament's veracity, authority, and continuing relevance when properly interpreted. In view of this, paucity of direct reference to Adam is no necessary indicator of his significance. However many times his name is mentioned, he serves centrally in the role in which the Old Testament casts him: the starting point of human existence, flourishing, and sin, with all its attendant woes. And because his sin was met with the seed of divine saving promise (Gen. 3:15), he is also at the root of human redemptive hope.

Adam is a dominant if unspoken presence in the redemptive narrations of the Gospels and Acts. From God's viewpoint in its canonical representation, Adam was the gateway through whom creation gave birth to all those to whom God has given life, as Acts 17:26–27 states: "And he made from one man every nation of mankind to live on all the face of the earth, having determined allotted periods and the boundaries of their dwelling place, that they should seek God."

From Christ's viewpoint Adam is the one who is part of a pristine "beginning" involving "male and female" (Matt. 19:4; see also 24:21), the aftermath of whose misdeeds Christ has come to address. Adam is implicit in the angel's reference to a "Son of the Most High" to whom "the Lord God will give . . . the throne of his father David" and who "will reign over the house of Jacob forever" (Luke 1:32–33). Rarity of reference to Adam in the Gospels and Acts does not mean that Jesus or his earliest followers were oblivious or indifferent to Adam and his implications, whether for his direct descendants all the way down to Jesus, for human nature universally, or for divine deliverance.

Romans 5:14

This verse appears in a passage whose details are disputed (Rom. 5:12–21). A full exegesis of the passage is not possible here. Nor is it necessary, since the text is treated fully by Thomas Schreiner in this volume. But four observations may be ventured.

First, Adam is central to Paul's soteriological understanding. Romans 5:14, which explicitly mentions Adam twice, is key in a literary unit that explains justification and reconciliation, two of Paul's most fundamental soteriological categories. Justification is mentioned in Romans 5:1 and 9, indicating this is a major theme of the chapter. In 5:10–11 Paul switches the explicit subject to reconciliation. But this is rightly regarded as an application and extension of justification. As Paul moves to death in Adam and life in Christ (5:12–21), he still has justification in mind (note "justification" in 5:16, 18; "the free gift of righteousness" in 5:17; "made righteous" in 5:19). While it is possible that Paul had never made the connection between justification, on the one hand, and Christ's role in relation to Adam, on the other, this is unlikely given the tie between Adam and Christ seen in 1 Corinthians 15, written some years prior to Romans. It is more likely that as an observant Jew, Paul had always affirmed the Old Testament account of human origins (see Acts 17:26), much as Jesus instinctively looked to Genesis 1–2 for his understanding of marriage (Matt. 19:4–6; see also Mark 10:6–9). The very fact that Paul pairs Adam with Christ in the way he does at this key point in Romans—just after defining saving "faith" via Abraham (chap. 4) and just before turning to objections to his soteriological affirmations (chaps. 6–7)—suggests that the logic of justification and its benefits hinges to a considerable degree on the understanding of man and sin that the Adam narratives support.

Second, the sin of Adam who was made in God's image (Gen. 1:26–27; 5:1) had consequences for those after him, who were "in his own [i.e., Adam's] likeness, after his image" (Gen. 5:3). They were, namely, subject to sin and death. "Sin came into the world through one man," Paul summarizes in Romans 5:12. (This is not to minimize Eve's importance but to affirm Adam's representative status as the father of humankind.) He continues, "And death [came into the world] through sin." That would surely be Adam's sin, or Eve's and Adam's together viewed in its composite cataclysmic effect. The result will turn out to be pervasive for each and every one of their offspring. (They produce no morally pristine children, according to the Bible's narrative, but quite the opposite.) It will also prove remediable through one and only one avenue: trust in the gracious saving provision of the God who gave humans life to begin with.

Third, Adam is far more pervasive in Romans 5:12–21 than occurrences of his name indicate. There is need to avoid the word-concept fallacy.[39] This fallacy assumes that for a thing (in the case "Adam") to be present in a discourse, a single precise word denoting that thing must appear. In this view, "Adam" is not that significant to the discourse of Romans because his name occurs there in just one verse.

But there is a more plausible way to view the matter. First, Romans 5:12–21 is not just some random juncture in Romans but is near the pinnacle of Paul's

---

39. See also J. S. Duvall and J. D. Hays, *Grasping God's Word*, 2nd ed. (Grand Rapids: Zondervan, 2005), 135.

account of justification, reconciliation, how the need for these divine actions arose (namely, due to Adam's sin), and what those actions were (namely, Christ's saving work perfectly offsetting Adam and his misdeed). This is one of several climactic passages in the entire epistle widely regarded as the theological crossroads of the entire New Testament. Second, in this pivotal section "Adam" is not only mentioned in Romans 5:14: he is also alluded to directly in numerous additional ways, as the table below indicates.

Romans 5, verse	Reference to Adam
12	"sin came into the world through one man"
13	"sin . . . in the world before the law was given"
15	"the trespass" "through one man's trespass"
16	"the result of that one man's sin" "the judgment following one trespass brought condemnation"
17	"because of one man's trespass" "death reigned through that one man"
18	"one trespass led to condemnation for all men"
19	"by the one man's disobedience the many were made sinners"
20	"the trespass"
21	"sin reigned in death"

The chart shows that Adam is referred to not just once in this passage but over a dozen times. By name or by other direct reference, he is as integral to the logic of redemption in this passage as Christ is. The former is the foil for the latter, whose person and work are the comprehensive and perfect antidote to the ills Adam's misdeed spawned. Paul's soteriology, Christology, theological anthropology, and hamartiology come together in these ten terse verses, none of which is intelligible without Adam in his historical existence and real aftereffects, which Christ came to address and remedy.

A fourth observation regarding Adam in Romans is in order. His presence in this epistle may not be limited to Romans 5:12–21. Dunn proposes clear allusions to Adam in Romans 3:23, 7:7–13, and 8:19–22.[40] Brief examination of these three passages is in order.

Romans 3:23

Do the words "all have sinned and fall short of the glory of God" (Rom. 3:23) allude to Adam? Due to background considerations, Dunn answers yes. He notes that in the Apocalypse of Moses 20:2, Adam laments God's depriving

---

40. "Adam (Person)," *EBR* 1:309–10.

him of the glory with which he had previously been clothed. Adam repeats this lament when he denounces Eve in 21:6: "O wicked woman! what have I done to thee that thou hast deprived me of the glory of God?"[41] Observes Dunn: Pauline and Jewish soteriology both "understood salvation in terms of the restoration or enhancement of the original glory."[42] Therefore when Paul in Romans 3 speaks of sin in connection with human loss of glory, he must be drawing on the Adam account in Genesis, or at the very least on Jewish tradition associated with it. D. Moo loosely concurs: "the absence of glory" to which Paul calls attention in Romans 3:23 "involves a declension from the 'image of God' in which human beings were first made."[43]

In this connection, Dunn proceeds to implicate several other Pauline passages with Adamic representations, namely 2 Corinthians 3:18, Philippians 3:21, and Colossians 3:10. All these passages speak of new creation. Dunn thinks that the resurrected Christ serves as "the template on which the divine image of the first creation is recreated."[44] That Christ serves as such a template, and more, is indisputable. Whether Paul has Adam so much in view that these verses can be seen as allusions to him depends in part on the definition of "allusion." It seems unverifiable that Paul necessarily had Genesis 1–3 in mind when he penned these passages.[45] For that reason it is not compelling to assert that he was alluding to Adam. Yet if "allusion" means the unconscious assumption of Adam's historical existence, of sin's universal effect on humans in Adam's train, and of Christ's conferral of eschatological glory on his people as the Second Adam, Dunn's point has merit. This would be another example of the need to transcend the word-concept fallacy in gauging Adam's importance for New Testament writers.

Romans 7:7–13

Did Paul, as Dunn suggests, intend the "I" passage of Romans 7:7–13 "to evoke the Genesis story of Adam's original sin in coveting likeness to God in knowing good and evil (Gen. 3:5)"?[46] In various forms this view has a hoary heritage dating to "the earliest days of the church."[47] Yet it seems unlikely, as Paul explicitly describes Adam's sin as occurring in a context that predated

41. *The Apocalypse of Moses*, trans. R. H. Charles, Christian Classics Ethereal Library (website), accessed September 17, 2012, http://www.ccel.org/c/charles/otpseudepig/apcmose.htm.
42. Dunn, "Adam (Person)," *EBR* 1:310.
43. Douglas J. Moo, *The Epistle to the Romans* (Grand Rapids: Eerdmans, 1996), 226.
44. Dunn, "Adam (Person)," *EBR* 1:310.
45. Gordon Fee, e.g., in his *Pauline Christology* (Peabody, MA: Hendrickson, 2007), 180–83, explains 2 Cor. 3:18 with reference to Moses and Exodus, not Adam and Genesis.
46. Dunn, "Adam (Person)," *EBR* 1:310.
47. Moo, *Epistle to the Romans*, 425.

the giving of the law (Rom. 5:13). But in Romans 7, Paul speaks of someone's (and possibly his own) coveting because of what the law commanded him. Each verse from verse 7 to verse 13 mentions "law" or "commandment" or both. So while mention of sin producing death (v. 13) is reminiscent of Adam's sin, Paul's ubiquitous reference to the law and its commandments is unfavorable to the notion that he has Adam's sin in particular in mind in this passage.[48] The undeniable formal similarity (temptation to sin) is offset by the categorical differences between Paul's setting (where the law was at work) and Adam's (where the law was not a factor in the way it was for the Romans 7 figure, and where, moreover, a negative divine stipulation ["you shall not eat of it"] must have interacted with Adam's sinless nature in a different way than Paul depicted or possibly experienced).

Romans 8:19–22

Does Romans 8:19–22 constitute a "strong allusion to the Genesis narrative," as Dunn affirms?[49] A positive answer seems undeniable. In the curse of Genesis 3, God clearly in some sense subjects creation to futility (see also Rom. 8:20). Since the fall, all humans have inhabited a world of "bondage to corruption" (v. 21), a world longing for better things (v. 19) and "groaning" in travail (v. 22). Adam (and Eve) stand at the onset and the core of this most doleful of cosmic portraits, mitigated only by the strands of gospel redemption interwoven through it. Dunn could have extended the allusion one more verse, since the phrase "we wait eagerly for adoption as sons, the redemption of our bodies" (v. 23) might easily be pressed to depict the reversal of the earthly and bodily curses inflicted on the Edenic pair.

In sum, in numerous passages and manners Romans refers significantly to Adam, his existence and fall, and his universal importance for human nature and destiny in the times between Christ's first and second comings. Paul's consciousness of Adam is by no means limited to explicit references in one verse of chapter five.

1 Corinthians 15:22, 45

In 1 Corinthians emphasis shifts ultimately to Adam's importance, not only in the past and for the present but also for the age to come. Paul writes, "For as in Adam all die, so also in Christ shall all be made alive" (15:22). He states this to confirm an assertion made two verses earlier: "But in fact Christ has been raised from the dead, the firstfruits of those who have fallen asleep"

---

48. So also ibid., 426–30.
49. Dunn, "Adam (Person)," *EBR* 1:310.

(v. 20). In what sense is Christ "the firstfruits"? The next verse explains: "For as by a man came death, by a man has come also the resurrection of the dead" (v. 21). Here Adam is mentioned ("by a man came death"), though not by name. Adam is the prototype of all people in that he preceded them in death and fatefully contributed to why this death happens: his sin established a pattern and outcome that since that time none has managed to elude.[50]

Yet Paul's point is one of hope, not blame or despair. "In Adam all die," it is true. Yet by the same token "so also in Christ shall all be made alive" (v. 22). Recent commentators underscore three ways in which this confirms Adam's importance.

First, Paul's offhand mention of Adam presupposes that his Corinthian readers would have been familiar with the Genesis 1–3 narrative. It is evident, E. Schnabel writes, that in Paul's instruction of the Jesus-believers in Corinth some three years previous he had taught them "the Old Testament account of creation and the fall."[51] Schnabel continues: "We have here another example of how the Holy Scriptures of Israel furnished the 'symbolic world' within which Paul understood and explained the significance of the person and the work of Jesus."[52] From the first days of the early church, an Adamic background for New Testament Christology (in this case Christ's resurrection) may have been instilled in new converts—although many would have been familiar with this account of human origins already from synagogal participation.

Second, Paul's understanding of Adam was definitely not the result of acceptance of a gnostic primal-man myth, as Bultmann and others maintained.[53] Nor are the similarities to Philo's interpretation of Genesis 1–2[54] sufficient to account for Paul's outlook, which contrasts sharply with Philo's, contra Wallace's proposal that "Paul could well be using the type of exegesis Philo exhibits in his discussion of Genesis."[55] Several observations should be made: (1) For Paul only the second Adam (who as incarnate deity is categorically distinct from the first Adam) has saving power; Philo seems to predicate redemptive potential of the intellectual nature of the Genesis 1–2 figure. (2) For Paul there is no heavenly first Adam, whereas Philo seems to impute heavenly essence to the uncreated, rational component instilled in Adam at creation. (3) Paul's Adam is not a timeless concept as Philo envisioned: "Man, made according to

---

50. Exceptions in biblical annals are Enoch and Elijah (Gen. 5:24; 2 Kings 2:11).

51. Eckhard Schnabel, *Der erste Brief des Paulus an die Korinther* (Wuppertal: Brockhaus; Giessen: Brunnen, 2006), 921. Here and elsewhere, quotes of this source are my translations.

52. Ibid.

53. Ibid. Rejection of Bultmann's view here may be regarded as a consensus today.

54. *Legum Allegoriae*, 1:31–32; *De Opificio Mundi*, 134–35.

55. Howard N. Wallace, "Adam (Person)," in *Anchor Bible Dictionary*, ed. D. N. Freedman (New York: Doubleday, 1992), 1:64.

the image of God, was an idea, or a genus, or a seal, perceptible only by the intellect, incorporeal, neither male nor female, imperishable by nature";[56] for Paul he is a historical reality whose physical essences do not admit of facile dualistic partitioning from his conceptual competencies.[57] In sum, the Adam of 1 Corinthians 15:22 is important to Paul but in ways sharply different from gnostic thought of later centuries or Alexandrian Jewish thought (Philo) of his own day. This was not least because Philo had no properly divine incarnate man to speak of, whereas for Paul such a figure occupied center stage, as G. Fee has made clear.[58]

Third, Paul's reference to Adam "assumes solidarity" of "those at the beginning of a line with those . . . who follow."[59] This solidarity is transparent in the pan-biblical conviction that the human race traces back to the creation of Adam and Eve, just as the brokenness and thorns and thistles of this life trace back to the curse of Genesis 3. Fourth Ezra (2 Esdras) 7:118 states, "O Adam, what have you done? For though it was you who sinned, the fall was not yours alone, but ours also who are your descendants" (RSV). By virtue of Old Testament Scriptures and Second Temple convictions, it is easily understandable that Paul would see an analogy between all humanity dying "in Adam," while all who are "in Christ shall . . . be made alive" (1 Cor. 15:22).

Much can be debated regarding the meaning and implications of 1 Corinthians 15:22: "For as in Adam all die, so also in Christ shall all be made alive." What cannot be denied is that at a climactic juncture of this epistle, in chapter 15 with its restatement of the gospel message (vv. 1–9) and insistence on the reality of the resurrection, Paul adduces Adam as a central plank in his rhetorical, apologetic, and theological platform.

Adam's importance is seen again later in the same chapter: "Thus it is written, 'The first man Adam became a living being'; the last Adam became a life-giving spirit" (v. 45). I have already commented above on Paul's adaptation of the Masoretic Text in this rendering; he did not twist grammar or word meanings.[60] There are actually multiple references to Adam in this context, as the table below indicates.

---

56. *De Opificio Mundi*, 134: ὁ δὲ κατὰ τὴν εἰκόνα ἰδέα τις ἢ γένος ἢ σφραγίς, νοητός, ἀσώματος, οὔτ᾽ ἄρρεν οὔτε θῆλυ, ἄφθαρτος φύσει.

57. See Schnabel, *Der erste Brief des Paulus an die Korinther*, 922. See also Dunn, "Adam (Person)," *EBR* 1:308. Schnabel lists three additional distinctions between Philo and Paul in their regard for Adam.

58. Fee, *Pauline Christology*, 500–512.

59. David Garland, *1 Corinthians* (Grand Rapids: Baker Academic, 2003), 707.

60. See Ciampa and Rosner, "1 Corinthians," 747.

1 Corinthians 15, verse	Reference to Adam	Reference to Christ
42	"what is sown is perishable"	"what is raised is imperishable"
43	"sown in dishonor," "weakness"	"raised in glory," "power"
44	"sown a natural body"	"raised a spiritual body"
45	"first Adam became a living being"	"last Adam became a life-giving spirit"
46	"first the natural"	"then the spiritual"
47	"the first man was from the earth, a man of dust"	"the second man is from heaven"
48	"the man of dust"	"the man of heaven"
49	"we have borne the image of the man of dust"	"we shall also bear the image of the man of heaven"

Several observations may be made. (1) As was the case in Romans 5, Adam is more prominent in 1 Corinthians 15 than a concordance check might suggest. There are not just the two citations of his name in verse 45 but a sustained and "complex"[61] analogy extending over eight verses. (2) Comparison with Romans 5 is fruitful in a second sense. Just as Adam was foundational to Paul's reasoning about the core truths of justification and reconciliation in Romans, Adam is essential to Paul's reasoning about the gospel and its assertion of the truth and nature of bodily resurrection as per the Pauline kerygma in 1 Corinthians. (3) Implicit in Paul's reference to Adam in this context are not only assumptions about Adam's existence and createdness but also convictions regarding his sin. Words like "perishable," "dishonor," and "weakness" do not comport with the Adam of a pristine creation. They do answer to Adam's state following the fall. But this means that just as all humans owe their very being to their ancestor Adam, their sin that culminates in universal human death and need for redemption is linked to Adam too.

In a word, since "flesh and blood cannot inherit the kingdom of God, nor does the perishable inherit the imperishable" (v. 50), all humans face hopelessness unless they can transcend their Adamic identity, nature, and destiny. "The first man Adam" (v. 45), the "natural" man (v. 46), "the man of dust" (vv. 47–49), founded a fellowship of curtailed glory and ultimately loss and woe. But in God's economy, "the last Adam became a life-giving spirit" (v. 45), who fully shared Adam's createdness but did not follow him into sin and bondage. Instead, Paul preached that Christ, the last Adam, endured the cross for the sake of sinners' salvation (see also 1:18; 15:3); worked their washing,

---

61. Fee, *Pauline Christology*, 516–17. Fee uses "complex" or "complexities" four times in three paragraphs explaining 1 Cor. 15:44–49.

sanctification, and justification (6:11); and proved to be "the man of heaven" (15:48–49) in whom Adam's seed, like him transgressors of the Creator's will, may place their hope. Paul's doctrine of Christ and redemption functions in tandem with his understanding of Adam, sin, and its baleful consequences.

1 Timothy 2:13–14

For many these verses are of little relevance to Paul's view of Adam because in their view Paul did not write 1 Timothy. Then who did? One best guess is that 1 Timothy (along with 2 Tim. and Titus) was written by someone else during "the last third of the first century, after the death of Paul."[62] Another theory is that these pseudepigraphic verses are witness to early Christian power politics and polemical use of traditions, not apostolic doctrine.[63] The (non-Pauline) author of 1 Timothy "is pulling a power play."[64] From yet another viewpoint, the scandal of these verses in appearing to limit women's access to leadership positions in the church so dominates the discussion that little is made of the Adam references.[65] Yet recent commentaries by L. T. Johnson,[66] W. Mounce,[67] and P. Towner,[68] as well as other studies[69] have made strong cases for Pauline authorship. There is ample justification for drawing on these verses for what they might tell us about Paul's assessment of Adam.

Recent research points out the following. (1) Paul is *not* reflecting then-current "Jewish chauvinistic belief in the inherent gullibility of women."[70] Given the high status in ministry Paul accords women elsewhere, Jewish chauvinism "is irrelevant to a discussion of the argument in 1 Timothy 2."[71] (2) Paul draws

62. P. Achtemeier, J. Green, and M. Meye Thompson, *Introducing the New Testament* (Grand Rapids: Eerdmans, 2001), 464.
63. D. Krause, *1 Timothy* (London: T&T Clark, 2004), 59.
64. Ibid., xii.
65. See I. H. Marshall with P. Towner, *The Pastoral Epistles* (London: T&T Clark, 1999), 460–67.
66. L. T. Johnson, *The First and Second Letters to Timothy* (New York: Doubleday, 2001).
67. W. Mounce, *The Pastoral Epistles* (Waco: Word, 2000).
68. P. Towner, *The Letters to Timothy and Titus* (Grand Rapids: Eerdmans, 2006).
69. E.g., E. Schnabel, "Paul, Timothy, and Titus: The Assumption of a Pseudonymous Author and of Pseudonymous Recipients in the Light of Literary, Theological, and Historical Evidence," in *Do Historical Matters Matter for Faith? A Critical Appraisal of Modern and Postmodern Approaches to Scripture*, ed. J. K. Hoffmeier and D. R. Magary (Wheaton: Crossway, 2012), 383–403; A. Köstenberger and T. Wilder, eds., *Entrusted with the Gospel: Paul's Theology in the Pastoral Epistles* (Nashville: Broadman & Holman, 2010); see esp. the chapter by Wilder that applies to Philippians the same tests used to prove Paul did not write the Pastorals. Measured by those standards, Philippians turns out to be pseudepigraphic too.
70. P. Towner, "1–2 Timothy and Titus," in Beale and Carson, *Commentary on the New Testament Use of the Old Testament*, 896.
71. Ibid.

directly on the Genesis account. Moreover, this is not an innovation, "since Paul also earlier makes the point that 'the serpent deceived Eve by its cunning' (2 Cor. 11:3), though he does not thereby exculpate Adam."[72] (3) In an ecclesial setting where good gifts like food and marital sexuality are disparaged (1 Tim. 4:1–3) and the resurrection itself is misunderstood (2 Tim. 2:18), Paul's words "Adam was formed first, then Eve" (1 Tim. 2:13) are "a reminder that the creation order is still in effect."[73] (4) In that same setting, where the Genesis narrative may have been twisted and "somehow influenced women to think that they were free from the constraints and limitations brought on by the fall," 1 Timothy 2:14 "reminds women of their role in the fall and of the present unfinished nature of Christian existence."[74]

It may be concluded that Paul's references to Adam and Eve in 1 Timothy 2 (in conjunction with related references in 1–2 Corinthians, Romans, and elsewhere) confirm his conviction that their creation and fall were in many respects determinative for all people everywhere. Moreover, details and sequence in the Genesis 1–3 account continue to serve in doctrinally foundational ways for thought and practice regarding male-female identity in Christ and church order.

Conclusion

The aim of this chapter has been to clarify exegetically what the New Testament says about Adam. Not surprisingly, this was found to be closely related to what the Old Testament records, particularly in Genesis 1–3, confirming G. Beale's observation that "the NT community's presuppositions are rooted in the OT."[75]

What we make of New Testament claims will depend on variables too complex to size up here—one could speak of something like "the hermeneutics of Adamic appropriation" (or resistance thereunto). But two concluding observations may be ventured.

The first stems from the fact that much of what the New Testament says about Adam comes via Paul. It can be argued that Paul was deeply cognizant of Jesus's teaching and heritage[76] and that he did not distort but faithfully represented Jesus's intent and commission.[77] Yet even if the Jesus connection (affirmed in every Pauline reference to his apostleship) were called into ques-

---

72. Dunn, "Adam (Person)," *EBR* 1:308.
73. Towner, "1–2 Timothy and Titus," 897.
74. Ibid.
75. G. Beale, *Handbook on the New Testament Use of the Old Testament* (Grand Rapids: Baker Academic, 2012), 101.
76. See, e.g., Fee, *Pauline Christology*, 524–29.
77. See, e.g., Paul Barnett, *Paul, Missionary of Jesus* (Grand Rapids: Eerdmans, 2008).

tion, Paul understood three things that British theologian Stephen Williams has wisely noted about our own coming days:

> Theological accomplishments will in the future happen largely in the valley of growing *persecution*, a phenomenon that in its way forced Bonhoeffer, who endured suffering, to reflect on the place of words today. It will happen only in the *flight from materialism* as Cone, like many others, has said. It will happen, as Luther knew as well as anyone, only in the *communion of Christ*.[78]

Paul's firsthand experience of persecution (see 2 Cor. 11:23–12:10), his repudiation of materialism in favor of pursuit of God (see Phil. 3:8), and his grasp of communion with Christ are in some ways unrivalled since apostolic times. Paul likely therefore remains a wise and perhaps even authoritative guide for those sharing his faith in Christ and his commitment to live out Christ's gospel in all its dimensions including its purported rootage in Adam.

The second concluding observation is that there are, broadly speaking, two approaches to the New Testament's representations of Adam and his importance. One view is minimalist; it looks, not to avowed messengers of the God who made all things and who in the view of those messengers gave Scripture, but to latter-day prophets. Gary Dorrien has recently underscored the determinative role of Kant, Schleiermacher, Schelling, and Hegel in what he calls "modern theology."[79] This describes to a large extent Western Protestant religious thought in traditions that accepted the Enlightenment's rejection of historic Christian theology and replacement of that theology with autonomous idealism. In this cognitive culture, biblical Adam passages will not serve to tell us anything much about our origin, our identity, our duties, or a divine savior sharing Adamic essence in ways that we glimpse in Paul.

While a minimalist view is dominant in mainline circles where the numbers of Christians are dropping precipitously, in parts of the world where the church has exploded numerically, Adam passages are interpreted in maximalist ways that comport with Paul's understanding and application of them. African interpreter Samuel Ngewa, for example, relates 1 Timothy 2:13–14 simply, directly, and plausibly to the family and the church today; the verses are not about male or female ability but focus rather "on good order," "because God has put [men] in" leadership positions "for the sake of order in the family and in larger groups, such as the church."[80]

---

78. Stephen Williams, "The Theological Task and Theological Method," in *Evangelical Futures: A Conversation on Theological Method*, ed. J. G. Stackhouse Jr. (Grand Rapids: Baker Academic; Leicester, UK: Inter-Varsity; Vancouver, BC: Regent College, 2000), 176–77, emphasis added.

79. Dorrien, *Kantian Reason and Hegelian Spirit*.

80. Samuel Ngewa, *1 & 2 Timothy and Titus* (Grand Rapids: Zondervan, 2009), 55.

Post-Christian biblical minimalism and majority world biblical maximalism serve as somewhat opposite ideals and models for understanding Adam, Scripture, ourselves, and the relevance, if any, of the last Adam. Conclusions regarding "Adam in the New Testament" will accordingly vary depending on where interpreters locate themselves in relation to these fundamentally antithetical options.

3

ADAM AND MODERN SCIENCE

William Stone
(a pseudonym)

Although Charles Darwin carefully avoided the topic of human evolution when he published his *Origin of Species* in 1859, hinting only that "light will be thrown on the origin of man and his history,"[1] his contemporaries were quick to realize the implications of his theory of evolution. Controversy was provoked by Thomas Henry Huxley's book *Evidence as to Man's Place in Nature*, published in 1863, in which he argued that similarities between humans and apes indicate common descent (this was before Darwin published his own account of human origins, *The Descent of Man*, in 1871). At the time, the lack of potential fossil ancestral species made the theory of human evolution highly speculative, and some scientists, such as Richard Owen, argued for the special status of humans as separate from animals.[2]

Neanderthal bones had been found in Engis, Belgium, in 1829, in Forbes' Quarry, in Gibraltar, in 1848, and in the Neander Valley, in Germany, in 1856, although initially their significance was not realized. Debate raged about the antiquity of man, as evidence accumulated for the co-occurrence of stone tools and extinct animals, such as the mammoth. With the 1891 discovery of

1. Charles Darwin, *On the Origin of Species by Means of Natural Selection* (London: John Murray, 1859), 488.
2. N. A. Rupke, *Richard Owen: Biology without Darwin*, rev. ed. (Chicago: University of Chicago, 2009).

Java Man (originally named *Pithecanthropus erectus*, now known as *Homo erectus*), there was an Asian candidate for human ancestry. However, when the Taung child (*Australopithecus africanus*) was unearthed in South Africa in 1924, the emphasis shifted to Africa, and over the next half-century further fossils were found in southern and eastern Africa and attributed to various potentially "transitional" species.

The evidence put forward by modern paleoanthropology, the study of human fossils, is often regarded as the "smoking gun" against Adam's historicity.[3] While some Christian scholars have sought to locate Adam within the paleoanthropological record somewhere along the evolutionary line leading up to modern humans,[4] whether as a historical figure or as some type of representative of humanity,[5] such a strategy forces a redefinition of the traditional doctrine of original sin. This chapter aims to bring the traditional doctrines of Adam and the fall into conversation with the scientific data by outlining the expectations we harbor for the human fossil record based on the biblical witness and comparing these expectations with current data and theories in paleoanthropology.

Adam's Historicity and the Fossil Record

If we accept the historicity of Adam and the fall, several key aspects of the biblical witness have a bearing on our expectations from the fossil record. Here we immediately encounter a problem: our account of earth's history, and in particular the age of the earth and the extent and impact of Noah's flood, strongly influences our views of early human history. These are highly complex and contested issues that require interaction with a wide range of topics, such as biblical hermeneutics, geology, radiometric dating, and biogeography. Such a comprehensive treatment is outside the scope of this volume and this chapter. The exposition here is therefore necessarily restricted to

3. E.g., R. Collins, "Evolution and Original Sin," in *Perspectives on an Evolving Creation,* ed. K. B. Miller (Grand Rapids: Eerdmans, 2003), 469–501.

4. Modern humans: our own species, *Homo sapiens*. Anatomically modern humans are fossils whose skeletal remains are indistinguishable from those of our own species, *Homo sapiens*, although the behavioral evidence associated with these skeletal remains may not necessarily be similar to that of people living now.

5. E.g., B. Ramm, *The Christian View of Science and Scripture* (Grand Rapids: Eerdmans, 1954); J. J. Davis, "Genesis, Inerrancy, and the Antiquity of Man," in *Inerrancy and Common Sense*, ed. R. Nicole and J. R. Michaels (Grand Rapids: Baker, 1980), 137–59; J. P. Hurd, "Hominids in the Garden?" in Miller, *Perspectives on an Evolving Creation,* 208–33; D. R. Alexander, *Creation or Evolution: Do We Have to Choose?* (Oxford: Monarch Books, 2008).

those aspects of the biblical witness that have a direct bearing on the skeletal remains of fossil humans.

I here affirm (based on the biblical witness) that all of humankind is connected by a line of ancestry to a *single pair of specially created* humans, Adam and Eve. Despite the diversity seen in modern humans today, both in physical characteristics, such as skin color and facial features, and in behavioral and cultural characteristics, there is a fundamental *unity* to humanity. Although humans were created with a body composed of the same material as animal bodies, I start with the assumption that there is *no ancestral lineage*[6] that links humans reproductively with any other living or extinct animal species, including the apes and any fossil apelike creatures.

Based on these starting points, I expect the paleoanthropological record:

a. to show that humans belong to a distinct "kind" from other primates;
b. to be consistent with a single human lineage.

Exactly how we can recognize different "kinds," or even what the term "kind" means from a biological point of view, is debatable.[7] But regardless of such discussions, contemporary Christian scholars, including those who accept an ancestral lineage for humanity, acknowledge a discontinuity between humans and the animals. If I accept an ancestral lineage, such a discontinuity must be of a purely spiritual nature. Since I reject an ancestral lineage, given a traditional doctrine of Adam and the fall, the question then remains to what extent this discontinuity is expressed in morphological, and especially skeletal, differences between humans and other primates, the mammalian order that most closely resembles humans.[8] And at what level of taxonomy should we expect such a discontinuity to be expressed? At the level of species, genera, or even higher levels? Or is the discontinuity primarily behavioral, and should we look for it in the archaeological evidence rather than in the fossils?

6. Ancestral lineage: the line of ancestral organisms that provide a continuous link between humans and a common ancestor shared with chimpanzees.

7. See, e.g., the review in T. C. Wood et al., "A Refined Baramin Concept," *Occasional Papers of the Baraminology Study Group* 3 (2003): 1–4.

8. The taxonomy, or classification, of fossil and extant species used in this chapter follows the hierarchical classification system originally proposed by Carolus Linnaeus in his *Systema Naturae* in 1735. In this system, animals are grouped in increasingly wider categories based on similarities and differences with other living organisms. For instance, humans are classified in the Class Mammalia, the Order Primates, the Family Hominidae, the Tribe Hominini, the Genus *Homo* and the Species *Homo sapiens*.

An Overview of Current Paleoanthropology

What exactly does the paleoanthropological record look like, and how does that compare to my expectations outlined above? Before I can address the question of whether modern paleoanthropology really poses critical problems for the traditional doctrine of Adam and Eve, I shall investigate the current state of knowledge regarding the fossil origins of humans. I will trace the story of paleoanthropology from modern humans to the earliest known fossils that are included in the human tribe, the earliest members of the Hominini.[9] I will largely follow the taxonomy proposed by B. Wood and N. Lonergan.[10] For the current scientific consensus regarding the dating of the species mentioned, see figure 3.1.[11]

The Genus Homo

The earliest fossils whose skeletal remains are indistinguishable from those of our own species, *Homo sapiens*, also described as "(anatomically) modern humans," are known from the Kibish Formation in Ethiopia.[12] These specimens are dated to about 200,000 years ago. From Africa, modern humans first spread to Asia from around 120,000 years ago, reaching Europe and Australia 40,000–50,000 years ago, and the Americas 20,000 years ago. In Africa, several fossil specimens link modern humans with their proposed ancestor species, *Homo heidelbergensis*, which differs from modern humans mainly in its very robust bones[13] and projecting face. Fossils of *Homo heidelbergensis* have also been found in the Near East and Europe.[14]

In Europe and the Near East, *Homo heidelbergensis* is thought to have given rise to *Homo neanderthalensis*, a well-known fossil species with a robust morphology that is in many ways adapted to life in a harsh, ice age environment. Their demise has often been seen as a result of being outcompeted by the cognitively superior modern humans, but factors such as population density and subsistence strategies may have been more important.[15] Recent research indicates that the

9. B. Wood and B. G. Richmond, "Human Evolution: Taxonomy and Paleobiology," *Journal of Anatomy* 196 (2000): 19–60.

10. B. Wood and N. Lonergan, "The Hominin Fossil Record: Taxa, Grades, and Clades," *Journal of Anatomy* 212 (2008): 354–76.

11. Dates mentioned in this chapter follow the scientific literature. Although not all Christians will accept these dates, this procedure intends to give the reader an insight into the current scientific consensus regarding the age of the fossils.

12. I. McDougall et al., "Stratigraphic Placement and Age of Modern Humans from Kibish, Ethiopia," *Nature* 433 (2005): 733–36.

13. In the context of skeletal morphology, "robust" refers to the sturdiness of the bones, while "gracile" refers to their slenderness.

14. Wood and Lonergan, "Hominin Fossil Record," 354–76.

15. J. R. Stewart, "Neanderthal Extinction as Part of the Faunal Change in Europe during Oxygen Isotope Stage 3," *Acta Zoologica Cracoviensia* 50A (2007): 93–124; W. E. Banks et al., "Neanderthal Extinction by Competitive Exclusion," *PLOS ONE* 3 (2008): e3972.

Fig. 3.1

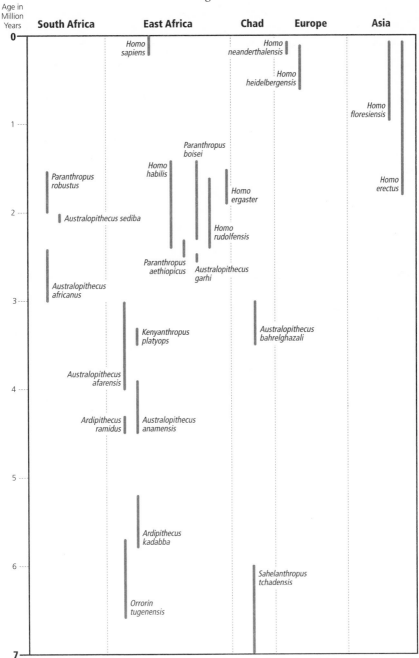

Hominin species, their distribution, and current scientific consensus regarding their dating based on dates from R. Pickering et al., "*Australopithecus sediba* at 1.977 Ma and Implications for the Origins of the Genus *Homo*," *Science* 333 (2011): 1421–23. Data for all other species drawn from Wood and Lonergan, "The Hominin Fossil Record: Taxa, Grades and Clades."

Neanderthals, and an Asian group of archaic *Homo* called the Denisovans, have contributed genetic material to modern humans, which is interpreted as evidence for interbreeding between these groups and modern humans.[16]

Preceding these archaic humans are the closely related species *Homo ergaster* (Africa, 1.9–1.5 million years ago) and *Homo erectus* (Asia, 1.8 million years ago–30,000 years ago). Though more robust, they are the first hominins in the fossil record whose postcranial[17] skeleton is very similar to that of modern humans.[18] The skull, in contrast, is robust with a projecting face and a cranial volume smaller than in modern humans. Famous fossils include the nearly complete skeleton of a young male known as "Nariokotome boy," discovered in Kenya; "Java Man"—the first fossils found for *Homo erectus*, discovered in East Java Province, Indonesia; and the "Peking Man" fossils from Zhoukoudian Cave in China, for which only casts remain because the original fossils went missing when they were shipped to the United States in 1941. The small-bodied *Homo floresiensis* (known as the "hobbit") from the Indonesian island of Flores is regarded by some as a separate species, but others identify it as an island dwarf form or diseased individuals of *Homo erectus*. Clearly, the last word has not been said concerning these intriguing fossils.[19]

At this point, around 1.9 million years ago, proposed classifications start to diverge. Traditionally, a collection of skulls and cranial fragments, alongside a few postcranial remains, is included in a transitional species called *Homo habilis*. A contemporary species, *Homo rudolfensis*, is characterized by a somewhat different mixture of primitive and derived features.[20]

16. R. E. Green et al., "A Draft Sequence of the Neanderthal Genome," *Science* 328 (2010): 710–22; J. Krause et al., "The Complete Mitochondrial DNA Genome of an Unknown Hominin from Southern Siberia," *Nature* 464 (2010): 894–97; D. Reich et al., "Genetic History of an Archaic Hominin Group from Denisova Cave in Siberia," *Nature* 468 (2010): 1053–60.

17. Postcranial skeleton: the skeleton apart from the skull (cranium and mandible; the cranial skeleton).

18. R. H. Crompton et al., "Locomotion and Posture from the Common Hominoid Ancestor to Fully Modern Hominins, with Special Reference to the Last Common Panin-hominin Ancestor," *Journal of Anatomy* 212 (2008): 501–43; B. Wood and J. Baker, "Evolution in the Genus *Homo*," *Annual Review of Ecology, Evolution, and Systematics* 42 (2011): 47–69.

19. M. J. Morwood et al., "Archaeology and Age of a New Hominin from Flores in Eastern Indonesia," *Nature* 431 (2004): 1087–91; M. J. Morwood and W. L. Jungers, "Conclusions: Implications of the Liang Bua Excavations for Hominin Evolution and Biogeography," *Journal of Human Evolution* 57 (2009): 640–48.

20. B. Wood, "Origin and Evolution of the Genus *Homo,*" *Nature* 355 (1992): 783–90. In evolutionary biology, "primitive" features are features that are shared with other species descended from the same ancestral species; such features are deemed to have been inherited from that ancestral species. In contrast, "derived" features are those features that are unique to a particular group and are not found in its ancestral species or other species descended from the same ancestral species.

The Australopithecines

The australopithecines are a group of primates thought to be most closely related to humans; they fall outside the genus *Homo* but within the tribe Hominini. Although debated,[21] most researchers are now convinced that these australopithecines were capable of bipedal (upright) locomotion, although—unlike the genus *Homo*—they were not able to sustain bipedal locomotion for extended periods of time.[22] They also retained a significantly greater ability to move in trees.[23] The australopithecines are classified into two genera, *Australopithecus* and *Paranthropus*.

Two australopithecine species lived alongside the early *Homo* species, *Paranthropus boisei* in East Africa and *Paranthropus robustus* in South Africa. These species are characterized as "robust australopithecines," along with the somewhat older, closely related but less specialized East African species *Paranthropus aethiopicus* and *Australopithecus garhi*. These species had large cheek teeth and a skull adapted to heavy chewing of plant materials. Not much is known about their postcranial skeleton.

The earliest australopithecines were more omnivorous and gracile, and include the species *Australopithecus africanus* in South Africa; *Australopithecus anamensis*, *Australopithecus afarensis*, and *Kenyanthropus platyops* in East Africa; and *Australopithecus bahrelghazali* in Chad.[24] The most famous australopithecine fossil is the partial skeleton of an *Australopithecus afarensis* individual known as "Lucy." It was thought that the gracile australopithecines had given way to the robust species, until the recent find of *Australopithecus sediba* at Malapa in South Africa, which shows a combination of gracile australopithecine features with some characteristics that are more similar to *Homo*.[25]

21. E.g., C. O. Lovejoy, "Evolution of Human Walking," *Scientific American* 259.5 (1988): 118–25; J. T. Stern, "Climbing to the Top: A Personal Memoir of *Australopithecus afarensis*," *Evolutionary Anthropology* 9 (2000): 113–33; C. V. Ward, "Interpreting the Posture and Locomotion of *Australopithecus afarensis*: Where Do We Stand?" *Yearbook of Physical Anthropology* 45 (2002): 185–215.

22. D. M. Bramble and D. E. Lieberman, "Endurance Running and the Evolution of *Homo*," *Nature* 432 (2004): 345–52.

23. Crompton et al., "Locomotion and Posture."

24. M. Brunet et al., "The First Australopithecine 2,500 Kilometres West of the Rift Valley (Chad)," *Nature* 378 (1995): 273–75; M. Brunet et al., "*Australopithecus bahrelghazali*, une nouvelle espèce d'Hominidé ancien de la région de Koro Toro (Tchad)," *Comptes rendus de l'Académie des sciences de Paris, Série IIa, Sciences de la terre et des planètes* 322 (1996): 907–13; M. G. Leakey et al., "New Four-Million-Year-Old Hominid Species from Kanapoi and Allia Bay, Kenya," *Nature* 376 (1995): 565–71; M. G. Leakey et al., "New Hominin Genus from Eastern Africa Shows Diverse Middle Pliocene Lineages," *Nature* 410 (2001): 433–40; R. Lewin and R. A. Foley, *Principles of Human Evolution*, 2nd ed. (Malden, MA: Blackwell, 2004).

25. L. R. Berger et al., "*Australopithecus sediba*: A New Species of *Homo*-like Australopith from South Africa," *Science* 328 (2010): 195–204; R. Pickering et al., "*Australopithecus sediba*

Early Hominini

The period between the earliest occurrence of an australopithecine species, *Australopithecus anamensis*, at about 4.5 million years ago and the commonly proposed divergence date of 7 million years ago between the lineage leading to *Homo* and the lineage leading to *Pan* (chimpanzees) is populated by very few fossil species and specimens. These species are mostly characterized by a mosaic of generalized African ape, chimpanzee, and australopithecine features. The two species of the East African genus *Ardipithecus*, *Ardipithecus ramidus* and the earlier species *Ardipithecus kadabba*, show limited evidence for facultative bipedalism.[26] Also from East Africa, *Orrorin tugenensis* fossils have apelike teeth and arms, but in some respects the thigh bone is more like *Homo* than *Australopithecus*.[27] Finally, *Sahelanthropus tchadensis* from Chad has a hominin-like facial morphology, but other parts of the skull are more apelike.[28] Considerable debate surrounds the status of these species and their position in the human lineage.[29]

The Smoking Gun against Adam's Historicity

As we have seen, the fossil record contains a great diversity of hominin species with different adaptations. These hominin fossils are regularly referred to when the traditional doctrine of Adam and Eve is called into question. In particular, it is claimed that the scientific data refute Adam's historicity because the fossil record does not conform to the expectations stated above. Instead, the fossil

---

at 1.977 Ma [million years ago] and Implications for the Origins of the Genus *Homo*," *Science* 333 (2011): 1421–23.

26. "Facultative bipedalism" means that walking on two legs is part of the behavioral repertoire of the species, but not its preferred mode of locomotion; T. D. White, G. Suwa, and B. Asfaw, "*Australopithecus ramidus*, a New Species of Early Hominid from Aramis, Ethiopia," *Nature* 371 (1994): 306–12; T. D. White, G. Suwa, and B. Asfaw, "Corrigendum: *Australopithecus ramidus*, a New Species of Early Hominid from Aramis, Ethiopia," *Nature* 375 (1995): 88; T. D. White et al., "*Ardipithecus ramidus* and the Paleobiology of Early Hominids," *Science* 326 (2009): 75–86; Y. Haile-Selassie, "Late Miocene Hominids from the Middle Awash, Ethiopia," *Nature* 412 (2001): 178–81; Y. Haile-Selassie, G. Suwa, and T. D. White, "Late Miocene Teeth from Middle Awash, Ethiopia, and Early Hominid Dental Evolution," *Science* 303 (2004): 1503–5; for a critique, see E. E. Sarmiento, "Comment on the Paleobiology and Classification of *Ardipithecus ramidus*," *Science* 328 (2010): 1105; B. Wood and T. Harrison, "The Evolutionary Context of the First Hominins," *Nature* 470 (2011): 347–52.

27. B. Senut et al., "First Hominid from the Miocene (Lukeino Formation, Kenya)," *Comptes rendus de l'Académie des sciences de Paris, Série IIa, Sciences de la terre et des planètes* 332 (2001): 137–44.

28. M. Brunet et al., "A New Hominid from the Upper Miocene of Chad, Central Africa," *Nature* 418 (2002): 145–51.

29. Reviewed in B. Wood and T. Harrison, "The Evolutionary Context of the First Hominins."

evidence is taken to point to a continuity of descent between humans and fossil primate species, with a multitude of species characterizing the human lineage.

Continuity between Humans and Earlier Primates

Darwin wrote, "In a series of forms graduating insensibly from some apelike creature to man as he now exists, it would be impossible to fix on any definite point when the term 'man' ought to be used."[30] If humans evolved from primates, we should find, going back in time, a continuous lineage of ancestral species that are increasingly and incrementally less humanlike and more like a generalized ape. Eventually, this ancestral lineage of humanlike species should coalesce with the ancestral lineages of the great apes. This would falsify the Adamic prediction that there is discontinuity between humans and apes.

Although there is much controversy about the actual pathway of evolution and the position of particular species on the trajectory from hominin to human, the overwhelming consensus among paleoanthropologists is that there are enough similarities between earlier hominins and early species in the genus *Homo* to accept the hypothesis that these earlier hominins were ancestral to humans.[31] Evidence for continuity of descent can be grouped into three categories: morphological, genetic, and behavioral.[32] (Chronological information provides the context for the argument for continuity.) Important morphological trends in the human lineage include those tending to bipedalism and relatively large brain size. Morphological and genetic characteristics form the substrate for the more complex behavioral traits. Meat eating, social structure, language, tool use, and advanced cognitive abilities, expressed in, for example, the ability to plan ahead, adornment of the body, burial of the dead, and symbolic behavior, are thought to have gradually developed over the course of human evolution. These changes took place against a background of environmental change and migration, which are thought to have shaped humans into the species we are now.

30. Charles Darwin, *The Descent of Man and Selection in Relation to Sex*, 2nd ed. (London: John Murray, 1874), 188.

31. W. H. Kimbel, "The Origin of *Homo*," in *The First Humans—Origin and Early Evolution of the Genus* Homo, Contributions from the Third Stony Brook Human Evolution Symposium and Workshop, October 3–October 7, 2006, ed. F. E. Grine, J. G. Fleagle, and R. E. Leakey (Dordrecht: Springer, 2009), 31–37. Hominin species, their distribution, and current scientific consensus regarding their dating based on dates from R. Pickering et al., "*Australopithecus sediba* at 1.977 Ma and Implications for the Origins of the Genus *Homo*," *Science* 333 (2011): 1421–23. Data for all other species drawn from Wood and Lonergan, "The Hominin Fossil Record: Taxa, Grades and Clades."

32. The scope of this chapter does not allow us to do justice to the genetic data and thus is limited to morphological and behavioral data.

Multiple Contemporaneous Species

The contemporaneity of multiple species in the human lineage is put forward as evidence against the other prediction following from Adam's historicity—that of the unity of the human lineage. As in most animal groups, speciation[33] in the hominins follows a bushlike pattern rather than a single, directional path of transformation. A unique line of descent from a common human ancestor to modern humans seems to be absent. The colonization of Europe by modern humans from Africa is thought to have caused the demise of the Neanderthals during a period when the two species coexisted. Deposits dated 50,000–120,000 years ago at sites such as Tabun, Skhul, Qafzeh, and Kebara in the Near East give evidence for alternating occupation by *Homo neanderthalensis* and early modern humans.[34] What is more, over the last decade evidence has accumulated for interbreeding between different species of *Homo*, specifically between *Homo sapiens* and *Homo neanderthalensis*, as well as the newly discovered Denisovan group. The earlier history of the genus *Homo* shows an even greater proliferation of co-occurring species, with *Homo ergaster*, *Homo rudolfensis*, and *Homo habilis* all occurring in Africa, and *Homo erectus* in Asia, while at the same time the australopithecines *Paranthropus robustus* and *Australopithecus sediba* lived in South Africa and *Paranthropus boisei* in East Africa. Some of these species are even found in the same sediments, demonstrating real co-occurrence, such as at Swartkrans in South Africa, where fossils of *Paranthropus robustus* and *Homo ergaster* were recovered from the same sediments.[35]

Where in this forest of species should we place Adam, and what does that mean for other hominin species that existed at the same time? If we place Adam close to the origin of *Homo sapiens*,[36] there would be an influx of "non-Adamite" DNA later on in the history of the species through interbreeding with Neanderthals and Denisovans. This raises theological problems related to the human or nonhuman status of these hybrids and their descendants in people groups still living now.[37] Alternatively, a late date for Adam would require a redefinition of Adam as the first man to whom God revealed himself in order to

---

33. Speciation: the process by which new species evolve from ancestral species.
34. J. J. Shea, "Neanderthals, Competition, and the Origin of Modern Human Behavior in the Levant," *Evolutionary Anthropology* 12 (2003): 173–87.
35. Lewin and Foley, *Principles of Human Evolution*.
36. See F. Rana and H. Ross, *Who Was Adam? A Creation Model Approach to the Origin of Man* (Colorado Springs: NavPress, 2005).
37. T. C. Wood, "Who Were Adam and Eve? Scientific Reflections on Collins's *Did Adam and Eve Really Exist?*," *Journal of Creation Theology and Science Series B: Life Sciences* 2 (2012): 28–32.

have fellowship with him (the "*Homo divinus*" model).[38] Locating Adam earlier in the human lineage raises the issue of the unity of humankind. If Adam is the progenitor of the entire human lineage, what is the status of the different species that are recognized in the fossil record? Is Adam the progenitor of multiple human species? Could several human species have co-occurred after Adam?

Some Provisos regarding the Paleoanthropological Evidence

Before we examine the paleoanthropological data in more detail to establish whether these objections to a historic Adam are well founded, let us pause briefly to consider the nature of the evidence and the inferences drawn from it. What is the quality of the record? How do ideas about human evolution relate to the fossils and other scientific data on which they are based?

Fossil Remains

The fossil record is inherently incomplete. Fossil remains are scarce, and the distribution of fossil finds may have little connection with the actual past occurrence of living individuals. Other factors are often in play, including the conditions for preservation and movement of skeletal remains (both at the time the fossil was formed and afterward) and research history, which is influenced by a host of factors including politics, quarrying activities, and the presence of local collectors. New fossil discoveries have the potential to radically alter current ideas about human evolution. Indeed, half of the hominin species in figure 3.1 were recognized after 1990, and six of them were described after 2000. Hominin fossils are often highly fragmented when they are found, and many fossils have been deformed during the time that they were buried in sediment. Clear associations of cranial and postcranial material (i.e., full or partial associated skeletons) are rare. Thus many hominin species were defined based on cranial material only, and it is unclear what the postcranial characteristics of such species are. For some species, no postcranial material is known whatsoever, and other species are represented only by a very limited amount of material. For those species for which we do have postcranial remains, it can be difficult to translate skeletal morphology into a living skeletal structure. If a fossil has a mosaic of traits that do not occur in that combination in any extant species, it is hard to reconstruct the details of its locomotor strategy.[39]

---

38. See J. R. W. Stott, *Understanding the Bible* (London: Scripture Union, 1972); Alexander, *Creation or Evolution.*

39. See, e.g., the discussion of traits related to bipedalism in Wood and Harrison, "Evolutionary Context of the First Hominins."

Although skeletal structure puts constraints on what movements are possible, locomotor behavior is to some degree flexible. However, despite the incompleteness of the fossil record and the interpretive problems outlined above, the available evidence suggests key differences exist between the australopithecines and species of the genus *Homo*.[40]

Cultural Remains

The difficulties surrounding species attribution of particular fossils are exacerbated when we consider the behavioral and cultural evidence. Evidence for subsistence practices is sought in the characteristics of hominin teeth and remains of animals that may have been exploited for meat, marrow, and possibly other animal resources, such as hides. Fossils can also help establish whether particular species had the physical capacity for speech and the manual dexterity to produce the stone tools found in the same deposits. As with the morphological characteristics discussed previously, the scant nature of the fossils limits the inferences that can be drawn from them. Moreover, behavior is a far more plastic trait than anatomy. For example, even if a species was in principle physically capable of producing speech, this does not necessarily imply that it used language.

As is widely acknowledged among archaeologists, the archaeological record has similar limitations to the fossil record: it is incomplete and influenced by movement and research history.[41] Preservation issues lead to a highly biased record, reflected in the almost complete lack of organic remains other than bone surviving from early prehistoric sites. Interpreting spatial associations between fossils and archaeological finds as evidence that the species represented in the fossil remains produced the artifacts is controversial.[42] When we consider the more obvious cases of highly developed cognitive abilities, such as body adornment, burial of the dead, and art, that clearly set humans apart from all the animals, interpretation of the archaeological finds is not always straightforward.

What Makes Us Human?

Earlier we asked how the discontinuity we expect to see between humans and animals is expressed, and whether we can recognize this in the fossil and

40. D. E. Lieberman et al., "The Transition from *Australopithecus* to *Homo*," in *Transitions in Prehistory: Essays in Honor of Ofer Bar-Yosef*, ed. J. J. Shea and D. E. Lieberman (Oxford: Oxbow Books, 2009), 1–22.

41. See, e.g., the seminal discussions in L. R. Binford, *Bones: Ancient Men and Modern Myths* (New York: Academic Press, 1981) and M. B. Schiffer, *Formation Processes of the Archaeological Record* (Albuquerque: University of New Mexico Press, 1987).

42. See, e.g., "Behavioral Criteria–Tool Use" below for evidence for tool use by australopithecines.

archaeological record. As we have seen, paleoanthropologists answer the question "What makes us human?" by referring to certain morphological, genetic, and behavioral characteristics. Most treatments of the fossil record from a Christian perspective accept these basic categories.[43] But questions remain: How different from or similar to animals can we expect humans to be? Which characteristics are important in deciding whether a fossil represents a human? And how much variation can we accommodate within the human lineage?

On a biological level, there are many similarities between humans and apes, for example in subsistence activities, basic levels of tool use, and social organization. Therefore, it comes as no surprise that there are many morphological and genetic similarities between humans, fossil hominins, and the great apes. Although there are some clear differences in morphology, most notably in brain size and skeletal features related to fully bipedal locomotion, we have seen how difficult it can be to draw inferences about the presence or absence of these features in fragmentary fossils. In contrast, a qualitative gap at the behavioral level can be observed between humans and great apes. Modern humans show a remarkable richness of cultural inventiveness and much greater cognitive abilities and associated behavior. But a highly biased and incomplete fossil and archaeological record can be interpreted in multiple valid ways.

How then can we recognize humans in the fossil and archaeological record? Morphologically, relative brain size and fully human, habitual bipedalism seem to be relatively unproblematic criteria. However, we need to keep in mind that brain structure is important too, that we know very little about the way the human brain operates, and that we do not actually have any fossil brains, only casts of the insides of skulls. We should be careful not to overinterpret small, fragmentary samples of postcranial material. The behavioral and cultural evidence is much harder to interpret. Human capacities for creativity and symbolic behavior have frequently been connected with the image of God.[44] We can safely assume that indications of such behavior in the archaeological record imply a human status for their makers. Conversely, the absence of such

---

43. E.g., M. L. Lubenow, *Bones of Contention: A Creationist Assessment of Human Fossils* (Grand Rapids: Baker, 1992); S. Hartwig-Scherer, "Apes or Ancestors? Interpretations of the Hominid Fossil Record within Evolutionary and Basic Type Biology," in *Mere Creation: Science, Faith, and Intelligent Design*, ed. W. A. Dembski (Downers Grove, IL: InterVarsity, 1998), 212–35; Rana and Ross, *Who Was Adam?*; T. C. Wood, "Baraminological Analysis Places *Homo habilis, Homo rudolfensis*, and *Australopithecus sediba* in the Human Holobaramin," *Answers Research Journal* 3 (2010): 71–90.

44. J. W. Van Huyssteen, *Alone in the World? Human Uniqueness in Science and Theology* (Grand Rapids: Eerdmans, 2006).

indicators does not necessarily imply that the capacities, or even the behavior, were not present. We therefore need to approach the fossil and archaeological evidence with great caution.

Adam and Modern Paleoanthropology

With these provisos in mind, let us now contrast the paleoanthropological status quo with the expectations we set out for the fossil record based on Adam's historicity and examine whether paleoanthropology really provides the alleged smoking gun against Adam's historicity. It is impossible to comprehensively discuss all the evidence here, but we will touch on some recent finds and their implications for the hominin lineage.

First of all, let us consider the evidence offered for the existence of a hominin ancestral lineage. For a long time, the origin of modern humans and their relationship with earlier and contemporaneous species of the genus *Homo* were fiercely debated.[45] Adherents of the "Out-of-Africa" model stated that modern humans evolved in Africa and spread from there to other parts of the world without any significant admixture with other species of *Homo*. In contrast, advocates of the "multiregional continuity" model held that modern humans evolved simultaneously in Africa, Asia, and Europe from several earlier *Homo* species and formed a single species due to interbreeding between the different regions. Recent findings of traces of interbreeding between modern humans, Neanderthals, and Denisovans indicate a more complex story that combines aspects of both models.

Much controversy surrounds the inclusion of particular fossils in *Homo habilis*, and some paleoanthropologists have suggested that at least some of the *Homo habilis* specimens are more similar to australopithecines and should thus be excluded from the genus *Homo*.[46] In some sites, *Homo habilis* and *Paranthropus boisei* occur alongside each other. Skull remains of both species are easy to differentiate from each other because of the robust nature of the *Paranthropus* skulls. However, very little postcranial material occurs in

45. C. Stringer, "Rethinking 'Out of Africa,'" *Edge* (website), November 12, 2011, www.edge.org/conversation/rethinking-out-of-africa; J. R. Stewart and C. B. Stringer, "Human Evolution out of Africa: The Role of Refugia and Climate Change," *Science* 335 (2012): 1317–21.

46. H. M. McHenry and K. Coffing, "*Australopithecus* to *Homo*: Transformations in Body and Mind," *Annual Review of Anthropology* 29 (2000): 125–46; M. Collard and B. A. Wood, "Defining the Genus *Homo*," in *Handbook of Paleoanthropology*, vol. 3, *Phylogeny of Hominids*, ed. W. Henke and I. Tattersall (Berlin: Springer, 2007), 1575–1610; B. A. Wood, "Where Does the Genus *Homo* Begin, and How Would We Know?," in Grine, Fleagle, and Leakey, eds., *The First Humans*, 17–28.

association with these cranial remains, and it is often impossible to identify the species associated with the fragmented postcranial remains. Any evaluation of *Homo habilis* postcranial morphology is therefore tentative. The large temporal overlap between *Homo habilis* and more advanced species such as *Homo ergaster* also complicates any assessment of their relationship.

Until recently, none of the known later australopithecine species could be directly linked in terms of morphology to early *Homo* species.[47] Candidates for ancestral status have mainly been sought among the robust species. Important proposals include *Australopithecus garhi*, which was found in association with butchered bones in the Bouri Formation of the Middle Awash Valley (Ethiopia), and *Australopithecus africanus*, which has a somewhat more humanlike skull than other australopithecine species.[48] Examination and publication of the three partial skeletons of *Australopithecus sediba*, found recently in Malapa in South Africa, are ongoing.[49] This species has australopithecine characteristics but also shares more derived traits with *Homo erectus* than any other australopithecine species; it has been hailed as the transitional species between *Australopithecus africanus* and the earliest representatives of the genus *Homo*. It is unclear where *Homo habilis* and *Homo rudolfensis* fit in this scenario, as *Australopithecus sediba* shares several derived features of the hip bone and the cranium with *Homo erectus* that do not appear in these earlier *Homo* species. Some paleoanthropologists dispute the status of *Australopithecus sediba* as an ancestor of *Homo* based on the earlier date for some specimens of *Homo rudolfensis*.[50] As only initial assessments of the morphology of *Australopithecus sediba* are currently available, and the species as yet has only been subject to a small number of studies, it is difficult to judge its status. It may turn out to be more closely related to humans than it was thought at first (in which case its current inclusion in *Australopithecus* rather than *Homo* may need to be revised), or alternatively, further research may show that the species is part of the australopithecine variation.[51]

47. McHenry and Coffing, "*Australopithecus* to *Homo*"; Kimbel, "Origin of *Homo*"; Wood and Harrison, "Evolutionary Context of First Hominins."

48. B. Asfaw et al., "*Australopithecus garhi*: A New Species of Early Hominid from Ethiopia," *Science* 284 (1999): 629–35; de Heinzelin et al., "Environment and Behavior of 2.5 million-year-old Bouri Hominids," *Science* 284 (1999): 625–29.

49. L. R. Berger, "The Mosaic Nature of *Australopithecus sediba*," *Science* 340 (2013): 163–65; Berger et al., "*Australopithecus sediba*: A New Species of *Homo*-like Australopith from South Africa." W. H. Kimbel, "Palaeoanthropology: Hesitation on Hominid History," *Nature* 497 (2013): 573–74; series of publications in *Science* 333 (2011): 1402–23 and *Science* 340 (special issue, April 12, 2013).

50. M. Balter, "Candidate Human Ancestor from South Africa Sparks Praise and Debate," *Science* 328 (2010): 154–55; see also the critical notes on morphology in Wood and Harrison, "Evolutionary Context of First Hominins"; and Kimbel, "Palaeoanthropology."

51. T. C. Wood, "Baraminology, the Image of God, and *Australopithecus sediba*," *Journal of Creation Theology and Science Series B: Life Sciences* 1 (2011): 6–14.

The species *Kenyanthropus platyops* adds further complexity to the argument. Its skull has an unusually flat face, similar to the species *Homo rudolfensis*.[52] This has been taken by some as an indication that the species was part of an evolutionary side branch that led to *Homo*, bypassing the other australopithecines. However, other paleoanthropologists regard the fossil as distorted and the flat face as an artifact of geological processes.[53]

It is therefore by no means clear which species are part of the ancestral line of humans and which species represent side branches or even an entirely separate group of species. Let us briefly consider what light the morphological and behavioral criteria mentioned previously can shed on this issue.

Morphological Criteria

Bipedalism

One of the distinguishing characteristics of all the fossil species that are proposed as part of the human lineage is their ability to walk bipedally, as inferred from sparse postcranial remains and the way the head is balanced on the neck. Unlike the great apes, which are capable of a facultative form of bipedal locomotion over short distances but cannot sustainably use it as their preferred mode of locomotion, some australopithecine species are thought to have been habitually bipedal. However, it is also clear that bipedalism in many hominins existed alongside various forms of arboreal locomotion[54] and was of a different character than modern human locomotion.

Studies of a track of footprints that were preserved in volcanic ash at Laetoli and dated to about 3.6 million years ago almost unanimously come to the conclusion that these footprints were left by individuals utilizing fully human bipedal locomotion.[55] The footprints are attributed to *Australopithecus afarensis* based on the occurrence of several teeth and bone fragments of this species with a roughly similar date in the same site. In a comprehensive study of the then-available postcranial remains, including that of the famous partial skeleton known as Lucy (catalog number AL 288–1), researchers concluded that *Australopithecus afarensis* from Hadar, Ethiopia, did not possess fully humanlike bipedal locomotion and was fundamentally adapted to arboreal

52. Leakey et al., "New Hominin Genus from Eastern Africa."
53. T. White, "Early Hominids—Diversity or Distortion?" *Science* 299 (2003): 1994–97.
54. Arboreal locomotion: the ability to skillfully negotiate moving around in trees.
55. Summarized in Raichlen et al., "Laetoli Footprints Preserve Earliest Direct Evidence of Human-like Bipedal Biomechanics," *PLOS ONE* 5 (2010): e9769.

locomotion.[56] Many authors have since concluded that *Australopithecus afarensis* was a habitual biped, but most researchers stress that this bipedalism differed from that of modern humans.[57]

Each australopithecine species shows a mosaic of primitive and derived traits,[58] and there is no net trend toward an increased number of derived traits. Indeed, some derived traits occur relatively early on in the australopithecine lineage, with a reversal to the primitive trait in later species.[59] For example, the size of the forelimb relative to the hind limb is larger, and thus more apelike, in *Australopithecus africanus* and *Homo habilis* than in the earlier species *Australopithecus afarensis* and *Australopithecus anamensis*, whereas the teeth are more primitive in the latter two species.[60] A clear trend toward a fully human form of bipedalism cannot be observed in the australopithecines. In contrast, the earliest *Homo ergaster/erectus* specimens are highly similar to modern humans in this respect, from the oldest preserved hind limb and foot bones of the genus *Homo* from the site Dmanisi (Georgia) onward, although there are slight differences in morphology.[61]

Brain Size and Its Relationship to Cognitive Ability

Humans are unique among all living creatures for their great cognitive capabilities. Intelligence is rooted in the brain, which is very large relative to body size in modern humans. How does our brain compare to the brains of earlier hominins? Brain size was roughly similar in all australopithecine species with an

56. J. T. Stern and R. L. Susman, "The Locomotor Anatomy of *Australopithecus afarensis*," *American Journal of Physical Anthropology* 60 (1983): 279–317.

57. For an overview of the discussion, see Stern, "Climbing to the Top"; W. H. Kimbel and L. K. Delezene, "'Lucy' Redux: A Review of Research on *Australopithecus afarensis*," *Yearbook of Physical Anthropology* 52 (2009): 2–48; new fossils have recently stirred up the debate, see Y. Haile-Selassie et al., "An Early *Australopithecus afarensis* Postcranium from Woranso-Mille, Ethiopia," *Proceedings of the National Academy of Sciences* 107 (2010): 12121–26; J. M. DeSilva and Z. J. Throckmorton, "Lucy's Flat Feet: The Relationship between the Ankle and Rearfoot Arching in Early Hominins," *PLOS ONE* 5 (2010): e14432; C. V. Ward et al., "New Postcranial Fossils of *Australopithecus afarensis* from Hadar, Ethiopia (1990–2007)," *Journal of Human Evolution* 63 (2012): 1–51.

58. A short overview can be found in D. E. Lieberman, "Human Evolution: Those Feet in Ancient Times," *Nature* 483 (2012): 550–51.

59. H. M. McHenry, "Origin and Diversity of Early Hominin Bipedalism," in *African Genesis: Perspectives on Hominin Evolution*, ed. S. M. Reynolds and A. Gallagher (Cambridge: Cambridge University Press, 2012), 205–22.

60. H. M. McHenry and L. R. Berger, "Body Proportions in *Australopithecus afarensis* and *A. africanus* and the Origin of the Genus *Homo*," *Journal of Human Evolution* 35 (1998): 1–22.

61. McHenry and Coffing, "*Australopithecus* to *Homo*"; Bramble and Lieberman, "Endurance Running"; H. Pontzer et al., "Locomotor Anatomy and Biomechanics of the Dmanisi Hominins," *Journal of Human Evolution* 58 (2010): 492–504.

average of around 450–550 cubic centimeters,[62] especially taking into account the larger body weight of *Paranthropus* species (fig. 3.2). In early *Homo*, we see an increase to an average of around 700–850 cubic centimeters. However, given that these species also had a somewhat larger body weight, this is less significant than the large increase we see in *Homo heidelbergensis*, *Homo neanderthalensis*, and *Homo sapiens*, with mean values between 1250 and 1450 cubic centimeters.[63] The basic pattern is one of stasis in the australopithecines and an increase in brain size in the genus *Homo*. But although (relative) size matters, it is not the only variable determining cognitive capacities.[64] Brain organization may be a more reliable indicator of intelligence than brain size. A long-standing controversy exists between researchers who argue that brain reorganization from an apelike structure to a humanlike organization was already under way in the australopithecines and researchers holding the view that the australopithecine brain is essentially apelike, with modern features first manifesting themselves in early species of *Homo*.[65] We can conclude that it is very difficult to make connections between brain size, brain structure, and cognitive abilities in general or specific capabilities. It therefore seems more fruitful to rely on the archaeological record for indications of intelligence and complex behaviors.

Behavioral Criteria

There is a great variety of archaeological evidence, and here we can only scrape the surface of the available data. We will focus on three aspects of human behavior that are documented relatively extensively in the fossil record.

Meat Eating

Most primates are herbivorous, although meat eating and even active hunting is well documented for chimpanzees.[66] Evidence from the wear and chemical composition of teeth indicates that the diet of the early australopithecines was

62. McHenry and Coffing, "*Australopithecus* to *Homo*"; D. E. Lieberman, *The Evolution of the Human Head* (Cambridge, MA: Harvard University Press, 2011).

63. Wood and Harrison, "Evolutionary Context of First Hominins."

64. See the review in T. W. Deacon, "What Makes the Human Brain Different?," *Annual Review of Anthropology* 26 (1997): 337–57.

65. D. Falk, "Hominid Paleoneurology," *Annual Review of Anthropology* 16 (1987): 13–30; D. Falk et al., "Early Hominid Brain Evolution: A New Look at Old Endocasts," *Journal of Human Evolution* 38 (2000): 695–717; see also the review in P. T. Schoenemann, "Evolution of Size and Functional Areas of the Human Brain," *Annual Review of Anthropology* 35 (2006): 379–406.

66. J. C. Mitani and D. P. Watts, "Why Do Chimpanzees Hunt and Share Meat?," *Animal Behaviour* 61 (2001): 915–24; J. D. Pruetz and P. Bertolani, "Savanna Chimpanzees, *Pan troglodytes verus*, Hunt with Tools," *Current Biology* 17 (2007): 412–17.

Fig. 3.2

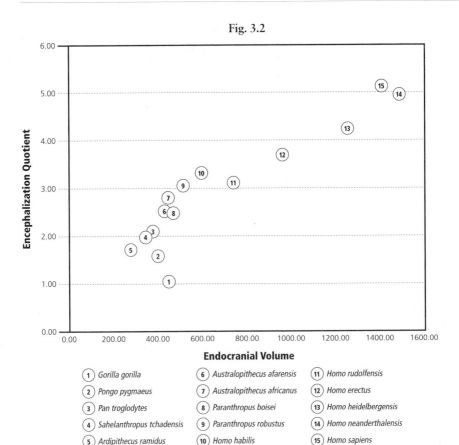

Relative brain size for *Homo rudolfensis*, expressed through the encephalization quotient (a measure for brain size adjusted for differences in body weight) and endocranial volume (volume of the inside of the braincase), based on data from McHenry and Coffing, "*Australopithecus to Homo*," 127. Data for all other species drawn from D. E. Lieberman, *The Evolution of the Human Head* (Cambridge, MA: Belknap Press of Harvard University Press, 2011), 193.

similar to that of chimpanzees, gorillas, and geladas, and consisted mainly of soft fruits and leaves.[67] In the later australopithecines, a broadening of the diet can be observed, which in the robust australopithecines involved feeding on harder, brittle foodstuffs or tough, low-quality fibrous plant resources.

The incorporation of high-energy food resources, especially meat, in the diet of early hominins is thought to have made it possible to evolve a large, energy-consuming brain, which in turn provided the cognitive powers necessary to successfully hunt large animals.[68] A long-standing controversy surrounds

67. F. E. Grine et al., "Dental Microwear and Stable Isotopes Inform the Paleoecology of Extinct Hominins," *American Journal of Physical Anthropology* 148 (2012): 285–317.

68. R. B. Lee and I. Devore, *Man the Hunter* (Chicago: Aldire, 1968); L. C. Aiello and P. Wheeler, "The Expensive-Tissue Hypothesis: The Brain and the Digestive System in Human and Primate Evolution," *Current Anthropology* 36 (1995): 199–221.

the character of hominin use of animals, known as the "man the hunter vs. man the scavenger" debate. Far-reaching conclusions have been drawn from the presence of animal bones in sites with hominin fossils or archaeological remains. Hunting as a subsistence strategy requires the hunter to range widely, and this has been taken to imply food-sharing in complex social environments and a sexual division of labor as pregnant or breast-feeding females are less able to partake in hunting parties but contributed to the diet through the gathering of plant resources.[69] In contrast, other researchers have claimed that hominins only scavenged the leftover scraps of carnivore meals.[70] Marks left on animal bones during the butchering process provide direct evidence of hominin use of the bones but do not necessarily imply that the carcass was obtained by hunting.

Evidence for the inclusion of meat in the australopithecine diet is scant; butchered bones have been found in the Bouri Formation of the Middle Awash Valley and Gona in Ethiopia.[71] However, the evidence is clearer once *Homo ergaster* appears in the fossil record, with a much stronger association with larger numbers of mammalian bones, some of which evidence human access to carcasses preceding carnivore access, a sign that such carcasses were obtained by hunting.[72] Various strands of evidence, most importantly the reduction in size of the cheek teeth, chewing muscles, and the gut, indicate that cooking of food may have been important to species of the genus *Homo* from *Homo erectus/ergaster* onward.[73] There is good evidence for the control of fire by Neanderthals and modern humans.[74] Further back in time, burnt flint artifacts and wood at the site of Gesher Benot Ya'akov (Israel) attest to the presence of hearths.[75] A recent analysis of sediments and archaeological remains from

69. G. Isaac, "The Food-Sharing Behaviour of Proto-Human Hominids," *Scientific American* 238 (1978): 90–108.

70. Binford, *Bones*; L. R. Binford, "Human Ancestors: Changing Views of Their Behavior," *Journal of Anthropological Archaeology* 4 (1985): 292–327.

71. De Heinzelin et al., "Environment and Behavior of Bouri Hominids"; M. Domínguez-Rodrigo et al., "Cutmarked Bones from Pliocene Archaeological Sites at Gona, Afar, Ethiopia: Implications for the Function of the World's Oldest Stone Tools," *Journal of Human Evolution* 48 (2005): 109–21.

72. Lewin and Foley, *Principles of Human Evolution*; P. S. Ungar, F. E. Grine, and M. F. Teaford, "Diet in Early *Homo*: A Review of the Evidence and a New Model of Adaptive Versatility," *Annual Review of Anthropology* 35 (2006): 209–28.

73. McHenry and Coffing, "*Australopithecus* to *Homo*"; R. W. Wrangham, *Catching Fire: How Cooking Made Us Human* (London: Profile, 2010); C. Organ et al., "Phylogenetic Rate Shifts in Feeding Time during the Evolution of *Homo*," *Proceedings of the National Academy of Sciences* 108 (2011): 1455–59.

74. W. Roebroeks and P. Villa, "On the Earliest Evidence for Habitual Use of Fire in Europe," *Proceedings of the National Academy of Sciences* 108 (2011): 5209–14.

75. N. Goren-Inbar et al., "Evidence of Hominin Control of Fire at Gesher Benot Ya'akov, Israel," *Science* 304 (2004): 725–27.

Wonderwerk Cave in South Africa provides evidence of the use of fire by *Homo ergaster*.[76] The activity of cooking itself is harder to demonstrate, but there are indications for cooking from Neanderthal times onward.[77] The implications of the control of fire are wide-ranging. Besides food preparation, hearths make it possible to survive in colder climates. They provided light and safety for a hominin that, in contrast to primates with better tree-climbing abilities who can sleep in trees, most likely slept on the ground, a dangerous course of action in an environment where large carnivores abounded.[78]

Tool Use

Chimpanzees are well known for using tools, especially for food acquisition.[79] But animals do not have elaborate toolkits that are stable in design and production strategy over large areas or long periods of time, and the degree of tool use and variety in tool types is much higher in humans.

The earliest known stone tools are from Gona, Ethiopia, and are dated to about 2.5 million years ago.[80] Scattered stone tools with similar dates have been found in the Bouri Formation of the Middle Awash Valley in Ethiopia.[81] The association between stone tools and particular hominin species is problematic. For example, it is unclear whether *Australopithecus garhi* was the maker and user of the stone tools from Gona and Bouri since the earliest species of the genus *Homo* are also dated to this time span, and the stone tools are not found in direct association with butchered animal bones or *Australopithecus garhi* fossils.[82] The stone and bone tools at Swartkrans, dated to 1.8 million years ago, come from deposits where *Paranthropus robustus* and *Homo ergaster*

76. F. Berna et al., "Microstratigraphic Evidence of In Situ Fire in the Acheulean Strata of Wonderwerk Cave, Northern Cape province, South Africa," *Proceedings of the National Academy of Sciences* 109 (2012): E1215–E1220.

77. E.g., E. Lev, M. E. Kislev, and O. Bar-Yosef, "Mousterian Vegetal Food in Kebara Cave, Mt. Carmel," *Journal of Archaeological Science* 32 (2005): 475–84; R. Blasco and J. F. Peris, "Middle Pleistocene Bird Consumption at Level XI of Bolomor Cave (Valencia, Spain)," *Journal of Archaeological Science* 36 (2009): 2213–23; A. G. Henry, A. S. Brooks, and D. R. Piperno, "Microfossils in Calculus Demonstrate Consumption of Plants and Cooked Foods in Neanderthal Diets (Shanidar III, Iraq; Spy I and II, Belgium)," *Proceedings of the National Academy of Sciences* 108 (2011): 486–91.

78. Wrangham, *Catching Fire*.

79. E.g., C. Boesch and H. Boesch, "Tool Use and Tool Making in Wild Chimpanzees," *Folia primatologica* 54 (1990): 86–99; A. Whiten et al., "Cultures in Chimpanzees," *Nature* 399 (1999): 682–85.

80. S. Semaw, "The World's Oldest Stone Artefacts from Gona, Ethiopia: Their Implications for Understanding Stone Technology and Patterns of Human Evolution between 2.6–1.5 Million Years Ago," *Journal of Archaeological Science* 27 (2000): 1197–1214.

81. De Heinzelin et al., "Environment and Behavior of Bouri Hominids."

82. Ibid., 627; Ungar et al., "Diet in Early *Homo*."

occur alongside each other, complicating the question of which species had sufficient manipulative skills for the task.[83]

These earliest toolkits consist mainly of pebbles with one or more sharpened edges, known as the Oldowan industry. Not long after the appearance of *Homo ergaster*, tool production became considerably more complex, leading to the creation of the Acheulean industry characterized by hand axes. In contrast to the earliest sites with stone tools, sites associated with *Homo ergaster* contain a larger quantity of stone tools and have a clearer structure.[84] Unfortunately, tools made out of organic material do not often fossilize, but where they do, they show a mastery of materials, for example in the oldest wooden artifacts, the Schöningen spears, dated to 400,000 years ago.[85]

Cognitive Abilities

Modern humans are qualitatively different from primates and other animals in a wide range of cognitive abilities. The origin of the modern human behavioral repertoire has been termed the "human revolution" because of the sudden appearance in the archaeological record of a range of technological and cultural innovations, including blade tools, grinding and pounding tools, systematic use of bone and antler, musical instruments, body decoration, and art. Traditionally, this "modern human package" has been linked to the supposedly superior cognitive ability of *Homo sapiens* as compared with other *Homo* species. Paradoxically, the appearance of the classic "modern human package" does not coincide with the appearance of anatomically modern humans[86] but postdates them by about 100,000 years. The correlation with an increase in brain size is even weaker. As a further complication, many elements of the package appear around 65,000–100,000 years ago in South African sites,[87] such as the iconic site of Blombos Cave, where the world's earliest art object was found alongside stone and bone tools and shell jewelry.[88] Following their

83. Lewin and Foley, *Principles of Human Evolution*; M. W. Tocheri et al., "The Evolutionary History of the Hominin Hand since the Last Common Ancestor of *Pan* and *Homo*," *Journal of Anatomy* 222 (2008): 544–62.

84. Lewin and Foley, *Principles of Human Evolution*.

85. H. Thieme, "Lower Palaeological Hunting Spears from Germany," *Nature* 385 (1997): 807–10.

86. McDougall, Brown, and Fleagle, "Stratigraphic Placement"; A. Nowell, "Defining Behavioral Modernity in the Context of Neanderthal and Anatomically Modern Human Populations," *Annual Review of Anthropology* 39 (2010): 437–52.

87. S. McBrearty and A. Brooks, "The Revolution That Wasn't: A New Interpretation of the Origin of Modern Human Behavior," *Journal of Human Evolution* 39 (2000): 453–63.

88. C. S. Henshilwood et al., "Emergence of Modern Human Behavior: Middle Stone Age Engravings from South Africa," *Science* 295 (2002): 1278–80.

first appearance, these innovations disappear from the archaeological record, to reappear 25,000 years later, at which point they rapidly spread to human populations throughout the world.[89] Moreover, some researchers argue that many elements of the modern human package, such as blade tools, use of pigments and body adornment, and burial practices, were also independently developed by Neanderthals, or even earlier species of *Homo*.[90] Together, these observations indicate that factors other than cognitive ability were involved in the appearance of the modern human package. Recent modeling suggests that innovations could be maintained and transmitted to future generations only when a certain population density threshold was crossed.[91]

It remains difficult to interpret indications of modern human behavior in earlier *Homo* species. For example, did Neanderthals bury their dead for hygienic reasons only or did they have a concept of an afterlife? Do cutmarks and defleshing marks on Neanderthal skeletons from sites like Moula-Guercy (France) and Krapina (Croatia) indicate that Neanderthals considered their conspecifics (members of the same species) as a source of meat, or are they indicative of ritual and mortuary behavior similar to that found in some present human populations?[92] And what are the implications of the absence of evidence for advanced cognitive behavior in light of preservation conditions? The older the site, the less likely it is that fragile materials will survive to this day. Consider for example the major difference between modern humans and Neanderthals in their spatial behavior. Neanderthal living spaces tend to be much less structured than modern human living spaces.[93] The Neanderthal lifestyle seems to have been more localized, as evidenced in the shorter distances

89. J. Zilhão, "The Emergence of Ornaments and Art: An Archaeological Perspective on the Origins of 'Behavioral Modernity,'" *Journal of Archaeological Research* 15 (2007): 1–54.

90. F. d'Errico et al., "Archaeological Evidence for the Emergence of Language, Symbolism, and Music—An Alternative Multidisciplinary Perspective," *Journal of World Prehistory* 17 (2003): 1–70; J. Zilhão, "Emergence of Ornaments"; J. Zilhão et al., "Symbolic Use of Marine Shells and Mineral Pigments by Iberian Neanderthals," *Proceedings of the National Academy of Sciences* 107 (2010): 1023–28.

91. A. Powell, S. Shennan, and M. G. Thomas, "Late Pleistocene Demography and the Appearance of Modern Human Behavior," *Science* 324 (2009): 1298–1301.

92. M. D. Russell, "Mortuary Practices at the Krapina Neanderthal Site," *American Journal of Physical Anthropology* 72 (1987): 381–97; A. Defleur et al.,"Neanderthal Cannibalism at Moula-Guercy, Ardèche, France," *Science* 286 (1999): 128–31; S. A. Hurlbut, "The Taphonomy of Cannibalism: A Review of Anthropogenic Bone Modification in the American Southwest," *International Journal of Osteoarchaeology* 10 (2000): 4–26; S. Lindenbaum, "Thinking about Cannibalism," *Annual Review of Anthropology* 33 (2004): 475–98.

93. J. Kolen, "Hominids without Homes: On the Nature of Middle Palaeolithic Settlement in Europe," in *The Middle Palaeolithic Occupation of Europe*, ed. W. Roebroeks and C. Gamble (Leiden: University of Leiden Press, 1999), 139–63.

over which they transported raw materials.[94] In contrast, modern humans invested more in living structures and transported raw materials over much greater distances. However, this may be related to the potentially extremely ephemeral nature of the living spaces of highly mobile populations,[95] as seen in the sparse material culture of groups like the Selk'nam, who live in the hostile conditions of Tierra del Fuego in southern Argentina. Neanderthal body proportions, and thus energy requirements and expenditure, may have forced them to have relatively small home ranges and move camp frequently, covering relatively small annual ranges.[96] Therefore, even if we discount preservation issues, these patterns could be explained by cultural and physical factors and do not necessarily imply that Neanderthals had lower cognitive abilities.

Where Do We Place Adam?

Taking stock of the evidence presented in the preceding paragraphs, where does Adam fit in this picture? Is there space for assimilating the biblical doctrine of Adam and Eve into this overview of modern palaeoanthropology?

The morphological evidence suggests that the genera *Australopithecus/ Paranthropus* and *Homo* (potentially excluding *Homo habilis*) differ in crucial respects. Key skeletal traits related to locomotion show a combination of habitual bipedalism of a nonhuman form with arboreal locomotion in the australopithecines. In contrast, species in the *Homo* lineage from *Homo erectus/ergaster* onward are characterized by fully human bipedalism. Differences between the postcranial skeletons of these two groups abound and the examples given here can be complemented by similar patterns observed in a variety of other skeletal elements.[97]

94. N. Rolland and H. L. Dibble, "A New Synthesis of Middle Paleolithic Variability," *American Anthropology* 55 (1995): 480–99; A. Scheer, "The Gravettian in Southwest Germany: Stylistic Features, Raw Material Resources and Settlement Patterns," in *Hunters of the Golden Age: The Mid-Upper Palaeolithic of Eurasia 30,000–20,000 BP*, ed. W. Roebroeks et al. (Leiden: Leiden University Press, 1999).

95. W. Roebroeks and A. Tuffreau, "Palaeoenvironment and Settlement Patterns of the Northwest European Middle Palaeolithic," in *Middle Palaeolithic Occupation*, ed. Roebroeks and Gamble, 121–38.

96. K. MacDonald, W. Roebroeks, and A. Verpoorte, "An Energetics Perspective on the Neanderthal Record," in *The Evolution of Hominin Diets: Integrating Approaches to the Study of Palaeolithic Subsistence*, ed. J.-J. Hublin and M. P. Richards (Leipzig: Springer, 2009), 211–20.

97. E.g., the mandible: Y. Rak, A. Ginzburg, and E. Geffen, "Gorilla-like Anatomy on *Australopithecus afarensis* Mandibles Suggests *Au. afarensis* Link to Robust Australopiths," *Proceedings of the National Academy of Sciences* 104 (2007): 6568–72; the inner ear: F. Spoor, B. Wood, and F. Zonneveld, "Implications of Early Hominid Labyrinthine Morphology for Evolution of Human Bipedal Locomotion," *Nature* 369 (1994): 645–48; arms and hands: B. G. Richmond and

As we have seen, preservation problems and our limited understanding of the impact of differences in brain structure prevent us from assessing the cognitive abilities of early hominins. All we can conclude is that although there is no clear gap in relative brain size between *Homo* and the australopithecines, brain size is clearly larger in *Homo* and no directional trend toward larger brain size can be observed in the *Australopithecus/Paranthropus* lineage.

Turning to the behavioral evidence, again we can observe a step change between the australopithecines and *Homo* in several important traits. While the australopithecines were primarily plant-eaters, some of whom may occasionally and opportunistically have incorporated meat into their diet, meat was a far more important food source for *Homo erectus/ergaster*, with evidence of active hunting long predating modern humans. This difference in subsistence methods is thought to be correlated with fundamental differences in social organization, control of fire, and food preparation. Although there is some evidence for tool use in later australopithecine species, their technology was simple and ad hoc. When *Homo ergaster* enters the scene, use of technology becomes more complex and planned. Evidence for symbolic behavior is not synchronous with the appearance of anatomically modern humans, and some indications of advanced cognition also occur earlier in the archaeological record. The fossil and archaeological records can therefore be seen to support a clear difference between the australopithecines and *Homo*.[98] Researchers working from a Christian perspective have mostly drawn the line between human and nonhuman at exactly this juncture,[99] and the recent evidence presented above tends to strengthen rather than erode this position. Paleoanthropologists overstate their case when they claim that the evidence unequivocally supports the idea that the australopithecines were the ancestors of the *Homo* lineage. Even when we take the imperfection of the fossil and archaeological record into account, the fact remains that in several crucial respects, the australopithecines were very different from us.

D. S. Strait, "Evidence that Humans Evolved from a Knuckle-Walking Ancestor," *Nature* 404 (2000): 382–85; J. Arias-Martorell et al., "3D Geometric Morphometric Analysis of the Proximal Epiphysis of the Hominid Humerus," *Journal of Anatomy* 221 (2012): 394–405; Tocheri et al., "The Evolutionary History of the Hominin Hand"; adaptations for endurance running: Bramble and Lieberman, "Endurance Running."

98. J. Hawks et al., "Population Bottlenecks and Pleistocene Human Evolution," *Molecular Biology and Evolution* 17 (2000): 2–22; McHenry and Coffing, "*Australopithecus* to *Homo*"; E. Mayr, *What Makes Biology Unique? Considerations on the Autonomy of a Scientific Discipline* (Cambridge: Cambridge University Press, 2004), 198; Lieberman et al., "The Transition from *Australopithecus* to *Homo*."

99. E.g., Lubenow, *Bones of Contention*; Hartwig-Scherer, "Apes or Ancestors?"; T. C. Wood, "Baraminological Analysis."

There is no clear trend toward more humanlike morphologies and behaviors, but instead the australopithecine lineage is largely unique. Although changes did occur between *Homo erectus/ergaster* and *Homo sapiens*, particularly in brain size and the evidence for complex behavior, the scale of these changes is relatively small when contrasted with the differences between australopithecines and *Homo*.

Where then do we place Adam? The step change from australopithecines to *Homo* suggests that Adam could be placed at the root of the *Homo erectus/ergaster* to *Homo sapiens* lineage around 1.8 million years ago. This is in contrast to Rana and Ross (2005) but in accordance with the "basic type" classification developed by Hartwig-Scherer (1998). This proposal does justice to morphological similarities and indications of complex behavior in the earlier *Homo* species, as well as to the recent evidence of Neanderthal and Denisovan contributions to our genome. However, it does imply that Adam's progeny split into different species, a model which is sometimes seen as problematic by Christians, because they identify humans, bearers of the image of God, exclusively with our own species.[100]

Accommodating the Presence of Multiple Species in the *Homo* Lineage

We are all familiar with the enormous potential for variation present in the genome of a single species. A brief look at the breeds of domesticated animals (cats, dogs, horses) reveals a bewildering array of variations in conformation, coloration, appendages, and temperament. This amazing ability of nature to produce an ever greater variety of species was one of the observations that Darwin used to explain the idea of evolution in the first place. Modern humans at present show lower levels of genetic variability than most animal species, including great apes, reflecting a reduced gene pool due to past population bottlenecks, low population sizes, and local extinction events.[101] Even our relatively homogeneous genome is capable of producing individuals with widely differing physical, cognitive, and behavioral characteristics. Thus, it is not unreasonable to assume that our ancestral genome had great potential for variation.

Since humans are embodied creatures, it should not surprise us that our bodies are subject to the same natural processes as the bodies of primates and

---

100. Rana and Ross, *Who Was Adam?*
101. H. Kaessman et al., "Great Ape DNA Sequences Reveal a Reduced Diversity and an Expansion in Humans," *Nature Genetics* 27 (2001): 155–56.

other animals. This could potentially include speciation—the process by which new species arise. For example, different groups of the same human species could have become geographically isolated, and some genetic traits may have been present in one group but not in another. In addition, over time different genetic traits could have been selected and passed down through the generations of the separated groups. Eventually, this would result in significantly different genomes. Furthermore, we should keep in mind that the fossil species concept used by paleoanthropologists is not the same as that used by biologists, who study living species. The "biological species concept" defines species on the basis of reproductive isolation from other species: a species is a population of individuals that interbreed with each other but not with individuals of other species.[102] However, this criterion can only rarely be applied to fossil species, where interbreeding can seldom be investigated.[103] Paleoanthropologists therefore use mainly morphological characteristics to identify species. As we have seen, species identification can be difficult in the face of small, distorted, and/or biased samples, especially if postcranial fossils are missing or not associated with cranial remains. Furthermore, it is by no means clear how much variation we should allow for within a single species, especially if there are large morphological differences between males and females of the species. Finally, in many cases it is hard to ascertain how morphological differences relate to cognitive and behavioral differences.

The differences between earlier and later species of the genus *Homo* are mainly in cranial traits and evidence for behavioral characteristics. As we have seen, the interpretation of many of these differences is surrounded by difficulties. Do they amount to differences at the level of a biological species? Recent evidence for interbreeding between modern humans and Neanderthals and Denisovans indicates that these "species" were not fully separated genetically, even if present thinking is they were rarely in contact for some 150,000 years. But even if the fossil species do represent real biological species, this is not problematic in the light of the biblical account of Adam, as long as he is the father of all such species.[104] After all, the fall affected all Adam and Eve's descendants, and Christ offers redemption to all humans who trust in his death and resurrection.

102. E. Mayr, *Systematics and the Origin of Species* (New York: Columbia University Press, 1942).

103. Interbreeding in fossil species can only be investigated through studies of ancient DNA still remaining in the fossils. Although the recent sequencing of the Neanderthal genome shows that this is sometimes possible, such cases are rare, especially since DNA does not survive for longer than about 50,000 years, and only under conditions favorable to preservation.

104. T. C. Wood, "Baraminology, the Image of God."

Conclusion

The findings of modern paleoanthropology are often presented as the "smoking gun" that exposes the biblical account of human origins and the fall as false or at best mythical. However, Adam's historicity and the human fossil record are not necessarily in conflict. The evidence considered in this chapter confirms the expectation of a discontinuity between the genus *Homo* and the australopithecine genera. If we place Adam at the root of the genus *Homo* then this discontinuity can be seen as the dividing line between humans and nonhumans. Under the conventional chronology, this would place Adam at around 1.8 million years ago.

Many have preferred to place Adam later in the record, placing the dividing line between humans and nonhumans within the genus *Homo*. But these models face two challenges from the paleoanthropological record. First, these models are faced with the lack of a clear morphological and behavioral division between what are regarded as humans and what are regarded as nonhumans. In recent years new data have slowly pushed further back in time the appearance of features that were thought to be unique to modern humans, and the genetic evidence for interbreeding between different *Homo* species is accumulating, so that any such division within the genus *Homo* is increasingly difficult to support. Second, these models need to account for the morphological and behavioral gap between the australopithecine genera and the genus *Homo*. The australopithecines form a uniquely distinct group of primates, and the identity of the hypothesized ancestor of the genus *Homo* remains shrouded in mystery.

In conclusion, when the paleoanthropological data are considered in isolation, the evidence points to placing Adam at the root of the genus *Homo*. This proposal also solves some difficult theological issues that encumber other models for the integration of the biblical witness and the fossil record. It enables us to fully affirm the traditional doctrine of Adam and Eve's historicity, their special creation, and the fall and original sin. Taking the embodied nature of humans into account, we should not be surprised by the variation in physical features observed in the fossil record of *Homo*. Instead, we can affirm the humanity of all fossil *Homo* species and recognize them as descendants of a common father and mother, in accordance with our expectation of the unity of the human lineage.

In this chapter I have focused mainly on the historicity of Adam in light of the paleoanthropological data. In important respects, then, my conclusions here are somewhat contingent on the acceptance of a number of presuppositions bound up with current paleoanthropological models—and yet, such methodological presuppositions or assumptions are by no means inviolable or beyond critique. For instance, I have not addressed the wider issues of how to relate the human fossil record to the biblical narrative. An important problem concerns chronology: did Adam live about 1.8 million years ago, the conventional date for the origin of *Homo erectus*? If so, what does that mean for our reading of the genealogies and the apparently Bronze or Iron Age context of Genesis 4–5? Or do we need to consider a radical revision of the scientific chronological framework? And how does our interpretation of the paleoanthropological record interact with our understanding of Noah's flood and the spread of humankind over the earth? Much work remains to be done, but I am confident that with an investment of time and research, it will be possible to construct models that do justice both to the biblical narrative and the scientific data.

PART 2

Original Sin in History

4

ORIGINAL SIN IN PATRISTIC THEOLOGY

Peter Sanlon

Augustine imagined that a baby, able to speak, would complain, "Why do you regard me simply as an infant? Admittedly you cannot see the load of sin I carry, but I was conceived in iniquity."[1] Rhetorical flourishes such as this were founded on the doctrine of original sin—a controversial, offensive teaching forever associated with the name of Augustine. Original sin "generally denotes the sinfulness or fault inherent in human beings prior to anything they do."[2] More comprehensively:

> The Augustinian doctrines of the fall and original sin affirm (1) that Adam and Eve's violation of God's primordial commandment against eating from the tree of the knowledge of good and evil caused a fundamental deformation in humanity's relationship to God, each other, and the rest of creation; and (2) that this "fall" includes among its consequences that all human beings thereafter are born into a state of estrangement from God—an "original" sin that condemns all individuals prior to and apart from their committing any "actual" sins in time and space.[3]

1. Augustine, *Expositions of the Psalms*, 2 of 6 of *The Works of Saint Augustine: A Translation for the 21st Century*, ed. J. Rotelle, trans. M. Boulding (New York: New City Press, 2000), 50.10.
2. Risto Saarinen, "Original Sin," in *Religion Past and Present: Encyclopedia of Theology and Religion*, ed. H. D. Betz, D. S. Browning, B. Janowski, and E. Jungel (Leiden: Brill, 2011), 9:380.
3. I. A. McFarland, *In Adam's Fall: A Meditation on the Christian Doctrine of Original Sin* (Malden, MA: Wiley-Blackwell, 2010), 29–30.

Did Augustine Invent Original Sin?

"It is virtually an axiom of historical theology that the doctrine of original sin . . . cannot be traced back beyond Augustine."[4] Augustine is accused of "having concocted a doctrine that is found neither in the gospels nor in the Pauline epistles nor in the Greek patristic tradition."[5] Many believe that "Research has shown that Augustine's thought on original sin ultimately introduced a hitherto unknown element into Christian theology."[6] Some castigate Augustine for inventing an immoral doctrine that turns a person into a "puppet."[7] Others praise Augustine's theological constructiveness as earning him a place among theological giants: "Augustine may be accounted the originator of the doctrines of original sin and sovereign grace, Anselm the doctrine of satisfaction, and Luther that of justification by faith."[8]

Augustine was outraged when his Pelagian opponent, Julian of Eclanum, accused him of inventing the doctrine of original sin. Augustine fulminated, "It is not I who made up original sin! The catholic faith has believed it from its beginnings. But you who deny it are undoubtedly a new heretic."[9] Those who reject Augustine's teaching on original sin must, as A. Jacobs points out, "see him as Paul's misinterpreter. . . . In North Africa, at least, Augustine's reading of Paul is amply anticipated."[10]

Auguries of Original Sin Pre-Augustine

The Pelagian controversy was ostensibly about Augustine's doctrine of original sin. However, the dispute had begun without Augustine's knowledge when a deacon, Paulinus of Milan, accused one of Pelagius's disciples, Caelestius, of heresy. A tribunal (not involving Augustine) at Carthage in AD 411 or 412 condemned Caelestius for teaching that "the sin of Adam harmed him

4. Gerald Bray, "Original Sin in Patristic Thought," *Churchman* 108.1 (1994): 37.
5. H. Rondet, *Original Sin: The Patristic and Theological Background* (Shannon, Ireland: Ecclesia Press, 1972), 21.
6. Anthony Dupont, Gratia *in Augustine's* Sermones ad Populum *during the Pelagian Controversy: Do Different Contexts Furnish Different Insights?*, ed. Wim Janse, Brill's Series in Church History (Leiden: Brill, 2013), 48.
7. John Rist, "Augustine on Free Will and Predestination," *Journal of Theological Studies* 20.2 (1969): 440.
8. B. B. Warfield, *Studies in Tertullian and Augustine*, vol. 4 of *The Works of Benjamin Breckinridge Warfield* (1930; Grand Rapids: Baker, 1981), 19.
9. Augustine, *Marriage and Desire*, 2.12.25, in *Answer to the Pelagians*, vol. 2 of 4 (Hyde Park, NY: New City Press, 1998).
10. A. Jacobs, *Original Sin: A Cultural History* (New York: HarperCollins, 2009), 32.

alone and not the human race."[11] Paulinus was Ambrose's secretary and biographer—the conviction that original sin was part of the catholic church's
faith appears to have been upheld by Ambrose. Ambrose had written, "We
are conceived in the sin of our parents, and we are born in their transgressions. Birth itself has its own infections, and nature itself does not have only
one infection."[12] He also observed that "Adam perished, and all perished in
him."[13] Augustine cited Ambrose as an authority who agreed with his views
on original sin: "All of us human beings are born under the power of sin, and
our very origin lies in guilt."[14]

Augustine maintained that the Pelagians' denial of original sin was an
assault on the historic catholic faith: "You attack the catholic faith. . . . The
Church, then, has taken fright at the profane words of your new teaching."[15]
The newness of the Pelagians' doctrine was decried by Augustine: "You Pelagian heretics construct new stratagems and prepare new attacks against
the walls of the most ancient truth."[16] Against Julian's "wretched insanity"
Augustine claimed to have "many holy, outstanding, and renowned teachers
of the catholic truth: Irenaeus, Cyprian, Reticius, Olympius, Hilary, Gregory,
Basil, Ambrose, John, Innocent, Jerome, and other companions and colleagues
of theirs, as well as the whole Church of Christ."[17] Various of these and others
are cited by Augustine. Hilary is noted for saying, "In Adam's offense we lost
the richness of that first and blessed creation."[18]

As one of the earliest authorities, Irenaeus was of particular importance
in establishing the catholicity of original sin. Augustine was aware of this and
drew attention to Irenaeus's antiquity:

> Irenaeus, the bishop of Lyons, lived not long after the time of the apostles. He
> said, "Human beings can be saved from the ancient wound of the serpent in no
> other way than by believing in him who, when he was raised up from the earth

11. Augustine, *The Grace of Christ and Original Sin*, 2.2.2, in *Answer to the Pelagians*, vol.
1 of 4.

12. Ambrose, *Explanation of David the Prophet*, 1.11.56. Cited by Augustine in *Answer to
Julian*, 1.3.10, in *Answer to the Pelagians*, vol. 2 of 4.

13. Ambrose, *Commentary on Luke*, 7:23–4. Cited from Augustine, *Unfinished Work in
Answer to Julian*, 1.112., in *Answer to the Pelagians*, vol. 3 of 4.

14. Ambrose, *Penance*, 1.3.13. Cited from Augustine, *Answer to Julian*, 2.3.5, in *Answer to
the Pelagians*, vol. 2 of 4.

15. Augustine, *Answer to Julian*, 2.10.37. Cited from Augustine, *Answer to Julian*, in *Answer
to the Pelagians*, vol. 2 of 4.

16. Ibid., 3.17.32. Cited from Augustine, *Answer to Julian*, in *Answer to the Pelagians*, vol.
2 of 4.

17. Ibid., 2.10.37. Cited from Augustine, *Answer to Julian*, in *Answer to the Pelagians*, vol.
2 of 4.

18. Hilary, *Commentary on Job*, cited in ibid., 2.8.27.

on the tree of martyrdom in the likeness of sinful flesh, drew all things to himself and gave life to the dead." Likewise, the same Irenaeus said, "Just as the human race was subjected to death by a virgin, so it was justly released by a virgin; the disobedience of a virgin balanced by the obedience of a virgin. For, when the sin of the first-formed human being was corrected by the rebuke of the firstborn Son and the cunning of the serpent was defeated by the simplicity of the dove, we were released from the chains which bound us to death."[19]

Augustine was adamant that the doctrine of original sin was not his invention. In antiquity Irenaeus believed it; in the Eastern church Gregory[20] and Basil[21] concurred. The greatest of African bishops, Cyprian, agreed: "A newborn has no sin at all except that it has contracted by its first birth the contagion of the ancient death, because it was born in the flesh from Adam."[22] Establishing the nonoriginality of his teaching was a matter of great import to Augustine. His citations are copious. The *Council of Carthage* (May 418 AD) agreed that Augustine's doctrine of original sin was the historic catholic belief:

> If any deny that little ones fresh from their mothers' wombs must be baptized or say that they are baptized for the forgiveness of sins, but that they do not contract from Adam any original sin that is wiped away in the bath of rebirth . . . let them be anathema. The words of the apostle, "Through one human being sin came into the world, and through sin death, and so it passed on to all human beings in whom all have sinned" (Rom. 5:12) are not to be understood in any other sense than that in which the Catholic Church spread throughout the world has always understood them.[23]

Nevertheless not all subsequent readers have been satisfied. For many historians "original sin in the precise meaning of the term is an invention of St. Augustine."[24] The explanation for disagreements over the originality of Augustine at this point lies in the interpretive framework relied on to bring intellectual cogency to dogma. The determinative factor is the relative weighting given to either historical development or doctrinal explication.

19. Augustine, *Answer to Julian*, 1.3.5 (see also 1.7.32), in *Answer to the Pelagians*, vol. 2 of 4, citing Irenaeus, *Against Heresies*, 4.2.7; 5.19.
20. Augustine, *Answer to Julian*, 1.5.15.
21. Ibid., 1.5.16.
22. Cyprian, *Letter to Fidus*, 64.5, cited in ibid., 1.3.6.
23. Canon 2 of the Council of Carthage. Augustine, *Answer to the Pelagians*, vol. 1 of *The Works of Saint Augustine: A Translation for the 21st Century*, ed. J. Rotelle, trans. M. Boulding (New York: New City Press, 1997), 378.
24. Rondet, *Original Sin*, 122. See also J. Gross, *Entstehungsgeschichte des Erbsündendogmas: Von der Bibel bis Augustinus*, vol. 1 (Munich: Ernst Reinhardt, 1960), 218; J. Turmel, "Le dogme du péché originel dans Saint Augustin," *Revue d'Histoire Ecclésiastique* 6 (1909): 404.

Skating on the Surface: Historical Development

The most common approach adopted for interpreting the role of Augustine in formulating the doctrine of original sin is to chart a course of historical development, in which Augustine expropriates the role of the preeminent innovator.

It can prove a challenge to be evenhanded and consistent in sketching this sort of historical development. For example, a scholar can, on the one hand, emphasize discontinuity, arguing that Augustine marked a "transition from a loosely conceived, broadly ecumenical doctrine of the fall to a much more tightly formulated doctrine of original sin. . . . Augustine's thought decisively redirected Christian interpretation of the fall."[25] Yet no sooner than such a reading is proffered, it requires qualification: "The shift did not constitute a sharp break with established patterns of Christian reflection."[26] How can the evidence be so resistant to coherent elucidation that a historian is driven to portray Augustine's role in doctrinal formulation as one which "decisively redirected Christian interpretation" while simultaneously it "did not constitute a sharp break with established patterns of Christian reflection"?

Despite the palpable tension in readings, there have been many attempts to explain Augustine's role in terms of historical development. It has been argued that early engagements with original sin were chiefly theodicies prompted by the challenge of gnosticism.[27] Another historical development narrative portrays Irenaeus as teaching a multiplicity of factors as contributing to the fall; Tertullian, Clement of Alexandria, and Origen follow by stressing different strands, all of which are found in Irenaeus.[28] One of the most thorough studies of original sin in the patristic tradition devotes detailed chapters to individual authors and attempts to understand their interests on their own terms. Some connections are made to give a sense of historical development; for example, it is observed that "Tertullian appears to have read Irenaeus. Like him, he sets himself in opposition to Gnostic deviations."[29] Nevertheless, the more detail given on individual figures, the less a sense of coherent historical development is communicated.

Those who attempt to explain the extent of Augustine's inventiveness in formulating the doctrine of original sin by means of constructing a historical narrative struggle with contradictory impulses. Some of these narratives are extraordinarily tenuous; for example, there is the claim that while Augustine

---

25. McFarland, *In Adam's Fall*, 32.
26. Ibid.
27. N. P. Williams, *The Ideas of the Fall and Original Sin: A Historical and Critical Study* (London: Longman, 1927).
28. Bray, "Original Sin in Patristic Thought," 38–39.
29. Rondet, *Original Sin*, 51.

did not invent the doctrine of original sin, he derived it from the Encratites and Messalians—heretical ascetic groups.[30] The study that puts forward this case has been described as a "brilliant book,"[31] but it is probably more accurate to observe that

> in his efforts to fit Augustine and his teaching about original sin into the Encratite and Messalian framework, Beatrice has presented us with his own preconceived, monstrous hybrid, a cross-bred entity, which is neither Encratite, nor Messalian, nor Augustinian. . . . [His] slender evidence will be objected to at almost every point.[32]

Some historical narratives are burdened by self-contradiction, some emphasize discontinuity, and others present a moderate continuity. A good example of the latter is the conclusion of J. N. D. Kelly: "Though falling short of Augustinianism, there was here the outline of a real theory of original sin. The Fathers might well have filled it in and given greater sharpness of definition had the subject been directly canvassed in their day."[33]

Historical development narratives—regardless of where they lie on the spectrum of continuity and discontinuity—have the appearance of being self-evidently reasonable. In reality extraordinarily subjective judgments are necessarily made at each juncture. What, for example, should be made of the first-century Jewish text, 2 Esdras 7:118–31? In this document, Ezra is portrayed as complaining that Adam's sin has caused the condemnation of all his progeny: "O Adam, what have you done? For though it was you who sinned, the fall was not yours alone, but ours also who are your descendants."[34]

In response to this statement, an angel reassures Ezra that Adam's sin will not condemn his descendants; they will be judged on their self-control and obedience to the Mosaic law. This text can be taken to signify either widespread awareness of a doctrine of original sin or a studied rejection of original sin. Either is possible.

Some attempt at reconstructing the historical development of doctrine is necessary; however, the post-Darwinian, modernist mindset attributes too

30. P. F. Beatrice, *Tradux peccati: alle fonti della dottrina agostiniana del peccato originale,* vol. 8 (Milano: Studia Patristica, 1978).

31. G. Quispel and J. Oort, *Gnostica, Judaica, Catholica: Collected Essays of Gilles Quispel* (Leiden: Brill, 2008), 361.

32. R. J. De Simone, "Modern Research on the Sources of Saint Augustine's Doctrine of Original Sin," *Augustinian Studies* 11 (1980): 223.

33. J. N. D. Kelly, *Early Christian Doctrines,* 3rd ed. (London: A&C Black, 1965), 351.

34. 2 Esdras 7:118. Howard Clark Kee, ed., *Cambridge Annotated Study Apocrypha* (Cambridge: Cambridge University Press, 2008), 218.

much certainty and significance to developmental narratives. Debates over the veracity of narratives that attribute or deny theological inventiveness to Augustine regarding original sin are particularly invidious for the simple reason that they set aside Augustine's own interpretation of the situation. Augustine was fully aware of the manner in which beliefs could develop and decline over time—his *City of God* evidences that. Augustine was accused by Julian of inventing original sin. Nevertheless, Augustine rejected this accusation and staked his catholic orthodoxy on his understanding that "the Catholic faith does not doubt that there is original sin, and not little boys, but serious and solid men, who were taught in the Church and have taught the Church, defended this faith up to the day of their death."[35]

As mentioned above, the Council of Carthage affirmed Augustine's assessment. All the varied historical narrative reconstructions that aim to determine whether Augustine invented the doctrine of original sin skate on the surface of history since they impede thoughtful engagement with Augustine's self-understanding. Augustine presented in his writings a theological explanation of how he could be exonerated from the charge of inventing a new teaching. Good historians seek to empathically discern the self-interpretations of protagonists. Overemphasis on historical developmental narratives obscures Augustine's self-understanding. The historian must go deeper to unearth the doctrinal connections on which Augustine based his claim to catholicity.

Going Deeper: Doctrinal Explication

A number of unsurprising strategies were employed by Augustine to commend his claim that original sin was no innovation: citations from Scripture, church fathers, and councils. Augustine coined an epithet for the Pelagians, who denied original sin. They were the *novi heretici*, "new heretics."[36] All of these were parts of Augustine's denial of originality; the deeper doctrinal explication formulated by Augustine revolved around infant baptism. The connections Augustine made have abiding significance for our understanding of how Christian doctrine is discerned.

Augustine agreed with the Pelagians that a baby had committed no actual sins. Indeed he regarded the matter as self-evident:

---

35. Augustine, *Unfinished Work in Answer to Julian*, 4.136.1, in *Answer to the Pelagians*, vol. 3 of 4.

36. Augustine, *Revisions*, vol. 1.2 of *The Works of Saint Augustine: A Translation for the 21st Century*, ed. R. Teske, trans. B. Ramsey (New York: New City Press, 2010), 1.9.3, 1.9.4, 2.22.2; 33; 36; 53.

Look at their great weakness of mind and body, their ignorance of everything, their complete inability to obey a command, their inability to understand or observe any law, whether natural or written, and their lack of the use of reason. . . . [D]oes not all this proclaim and demonstrate their freedom from personal sin? Let the very obviousness of the matter speak for itself, for I am never so at a loss for words as when the matter under discussion is more obvious than anyone can say.[37]

With more than a hint of sarcasm Augustine derided the idea that his views attributed actual sinful acts to babies: "Perhaps an infant cries and bothers adults, but I would be surprised if this should be attributed to sinfulness and not rather to unhappiness."[38]

While everybody agreed that babies were innocent of sin, Augustine and other near contemporaries reveal in numerous asides and observations that infant baptism was widely accepted.[39] According to Augustine, it was not uncommon for a mother to be rushing to church to get her baby baptized, only for the child to die en route.[40] The tragic scene makes sense only in a setting where infant mortality is common and infant baptism highly esteemed. Augustine reasoned that baptism is a sacrament of forgiveness and grace. Baptizing infants evidenced an assumption that they had to be forgiven something—if not actual sins, then the original sin contracted from Adam. Augustine wrote:

What shall I say about the very form of the sacrament? . . . What does my exorcism do for the child, if it is not held in servitude to the devil? These persons would have to make responses to me on behalf of the little one whom they present, because the child could not make responses on its own. How, then, are they going to say that the child renounces the devil, if the devil had no claim on the child? How are they going to say that the child is turning back to God, if the child had not been turned away? How are they going to say . . . that the child believes in the forgiveness of sins, if the child receives no forgiveness?[41]

Augustine did not hesitate to say that he would refuse to let a person make promises on behalf of a baby, if the adult concerned did not believe forgiveness

---

37. Augustine, *The Punishment and Forgiveness of Sins and the Baptism of Little Ones*, 1.35.65, in *Answer to the Pelagians*, vol. 1 of 4.

38. Ibid., 1.35.66, in *Answer to the Pelagians*, vol. 1 of 4.

39. Everett Ferguson, *Baptism in the Early Church: History, Theology, and Liturgy in the First Five Centuries* (Grand Rapids: Eerdmans, 2009), chaps. 51–52.

40. Augustine, *Epistles*, 217.19.

41. Augustine, *The Punishment and Forgiveness of Sins and the Baptism of Little Ones*, 1.34.63, in *Answer to the Pelagians*, vol. 1 of 4. In Augustine's baptism service, exorcism of the devil's authority featured more prominently than in modern liturgies. Nevertheless in the traditional Anglican BCP liturgy, parents are still asked if they "in the name of this child, renounce the devil and all his works."

of the child was necessary.[42] The Pelagians, in an attempt "to avoid admitting original sin, claim that little ones have no sin at all."[43] Such an approach masqueraded as compassionate but in reality destroyed the sacrament of baptism and proclaimed that Christ was not a savior of children. Augustine insisted that Jesus was indeed a savior of children.[44] Accepting this meant believing that children were born needing salvation from sin. Unable to commit any actual sins, the sin babies needed rescuing from had to be original sin.

The Pelagians' denial of original sin left them vulnerable to accusations of inconsistency and deception:

> The Pelagians do not dare reject the sacraments of the Church which she celebrates with the authority of such an ancient tradition, though they suppose they are administered as a pretense rather than as a reality, in the case of children. These sacraments of the holy Church indicate quite clearly that little ones, who have just been born, are freed from slavery to the devil by the grace of Christ. . . . They are baptized for the forgiveness of sins by a rite that is not false, but true.[45]

All of this enabled Augustine to make doctrinal explications that undergirded his conviction that Christians had always believed in original sin. Although it is not until the start of the third century that we find unequivocal evidence for infant baptism, the most natural explanation of data left from the first two centuries is that in Apostolic times there was a variety of practices.[46] Augustine saw in infant baptism evidence that Christians instinctively grasped that infants needed salvation from a sinfulness that had to be original sin—it being obvious that babies could commit no actual sins. The "new heresy" of Pelagianism was calling into question the nature of forgiveness, baptism, and the grip of sin and Satan that were taught by the ancient church. Engaging with the Pelagians led Augustine to clarify and expand his teaching on original sin, but he understood himself in doing that not to be inventing a new doctrine but defending the vision of grace that he had years previously expounded in his *Confessions*.

Augustine's use of infant baptism to defend the catholic antiquity of original sin challenges us to reflect on how we view the formulation of Christian

---

42. Ibid.

43. Ibid., 1.34.64, in *Answer to the Pelagians*, vol. 1 of 4.

44. Augustine, *Sermons*, 174.7, in *Sermons*, vol. 5 of 11 (Hyde Park, NY: New City Press, 1992), 293.11.

45. Augustine, *The Grace of Christ and Original Sin*, 2.39.45, in *Answer to the Pelagians*, vol. 1 of 4.

46. Tony Lane, "Did the Apostolic Church Baptise Babies? A Seismological Approach," *Tyndale Bulletin* 55.1 (2004): 109–30. Available at: http://www.tyndalehouse.com/TynBul/Library/TynBull_2004_55_1_06_Lane_BaptiseBabies.pdf.

doctrine generally. Many theologians from diverse eras have recognized that in some manner there is development and change in doctrinal beliefs. So Gregory the Great wrote, "With the progress of the times the knowledge of the spiritual Fathers increased; for, in the science of God, Moses was more instructed than Abraham, the Prophets more than Moses, the Apostles more than the Prophets."[47] The Puritan John Robinson preached, "I am verily persuaded the Lord hath more truth yet to break forth out of His Holy Word."[48]

Against the backdrop of such observations, Augustine's use of infant baptism to deny the newness of his doctrine of original sin is counterintuitive. The most common interpretation of his approach is indebted to Roman Catholicism and claims that Augustine is extrapolating his doctrine from ecclesiastical practice. Church practice becomes prior and is the constant. Scripture is then subordinated to the church. So one Roman Catholic theologian contends: "For Augustine, the scriptures are prior by nature but the church is prior in time. That he should formulate such a view is not surprising, given his experience. Augustine went from the church to scripture, not vice versa."[49] Elsewhere the same author argued that for Augustine, "by the very fact that Catholic Christians so believed and acted, these beliefs and practices had authority."[50]

It is easy to see how Augustine's use of infant baptism against the Pelagians can be represented as exalting the church to a preeminent position in safeguarding the constancy of catholic doctrine. However, there is another interpretation that grants a higher authority to Scripture.

Augustine would then be understood to believe that the Scriptures comprise a uniquely authoritative and final revelation.[51] That revelation includes many things that are implicitly believed by the church in her practices. They are assumed within the theological grammar of ecclesiastical practices, such as the sacraments. Such an approach permits Augustine to reason from ecclesiastical realities, without suggesting that the church usurps the supreme position of Scripture. The appearance of development and change in doctrine evidences not an antecedent, preeminent church but rather an ongoing task of rendering

47. Gregory the Great, *Sermons on Ezekiel*, 2.4.12, cited in Karl Keating, *Catholicism and Fundamentalism* (San Francisco: Ignatius Press, 1988), 142.

48. D. Neal, *The History of the Puritans, or Protestant Nonconformists: From the Reformation in 1517, to the Revolution in 1688* (New York: Harper & Brothers, 1843), 269.

49. R. Eno, "Authority," in *Augustine through the Ages: An Encyclopedia*, ed. Allan Fitzgerald (Grand Rapids: Eerdmans, 1999), 80.

50. R. Eno, *Teaching Authority in the Early Church*, vol. 14 of *Message of the Fathers of the Church* (Wilmington, DE: Michael Glazier, 1984), 134.

51. Augustine, *Epistles*, 82.3, in *Letters*, vol. 1 of 4; *Sermons* 162c.15, in *Sermons*, vol. 5 of 11; *Against Faustus*, 26.7, 11.5, in *Answer to Faustus a Manichean*, Works of Augustine, vol. 1.20.

explicit what is revealed in Scripture but held implicitly in the church. As the Reformed theologian Herman Bavinck taught:

> The dogmas have never been fully incorporated in the church's creedal statements and ecclesiastically fixed. The life and faith that the church possesses is much richer than what comes to expression in its creedal statements. The church's confession is far from formulating the entire content of the Christian faith. To begin with, a confession generally comes into being in response to specific historical events and arranges its content accordingly. . . . [There may be] a truth concealed in Scripture that has not yet been assimilated by the church.[52]

Augustine's doctrinal explication of original sin as an ancient and catholic belief revealed a close relationship between the Bible's teaching on original sin and the sacrament of baptism. Children "believe by another, because they sinned by another."[53] In his response to Pelagianism, "Augustine did not invent original sin, but he rendered explicit a tradition which, through various formulas, was slowly coming to the surface."[54] As another scholar concludes his study, "While Augustine was the great systematizer, developer, and defender of the doctrine of original sin, he was not its inventor."[55] The claim that original sin was authoritatively revealed in Scripture and implicitly assumed in ecclesiastical practice is something that can be said for other major doctrines of the Christian faith:

> The doctrine of original sin is marked precisely by the attempt to do equal justice to Biblical language suggesting both human responsibility for and human powerlessness with respect to sin. This is not to claim that the doctrine can be read directly off Scripture. Like most of the classical doctrines of Christianity (e.g., the Trinity, creation from nothing), it cannot be derived so straightforwardly.[56]

The idea that major doctrines of the Christian faith were simply invented by theologians (such as Augustine) in response to challenges (such as Pelagianism) is a naïve interpretation, which Augustine repudiated vigorously. The reading ventured above, that Augustine explicated the teaching of Scripture, which was implicit in the sacrament of baptism, does justice to Augustine's

52. Herman Bavinck, *Reformed Dogmatics*, vol. 1, *Prolegomena* (Grand Rapids: Baker Academic, 2003), 31.
53. Augustine, *Sermons*, 294.12, in *Sermons*, vol. 8 of 11.
54. Rondet, *Original Sin*, 122.
55. Jesse Couenhoven, "Augustine's Doctrine of Original Sin," *Augustinian Studies* 36.2 (2005): 389.
56. McFarland, *In Adam's Fall*, 19.

self-interpretation and holds more promise for a constructive relating of church history, doctrine, and Scripture to the church.

Augustine's engagement with Pelagian denials of original sin addressed such a foundational doctrine that the territories traversed were necessarily wide-ranging. Disagreements over original sin amounted to nothing less than radically divergent visions of metaphysics and the Christian life. Augustine interpreted the denial of original sin as a proud refusal to embrace the grace through which God awakens sinners to the beauty of his love. To understand the patristic doctrine of original sin, we must see the denial or belief in original sin as demarcating two opposing patterns of praxis, rooted in alternative doctrines of God. So we turn to consider the Pelagian and Augustinian worldviews.

Pelagianism: Life without Original Sin

Rejecting original sin led naturally to the view that "there is no sin at all in newborns."[57] This meant that, for the Pelagian, the essence of sin was imitation. Adam's sin is subsequently copied by people of rational, culpable maturity.[58] Augustine argued that the idea of Adam as an example was truthful but not adequate:

> Of course, all those who through disobedience transgress God's commandment imitate Adam, but it is one thing for him to be an example for those who sin by the will; it is another thing for him to be the origin of those born with sin. After all, the saints also imitate Christ in their pursuit of righteousness . . . but apart from this imitation his grace also produces within us our enlightenment and justification.[59]

In a world without original sin, the human will is ascribed overweening power and freedom. Pelagians, such as Julian, held that unless the human will had the power to choose sin or virtue, it could not be held culpable for sin. Original sin makes sin inevitable and necessary. Holding agents guilty of sin that was unavoidable appeared manifestly unjust. Julian explained his Pelagian understanding of sin and freedom: "Sin is nothing but the will to do that which

57. Augustine, *The Punishment and Forgiveness of Sins*, 1.9.9, in *Answer to the Pelagians*, vol. 1 of 4.

58. The Church of England's Article 9 demands that its ministers reject this Pelagian belief: "Original Sin standeth not in the following of Adam (as the Pelagians do vainly talk); but is the fault and corruption of the nature of every man, that naturally is engendered of the offspring of Adam."

59. Augustine, *The Punishment and Forgiveness of Sins*, 1.9.10, in *Answer to the Pelagians*, vol. 1 of 4.

justice forbids and from which one is free to hold back. . . . Human beings are
not forced to have the will they choose, but they have it as something possible.
The evil they do, however, entails the necessity of guilt."[60]

Julian assumed that for a person to be held guilty of sin, he or she had to
have chosen sin in a manner that included within it the possibility of not sinning. On Julian's assumptions about justice and responsibility: "Justice does
not impute something as a sin unless one is free to hold back from it. . . . This
definition then is excellent and complete: sin is the will to do that which justice
forbids and from which one is free to hold back."[61] If the will was compelled
by something other than itself—such as original sin—then it could not be
held accountable. Augustine's initial response to this core aspect of the Pelagian worldview was to cite Romans 7:19: "The one who says, 'I do not do the
good that I will, but I do the evil that I do not will,' shows that he does evil
by necessity, not by will, and weeping over his wretchedness, he mocks your
definitions."[62]

The Pelagian worldview had an instinctual and deep respect for the human
will. Human freedom could not be undermined or sullied—that would destroy
the supporting framework of assumed views of justice and sin. As he pon-
dered this feature of Pelagianism, Augustine recognized affinities with pagan
metaphysics and ethical theories, specifically, the views of Aristotle and the
Stoics. "Pelagianism smuggles Stoic cosmology into Western Christian thought
and practice."[63] Augustine had earlier in his life defended a similar view of
the will—in his erstwhile treatise *On Free Choice*. "This early Augustine is
blandly Stoic, at least when it comes to his ethics, but Augustine soon comes to
outgrow his Stoicism."[64] His previous tacit acceptance of Stoic ethics enabled
Augustine to detect them when they resurfaced in Pelagianism.

The Stoics viewed ethics as a series of choices: decisions to be made for or
against virtue. Resolve, willpower, and inner determination were paramount.
Augustine saw Stoicism lurking behind Pelagian views of the will. Though once
he had thought Stoic philosophy could support Christian ethics, Augustine
came to see such an ethical project as an anti-Christian worldview that had no

60. Augustine, *Unfinished Work in Answer to Julian*, 5.51, in *Answer to the Pelagians*, vol.
3 of 4.

61. Ibid., 5.28.2, in *Answer to the Pelagians*, vol. 3 of 4. The rhetoric of this debate over
defining sin was particularly frustrating for Augustine, as Julian was utilizing a definition Augustine had formulated previously but had come to see as incomplete at best and incorrect when
applied to all aspects of sin.

62. Ibid. 5.50.2, in *Answer to the Pelagians*, vol. 3 of 4.

63. Michael Hanby, *Augustine and Modernity* (London: Routledge, 2003), 106.

64. James Wetzel, "Augustine," in *The Oxford Handbook of Religion and Emotion*, ed. John
Corrigan (Oxford: Oxford University Press, 2007), 350.

room for original sin. To Julian Augustine cried, "Your statements are monstrous. Your new doctrines—the paradoxes of the Pelagian heretics—are more astounding than those of the Stoic philosophers. . . . If they are saved, what sort of illness did they have? If they are set free, what held them in the bonds of slavery?"[65] Recording some of Julian's citations from Stoics, Augustine wrote, "I beg of you, do not hold the philosophy of the pagans superior to our Christian philosophy which is the one true philosophy."[66] While Julian approvingly quoted Zeno the Stoic's definition of justice, Augustine viewed Stoic assumptions as opposed to Christian beliefs: "As someone who is more a Pelagian than a Christian, you do not understand the grace of God nor the justice of God."[67]

Without original sin, the Pelagian outlook on life was based on Stoic assumptions. People were viewed as primarily rational, willing, choosing beings. To avoid sin one must simply resolve to choose virtue. Godliness was a matter of grit and determination. In order for justice to be preserved, human free will could not be challenged. The sovereignty of humanity's will pushed God to the periphery of his universe. In the midst of daily life, surrounded by temptations, sovereign creatures may be commanded—but not empowered—by God. "He admits the grace by which God discloses and reveals to us what we ought to do, but not the grace by which he gives us his help so that we act. Yet, if the help of grace is lacking, the knowledge of the law can only bring about transgression. . . . The law is so sharply distinguished from grace that the law is not merely of no benefit, but even does much harm, if grace does not provide help."[68] God's "grace"—such as it was in the Pelagian worldview—was little more than an empty, powerless, and cold commandment to obey laws:

> Pelagius locates the grace and help of God which helps us not to sin either in nature and in free choice or in the law and teaching. Thus when God helps one to "turn away from evil and do good" (1 Pet. 3:11), Pelagius thinks that God helps by revealing and showing us what to do, but not by . . . pouring love into us (Rom. 5:5) so that we do what we know we should do.[69]

65. Augustine, *Answer to Julian*, 3.3.8. Augustine connected Aristotelian anthropology to Stoic exaltation of the will: "You obfuscate the minds of the uneducated with the categories of Aristotle," 6.20.64. *Answer to the Pelagians*, vol. 2 of 4.

66. Ibid., 4.14.72, in *Answer to the Pelagians*, vol. 2 of 4.

67. Augustine, *Unfinished Work in Answer to Julian*, 1.35, in *Answer to the Pelagians*, vol. 3 of 4.

68. Augustine, *The Grace of Christ and Original Sin*, 1.8.9, in *Answer to the Pelagians*, vol. 1 of 4.

69. Ibid., 1.3.3, in *Answer to the Pelagians*, vol. 1 of 4.

Original sin may initially appear a stern, unjust, demotivating, and ungracious doctrine. Pelagianism strove for many years—under the tutelage of brilliant thinkers working with sophisticated Stoic and Aristotelian philosophical concepts—to commend a better worldview. The results of Pelagian efforts to banish original sin bequeathed a vision of life that revolved around human effort, potential, resolve, moral ability, and decision. Inevitably, Pelagian denials of original sin led to a cosmology more Stoic than Christian. As the eloquent study from Michael Hanby argues at length, Stoic and Pelagian instincts weighed against not just Augustine's ethics but also his doctrine of God:

> The grammar of divine simplicity; Augustine's insistence upon the radical transcendence and absolute difference of the Trinity; the refusal of any passivity in the generation and procession of the Son and Spirit; and the location of the *imago dei* in the active participation in divine love, all serve to differentiate the "mechanics" of *creatio ex nihilo*, from the cosmogony of the Stoics.[70]

In other words, original sin may be denied for supposedly ethical reasons. However, such a theological move has given birth to a vision of life that can function only by eviscerating the Christian doctrine of God. Augustine believed that the ugliness of original sin belied a beautiful vision of a gracious God, worth loving and confessing.

Augustinianism: The God beyond Original Sin

Augustine believed that Adam's sin did more than offer a possible example; it was a direful act that engulfed all his posterity in the mire of sin. Ironically, as the shackles of sin tighten ever more firmly on all Adam's progeny, the impact may be to deepen not depression and despair, but relief. Augustine reasoned, "My conscience . . . [is] more secure in the hope of your mercy than in its own innocence."[71] Augustine knew that his teaching on original sin was more severe than that of the Pelagians. However, as a theologian and pastor, he intuited the biblical connections between doctrines. One's view of sin shapes a vision of God, people, and ethics. Augustine refused to accept views that diverged from his articulation of original sin because only his doctrine of original sin fitted with the gloriously grace-filled God he found in Scripture.

Adam's rebellion and original sin preclude humanity willing a choice of the good, leaving God's grace as our only hope: "On your exceedingly great

---

70. Hanby, *Augustine and Modernity*, 110.

71. Augustine, *Confessions*, vol. 1.1 of *The Works of Saint Augustine: A Translation for the 21st Century*, ed. J. Rotelle, trans. M. Boulding (New York: New City Press, 1997), 10.3.4.

mercy rests all my hope. Give what you command, and then command whatever you will."[72]

Adam's sin enslaved his descendants such that mere commandments from
God could not be followed. God's grace would have to be more than just instructions—it had to include spiritual empowerment and transformation. In
his final years of engagement with Semi-Pelagianism, Augustine reflected on
the impact the above words made on Pelagius. He observed that though the
Confessions had been his best received treatise, "when these words of mine
were recited at Rome by some brother and fellow bishop of mine in Pelagius'
presence, he could not tolerate them and, attacking them somewhat emotion-
ally, he almost came to blows with the one who cited them."[73]

Pelagius thought Augustine's teaching cheapened grace and promoted immorality. Rather, it ushered grace into the citadel of morality—the heart.
Caught up in Adam's original sin, Augustine's heart had "loved emptiness
and chased falsehood."[74] His career as a pagan orator had been to "peddle
lies"[75] because in his heart he "enjoyed being praised."[76] He had lived among
those who "try to make their own way back to you." Such people attracted
the attention of evil spiritual powers—"fitting accomplices and allies of their
pride."[77] Since his heart was infected with sin from birth, Augustine came to
see that he needed God to graciously work in his heart. New desires needed
to be implanted, proud longings had to be deadened. If Augustine was to
journey home to God, it would have to be God who took the first step: "Can
there be for us any route back to hope other than your mercy? . . . You began
by healing me of the itch to justify myself, so that you could be compassionate
to all my other iniquities as well."[78]

Augustine knew his own heart and humbly accepted Scripture's diagnosis
of its condition. He believed that if he was to be brought into relationship
with God, it was necessary for God's grace to transform his heart. He had
to be brought, by God, to love and depend on Jesus for salvation. His walls
of proud resistance would have to be broken down. God's grace encompassed so much more than simply words about God or instructions aiming at virtue. God's grace included the mysterious, emotional, enigmatic,
supernatural renewal of the heart's longings. All of creation commands

---

72. Ibid., 10.29.40.
73. Augustine, *The Gift of Perseverance*, 20.53, in *Answer to the Pelagians*, vol. 4 of 4.
74. Augustine, *Confessions*, 9.4.9, vol. 1.1 of *The Works of Saint Augustine*.
75. Ibid., 6.6.9.
76. Ibid., 10.37.61.
77. Ibid., 10.42.67.
78. Ibid., 10.36.58.

humanity to love God. Since we are in bondage to original sin, God must extend yet more grace:

> You pierced my heart with your word, and I fell in love with you. The sky and the earth, and everything in them—all these things around me are telling me that I should love you; and since they never cease to proclaim this to everyone, those who do not hear it are left without excuse. But you show mercy to anyone with whom you have already determined to deal mercifully, and will grant pity to whomsoever you choose. Were this not so, the sky and the earth would be proclaiming your praises to the deaf.[79]

This distinctively Augustinian vision of a God who lavishly pours out the grace of salvation on the grace of natural revelation is the God who stands behind original sin. Certainly original sin is dark, but the flame of God's grace burns all the more brightly for it.

Maintaining his beliefs about original sin and God's grace required that Augustine articulate an anthropology that allowed more penetrating and complex evaluations of human freedom and flourishing than the Stoic postulates that undergirded Pelagianism.

Before writing *Confessions* Augustine's style of writing was informed by Platonic academic dialogues, where clarity and rational argument are prized above all else. *Confessions* represented not just a new manner of writing for Augustine—it also introduced to the church a fresh tradition of relational, contemplative, autobiographical theological writing. Style and content fused to draw the reader's thoughts, imagination, memory, emotions, and longings toward God. Augustine sought to present more than rational arguments for God—he portrayed God as the beautiful one who was all too easily hidden behind our bondage to the love of created things. "Late have I loved you, Beauty so ancient and so new, late have I loved you," he lamented.[80]

The crucial factor in changing Augustine's manner of writing appears to have been that prior to and during the composition of *Confessions*, he was engaged in a close study of Scripture and regular expository preaching of it. This observation is borne out by a letter Augustine wrote to his bishop asking for a sabbatical to study Scripture more, as he felt he understood it himself but was ill-equipped to preach it to others.[81] It is also supported by the Scripture-saturated prose of *Confessions* and the concurrent project of *Teaching Christianity*—Augustine's manual on how to understand the Bible

79. Ibid., 10.6.8.
80. Ibid., 10.27.38.
81. Augustine, *Epistles*, 21.1–6, in *Letters*, vol. 1 of 4.

and preach it to others. These developments were linguistic and stylistic, but they were much more. They rested on a theological conviction that people are controlled not by their rational understanding of facts but by their emotional longing for love. As Augustine preached through the Bible (the psalms in particular), he found only such an anthropology could make sense of the passages he taught.

So Augustine observed, "In your gift we find rest, and there we enjoy you. Our true home is where we find rest. We are carried towards it by love, and it is your good Spirit who lifts our sunken nature up from the gates of death. . . . [A] body gravitates towards its proper place by its weight. . . . Now my weight is my love, and wherever I am carried it is this weight that carries me."[82] The heart's desires shape all a person's decisions. "It is not the swerving of my horse's body that alters my course, but the inclination of my own heart."[83] This life is a journey "travelled by the affections."[84] The battle and conflict Christians feel within themselves is not the result of insufficient data but is born of conflicting loves: "Two loves in this life wrestle each other in every temptation—love of the times and love of God. Whichever of these two overcomes, that one drags the lover as if by weight. For it is not by wings or feet, but by affections we come to God."[85]

This heart-shaped anthropology was more penetrating than the Pelagian alternative. Augustine's portrayal of the heart echoed the dark multifariousness of motivations delineated in Scripture as constitutive of people's slavery under original sin. Pride, lust, envy, self-deception, sloth, and prurient curiosity[86] infect the heart, shaping desires, longings, and motivations such that we are blinded to God's beauty.

Augustine's somber depiction of sin's grip on our hearts led him to appreciate that God's grace had to penetrate to the depths of our hearts. His heart-focused anthropology allowed not only for an original sin that grips the deepest recesses of our hearts, it also proclaimed a gracious God who is able to make his home in our hearts and refashion them according to his holy love. Promise of such deep heart work Augustine found in Romans 5:5, one of his most frequently quoted verses. The spiritual reality of this deep heart ministry astounded Augustine: "Who can give me peace in you? Who would give me

---

82. Augustine, *Confessions*, 13.9.10, vol. 1.1 of *The Works of Saint Augustine*.
83. Ibid., 10.35.57.
84. Augustine, *Teaching Christianity*, 1.17.16, vol. 1.11 of *The Works of Saint Augustine*.
85. Augustine, *Sermons*, 344.1, in *Sermons of Saint Augustine*, vol. 10 of 11.
86. In Augustine's theology, curiosity refers to a "knowing" fascination with the grotesque, akin to modern love of violent horror. See *Confessions*, 10.35.54–55.

this grace, that you would enter into my heart and inebriate it, enabling me to forget the evils that beset me, and embrace you, my only good?"[87]

Original sin may penetrate deep into the human heart and ravage all our desires and longings. Augustine held that the solution taught in the Bible was not to deny original sin but rather to embrace the saving grace of God, which penetrates to the depths of hearts born dead in Adam's sin.

A Vision of Reality

Augustine's account of original sin hangs together with his vision of God as abundantly gracious and people as incurably desirous. God's love initiates; a person's love is awakened and healed. The Augustinian account of ethics, which flows from all of this, follows the lead of Jesus, who drew attention to the centrality of love for God and neighbor (Matt. 22:36–40). Another feature of Augustine's approach to the Christian life, which is particularly due to his acceptance of original sin, is his acknowledgment of the ongoing disorder and perversity of human desires. Born in the bondage of original sin, all our desires are disordered, turned in on themselves toward the creature rather than toward God the Creator. The Spirit awakens in Christians a holy love for God, but the full renewal of our natures awaits the City of God's eschatological revelation. So Augustine lamented, "I have become an enigma to myself, and herein lies my sickness."[88]

Original sin was not, for Augustine, a merely legal or speculative doctrine. It certainly meant that all people born after Adam bore an actual status of guilt, but it meant much more. Original sin gave birth to what Augustine called "concupiscence." This is his favored term for the ongoing inner dislocation, alienation, and perversion that mark the inner desires of humans laboring under original sin. Concupiscence drove the young Augustine to steal the pears simply for the pleasure of sinning. Mature awareness of concupiscence led the older preacher to tell his congregation that his own nature could only lead him to be a bad bishop—any sense in which he was a good shepherd was "only by God's grace."[89]

Augustine's sense of inner alienation and twisting of loves pervades his entire corpus. It gave him a delicate compassion for the struggling Christian. Although the term "concupiscence" is not always present in his writings, the above concerns are ubiquitous. On at least one occasion he made explicit the theological connections between original sin and concupiscence:

87. Ibid., 1.5.5.
88. Ibid., 10.33.50.
89. Augustine, *Sermons*, 340.2, in *Sermons of Saint Augustine*, vol. 9 of 11.

Though concupiscence is present in those who have only been born and also those who have been born again, it is both present in and harms those who have only been born, but is present in those who have been born again without being able to do them harm. It is harmful to those who have been born again to the extent that, unless they are born again, they can derive no benefit from being born of parents who were born again. For the defect stemming from the origin remains in the offspring to make them guilty, even if the guilt of the same defect is washed away in the parents by the forgiveness of sins. Such is the case until all of the defect, by consent to which we sin, is destroyed in the final rebirth, that is, in the renewal of the flesh which is promised in the resurrection that is to come. Then, we will not only not commit any sins, but not have any sinful desires.[90]

Original sin is thus a doctrine profoundly concerned with ethics. It denotes not only a guilty status procured by Adam's sin; it also intimates the state of ongoing estrangement that is the lot of all born from Adam's line. "Concupiscence" has been a helpful term in the Christian tradition in that it distinguishes the inseparable existential angst from the rendering of judicial judgment. It also serves as shorthand for a multitude of biblical phrases that describe the condition of humanity under sin.

When original sin is brought into conversation with modern ethical theories, the idea that Augustine's teaching is tied to one or another of the particular theories of transmission that he considered is often thought a weakness. One of the best responses to this objection is Lane's wry observation: "Augustine's views on the mechanics of the transmission of original sin are not integral to his doctrine of original sin and the former can be abandoned without prejudicing the latter. It is a pity that Augustine was not right as we would otherwise now have a way to abolish original sin, namely In Vitro Fertilization."[91]

The ethical focus of Augustine's doctrine of original sin has led to particularly fruitful studies that draw on Augustine's insights to offer pastoral help to those reflecting on the horrors of child abuse[92] and addiction.[93] There are no simple answers to these pastoral matters, but Augustine's rich reflections on the nature of original sin and concupiscence have proven more compatible

---

90. Augustine, *The Grace of Christ and Original Sin*, 2.39.44, in *Answer to the Pelagians*, vol. 1 of 4.

91. A. N. S. Lane, "Lust: The Human Person as Affected by Disordered Desires," *Evangelical Quarterly* 78.1 (2006): 28–29.

92. A. McFadyen, *Bound to Sin: Abuse, Holocaust and the Christian Doctrine of Sin* (Cambridge: Cambridge University Press, 2000). See esp. chaps. 6–10 for the use of Augustine.

93. Christopher C. Cook, *Alcohol, Addiction and Christian Ethics* (Cambridge: Cambridge University Press, 2006). See esp. chaps. 4 and 6 for the use of Augustine.

with the biblical material than simplistic Pelagian/Stoic appeals to rationality, choice, and effort.

Since original sin is a doctrine that is closely connected to our view of God, ourselves, and daily life, the question must be faced—is original sin real? The inquiry actually addresses all the related matters—God, humanity, and ethics.

The reality of the Augustinian understanding of original sin is tied to the historical reality of Adam. "Many scholars who reject the idea of Adam as a real person whose sin has affected us all say that the notion of original sin comes from Augustine."[94] I contend that Augustine did not invent the doctrine of original sin. It remains then to state that Augustine recognized the same connections made by many modern thinkers between the historical reality of Adam and original sin. Augustine grasped that if Adam had not been an actual historical figure, then original sin would be meaningless. The Pelagian reading of sin (or a form of it) would be the only option. A world without original sin would also, tragically, find itself absent of the fundamentally gracious God Augustine loved.

It is particularly striking that Augustine recognized the necessity of Adam's historicity since many of his formative scholarly influences tended toward deprecating the material, favoring the conceptual ideal.[95] Throughout his life Augustine was fascinated with the relationship between "pagan" learning and Christian theology. Anticipating modern controversies, Augustine observed:

> It frequently happens that even non-Christians will have knowledge . . . that they can substantiate with scientific arguments or experiments. Now it is quite disgraceful and disastrous, something to be on one's guard against at all costs, that they should ever hear Christians spouting what they claim our Christian literature has to say on these topics, and talking such nonsense that they can scarcely contain their laughter when they see them to be . . . wide of the mark. What is so vexing is not that misguided people should be laughed at, as that our authors should be assumed by outsiders to have held such views and, the great detriment of those about whose salvation we are so concerned, should be written off and consigned to the waste paper basket as so many ignoramuses.[96]

94. C. John Collins, *Did Adam and Eve Really Exist?* (Nottingham, UK: Inter-Varsity, 2011), 84.

95. I develop this argument further in the article "Augustine's Literal Adam," The Gospel Coalition (website), June 14, 2011, http://thegospelcoalition.org/article/augustines-literal-adam/.

96. Augustine, *A Literal Interpretation of Genesis*, 1.39, in *On Genesis, The Works of Saint Augustine*, vol. 1.13.

Augustine revealed his humility by his willingness to alter his views of how best to interpret Genesis. At the start of his ministry he thought a spiritual reading was wise, as it sidestepped Manichean polemics against materiality. By the time he wrote *City of God*, Augustine had replaced his spiritual reading with a focus on redemptive-historical narrative. It is striking that throughout all these stages of development, Augustine believed Adam was a literal, historical figure. Even when his emphasis was on a spiritual reading, he did not overturn his belief in the historicity of Adam as a human being. While in his early writings Augustine did not see much significance in the historical reality of Adam, by the time of the Pelagian controversies, he ascribed considerable importance to the point. Adam was as real a person as Jesus, and the original sin Adam wrought was as genuine as the corresponding salvation from Christ.

> You will see that the anger of God came upon the human race through one man and that reconciliation with God comes through one man. This is for those who are graciously set free from the condemnation of the entire race. The first Adam was made from the earth; the second Adam was made from a woman. In the former flesh was made through a word, in the latter the Word was made flesh.[97]

Given all this, it is difficult to accept that "without an alternative available, Augustine presumed the historicity of Adam and Eve" and that "Augustine's insights into sin can be detached from the story."[98]

Augustine's vision of God, humanity, and ethics was thoroughly informed by his understanding of original sin. He perceived the architectonic connections between doctrines and knew that had Adam not been a historical person, then the reality of original sin, which shaped God's grace and its reception, would collapse.

Conclusion

Augustine's polyvalence means he has not always been well served by many who are indebted to his ministry. So influential has he been across such a range of theological loci that almost every strand of later Western Christianity can claim in some measure the label "Augustinian." This totemic standing has

---

97. Augustine, *Answer to Julian*, 6.24.77, in *Answer to the Pelagians*, vol. 2 of 4.

98. T. Wiley, *Original Sin: Origins, Developments, Contemporary Meanings* (Mahwah, NJ: Paulist Press, 2002), 74. Wiley proceeds to propose that such a nonhistorical Adam construction of original sin would consist of an appreciation of Adam's sin as "paradigmatic" of "pride." Refusing to allow for Adam's sin to be more than that is not to preserve Augustine's teaching on original sin but rather to deny it.

led far too many to imagine that Augustine invented the doctrine of original sin. Radical individuality and inventiveness may be (overly) prized by our age. Augustine despised these as the sin of proud curiosity. He had a deep-seated sense of his role being one of guarding the faith against innovations. He knew that his defense of original sin was open to being misunderstood as a form of personal idiosyncrasy. So Augustine took care to show that—as subsequent councils agreed—he was in line with earlier interpreters and was only rendering explicit what was taught in the Scriptures and had been implicitly accepted by the church in its practice of baptism.

Augustine ought not to be consulted as an authority who automatically settles debate. However, the connections he saw between doctrines surely should set the terms for debate and to continue to be respected today. The doctrine of original sin does indeed shape one's view of God, humanity, and ethics. The nature of salvation offered through the second Adam is inextricably tied to the historicity of Adam.

The organic interconnectedness of revealed theological knowledge makes it sad that down through the ages many have attempted to defend recognizably Augustinian visions of God, humanity, or the Christian life, while simultaneously shying away from the darkness of the original sin wrought by the historical Adam. Such theological truncations are doomed enterprises. Augustine's interpretations of Scripture may be accepted or rejected, but those who resist part of his theological vision would do well to respect the undergirding structures of revealed knowledge that he perceived. It is due to the reality of those connections that he reflected at the end of his life that his costly, long-drawn-out battle for the reality of original sin had in actuality been a contending for God's grace. When Augustine wrote about original sin it was "for the sake of those who . . . defend free choice in such a way as to deny God's grace."[99]

---

99. Augustine, *Revisions*, 2.66.93, in *The Works of Saint Augustine*, vol. 1.2.

5

THE LUTHERAN DOCTRINE
OF ORIGINAL SIN

Robert Kolb

Martin Luther's Doctrine of Original Sin

In 1537, as he prepared an agenda for the presentation of the Wittenberg concerns in his "Smalcald Articles" for the papally called council, Martin Luther included among the articles of faith that he wished to discuss among "learned, reasonable people or among ourselves" the topic of sin. He began with Romans 5:12 and labeled Adam's sin "the inherited sin," the normal German rendering of the Latin *peccatum originis*, and offered a synonym, "the chief sin" (*Häuptsunde*). He commented that "this inherited sin has caused such a deep, evil corruption of nature that reason does not comprehend it; rather, it must be believed on the basis of the revelation in the Scriptures," offering Psalm 51:5, Romans 5:12, Exodus 33:20, and Genesis 3:1–13 as proof. He listed eighteen fruits of this inherited sin. The first eight fruits all describe violations of the first commandment—to have no other gods before God. (Luther explained this commandment in his Small Catechism: "we are to fear, love, and trust in God above all things.")[1] Luther's last ten fruits summarize, with one or two

---

1. *Die Bekenntnisschriften der evangelisch-lutherischen Kirche*, 11th ed. (Göttingen: Vandenhoeck & Ruprecht, 1992), hereafter *BSLK*, 507; *The Book of Concord*, ed. Robert Kolb and Timothy J. Wengert (Minneapolis: Fortress, 2000), 351.

words each, the last nine commandments. The Smalcald Articles' list of these violations used descriptions of original or inherited, or the root, sin: "unbelief, false belief, idolatry, being without the fear of God, presumption, despair, blindness, and in short, not knowing and honoring God." As the key presupposition for his definition of sin he set down the source of all sin in Adam, "through whose disobedience all people became sinners and subject to death and the devil."[2] Luther simply took for granted that, because Scripture says that all sin is due to Adam and Eve (Rom. 5:12), and also because God does not create or cause evil and so could not be responsible for original sin, children receive this root sin just as they receive body and soul from their parents, through conception and birth. No other possibility fit with his understanding of human existence since the fall.

This definition of sin led Luther to propose that at the papal council a number of issues raised by scholastic theology be discussed, all for the purpose of rejecting errors in what he had heard as a student from his instructors. These errors included the teaching that "after the fall of Adam the natural powers of the human being have remained whole and uncorrupted and that each human being possesses by nature sound reason and a good will." Instead, he made clear the "pure error and blindness" of the claim that any human being since Eden had been conceived and born with natural powers to reject evil and choose the good (or vice versa), to love God above all things and their neighbors as themselves, to merit grace from God, that any human being could perform truly good, God-pleasing works apart from the Holy Spirit. Nor is sin something that inheres to the body but not to the soul, for conception and birth deliver this defect that shapes all of life to every human creature descended from the first parents. Luther labeled these contentions "purely pagan teachings" since they contradict Scripture and render the death of Christ for sin meaningless.[3]

The Smalcald Articles reflect how Luther proposed to talk with the scholastic theologians in the Roman camp, but they do not fully reveal his transformation of the understanding of "original sin" from medieval conceptions he had learned as a student to his own comprehension of what he also called the "root" sin.[4] In general, he emphasized, alongside the inheritance of sin,

2. *BSLK*, 433–34; *Book of Concord*, 310–11. See Werner Führer, *Die Schmalkaldischen Artikel* (Tübingen: Mohr Siebeck, 2009), 180–220, and Gerhard Ebeling, "Der Mensch als Spender," in *Lutherstudien III, Disputatio de Homine, Dritter Teil* (Tübingen: Mohr Siebeck, 1989), 74–107, esp. 75–96.

3. *BSLK*, 434–35; *Book of Concord*, 310–11.

4. Alan Jacobs states, "The Protestant Reformation did not bring about any substantially new teaching regarding original sin," in *Original Sin: A Cultural History* (New York: HarperOne, 2008), 106; "history" is a misleading label for this interesting personal confession of faith—he only indicates that he has not read, or at least not understood, the sources.

its overpowering influence on every aspect and every hour of fallen human existence. Original sin was no longer explained within the context of medieval Aristotelian anthropology as a quasi-substantial habitus that invaded the human creature. Just as he rejected recourse to Aristotelian physics in explaining the true, real presence of Christ's body and blood in the Lord's Supper, refusing to speculate in terms of that physics about a "transubstantiation" or a "consubstantiation," so he rejected Aristotle's analysis of human psychology in terms of "habitus" and simply insisted on the reality of the root sin that has its origin in Adam and Eve's doubt in the garden of Eden, its individual beginning in conception, and its continuing reality in human lives through the utter incapacity of all to fear, love, and trust in God above all things, with all the havoc that wreaks through actual sins in daily life. This is why Luther believed that, while there is a "natural" knowledge in all people of actual sin, of their own breaking of the standards set by self, society, or some higher power, a true knowledge of original sin comes only from the scriptural testimony. For only God's revelation of himself can persuade those "turned in on themselves," as Luther often described the sinful human nature, that the most deep-seated wrong in humanity is the individual's inborn inability to trust in the Creator and to be in fellowship with him.

The reformer had come to this conviction in the midst of his "evangelical maturation" in the 1510s. Some years before the process was completed, as he treated Romans 4 and 5 (1515–16) before his students, he concluded that in analyzing the universal human condition of sinfulness, searching for blame did not help one escape from its dilemma, its curse. Of original sin, inborn iniquity, he stated, "It is there whether I perform it or even know about it. I am conceived in it, but I did not do it. It began to rule in me before I began to live. . . . I was conceived in it without my consent. . . . My will approves and accepts this sin and consents to it because apart from grace I have not been able to overcome it in myself. It has overcome me, and I have become an actual sinner in addition to being under original sin."[5] When he came to Romans 5:12 in his lectures, he called on the authority not only of Paul but also of Christ Jesus to affirm that original sin is more than "the absence of a certain quality in the will" or "the deprivation of light in the mind or the power of the memory." It is "the absence of any bit of righteousness and of the power of all the faculties of both body and soul. . . . It is a predisposition

---

5. D. Martin Luthers Werke (Weimar: Böhlau, 1883–1993), hereafter WA (WA references are expressed with volume number [and where appropriate, subvolume number separated from volume by comma], followed by a colon, followed by the page number, followed by a comma, followed by line numbers), 56:287, 2–8, 10–14; Luther's Works (St. Louis: Concordia; Philadelpia: Fortress, 1958–86), hereafter LW, 25:274.

toward evil; the good makes me vomit, I loath light and wisdom, delight in error and darkness, flee from all good works and abhor them, I pursue evil."[6] In the context of Romans 5, it is clear that Luther held that the rejection of God in Eden had been passed from parents to children throughout history, infecting every new human being with the fatal virus of rejecting God as had Adam and Eve. Luther simply took that for granted.

Throughout his life Luther's major emphasis in his actual use of the doctrine of original sin fell upon its relational aspect, the breaking of the bond between Creator and human creature. Sin originated in the sinner's doubt of God's Word and denial of his lordship: thus, Luther's terms "root sin" and "chief sin" to convey this original sin as the broken relationship with God, which produces every other transgression of God's commandments. Luther's comments on Genesis 3, delivered to his students a year and a half before he penned the Smalcald Articles, reveal better how his reformational redefinition of Christianity required a reshaping of his understanding of original sin. He retained the medieval term but substantially altered its meaning by altering the framework for perception of reality.

Twenty years earlier, as his thought matured amid his escalating critique of medieval policy and piety, Luther had reworked his conception of what it meant to be Christian. He had grown up with a system that he later criticized for retaining too much of its pagan past. As a child and youth, he experienced Christianity as primarily a religion of ritual, in which the human performance of works, particularly sacred or religious activities, won God's favor and blessing. The benefits of performing this ritual were guaranteed by a hierarchy, from local priest to distant pope. Luther's study of Scripture, his personality and personal experiences, and his presuppositions inherited from both Ockhamism and monastic piety created the setting in which he redefined the Christian faith. He took as his new starting point the gracious nature and action of God, whom Scripture presents as a God of conversation and community. This God created through his Word, and through his Word is active in his world. Preaching and all other forms of his Word, given authoritatively in Scripture, engage and transform sinners, re-creating them into the people of God, called to serve him in his world, through the promise that delivers forgiveness won by Jesus Christ. Luther's ontology therefore arose out of his concept that reality rests on God's Word and consists fundamentally in the relationship between each person (or thing he created) and the Creator.[7] That

---

6. WA 56:312, 4–13; LW 25:299.

7. WA 42:17, 15–23, 17, 16–33; LW 1:21–24; see also his lecture on Ps. 2, 1532, WA 40, 2:230, 20–231, 28; LW 12:32–33.

reality, which is constituted by God's Word, is in no way ephemeral. Refusal to trust God's Word also determines the heart of human personhood for all those born in the line of Adam and Eve. Therefore, Luther labeled original sin "essential" or "natural" when he came to discussing the reality of the brokenness that plagues the heart of human life in its inborn incapacity to live in total and complete trust in God.

In this way of thinking, God's Word, especially in the form of his promise of new life through Christ, provided the key to the human being's existence. The trust that responds to God's person and promise is not merely one more characteristic of the human creature. Trust constitutes the very heart of humanity. Therefore, rejection of God's Word lay at the heart of human sin; it was the original sin that originated all other sins. The original sin was the doubt Adam and Eve displayed in their denial of the truth and reliability of God's Word in the command not to eat (Gen. 3:1–7). The serpent attacked the very will of God itself and God's image in the human being by attacking his Word, Luther told his students.[8] "When Satan had separated them from and deprived them of God's Word, nothing was not easy for him." A lie had separated Eve from God and his Word.[9] "The fountain from which all sin flows is unbelief, doubt, and abandonment of the Word," which are idolatry, denial of God's truth, the invention of new gods.[10]

God made human creatures through his Word, and he sustains them through his Word. Luther regarded the person who does not trust what God says as corrupted in his humanity to the very core. Nothing else comes out as it should be when trust in God does not define human life. Failure to trust God, Luther's Large Catechism posits, creates false gods, which always deceive and lead to ruin.[11] Satan invented a new god for Adam and Eve, for "when God's Word is altered or corrupted, then 'come new and freshly-invented gods whom our fathers did not worship.'"[12] Luther noted that Eve had not only rejected God's command but also distorted it by adding to it (Gen. 3:3).[13] For the Wittenberg reformer the most profound abuses of God's Word took place when the pious tried to master the Word rather than be mastered by it. As a result of this understanding of the root of sin, the original sin, Luther rejected the contention of some scholastic theologians that some elements of original righteousness were not lost through sin. He held that the loss of trust and assurance that

8. *WA* 42:110, 7–17; *LW* 1:146.
9. *WA* 42:111, 2–4; *LW* 1:147.
10. *WA* 42:112, 20–22; *LW* 1:149.
11. *BSLK*, 560–61; *Book of Concord*, 386–87.
12. *WA* 42:112, 6–8; *LW* 1:148.
13. *WA* 42:116, 40–117, 14; *LW* 1:154–55.

defined the human relationship with God permeates all of human existence.[14] The original sin grew from unbelief and disobedience into fear, hatred of God, flight from God, despair, and impenitence.[15]

This definition of "original sin" as an inborn characteristic of every human being, implanted and passed on by parents to children through conception and birth, which manifests itself in our breaking the relationship with God, given by God to Adam and Eve at creation as the heart of our being human, led Luther to another significant breach with the medieval concept behind the term: this definition affirmed that, though because of Christ's atoning work God does not regard original sin's presence in his chosen people, they contend with their inborn rebellion against God in their daily lives. Failure to trust God continues to invade even the most pious Christian consciousness each day. Therefore, Luther said that God's word of forgiveness restores the relationship with the Creator but that each day repentance is necessary as the Holy Spirit turns believers back to trusting Christ at the center of their lives and away from their life-determining trust in his creatures (even though obviously trust of other human beings is key to godly human relationships). Thus, the mystery of the continuation of sin and evil in the lives of the baptized caused Luther to make daily repentance the mark of the believer's daily existence. Salvation rests on the promise of God, which abides during the struggle of faith and unfaith in the individual (Rom. 7:13–25). This continuation of sin and evil in the lives of God's chosen people remains a mystery, beyond human solution in this life. Adam and Eve passed on this refusal to trust God to all their descendants in a way that is more profound than human reason or explanations can fathom or express.

Psalm 51:5, one of Luther's chief bases for his assertion of the total claim of sin on fallen human creatures, implied for Luther a traducianist position, that original sin is propagated by generation from parents to children. According to Werner Führer: from Augustine Luther borrowed this understanding of how sin moved from generation to generation, but at the same time the Wittenberg reformer paid little attention to the issue because he found no clear biblical support for speculation about it.[16] Oswald Bayer finds it totally misleading to define Luther's view of "inherited sin" as being simply a matter of transmission exclusively during sexual relationships. Bayer cites Luther's *Confession* of 1528; its treatment of sin makes every human being responsible for the inherited sin in spite of the temptation to evade the responsibility or to blame another person (one's father or mother). Luther emphasized the exact

14. *WA* 42:125, 21–32; *LW* 1:167.
15. *WA* 42:128, 20–24; *LW* 1:171.
16. Führer, *Die Schmalkaldischen Artikel*, 201–3, 223.

wording: "not: my mother conceived me by acting sinfully, but rather: I, I, I was conceived in sin." Even though, according to the grammar, "my mother" is the subject and "I" is the object, Luther reverses the order of words in his explanation, so that my nature as subject, as a person, and as one who cannot get out of my own responsibility, as one who has the nature of a sinner, is beyond all doubt: "My mother bore me in sin . . . means that I [!] grew from sinful seed in my mother's womb. . . . And the extensive passage that brings out most prominently that I am imprisoned in original sin in all its fullness and in all its radical nature establishes the constitutive connection between the inherited sin and the bound will."[17]

This accords with the reformer's interpretation of Psalm 51:5 a decade earlier. To be brought forth in iniquity and conceived in sin, as David had said, meant simply "that before you [God] I am such a sinner that my nature, my very beginning, my conception is sin, to say nothing of the words, works, thoughts, and life which follows. . . . I am an evil tree and by nature a child of wrath and sin." Such sinners can only pray God for forgiveness because "Adam must die and decay before Christ can arise completely, and this begins with a penitent life and is completed through death."[18] In 1532 he lectured again on Psalm 51, still focusing on original sin's result in the wrath of God and death and on its nature as perversion of the fear and love of God, which God created at the center of human life. This "original or innate sin" is "hidden from the whole world. . . . [W]e need God's Word from heaven to reveal this uncleanness or fault of our nature."[19] Luther set Psalm 51 within the context of David's biography—adultery with Bathsheba, the murder of Uriah—and found his example an apt illumination of the nature of the interconnectedness of all sins and their rootedness in defying and despising God, that is, in blasphemy.[20] This connection of the psalm, particularly its reminder that "I was born in sin, and in sin did my mother conceive me," with David's adultery and murder reveals that Luther in no way attributed the actual sinning of daily life merely to poor upbringing or natural potential. What gave every individual human being his body and soul had also bequeathed him the rejection of God that constitutes original sin. Luther did not need to develop a philosophical explanation for what he regarded as clear biblical truth. Death, which is the wages of sin (Rom. 6:23a), comes to every individual from Adam (Rom. 5:12), in whose lineage all become sinners by conception and birth. Luther's own experience only echoed

---

17. *WA* 26:503, 29–34; *LW* 37:363; see Oswald Bayer, *Martin Luthers Theologie. Eine Vergegenwärtigung*, 2nd ed. (Tübingen: Mohr Siebeck, 2004), 193.

18. *WA* 18:501, 31–502, 3; *LW* 14:169.

19. *WA* 40, 2:385, 22–27; *LW* 12:350–51.

20. *WA* 40, 2:318, 26–321, 16; *LW* 12:305–6.

what he believed on the basis of these Bible passages. His will had been bound from his very beginning in his mother's womb, and he was thus determined at every turn to find substitutes for the true God as his ultimate object of trust until the Holy Spirit moved his heart and mind to trust in Christ.

Luther viewed the whole of biblical teaching as a "body of doctrine"[21] and regarded the topic of original sin as vital for understanding the entirety of Scripture: "without [the doctrine of original sin] it is impossible to understand Scriptures correctly."[22] For he viewed its message as centered in the call to repentance and the subsequent forgiveness of sins. This repentance acknowledges both the root of sin in the doubt of God's lordship bequeathed by human parents to their children, and the practice of sin in the activities of daily life that rebel against his law. Repentant sinners are then turned by the Holy Spirit to trust in their Savior, Jesus Christ, in whose death and resurrection they find life and salvation. Luther regarded this as the Spirit's act of re-creation (2 Cor. 5:17). If the reality of original sin as an all-pervasive rejection of God's lordship that plagues all from birth is not taken seriously, then repentance will most likely be shallow, and trust will find the same level.

One of the doctrinal synonyms for original sin that played a significant role in Luther's public teaching was his understanding of the bound will. Original sin has bound the will of every human being from conception and birth to reject God and to attempt to frame life relying on false gods. He repudiated his scholastic teachers who had contended for some spark of positive potential in the inborn will. From conception and birth on, Luther insisted, above all in his engagement with Erasmus, his *De servo arbitrio* (literally "on bound choice"), that all human beings are so shaped by conception and birth into creatures turned away from God, turned in upon themselves (*incurvatus in se*).[23] Therefore, in Luther's preaching and teaching the focus on this root sin of disbelief or lack of trust determined the shape of his entire message.

Philip Melanchthon's Doctrine of Original Sin

Luther's partner in leading the Wittenberg faculty, Philip Melanchthon, largely shared his view of original sin as a broken relationship and rejection of God's

---

21. Irene Dingel, "Philip Melanchthon and the Establishment of Confessional Norms," *Lutheran Quarterly* 20 (2006): 146–69.

22. Lecture on Psalm 51:4, 1532, WA 40, 2:385, 27–29; LW 12:351.

23. WA 18:600–787, esp. 733, 8–18; LW 33:15–295. See also my *Bound Choice, Election, and Wittenberg Theological Method: From Martin Luther to the Formula of Concord* (Grand Rapids: Eerdmans, 2005), 22–66.

Word but added defiance of God's law to Luther's more exclusively relational definition. Melanchthon's 1540 commentary on Romans defined sin simply as not adhering to God's law, but it defined original sin with Anselm's words: "the lack of original righteousness," which Melanchthon defined as "wholeness of human powers, or rectitude which rendered perfect obedience to God's law, . . . doubt in human minds about God's will, lack of the fear, trust, and love of God, harboring dreadful impulses against God's law."[24] In the final edition of Melanchthon's *Loci communes* (1543) he defined original sin as "the lack of original righteousness," that is, the "loss of the light in the mind" "by which the human creature could firmly assent to God's Word," "a turning of the will away from God and a stubbornness of the heart." It is the absence of the image and likeness of God by which human minds know God and will to live in freedom, righteousness, and harmony with God's law. Melanchthon stated that he did not object to attributing individual guilt to Adam's fall into sin, but God does more than impute Adam's sin to his descendents. "Human nature itself" is marked by "a darkness and depravity," "another law in my members warring against the law of my mind" (Rom. 7:23), "something that contends against God's law." It is "defects and corrupt inclinations." From Romans 5:12–21; 7:23; 8:7; Ephesians 2:3; John 3:5; Psalm 51:5; Genesis 8:21; Psalm 25:7; and Jeremiah 17:9 Melanchthon concluded that sinners cannot perceive the depth of this original sin in themselves and that they "deceive themselves, minimize these evils, have doubts about God, neglect God, trust in their own wisdom and power, pride, ambition, and other flames of desires."[25] Melanchthon continued by insisting that God is in no way responsible for original sin: the evil will of Satan and of Adam and Eve brought the disorder to the relationship between God and his human creatures that produced "ignorance of God, doubts, lack of fear and love of God" in the human will. Melanchthon avoided further explanation, as Luther had. His use of Aristotle's framework for explanations led him to distinguish that which forms original sin (the guilt of defying God) from its material (the appetites created by God). Those appetites, originally good, were perverted at their very core when Adam and Eve's rebellion discarded their knowledge of God, their trust, fear, and love of him.[26] Melanchthon's "repetition" of the

24. *Corpus Reformatorum. Philippi Melanthonis Opera quae supersunt omnia*, ed. C. G. Bretschneider and H. E. Bindseil (Halle and Braunschweig: Schwetschke, 1834–60), 15:917; *Commentary on Romans. Philip Melanchthon*, 2nd ed., trans. Fred Kramer (St. Louis: Concordia, 2010), 133.

25. *Melanchthons Werke in Auswahl*, 7 vols., ed. Robert Stupperich (Gütersloh: Mohn, 1951–1975), 2, 1:257–58; *Philip Melanchthon, Loci Communes 1543*, trans. J. A. O. Preus (St. Louis: Concordia, 1992), 48–49.

26. *Melanchthons Werke* 2, 1:258–63; *Melanchthon, Loci communes*, 50–51.

Augsburg Confession, prepared for presentation at the second session of the Council of Trent in 1551, reaffirmed his position in the last decade of his life. "All people after the fall of the first parents, who are born by intercourse of husband and wife, are born bearing in themselves original sin," citing Romans 5:12 and Ephesians 2:3. Original sin is "the lack of original righteousness," which involved being able to assent to God's Word, turn the will to God, and obey his law with the heart. "Original sin is such that because of the fall of the first parents and because of this depravity which resulted from the fall, all are born under the wrath of God and worthy of eternal damnation if they do not receive remission [of sins] through the Mediator."[27]

Some might question whether Melanchthon's doctrine of original sin was not weakened by his alleged "synergism," but against this accusation stands his consistent insistence that original sin, passed from parents to their children, made it necessary for the Holy Spirit to move the hearts and minds that God has given every human being and that are necessary components of the psychological side of adult faith.[28]

The Formula of Concord on Original Sin

Luther's and Melanchthon's students largely took over this definition of original sin. Some fell into dispute over the formulation of this teaching when the issue of the role of human will in conversion arose in the 1560s. Viktorin Strigel (1524–69), in an effort to preserve the integrity of the human creature and the absolute goodness of God, used the conceptualization of Aristotelian physics to make clear that *original sin does not destroy human nature* though it does corrupt it: he called original sin an (Aristotelian) "accident." His colleague but rival at the University of Jena, Matthias Flacius Illyricus (1520–75), disagreed. Although Flacius initially wanted to avoid using an Aristotelian conceptual framework for interpreting biblical thinking, he finally followed Strigel into that way of explanation and argued that *original sin actually becomes the essence or substance—the determining factor—in human life after the fall.* Flacius distinguished the formal substance, that which shapes human life, from its material substance, the activities of reason, will, and the like. The latter were corrupted, Flacius argued, but the former had changed from fear, love, and trust in God to reliance on false gods.[29] Flacius cited Luther in his

27. *Melanchthons Werke*, 6:91–92.
28. Kolb, *Bound Choice*, 70–102.
29. Luka Ilic, "Theologian of Sin and Grace. The Process of Radicalization in the Theology of Matthias Flacius Illyricus," PhD diss., Lutheran Theological Seminary, 2012; Lauri Haikola, *Gesetz und Evangelium bei Matthias Flacius Illyricus* (Lund: Gleerup, 1952), 101–8; Günter

argument, particularly Luther's use of the phrases "essential sin" and "image of Satan" as a designation of the sinner's state after the fall.[30]

The Formula of Concord resolved many differences for a majority who claimed the Wittenberg legacy in 1577, including this controversy over original sin. Not all of Flacius's followers abandoned his position; a small group opposed the Formula.[31] The authors of the Formula agreed fully with Flacius's holding fast to Luther's concept that the will is bound in its ability to choose to serve or trust God.[32] It defined inherited or original sin as "the horrible, dreadful inherited disease corrupting their entire nature," "truly sin," indeed "the chief sin. . . . It is the root and fountainhead of all actual sins." "Our entire nature and person is sinful, that is, totally and thoroughly corrupted in God's sight and contaminated by original sin as with a spiritual leprosy." However, the fallen human creature remains God's created human being even though deeply corrupted since "God is not a creator, author, or cause of sin."[33]

This inherited sin is not only "a complete lack of all good in spiritual, divine matters but also at the same time it replaces the lost image of God in the human being with a deep-seated, evil, horrible, bottomless, unfathomable, and indescribable corruption of the entire human nature and of all powers, particularly of the highest, most important powers of the soul, in mind, heart, and will. . . . [T]he fallen heart is diametrically opposed to God and the highest commandments. Indeed, it is hostile to God, particularly in regard to divine, spiritual matters."

The Formula also makes it clear that original sin is passed from parents to children, not as a matter of activity that is imitated or learned, but through inheritance: "ever since the fall, the human being inherits an inborn evil way of doing things, an internal impurity of heart, and an evil desire and inclination, so that we all by nature inherit such a heart, mind, and way of thinking from Adam. Following its highest powers and in light of reason, this fallen heart is by nature diametrically opposed to God and his highest commandments. Indeed, it is hostile to God, particularly in regard to divine, spiritual matters," even though in the matters of this earth its weakened

---

Moldaenke, *Schriftverständnis und Schriftdeutung im Zeitalter der Reformation. Teil I. Matthias Flacius Illyricus* (Stuttgart: Kohlhammer, 1936), 104–18; and Kolb, *Bound Choice*, 118–20.

30. E.g., *WA* 42:47, 14–22; *LW* 1:63; *WA* 10, 1:508, 2–21; *LW* 52:152; *WA* 40, 2:327, 20–30, 385, 17–20; *LW* 12:311, 351.

31. Irene Dingel, *Concordia controversa, Die öffentlichen Diskussionen um das lutherische Konkordienwerk am Ende des 16. Jahrhunderts* (Gütersloh: Gütersloher Verlagshaus, 1996), 467–541.

32. Article II, *BSLK*, 866–912; *Book of Concord*, 543–62.

33. Article I, FC Solid Declaration, §5–7, *BSLK*, 816–17; *Book of Concord*, 533.

powers of understanding may make decisions that outwardly conform to God's law.[34]

The Concordists recognized that in the context of theological discussion clarity can be attained only through the clear demarcation from opposing ideas. Therefore, they added to their teaching on original sin rejections of specific scholastic points of view. "Against old and new Pelagians, we reject and condemn the following false opinions and teachings: that original sin is merely a *reatus* (obligation resulting from a debt incurred by someone else) without any corruption of our nature." The list continued: The Formula repudiated the idea "that sinful, evil desires are not sin but *conditions* (or created, essential characteristics) of our nature." Nor was original sin to be defined as a "lack and defect which . . . are not really and truly sin in God's sight, because of which the human being apart from Christ must be a child of wrath and condemnation and under the rule and the power of Satan." It is an error to hold that original sin is "only external, a simple, insignificant spot splashed on us, or a stain spilled on us, or a *corruptio tantum accidentium aut qualitatum* (that is, a corruption of something incidental to human nature); in spite of which and beneath which human nature still has and retains its goodness and power even in spiritual matters" or "that original sin is not a deprivation or lack of spiritual powers but only an external obstacle for such good, spiritual powers," and "that this 'spot' can be easily wiped away, like a smudge on the face or paint on the wall." "We also reject and condemn those who teach that human nature has indeed been greatly weakened and corrupted through the fall but has not completely lost all good that pertains to divine, spiritual matters."

There can be no biblically-based contention, the Formula affirmed, that "there is nevertheless something good left from our natural birth, such as the capability, aptitude, competence, or capacity to begin doing something, or to effect something, or to cooperate in spiritual matters. Whatever concerns external, temporal, and civil matters and activities, which are subject to human reason, the following article will treat." The Concordists explained these repudiations: "God's Word teaches that corrupted human nature in and of itself cannot accomplish any good thing in spiritual, divine matters, not even the slightest thing (such as producing a good thought). Not only that, in and of itself it can do nothing else but sin in God's sight (Gen. 6[:5], 8[:21])."[35]

34. Article I, Formula of Concord, Solid Declaration §11, *BSLK*, 848–49; *Book of Concord*, 533–34.

35. *BSLK*, 850–52; *Book of Concord*, 534–36.

But to preserve human integrity as a creature of God and to prevent God from being seen as the cause of evil, the Formula of Concord rejected the formulation that original sin is the substance or essence of the sinner, as Flacius argued; indeed, the Formula of Concord discouraged Flacius's substance/activities distinction in general, echoing Luther's conviction that human explanations necessarily fail to grasp the mystery of evil that besets and permeates every human being.[36]

Martin Chemnitz's Doctrine of Original Sin

Flacius's position affected all subsequent formulations of the Lutheran doctrine of original sin; added to the concerns that God not be seen as the author of evil and that the corruption of all human powers be taken with utmost seriousness was the concern that the debilitating nature of original sin not call into question God's almighty creative power, even in the midst of the mystery of the existence and the continuation of sin and evil in believers. Among those contending with Flacius's view, Melanchthon's student Martin Chemnitz (1522–86) stands out, both because of his prime role in the composition of the Formula of Concord and because of several works that substantially shaped the subsequent Lutheran dogmatic tradition. In 1569 Duke Julius of Braunschweig-Wolfenbüttel charged Chemnitz with the task of producing a manual for the review of Christian doctrine that pastoral candidates might use as they prepared for their examination for the pastorate and for regular examinations thereafter. Chemnitz adhered closely to what he had learned in Wittenberg by defining original sin as "not simply actual imitation of the bad example of Adam, nor only bare guilt because of the fall of Adam . . . [but it] is passed through one man into all, by carnal propagation, namely because nature in its very origin is conceived and born sinful." Sinners therefore have been poisoned so that they cannot bring their lives into conformity with God's Word and will. Created in God's image, Adam and Eve had, "seduced by the wiles of the devil," "of their own free will turned themselves away from God and obedience to him." Original sin therefore consists of "the defect or lack of original righteousness . . . *ataxia* [disorder], destruction and corruption of all human powers." This turns sinners by their nature to "the things that are repugnant to God's will."[37]

---

36. *BSLK*, 843–66; *Book of Concord*, 531–42.
37. Martin Chemnitz, *Die fürnemsten Heuptstu[e]ck der Christlichen Lehre* . . . (Wolfenbüttel: Horn, 1569); and *Ministry, Word, and Sacraments: An Enchiridion*, trans. Luther Poellot (St. Louis: Concordia, 1981), 57–58.

Chemnitz also taught his fellow pastors in Braunschweig in a kind of continuing education program. His lectures on Melanchthon's *Loci* provided a vital link between the Wittenberg reformers and later generations in the period called Lutheran orthodoxy. Chemnitz rejected the restriction of the terms "sin of origin" and "original sin" to Adam's sin and argued that, although the term does not occur in Scripture and probably dates from Augustine's time, it conveys biblical teaching, just as do words such as "essence," "person," or "consubstantial" in regard to the Trinity. He marshaled even more biblical passages than Melanchthon and added citations from ancient church fathers, engaging their opinions with critique when he found them and more recent "scholastic" teachers misleading or wrong.[38] These lectures reflected his critique of the Council of Trent and contemporary Roman Catholic theologians, which repeated his teachers' conviction that original sin brought the disorder and corruption of the breakdown of the relationship of fear, love, and trust in God that led to actual sins of every kind. Chemnitz spoke of Satan's tyranny but left no doubt of each individual human being's responsibility for this broken relationship, the corruption in will and heart that leads to all sinful activities.[39] He repeated Luther's assertion of the mystery of the continuation of sin and evil in the lives of the baptized that acknowledged that this failure to fear, love, and trust God above all things continues to disrupt the relationship of God's chosen children with their heavenly Father. Thus, Chemnitz insisted, as had Luther and Melanchthon, on the necessity of a life of continuing repentance and forgiveness.[40]

The Doctrine of Original Sin in Lutheran Orthodoxy

With the next generation, Lutheran theology moved into the more—though not completely—settled period dubbed "Orthodoxy." Wittenberg professor Leonhardt Hütter (1563–1616) published his *Compendium of Theological Topics from the Holy Scripture and the Book of Concord*, continuing to employ the definition of original sin he had inherited. Original sin is a "natural illness, an inborn contagion and defect, which deprives us of fear and trust in God and perverts us totally through concupiscence and makes us guilty of eternal damnation if we are not regenerated." Hütter takes for granted

---

38. Martin Chemnitz, *Loci Theologici . . .* (Wittenberg: Henckel, 1610), 216–52; *Loci Theologici. Martin Chemnitz*, trans. J. A. O. Preus (St. Louis: Concordia, 1989), 276–309.

39. *Examen Concilii Trinidentini. Martinum Chemnicium*, ed. Eduard Preuss (Berlin: Schlawitz, 1861), 103–6; Martin Chemnitz, *Examination of the Council of Trent, Part I*, trans. Fred Kramer (St. Louis: Concordia, 1971), 315–32.

40. *Examen*, 106–20; *Examination*, 337–74.

without discussion that it is bequeathed from parents to children and earns all sinners eternal death.[41]

Hütter's student Johann Gerhard (1582–1637) spent his teaching career at the University of Jena, producing between 1610 and 1625 his multivolume *Loci theologici*, the foundation for the further development of "orthodox" Lutheran thinking. His commentaries on Romans 5 and Genesis 3 reflected the same understanding of original sin found in his dogmatic work. In defining the "first and principle sin that formed all others," he turned to Luther's Genesis commentary: "unbelief and revolt against God's Word." The devil fostered human doubt of that Word—the primal sin.[42] In his Genesis commentary Gerhard explicitly rejected the designation of original sin as pride held by "Scholastics and Jesuits," insisting that it is "doubt of God's Word and unbelief; pride results from doubt and unbelief, and the root and beginning of conversion to God after the fall is faith (Heb. 11:6)."[43] In contrast to the primal state in paradise, where his human creatures enjoyed "bliss and the most blessed condition" of having God's gifts and blessings heaped upon them in superabundance, the perversion and infection of sin brought God's wrath and curse upon humankind.[44] Satan incited hatred of God and hostility toward other human beings in Adam and Eve, leading to their transgression of God's command and the destruction of their integrity. Eve's doubt turned into outright denial of God's Word.

Gerhard did not excuse Adam and Eve, however. Human creatures are responsible for their rejection of God; God is not responsible in any way for sin and evil.[45] Gerhard set forth the consequences of original sin in disobedience[46] and death,[47] detailed the case against Pelagius's false interpretation of the human condition and contemporary Roman Catholic variations on it, and refuted Flacius's equating original sin with the substance of the sinner while affirming that it does corrupt the entire sinful person.[48] Gerhard introduced

---

41. Leonhart Hütter, *Compendium locorum theologicorum ex Scripturis Sacris et Libro Concordiae*, ed. Johann Anselm Steiger (Stuttgart-Bad Cannstatt: Fromann-Holzbog, 2006), 1:154–60, 2:950–51.

42. *Ioannis Gerhardi Loci theologici*, ed. Eduard Preuss, 2 (Berlin: Schlawitz, 1864): 147a–b; see also the similar definition in Gerhard's *Commenatrius super Genesin* (Jena: Steinmann, 1637), 75–78.

43. Ibid., 86.

44. *Loci theologici*, 142a.

45. Ibid., 142b–43a, 144a–47a.

46. In his Genesis commentary Gerhard asserted that original sin produces "transgression of the whole law and all the commands of God (James 2:10)," *Commentarius super Genesis*, 88.

47. In his Romans commentary Gerhard made a special point of death's origin in sin, not in human nature as created by God, *Annotationes posthumae in Epistolam ad Romanos*, ed. Johann Ernst Gerhard (Leipzig/Jena: Fleischer, 1676), 170–72.

48. Ibid., 151b–69a.

the first extended Lutheran discussion of the manner in which original sin is propagated. Citing John 3:3; Psalm 51:7; Job 14:4; Ephesians 2:3; and Genesis 5:1, he argued that natural propagation "of the flesh" produced the nature that is, in another sense, "fleshly," that is, hostile to God. This explicit elaboration of the implicit "traducian" element in Lutheran dogmatics present from the beginning arose within the polemical context set by Roman Catholic positions, particularly of Robert Bellarmine, and especially in regard to the immaculate conception of the Virgin Mary.[49] Another way of conceiving the source of original sin simply lay beyond the possibilities of the basic definition of human sinfulness and its origin in Eden.

By the end of the seventeenth century the definition of original sin among "orthodox" Lutheran theologians had begun to shift. Johann Friedrich König (1619–64), professor in Greifswald and Rostock, defined "the sin of origin" as Adam's act that inflicted on human nature its complete corruption and that was passed on to his descendents, "in us today." Not God but Satan and the human mind and will bent to his temptation. Adam's transgression and disobedience constituted the original sin, which is passed on as a "natural accident." König did define the "form of sin" intrinsically as "doubt of the truth of the divine law" and extrinsically as the eating of the fruit. He repeated a definition of the "adamitic sin" as first, doubt or not having faith in God's Word; second, a lack of conformity to God; third, transgression of God's law and obedience to the devil; and fourth, carrying out all that this means.[50] The concepts of doubt and trust were receding in the understanding of original sin.

This is also apparent in the work of Johann Andreas Quenstedt (1617–88), professor in Wittenberg, who defined original sin not as coming from the very beginning, as if created by God, but from its origin in Adam, passed on from parent to child, and in all human creatures the origin of actual sins. When David confessed his sinful origin in Psalm 51:5, he indicated that his sin stemmed from his parents, passed on through conception.[51] The breaking of trust in God did not enter into Quenstedt's formulation of his basic definition of original sin. Instead, he claimed Luther's authority for his designating the failure to observe the "entire moral law" as the object of the original evil, which produced lack of original righteousness, the most profound corruption, in the

---

49. Ibid., 169a–79b. See also Gerhard, *Annotationes . . . Romanos*, 169, where he opposes the conveying of original sin through propagation to its taking hold of the sinner simply through imitation of sinners of the previous generation.

50. Johann Friedrich König, *Theologia Postivo-Acroamatica succinctis Annotationibus explicata* (Wittenberg/Servestae: Zimmermann, 1755), 235–43; König's discussion continues to 256.

51. Johann Andreas Quenstedt, *Theologia Didactico-Polemica, Sive Systema Theologicum* (Wittenberg: Quenstedt, 1701), 2:56–59.

human being. This resulted in corrupted desires, actual sins, and the punishments visited upon original sin, including death, both temporal and eternal.[52]

Quenstedt's younger contemporary Johann Wilhelm Baier (1647–95), professor in Jena and Halle, continued Quenstedt's centering of his definition on the transgression of God's law instead of the breaking of trust in God and his Word, thus inevitably focusing on human action rather than the relationship of God and human creature. He defined sin in general as not conforming to the "eternal and immutable wisdom and judgment of God," as known through his law.[53] Original sin is thus defined as "in part, the privation of original righteousness, and in part the inclination of the entire nature toward what is corrupt," the total absence of the spiritual light that not only recognizes God truly but also recognizes why God should be worshiped and that what is divinely revealed should be embraced with firm assent. Thus it consists in the lack of original holiness and powers to love God above all things and to carry through the dictates of proper thinking in the coercion of the appetites that in the will point human beings in the directions of sinful works.[54] Although the power to act, which belongs to the "appetites of the senses," is not considered sin precisely in itself, nevertheless, because it carries people to that end, it is rightly called sin.[55] This shift of focus to human performance rather than the entire inherited breakdown of trust in God may be related to the synergism of which Baier is sometimes accused. Luther's framework for thinking of the origin of sin and its root within each sinner has faded severely.

Philipp Jakob Spener's Doctrine of Original Sin

However, at the level of popular preaching and catechetics, Luther's insights still influenced those who were trying to reach the common people. Although often accused of departing from the Reformation's principles, Philipp Jakob Spener (1635–1705) reproduced essentials from Luther's teaching on the doctrine of original sin in his sermons and catechesis. Lutheran orthodox theologians had striven to reform daily life as well as to hold to correct biblical teaching,[56] and these efforts glided into the movement labeled "Pietism," the

---

52. Ibid., 2:59–62.

53. *Compendium Theologiae Positivae* (Jena: Oehrling and Leipzig: Fritsch, 1708), 435, edited for use in the United States by C. F. W. Walther (St. Louis: Concordia, 1879), 2:268.

54. *Compendium*, 1708, 455–59; 1879, 2:283–85.

55. *Compendium*, 1708, 461–62; 1879, 2:286. Baier's contemporary, David Hollaz (1648–1713), held a similar position, *Examen Theologicum Acromaticum* (Stargard: Ernesti, 1707), 2:114–51.

56. Jonathan Strom, *Orthodoxy and Reform: The Clergy in Seventeenth Century Rostock* (Tübingen: Mohr Siebeck, 1999).

"father" of which was Spener. Pietist preachers, famous for their harsh critique of sinful lives, tended not to dwell on original sin, but Spener did not shy away from it in his catechetical instruction and preaching. His *Catechism Tables* defined sin as "all that is against the divine law," originating not from God but from the devil and the perverted human will. Original sin is so called "because it is the origin of all other sins and was placed upon us before our own origin"; it is inherited and propagated by natural conception. It is "the inability to do anything good, a real inclination to all evil. In the mind it is darkness, uncertainty, an inclination to error; in the will it is a rebelliousness and totally perverted essence; in the emotions it is complete disorder, lethargy, and idleness, as well as an inclination to evil deeds and a greater readiness to everything but the good, . . . the opposite of the divine image, therefore a mask of the devil."[57] Spener also explained the concept as "the horrible perversion of our nature, that, in the place of the image of God which we were given, we are born into the world totally incapable of doing any good, without faith, fear, and knowledge of God, and in natural blindness, with a continual desire for all kinds of evil and all that opposes God; from this poisoned root arise all other evils."[58]

⚜

Martin Luther's revolutionary redefinition of the patristic and medieval term "original sin" reflects his dramatic redefinition of the defining framework of the Christian faith and life, as based in the creative and re-creative Word of the Creator and the human response of trust or faith. Luther's view is particularly helpful and apt as twenty-first-century Christians of all traditions struggle to deal with both the radicality and banality of the evil that takes concrete form in human sin, missing God's mark for human life. Luther's followers have caught in various degrees the precise shape of his understanding of what goes wrong with human life as we experience it. Twenty-first-century people from all cultures can profit from his recognition of the unsolvable paradox of the goodness of humanity in its reflection of the image and nature of God's goodness, alongside the experience of a corruption and infection that Scripture alone can fully reveal since it involves the human relationship with the Creator. The horrors of the several holocausts of the twentieth century must

---

57. Philipp Jakob Spener, *Catechismus Tabellen, Darinnen der gantze Catechismus D. Martin Luthers Deutlich und gru[e]ndlich erkla[e]ret*, ed. Johann Georg Pritius (Frankfurt am Main: Zunner and Adam, 1713), 83–85, author's translation.

58. Philipp Jakob Spener, *Einfache Erkla[e]rung der christlichen Lehre* (Erlangen: Palm, 1827), 144. His sermons on the catechism echo the same ideas: *Kurtze Catechismus-Predigten* (St. Louis: Volkening; Leipzig: Naumann, 1867), 138–43, author's translation.

convince us of Luther's certainty that all human beings are infected with this rejection of God's lordship through the existence bequeathed them by their parents: original sin is inborn and inevitable. Most helpful is Luther's definition of the original sin—at the beginning of human history in Eden and in every individual's daily experience—as doubt of God's Word, denial of his lordship, and destruction of love for him and trust in him. This emphasizes the fact that human creatures, at the core of their existence, are in relationship with their Creator, a relationship broken by our failure to trust the one who fashioned and sustains us. Thus, the mysterious nature of the continuation of sin and evil in the lives of God's chosen people highlights how deep that corruption goes and how totally dependent creatures are on the grace and mercy of their Creator, who has become in Jesus Christ their re-creator.

6

ORIGINAL SIN IN REFORMED THEOLOGY

Donald Macleod

The Reformed discussion of original sin addressed two distinct questions. First, there was the question of fact. Is it true, as the Articles of the Church of England asserted, that there is such a thing as "Birth Sin," whereby corruption is naturally engendered in the nature of every human, with the result that every human being "is very far gone from original righteousness, and is of his own nature inclined to evil, so that the flesh lusteth always contrary to the spirit; and therefore in every person born into this world, it deserveth God's wrath and condemnation" (Article IX).

Second, there was the question of explanation. How can we account for this fact? The answer, derived from Scripture, and shorn of its more subtle nuances, was that we sinned in Adam, lost our original integrity in the moment of his fall, and inherit from him a nature that is wholly corrupt.

Much learning, emotion, and energy would be spent on this latter question, particularly on the precise nature of the relation between Adam and his descendants. But it was never forgotten that however difficult it might be to explain how human nature came to be in this predicament, there could be no doubting the fact. Nor was it ever forgotten that the fact itself, the depravity of human nature, was what mattered supremely. The nineteenth-century Scottish theologian William Cunningham even went so far as to declare that "the prosperity of vital personal religion is more closely connected with correct views of the points involved in the Pelagian controversy, than even with correct views upon the subject of the Trinity and of the person of Christ."[1]

This, then, was the fundamental thing, and this is why Reformed theologians, particularly in the early days, showed some impatience with such questions as how sin is propagated from parents to children. William Perkins, for example, exclaims, "Whereas the propagation of sin is as a common fire in a town, men are not so much to search how it came, as to be careful how to extinguish it."[2]

Yet the fact itself raises a critical issue. How did it come about that the human race exists in such a state of depravity?

Created "Very Good"

The answer began with a strenuous insistence that man was not created sinful. On the contrary, he came into being in a state of moral and spiritual perfection. This was a fundamental part of Reformed theodicy. God could not be the author of sin; neither, then, could he be the creator of a depraved creature. On the contrary, at its point of origin the human species was "very good." Untainted by sin, Adam and Eve bore the image of God, "by which we mean," wrote Ursinus, "that he was created perfectly good, wise, just, holy, happy, and lord of all other creatures."[3] This was not simply a state of moral ambiguity or indifference, as if Adam and Eve were endowed with nothing more than a formal freedom of moral choice (as Pelagius argued), hovering ambivalently between good and evil. On the contrary, they were already holy, and in their original condition they were a credit to their Maker and brought him immense satisfaction. Sin, therefore, was not of the essence of their nature (otherwise Christ could never have taken it), but a perversion of it.

This concern to distance God from human sin is clearly apparent in Calvin's writing. Commenting on Paul's statement that we are *by nature* children of wrath (Eph. 2:3), Calvin writes, "Paul does not mean 'nature' as it was established by God, but as it was vitiated in Adam. For it would be most unfitting for God to be made the author of death. Therefore, Adam so corrupted

---

1. William Cunningham, *Historical Theology*, vol. 1 (1862; repr., London: Banner of Truth, 1960), 321.

2. William Perkins, *A Golden Chain or the Description of Theology* (1590), chap. 12. See *The Work of William Perkins*, intro. and ed. Ian Breward, Courtenay Library of Reformation Classics (Appleford, UK: Sutton Courtenay Press, 1970), 192.

3. *The Commentary of Dr. Zacharias Ursinus on the Heidelberg Catechism* (1591), trans. George W. Williard (1852; repr., Phillipsburg, NJ: P&R, n.d.), 28.

himself that infection spread from him to all his descendants."[4] God is not to be censured for the vices of humankind: "We have perished solely because we have degenerated from our original condition."[5]

Later Reformed theologians spoke to the same effect. "Sin," wrote Perkins, "is the corruption, or rather deprivation, of the first integrity."[6] From a different perspective, William Ames, discussing the causes of Adam's fall, insists, "God therefore was in no way the cause of his fall; neither did he lay upon man the necessity of sinning. Man of his own accord freely fell from God."[7]

This point has lost none of its force with the passing of the centuries. In the dominant modern discourse, humans emerge not by creation, but by evolution, and at their point of origin, they are neither saints nor sages, but savages. On this construction, sin has characterized humans from the beginning. Far from originating in a "fall," sin arises from the "independence of the sensuous functions," which inevitably inhibit the development of the "God-consciousness."[8] This throws the blame for sin on man's Maker (if he has one), and it makes sin an inevitable and inescapable fact of human existence. The latter is infinitely depressing, the former incompatible with the existence of God (assuming that "good" is part of the connotation of "God").

The Covenant of Works

The second key element in the Reformed doctrine of original sin is that from the beginning the relation between God and man was defined by a covenant. This is not explicit in Calvin, but the idea of a probationary command certainly is, and Calvin's comments on Genesis 2:17 make plain that he viewed this probation as including not only the threat of death but also the promise of life. Had he passed this test of his obedience, Adam "would have passed into heaven without death, and without injury."[9] It remains, however, that though Calvin refers frequently to "covenant," he traces it no further back than Abraham, and though Calvin speaks of the "old" and the "new" covenants, he is still referring only to the successive administrations of the Abrahamic

4. John Calvin, *Institutes of the Christian Religion*, 2 vols., ed. John T. McNeill, trans. Ford Lewis Battles, Library of Christian Classics (Philadelphia: Westminster, 1960), 2.1, 6.

5. Ibid., 2.1, 9.

6. Perkins, *A Golden Chain*, chap. 10, 189.

7. William Ames, *The Marrow of Theology*, 1623, trans. John Dykstra Eusden (Grand Rapids: Baker, 1997), 114.

8. Friedrich Schleiermacher, *The Christian Faith*, 2nd ed., 1830, trans. H. R. Mackintosh and J. S. Stewart (Edinburgh: T&T Clark, 1928), 273.

9. John Calvin, *Commentary on Genesis*, vol. 1 (Edinburgh: Calvin Translation Society, 1847; repr., London: Banner of Truth, 1965), 127.

covenant, first under the law and then under the gospel. He has no concept of an Adamic covenant.

Nor does the concept appear in the Zurich theologians Zwingli and Bullinger, often seen as the progenitors of federal theology. Zwingli limited his use of the covenant idea to defending infant baptism against the Anabaptists.[10] Bullinger was the author of the first dedicated treatise on the covenant, *De Testamento sive foedere Dei*, published in 1534,[11] and in the *Decades* (1550) he speaks of a "league" between God and man. This "league," he says, did not begin with Abraham, but God "did first of all make it with Adam." This was not, however, what later came to be known as the covenant of works. It was a post-fall league made "immediately upon his transgression."[12] The Heidelberg theologian, Caspar Olevianus, also used the covenant concept, even to the extent of deploying it as an organizing principle for the whole of Christian doctrine, but, like Calvin, he knows of only one covenant, the covenant of grace.[13]

The phrase "covenant of works" was first used by the Scottish theologian Robert Rollock, whose work *Tractatus de Vocatione Efficaci* was published in 1597 and appeared in an English translation in 1603.[14] Rollock prefaces his remarks with the comment that "all the word of God pertains to some covenant; for God speaks nothing to man without the covenant."[15] He then continues:

> The covenant of works, which may also be called a legal or natural covenant, is founded in nature, which by creation was pure and holy, and in the law of God, which in the first creation was engraven in man's heart. For after that God had created man after his own image, pure and holy, and had written his law in his mind, he made a covenant with man, wherein he promised him eternal life,

10. See, for example, Zwingli's treatise *Of Baptism* in *Zwingli and Bullinger*, ed. G. W. Bromiley, LCC (Philadelphia: Westminster, 1953), 119–75. He writes, for example, that baptism is "a covenant sign, which indicates that all those who receive it are willing to amend their lives and to follow Christ" (14).

11. See William Klempa, "The Concept of the Covenant in Sixteenth- and Seventeenth-Century Continental and British Theology," in *Major Themes in the Reformed Tradition*, ed. Donald K. McKim (Grand Rapids: Eerdmans,1992), 96. On the early development of covenant theology, see also Geerhardus Vos, "The Doctrine of the Covenant in Reformed Theology," in *Redemptive History and Biblical Interpretation*, ed. Richard B. Gaffin (Phillipsburg, NJ: P&R, 1980), 234–67.

12. Klempa, "Concept of the Covenant," 97.

13. For Olevianus see further Lyle D. Bierma, "Covenant or Covenants in the Theology of Olevianus?," *Calvin Theological Journal* 22.2 (1987): 228–50.

14. See *Select Works of Robert Rollock*, vol. 1, ed. William M. Gunn (Edinburgh: Wodrow Society, 1849), 1–288.

15. Ibid., 33.

under the condition of holy and good works, which should be answerable to the holiness and goodness of his nature, and conformable to his law.[16]

In *The Marrow of Modern Divinity*, published while the Westminster Assembly was still sitting, the covenant of works is taken for granted.[17] *The Marrow* is a compilation gathered from "modern" (post-Luther) divines, and the treatment of the covenant of works draws on Ball, Ames, Walker, Ursinus, Rollock, Grotius, Reynolds, Slater, Goodwin, Musculus, and Bolton. The phrase was clearly current, then, before the Westminster Confession became the first Protestant creed to adopt it, declaring, "The first covenant made with man was a covenant of works."[18]

The "covenant of works" has been heavily criticized from the beginning on the grounds that this precise form of words does not occur anywhere in Scripture. The objection is already raised by Nomista, one of the dialogue-partners in *The Marrow of Modern Divinity*: "But, Sir, you know there is no mention made in the book of Genesis of this covenant of works, which, you say, was made with man at the first." He receives what was to become the standard answer: "Though we read not the word covenant betwixt God and man, yet have we there recorded what may amount to as much," namely two parties, a promise, and a condition. In the nineteenth and twentieth centuries the covenant of works was rejected on more fundamental historical and theological grounds: first, as a betrayal of the gospel of the magisterial reformers, particularly Calvin; and, second, as setting the tone for an oppressive legalism in which human's primary relation to God was defined by law, not by grace.

In response to this, I should note, first of all, that there is a remarkable insistence throughout Reformed theology that the terms God laid down for Adam constituted a *promissory* covenant, which not only threatened death but also promised life: hence the alternative term "covenant of life" used, for example, in the Shorter Catechism.[19] This insistence is already clear, as we have seen, in Calvin: "Truly the first man would have passed to a better life, had he remained upright."[20] This same note is struck by Rollock, who speaks of the covenant as offering eternal life under the condition of "holy and good

---

16. Ibid., 34.

17. *The Marrow of Modern Divinity, with Notes by the Rev Thomas Boston* (New Edition, Edinburgh: 1818), 31–35.

18. Westminster Confession of Faith, 7:7. The Confession was completed in December 1646, almost two years before Cocceius published his *Summa doctrinae de foedere et testamento Dei* (Amsterdam: 1648).

19. Westminster Shorter Catechism, Answer 12.

20. Calvin, *Commentary on Genesis*, 1:180.

works";[21] by Ames, who links the original "law" not only to a promise of continuing animal life, but also to "a later exaltation to spiritual life";[22] and by Turretin, who portrays God as linking the demand for perfect obedience with the promise of life and eternal happiness.[23] There was also a consensus among Reformed theologians that the tree of life was a sacramental seal of "the immortality which would have been bestowed upon Adam if he had persevered in his first state."[24] The covenant held out the prospect not only of immortality but also of elevation to an even more glorious existence than Adam already enjoyed in Eden.

At the same time, it was stressed that to attach any promise to obedience was itself an act of grace and condescension on God's part. Humans, as the Westminster Confession points out, already owe obedience to God by virtue of his creation; God, on the other hand, is under no obligation to reward such obedience with eternal life.[25] That he does so is "a voluntary condescension on God's part, which he hath been pleased to express by way of covenant."[26] This implies a clear distinction between the law and the covenant. The law as such has no promise attached. It is simply a command that we are bound to obey. Furthermore, whereas knowledge of the law was naturally engraved on Adam's heart, knowledge of the terms of the covenant was not. He knew of the promise only by special revelation. Similarly, the probationary command was in its very nature such that Adam could have knowledge of it only because "the LORD God commanded the man" (Gen. 2:16). Taking these considerations together, the argument that the covenant of works reflects pure legalism is hard to sustain. Both the promise that God makes, and the covenant by which he binds himself, are pure grace.

Linked to this emphasis on the promissory nature of the covenant of works was an equally clear emphasis that Adam, as he was by nature, was fully competent to comply with the terms that God laid down: hence the frequent use of the term "the covenant of nature" deployed, according to Turretin, not because

21. Rollock, *Select Works*, 1:34.
22. Ames, *The Marrow of Theology*, 113.
23. Turretin, *Institutes of Elenctic Theology*, vol. 1, ed. James T. Dennison Jr., trans. George Musgrave Giger (Phillipsburg, NJ: P&R, 1992), 575.
24. Turretin, *Institutes*, 1:581.
25. Westminster Confession of Faith, 7:1. See also Turretin, *Institutes*, 1:574: "By his own right, God could indeed have prescribed obedience to man (created by him) without any promise of reward."
26. Westminster Confession of Faith, 7:1. See also Cocceius, "The distinctive thing is not that man is under the law, but that there is a promise annexed to the hearing of the law." Cocceius, *Summa doctrinae de foedere et testamento Dei*, Caput II:12. See Cocceius, *Opera Omnia* (Amsterdam: 1701), Tom. VII, 45.

God was under a "natural" obligation to man "but because it is founded on the nature of man (as it was at first created by God) and on his integrity of powers."[27] This was closely related to the divine justice: "it was not consistent with the justice and goodness of God to have required that of his creature, which he had not given him power to perform."[28] This power, as divine gift, was part of Adam's concreated holiness, which, as we have seen, left him not simply evenly balanced between good and evil but positively inclined to good.

But the question then emerges, How could a holy man fall? "It is most difficult," wrote Turretin, "to imagine in what way at length man in a state of integrity could fall."[29] Ursinus offered a succinct answer: "The first sin of man had its origin, not in God, but was brought about by the instigation of the devil and the free will of man."[30] The comprehensive Reformed answer stressed three points.

First, the persuasions of Satan. Usher, for example, devotes considerable attention to the serpent's arguments.[31] Care was taken, however, to avoid conveying the impression that the devil had *compelled* Adam to sin. He was only the "consulting and persuading cause," wrote Ames;[32] or, as Turretin put it, Adam "suffered himself to be deceived by the Devil and, Satan persuading but not compelling, freely departed from God."[33]

Second, the abuse of free will. Calvin had already sounded this note: "When we come to speak of man, he will be found to have sinned voluntarily, and to have departed from God, his Maker, by a movement of the mind not less free than perverse."[34] Perkins wrote to the same effect, "Thus without constraint they willingly fell from their integrity."[35] Ames is equally explicit: "The principal cause was man himself in the abuse of free will. . . . God therefore was in no way the cause of his fall; neither did he lay upon man a necessity of sinning."[36]

This stress on free will is a key element in Reformed theodicy. Man was created upright, but mutable, and this mutability hinged on the way Adam

27. Turretin, *Institutes*, 1:575.
28. From Thomas Boston's treatise, *On the Covenant of Works: The Complete Works of the Late Rev. Thomas Boston*, vol. 1, ed. Samuel Macmillan, 12 vols. (1852; repr., Stoke-on-Trent: Tentmaker Publications, 2002), 232.
29. Turretin, *Institutes*, 1:606.
30. Ursinus, *Commentary on the Heidelberg Catechism*, 34.
31. James Usher, *A Body of Divinitie* (London: 1653), 128–31.
32. Ames, *The Marrow of Theology*, 115.
33. Turretin, *Institutes*, 1:607.
34. Calvin, *Commentary on Genesis*, 1:158.
35. Perkins, *A Golden Chain*, chap. XI, 190.
36. Ames, *The Marrow of Theology*, 114.

would use his freedom of choice. His choice would not be "determined" by Satan's blandishments nor, indeed, by his own character as the sinless bearer of God's image. Nor may we confuse foreordination with a divine compulsion. Adam's choice was foreordained as a free act, not "caused" by any prior event or circumstance within the causal nexus (and, of course, the divine decree itself is not part of the causal nexus). He, himself, Adam, was the cause of his own decision, and had any third party been present as an intelligent observer they would have found it impossible to predict what choice Adam would make. "He could indeed stand if he wished," wrote Turretin, "but could also if he wished become evil."[37]

The one refinement offered on this is the suggestion that when Adam made his decision, he made it neither as one who was "whole" (holy) nor as one who was "corrupt." Instead, he made it as one who, "imbued with a false idea, corrupted himself."[38] This is a variant on the solution proposed by Ames to the question of the exact timing of Adam's transgression: "The first motion or step of this disobedience necessarily came before the act of eating, so that it may truly be said that man was a sinner before he did the eating."[39]

The third factor in the Reformed explanation of the fall is that God withheld efficacious or restraining grace. "They willingly fell from their integrity," wrote Perkins, "God upon just cause leaving them to themselves and freely suffering them to fall."[40] This implies, however, a distinction within the concept of grace. Adam, as Ames notes, had received in his creation sufficient grace to enable him to have remained obedient, had he chosen, and that grace was not taken from him before he sinned. But grace in another form *was* withheld in the moment of his probation: "the strengthening and confirming grace by which the act of sinning might have been hindered and the act of obedience effected was not given to him—and that by the certain wise and just counsel of God."[41]

This, however, was neither an excuse for man nor a ground of accusation against God: "Therefore man alone was the cause of his evil. He willingly sinned and freely and of his own accord without any compulsion or external force transgressed the command of God, though he was furnished with such strength and helps that he might easily have avoided sin, if he had wished."[42]

37. Turretin, *Institutes*, 1:607.
38. Ibid.
39. Ames, *The Marrow of Theology*, 114.
40. Perkins, *A Golden Chain*, chap. 190.
41. Ames, *The Marrow of Theology*, 114.
42. Turretin, *Institutes*, 1:608.

The Adamic Relationship

But amid such recondite discussions one fact was clear: Adam's breach of the covenant plunged not only himself but the whole human race into ruin. There was nothing distinctively Reformed or even Protestant about such a position. But how, in accordance with justice, could the one sin of one man have such calamitous consequences? The seminal answer had been given by Augustine: "we were all that one man" (*omnes eramus unus ille homo*).[43] But in what sense, precisely, were Adam and his posterity one? It is not a question to which Calvin gives much attention, probably because it was not an issue in the controversy with Rome, and when he does refer to it he is, if not inconsistent, at least ambivalent. At the most basic level he describes the Adamic relationship as simply a divine ordinance: "it had been so ordained by God that the first man should at one and the same time have and lose, both for himself and for his descendants, the gifts that God had bestowed upon him."[44] He does not quite stop there, however, but sees a rationale for this ordinance in the biological link between Adam and his progeny: "We must surely hold that Adam was not only the progenitor but, as it were, the root of human nature";[45] if so, there is nothing absurd in supposing that, "when Adam was despoiled, human nature was left naked and destitute, or that when he was infected with sin, contagion crept into human nature."[46]

Calvin's early successors in the Reformed tradition continued to deploy this same rationale. Rollock, for example, explains the fact that Adam's apostasy affected us all on the basis that "we were all as then in his loins, and as parcels of the substance and nature of the first man; and so we all fell in him, and with him, from the living God."[47] Perkins writes to similar effect: "when Adam offended, his posterity was in his loins from whom they should in the course of nature issue and therefore take part of the guiltiness with him."[48] In Perkins, however, the biological explanation lies side by side with the federal one: "Adam was not then a private man, but represented all mankind and therefore look what good he received from God, or evil elsewhere, both were common

43. Augustine, *On Forgiveness of Sins and Baptism*, bk. I.11, *Nicene and Post-Nicene Fathers*, series 1, vol. 5, 19.

44. Calvin, *Institutes*, II:I, 6, 7.

45. Ibid., 6.

46. Ibid., 7.

47. Rollock, *Select Works*, 1:168. Rollock's language offers some justification for the later claim of W. G. T. Shedd that the "older Calvinism" shared his view that the link between Adam and his posterity was realist and not merely federalist. See W. G. T. Shedd, *A Critical and Doctrinal Commentary on the Epistle of St Paul to the Romans* (1879; repr., Minneapolis: Klock and Klock, 1978), 128, 130.

48. Perkins, *A Golden Chain*, chap. XI, 191.

to others with him."[49] This link between the federal and the biological was never broken even in fully developed covenant theology. It appears clearly, for example, in the Westminster Confession, which highlights both that our first parents were the "root of all mankind" and that in the covenant of works God promised Adam life not only for himself but also for his posterity.[50] The Larger Catechism refers to Adam as "a public person,"[51] a phrase already used by Ames, but still keeping in view the biological connection: "because Adam was the first of mankind, from whom all men came, a law was given to him not only as a private person, as among the angels, but as a public person or the head of the family of man. His posterity were to derive all good and evil from him."[52] The link is also maintained in Turretin: "the bond between Adam and his posterity is twofold: (1) natural, as he is the father, and we are his children; (2) political and forensic, as he was the prince and representative head of the whole human race."[53]

This federal understanding of the relationship between Adam and his posterity became the standard Reformed position. There was, however, one exception: W. G. T. Shedd. Shedd was a prolific author in several academic departments, but his most valuable legacy was the theological work enshrined in his *History of Christian Doctrine* (1863), his *Commentary on the Epistle to the Romans* (1879), and his three-volume *Dogmatic Theology* (1889–94). In each of these he takes up, perforce, the question of original sin, and particularly the nature of the connection between Adam and his posterity. Throughout, Shedd maintains the realist view that the whole of human nature, and indeed every human being, was present in Adam and acted in him, in the moment of his fall.[54] We are not merely *reckoned* to have sinned in Adam; we *did* sin.

Contrary to the opinion of Shedd, however, the overall Reformed consensus has been that the union between ourselves and Adam was not real but federal. Yet, as we have seen, this federal headship is justified by his biological connection with the whole human species, and it receives further justification from the fact that Adam, our "root," was asked to complete his probation under ideal conditions. He was endowed with splendid graces, placed in a magnificent environment with the riches of paradise around him and the wonders of the world before him, given crystal-clear instructions, and furnished with the

49. Ibid.
50. Westminster Confession of Faith, 6:3 and 7:2.
51. Westminster Larger Catechism, Answer 22.
52. Ames, *The Marrow of Theology*, 113.
53. Turretin, *Institutes*, 616.
54. W. G. T. Shedd, *Dogmatic Theology*, 3 vols. (1889–94; repr., Grand Rapids: Zondervan, n.d.), 2:188.

most compelling of motives (obedience would bring life, disobedience would bring death). Yet "Adam at that one clap broke all the Ten Commandments."[55]

Imputation

What were the consequences of Adam's act of disobedience? The short answer is that, due to it, we are all born in a state of original sin. As used by Reformed theologians, however, this term is ambivalent. Most commonly, it refers to the state of depravity in which all of us are born. Ames, for example, defines it as "the corruption of the whole man,"[56] but Rollock had earlier laid down that "the matter of original sin is threefold": the guilt of Adam's apostasy, the lack of original righteousness, and a natural corruption "whereby we are made prone to all evil."[57] The three components are not, however, symmetrical: the lack of righteousness and the corruption of our nature are the twin effects of Adam's apostasy. From this point of view, the sin of Adam is the root cause of our sinfulness, and the sinfulness itself consists of the two elements, deprivation and depravity. Allowing for variations in vocabulary, this became the consensus among Reformed theologians, and though they did not always use the precise language of imputation, the idea of our being liable to the penalty due to Adam's sin is there from the beginning, due, no doubt, to the influence of Augustine, who had asserted that "even if there were but that one sin, it is sufficient, without any more, to lead to condemnation."[58] Though the fully fledged idea of "immediate imputation" appears only a hundred years after Calvin, we already read in Ursinus that "the whole human race is subject to the eternal wrath of God on account of the disobedience of our first parents."[59] In Usher, the concept of imputation is explicit. Having laid down that there are two sorts of sin, imputed and inherent, he goes on to ask, What is the sin imputed? and replies, "[It is] our sin in Adam, in whom as we lived, so also we sinned; for in our first parents every one of us did commit that first sinne which was the cause of all other, and so we all are become subject to the imputation of Adam's fall, both for the transgression and guiltiness."[60] By the end of the seventeenth century, Turretin is giving the doctrine its definitive expression: "the actual disobedience

55. Ames, *Marrow of Modern Divinity*, 41.
56. Ames, *The Marrow of Theology*, 120.
57. Rollock, *Select Works*, 1:167–70.
58. See the treatise, *On Marriage and Concupiscence*, bk. II.46, *Nicene and Post-Nicene Fathers*, series 1, vol. 5, 302.
59. Ursinus, *Commentary on the Heidelberg Catechism*, 40.
60. Usher, *A Body of Divinitie*, 144.

of Adam is imputed by an immediate and antecedent imputation to all his posterity springing from him by natural generation."[61]

The key words here are "immediate" and "antecedent": echoes of a debate that divided Reformed theologians in the middle of the seventeenth century. The point at issue was the relation between imputed guilt and inherited corruption. According to the advocates of *immediate* imputation, the guilt of Adam's sin was imputed to his posterity simply on the basis that they *were* his posterity. Corruption of nature follows as the punishment of our guilt. According to the advocates of *mediate* imputation, on the other hand, guilt is mediated through our corruption: God holds us guilty not simply because, irrespective of any depravity, he sees us as guilty of Adam's sin, but because he sees in us the corruption derived from Adam. We are condemned not as Adam's posterity, but as wicked and corrupt.

The leading advocate of this latter view was Josué de la Place (Placaeus, 1596–1665), a minister of the French Reformed Church and colleague to Moïse Amyraut at the Academy of Saumur.[62] In 1640, Placaeus published a volume titled, *De Statu Hominis Lapsi ante Gratiam* (*On the State of Fallen Man before Grace*). Five years later, the Third Synod of Charenton passed a decree (under the heading "Article of General Matters") that, *prima facie*, condemned the views of Placaeus. The relevant section was as follows:

> There was a Report made in the Synod of a certain Writing, both Printed and Manuscript, holding forth this Doctrine, that the whole Nature of Original Sin consisted only in that Corruption, which is Hereditary to all *Adam's* Posterity, and residing originally in all Men, and denieth the Imputation of his first Sin. This Synod condemneth the said Doctrine as far as it restraineth the Nature of Original Sin to the sole Hereditary Corruption of *Adam's* Posterity, to the excluding of the Imputation of that first Sin by which he fell, and interdicteth on pain of all Church-Censures all Pastors, Professors, and others, who shall treat of this Question, to depart from the common received Opinion of the Protestant Churches, who (over and besides that Corruption) have all acknowledged the Imputation of *Adam's* first Sin to his Posterity.[63]

Placaeus is not named in the decree, but John Quick, editor of the *Synodicon,* certainly understood it to refer to him because he appended a marginal note, "Mr. De la Place." Placaeus, however, denied that he had ever held the

---

61. Turretin, *Institutes*, 1:163.

62. For a sympathetic treatment of the historical background, see David Llewellyn Jenkins, *Saumur Redux: Josué de la Place and the Question of Adam's Sin* (Norfolk: Leaping Cat Press, 2008).

63. John Quick, *Synodicon in Gallia Reformata*, 2 vols. (London: 1692), 2:273.

view condemned by the Synod or ever questioned the imputation of Adam's sin. He clarified his position in *De Imputatione Primi Peccati Adami*, published in Saumur in 1655, and it was here that he introduced the distinction between immediate and mediate imputation. *Immediate* imputation meant that the guilt of chewing the forbidden fruit was imputed to Adam's descendants on the grounds, simply, that they are "sons of Adam," and this guilt led to two punishments: privation of original righteousness and eternal death. Imputation in this sense, Placaeus denied. *Mediate* imputation, on the other hand, follows upon God's sight of our hereditary corruption, derived from Adam: "For we share in the participation of this corruption by the sin of Adam, we habitually consent to it, as I say, and for that reason we are deserving, we who are reckoned with Adam the sinner."[64] In sum, according to Placaeus the corruption comes before the guilt, whereas according to the advocates of immediate imputation the guilt comes first and corruption is its penal consequence.

The Westminster Confession makes no reference to this debate, probably because news of it had scarcely reached Britain by the time the Confession was completed in 1646, though the divines may also have been reluctant to bind ministers too strictly on this question. By contrast, the Formula Consensus Helvetica, composed in 1675 by John Henry Heidegger of Zurich and Francis Turretin of Geneva, explicitly rejects the position of Placaeus: "we can not, without harm to Divine truth, give assent to those who deny that Adam represented his posterity by appointment of God, and that his sin is imputed, therefore, *immediately* to his posterity; and under the term *mediate and consequent* not only destroy the imputation of the first sin, but also expose the doctrine of hereditary corruption to great danger" (Canon XII). In an earlier canon (Canon X) the Consensus had stated unambiguously that the corruption of our nature could not be understood otherwise than as the penalty of imputed guilt: "there appears no way in which hereditary corruption could fall, as a spiritual death, upon the whole human race by the just judgement of God, unless some sin of that preceded, incurring the penalty (*reatum*) of that death. For God, the supremely just Judge of all the earth, punishes none but the guilty."[65]

The position of Heidegger and Turretin became the standard Reformed position, but Placaeus, and the Saumur school in general, claimed that theirs was a more faithful reflection of the position of Calvin. However, Calvin was operating a century before Placaeus, in a very different theological climate,

---

64. Quoted from de la Place, *Opera Omnia*, 280, in Jenkins, *Saumur Redux*, 14.

65. The translation is that published as appendix II in A. A. Hodge, *Outlines of Theology* (New Edition, London: Nelson, 1880), 656–63. A more recent translation by Martin I. Klauber can be found in *Trinity Journal* 11 (1990): 102–23.

and the question of mediate versus immediate imputation was never before his mind. Nevertheless, even Cunningham admitted that the Saumurian claim had some plausibility.[66] But is that the most that can be said? Calvin is certainly clear that the human race suffers the penal consequences of Adam's sin: "all were lost through the disobedience of one man."[67] He did not, however, subscribe to Augustine's view, already quoted, that that one sin, without the addition of any more, is enough to lead to condemnation. On the contrary, Calvin insisted that no one suffers eternal death on the ground of imputed sin alone:

> For since it is said that we become subject to God's judgement through Adam's sin, we are to understand it not as if we, guiltless and undeserving, bore the guilt of his offense but in the sense that, since we through his transgression have become entangled in the curse, he is said to have made us guilty. Yet not only has punishment fallen upon us from Adam, but a contagion imparted by him resides in us, which justly deserves punishment.[68]

Calvin interprets Romans 5:12, "death came to all men, because all sinned," along the same lines: "We have, therefore, all sinned," he writes, "because we are all imbued with natural corruption, and for this reason are wicked and perverse."[69]

These are not the sentiments of one who has not reflected on the nature and basis of imputation. They are the settled opinion of one fully convinced that there is no guilt apart from personal depravity.[70]

The idea that the loss of original righteousness and the corruption of nature were the penal consequences of imputed sin was not first introduced into Reformed theology by the debate on mediate and immediate imputation. It occurs already in Ursinus, who writes, "On account of the transgression of our first parents God, even whilst he creates the soul, at the same time deprives it of original righteousness. . . . [T]his want of righteousness in respect of God, who inflicts it on account of the sin of our first parents, is no sin, but a most just punishment."[71] Polanus similarly argued that the soul was created by God already afflicted with the punishment denounced against Adam, namely, the

---

66. William Cunningham, *The Reformers and the Theology of the Reformation* (Edinburgh: T&T Clark, 1862), 375.

67. Calvin, *Institutes*, II:I, 4.

68. Calvin, *Institutes*, II:I, 8.

69. Calvin, *The Epistles of Paul the Apostle to the Romans and to the Thessalonians*, trans. Ross Mackenzie (Carlisle, UK: Paternoster, 1995), 112.

70. Supporters of Placaeus also claim the support of Jonathan Edwards. See Jenkins, *Saumur Redux*, 30–31; and, *contra*, John Murray, *The Imputation of Adam's Sin* (Grand Rapids: Eerdmans, 1959), 52–64.

71. Ursinus, *Commentary on the Heidelberg Catechism*, 41.

loss of original grace, which Adam had lost not only for himself but for his posterity.[72] This, however, is more carefully nuanced than the statements of Turretin and Hodge, who argue that, not only the lack of original righteousness, but also the positive corruption of our nature, is a penal infliction.[73] The problem is exacerbated by the fact that Reformed theologians have tended to be creationists, holding that each soul originates in an immediate and direct creative act of God. It is one thing to argue that God creates the soul without original righteousness: the suggestion that he creates it corrupt takes us to another level. Quite apart from the moral issues it raises, it faces a serious logical problem. As Robert Dabney points out,[74] it represents all humans as having, for a moment at least, an independent personal existence in innocence until they are "depraved" by an act of God in retribution for the imputed guilt of Adam's sin. But there can be no such moment. We are *conceived* in guiltiness *and* sin: sinful from our first beginning (Ps. 51:5). We have no existence, even theoretically, except as depraved beings, and we come under no condemnation except as depraved beings.

But if we cannot account for "the corruption of our whole nature" as a direct penal infliction on account of Adam's sin, how then can we account for it? One way forward is suggested by a statement used by the Shorter Catechism to define the "misery" of man's fallen condition: "All mankind by their fall lost communion with God."[75] This defines man's loss in personal rather than abstract terms, and this loss of personal fellowship with God (communion with the Holy Spirit) explains, in turn, the corruption of our nature. Yet the loss of our communion with God was not a separate, subsequent experience, external to the first act of disobedience. The very act itself (and indeed the unbelief that was its prelude) grieved the Holy Spirit. It was tantamount, indeed, to a repudiation of him, and in that moment all is lost, not only to Adam but to his posterity. In Adam's choice, the race ceased to be *pneumatikos* and became *psuchikos* (1 Cor. 2:14–15). Such are we born, and such we remain until grace re-creates us.

We must bear in mind too the analogy between our experience of condemnation and our experience of justification. We are justified by the imputation to us of the righteousness of another, Jesus Christ, but this righteousness is imputed to us only in union with him, and in union with him we are not only

72. See Polanus, *Syntagma Theologiae Christianae* (Hanover: 1624), Lib. VI, Caput III.
73. See Turretin, *Institutes*, 1:622; Charles Hodge, *Systematic Theology*, vol. 2 (Edinburgh: Nelson, 1872), 193.
74. Robert L. Dabney, *Discussions: Evangelical and Theological*, vol. 1 (1890; repr., London: Banner of Truth Trust, 1967), 256.
75. Westminster Shorter Catechism, Answer 19.

justified, but also transformed. We are "made alive" together with Christ (Eph. 2:5), and although we are not justified on the basis of this renewal, no one is justified who is not also renewed; nor is the renewal subsequent to the justification. They are simultaneous, which is simply to say that in Christ we experience a *duplex gratia*, including both justification and sanctification.[76] Everyone who is in Christ is right with God, and everyone who is in Christ is a new creation.

The same sort of debate as to mediate or immediate as was raised in connection with the imputation of Adam's sin could also be raised, then, in connection with the imputation of Christ's righteousness. Is the renewal subsequent to the imputation? Is regeneration the reward of the imputation? Are we first put right with God and then given new hearts? The New Testament admits of no such sequence. We are united to Christ by faith, and in the moment of that union we are both justified and sanctified (definitively).[77] To state it provocatively: though we are not justified because we are saints, no one is justified who is not also a saint. By the same token, no one is condemned who is not also depraved.

Creationism and Traducianism

All Christians, Pelagians excepted, have believed that original sin is propagated by natural generation. Granted, however, that the seat of sin is the soul, questions arise: How does the soul originate? Is each soul directly created by God? Or is the soul propagated by procreation?

Creationism is not simply the idea that in some general sense God created souls, but the more specific idea that each individual soul is created separately from the body, ex nihilo, by a direct and immediate act of God, and then "infused" into the body.[78] This has been the prevailing view among Reformed theologians, but there have been notable exceptions, particularly Shedd, a powerful advocate of traducianism. Shedd argued that in the case of humans, as in the case of all other species, the total individual is propagated. The soul, no less than the body, is passed down from the parents through the act of procreation.[79]

Both theories have been deployed to explain original sin. According to creationists, as we have seen from Ursinus, when God creates the soul he withholds

---

76. See Paul Helm, *Calvin at the Centre* (Oxford: Oxford University Press, 2010), 196–226.
77. See John Murray, "Definitive Sanctification," in *Collective Writings of John Murray*, vol. 2 (Edinburgh: Banner of Truth, 1977), 277–84.
78. Turretin, *Institutes*, 1:477–82.
79. Shedd, *Dogmatic Theology*, 2:75–81.

original righteousness, and he does so as a punishment for the guilt we inherit due to Adam's sin. Otherwise, argues Turretin, the fact that all humans are corrupt is inexplicable and raises, indeed, serious questions about the justice of God. The only reason we can assign for the fact that God creates human souls destitute of original righteousness is "the secret judgement of God by which he wills to smite the children of Adam on account of the sin of the parent." The privation of original righteousness is a punishment for the first transgression.[80]

Our moral sense recoils from this. Would anyone *preach* it? But there is also a serious theological issue. Though body and soul may be distinguished, a human being is a psychosomatic unity, a fact that is brought out clearly in the story of creation. When God breathed into Adam's nostrils, he *became* a "living soul" (*nephesh hayyim*, Gen. 2:7). This implies that rather than "having" a soul, a person "is" a soul. Creationists (for example, Turretin) tried to press this text into the service of their own theory, arguing that it points to the separate creation of body and soul: first, God forms Adam's body from the dust of the ground, and then into this body, God breathes a soul. This became the paradigm for creationism,[81] but, as Calvin pointed out in no uncertain terms, "Moses intended nothing more than to explain the animating of the clayey figure, whereby it came to pass that man began to live."[82]

Shedd's traducianism must be distinguished from his realism (though they are closely linked in his own thinking). It is possible to hold that each soul is passed down from the parents through procreation without having to hold that each soul is, literally, a detached particle of the original soul created by God. Apart from offering a simple explanation for original sin as transmitted by reproduction, the great strength of traducianism lies precisely where creationism is weakest: in its stress on the psychosomatic unity of humans. The whole person is procreated.

Conclusion

Reformed theologians were unanimous in their belief in the doctrine of original sin, accepting without hesitation the Augustinian doctrine that all human beings are born with a propensity to sin and invariably act out that propensity in their daily lives. Every human being is by nature incapable of loving God as

80. Turretin, *Institutes*, 1:622.
81. Ibid., 478.
82. Calvin, *Commentary on Genesis*, 1:112.

God commands and, apart from the new birth, equally incapable of repenting of sin or believing in Christ.

Reformed theologians were also unanimous, however, that the responsibility for original sin could not be thrown back on the Creator. On the contrary, our first parents, the historical Adam and Eve, had been made in the image of God and were morally and spiritually perfect. Human depravity, then, was rooted not in creation but in a fall. Adam and Eve had engaged in a voluntary act of defiance, and this had calamitous consequences for their descendants, who share in the guilt of that first sin and inherit a nature corrupted by that primal disobedience.

But this consensus still left room for in-house discussions and disagreements. Why, for example, should the sin of Adam involve all his offspring in guilt? Was this no more than a sovereign divine arrangement? Or was it justified by the biological connection, Adam and Eve being "the root of all mankind"? Or was it, yet again, a matter of federal headship, the first Adam, like the last, acting as representative of the race? Each view was represented within Reformed orthodoxy.

Then there was the question of the relation between imputed guilt and inherited depravity. Is the depravity penal: a punishment for the guilt of that first sin? Or is it true that there is no guilt separate from the depravity: in other words, no one is guilty who is not also depraved?

And what of the origin of the soul? The majority argued that each soul was directly and immediately created by God. But there were some who argued strenuously that the soul was procreated, a position that may be said to gain some support from modern genetics.

Such discussions will, no doubt, continue, though with little hope of final agreement. The questions are too esoteric and the data too limited. And in any case the issues that troubled Turretin are now overshadowed by the challenges posed to the story of the fall by both biblical criticism and modern anthropology—challenges that, though scornful of the very notion of "sin," have the effect, paradoxically, of making sin an aboriginal and necessary fact of human nature.

If the doctrine of original sin is as important to the Christian plan of salvation as our theological forebears deemed it, we must address these contemporary challenges as a matter of urgency.

7

"But a Heathen Still"

The Doctrine of Original Sin in Wesleyan Theology

Thomas H. McCall

There is widespread confusion—among both the detractors and defenders of Wesleyan theology—about the doctrine of original sin in historic Wesleyanism. Don't Wesleyan theologians deny "total depravity"? Don't they believe in "free will" rather than enslavement to sin? Are they not "Semi-Pelagians" (if not outright Pelagians) rather than "Augustinians"? *What* doctrine of original sin? Don't Wesleyans just *deny* original sin? The short answer to such questions is simply no, but a full response is much more complicated. In this chapter, I seek to offer a modest overview of the formulations of the doctrine of original sin in historic Wesleyan theology, and I offer a few brief suggestions for the way forward.

Original Sin in the Wesleyan Tradition

In his oft-cited and influential account of the theological evolution in Wesleyan theology, Robert E. Chiles tells a tale of movement away from an emphasis on grace and toward an emphasis on freedom of the will.[1] While the story he tells needs nuance and should not lead us to ignore important exceptions to this tendency, it is still helpful in many ways.[2] A look at the theologies of representative and influential theologians is instructive here.

John Wesley and the Doctrine of Original Sin in Early Methodism

John Wesley was convinced of the universality and power of sin. Everyone, he insists, is a sinner, and the power of sin is so strong that it enslaves those under its dominion—humanity is "filled with all manner of evil," "wholly fallen," and "totally corrupted."[3] Students of Wesleyan theology are sometimes surprised to find (what is arguably) John Wesley's most extensive and densest treatise is on the doctrine of original sin. They are often even more surprised by what he says in this treatise. Here Wesley challenges the influential arguments of John Taylor's *The Scripture-Doctrine of Original Sin, Exposed to a Free and Candid Examination*. As Thomas C. Oden notes, Wesley was convinced that "Taylor was working out of a deistic theism, a Pelagian anthropology, a reductionist Christology, a works-righteousness ethic, and a universalist eschatology, all of which were undermining substantive Christian teaching."[4] Wesley argues for the traditional doctrine from human history and experience, from reason, and (ultimately) from Scripture. As Oden points out, "We see him first working with historical arguments, then experiential and sociological arguments, and finally with patristic and scriptural arguments."[5] Wesley sees sin everywhere in human history; it is recorded in both sacred texts (here Wesley's key text is Gen. 6:5) and secular texts of history. He also

1. Robert E. Chiles, *Theological Transition in American Methodism: 1790–1935* (New York: Abingdon, 1965).

2. We should also remember to locate the story of American Methodist theology within the broader context of American intellectual (and especially theological) history. Within this broader story we see that parallel changes were taking place in other theological traditions as well. See, e.g., Mark A. Noll, *America's God: From Jonathan Edwards to Abraham Lincoln* (Oxford: Oxford University Press, 2002) and E. Brooks Holifield, *Theology in America: Christian Thought from the Age of the Puritans to the Civil War* (New Haven: Yale University Press, 2003).

3. E.g., "Original Sin," in *Wesley's 52 Standard Sermons* (Salem, OH: Schmul Publishing, 1988), 456. This impacts freedom of the will: "Natural free-will, in the present state of mankind, I do not understand: I only assert, that there is a measure of free-will supernaturally restored to every man, together with that supernatural light which 'enlightens every man that cometh into the world,'" John Wesley, "Predestination Calmly Considered," in *The Works of John Wesley*, vol. 10 (Grand Rapids: Zondervan, n.d.), 229–30.

4. Thomas C. Oden, *John Wesley's Scriptural Christianity: A Plain Exposition of His Teaching on Christian Doctrine* (Grand Rapids: Zondervan, 1994), 159. Oden cites Wesley: in a letter to Augustus Toplady (December 9, 1758), Wesley expressed his deep concern about Taylor, "I verily believe no single person since Mahomet has given such a wound to Christianity as Dr. Taylor."

5. Ibid., 160.

points to the presence and perversity of sin everywhere in human cultures; warfare and slavery here stand out as powerful case studies in the reality and societal effects of sin. He argues that the situation is no better (or at least not appreciably better) in theistic cultures than elsewhere, and he is at pains to highlight the obvious and horrific results of sin within Western and especially Protestant cultures. His basic point, as Oden puts it, is this: "Sin is everywhere an empirical fact, even where civilized virtues attempt to shine brightest. . . . There is nowhere to look in human history where one will not find a history of injustice, a dismal account of the social and interpersonal transmission of sin and misery."[6] When it comes to Scripture, Wesley argues that the doctrine of original sin is attested to across the pages of both the Old and the New Testaments (rather than only in Rom. 5:12–21).

When considering the question of our relation to Adam, Wesley defends the very ground under assault by Taylor. More specifically—and perhaps more surprisingly to those who have only heard Wesley's views peddled second- or thirdhand—Wesley defends the federalism of the Westminster Catechism: "the covenant being made with Adam as a public person, not for himself only, but for his posterity, all mankind descending from him by ordinary generation, sinned with him, and fell with him, in that first transgression."[7] His primary reason for holding to federalism is christological. Scripture draws a clear parallel between Adam and Christ, and the biblical account clearly depicts Christ as representative. "But Adam was a type or figure of Christ; therefore, he was also, in some sense, our representative; in consequence of which, 'all died' in him, as 'in Christ all shall be made alive.'"[8] So although "neither representative, nor federal head, are scriptural terms" (and thus not strictly necessary), yet the main lines of the federal position are biblically correct.[9] At the same time, it is important to remember that Wesley himself held to a doctrine of prevenient grace, and he takes the parallel between the two "federal heads" to support a doctrine of universal atonement: "Christ was the representative of mankind, when God 'laid on him the iniquities of us all, and he was wounded for our transgressions.'"[10]

Wesley's legacy, however, is not completely unambiguous. As American Methodism was being organized (at the famous "Christmas Conference" of

6. Ibid., 165.
7. John Wesley says that although he has never subscribed to the Westminster Larger Catechism, he thinks that "it is in the main a very excellent composition, which I therefore shall cheerfully endeavor to defend, so far as I conceive it is grounded on clear Scripture." "The Doctrine of Original Sin," in *The Works of John Wesley*, vol. 9 (Grand Rapids: Zondervan, n.d.), 261–62.
8. Ibid., 332.
9. Ibid.
10. Ibid.

1784), Wesley provided a slightly abridged version of the Anglican Articles of Religion for adoption and use by American Methodists. Article VII (which corresponds to Article IX of the Anglican Articles) removes the affirmation of guilt and corresponding damnation for original sin. As we shall see, some later theologians in the Wesleyan tradition took such an omission as nothing less than an outright rejection of original guilt, with Daniel Whedon concluding that "Wesley rejects the doctrine of our personal desert of damnation . . . for the very good reason that it contradicts our intuitive sense of right and justice. That rejection removes a contradiction to the moral sense and to common sense from theology."[11] In other words, the mature Wesley has now come to reject his former and erroneous affirmation of the guilt of original sin.[12]

But this is not the only possible understanding of the changes in the wording of the Articles. For note that Wesley never *denies* his earlier position. And, interestingly, Article II *retains* the affirmation that Christ is a sacrifice "for original guilt" in addition to "actual sins."[13] Some interpreters have taken this difference to indicate a deep inconsistency, and some Wesleyan theologians have decided that the best way to iron out the inconsistency is to simply reject any notion of original guilt. But this is not the only way to understand the Articles. One explanation for the apparent discrepancy is simply this: Wesley continues to believe in the reality of original guilt (thus the statement in Article II); in its "natural" state of fallenness, all humankind is guilty of original sin. But Wesley also believes that Christ's work brings prevenient grace to all (thus the statement in Article II), and he wants to avoid the notion that any infant is actually damned by the guilt of original sin *alone* (thus Article VII).

Despite any ambiguity in the legacy left by Wesley for the American heirs of Methodism, however, his own views of original sin remain clear:

> Is man by nature filled with all manner of evil? Is he void of all good? Is he wholly fallen? Is his soul totally corrupted? Or, to come back to the text, is "every imagination of the thoughts of his heart evil continually?" Allow this, and you are so far a Christian. Deny it, and you are but a heathen still.[14]

11. Daniel D. Whedon, "Quarterly Book-Table," *Methodist Quarterly Review* (1882), 365. Whedon rejects the orginal (Anglican) article both "for the clumsiness of its form and the heresy of its doctrine."

12. Randy L. Maddox understands this to be an important shift from "the middle Wesley" to his more mature perspective, *Responsible Grace: John Wesley's Practical Theology* (Nashville: Abingdon, 1994), 75. Whedon similarly dismisses it as "written early in his life" ("Quarterly Book-Table," 365).

13. As is noted by John Miley, *Systematic Theology*, vol. 1 (New York: Methodist Book Concern, 1892), 525.

14. "Original Sin," 456. See the discussion in Kenneth J. Collins, *The Scripture Way of Salvation: The Heart of John Wesley's Theology* (Nashville: Abingdon, 1997), 37.

As Barry E. Bryant points out, "In a well-known letter to John Newton dated 14 May 1765, Wesley indicated there was not a 'hairs-breadth' separating him from Calvin" with respect to hamartiology.[15] For Wesley, any denial of the full-blown doctrine of original sin "saps the very foundation of all revealed religion."[16] On the contrary, a full recognition of the deprivation and depravation of sin is made possible—and indeed is required—by the gospel.

The Early Nineteenth Century

The theological successors of Wesley in general carry his concerns and commitments forward into the nineteenth century. Richard Watson, whose *Theological Institutes* (1823–29) was referred to by Henry C. Sheldon as "the unrivaled textbook of American Methodism" for "a considerable period" of time and is generally considered formative for early Wesleyan theology, forcibly rejects, on one hand, the optimism, and, on the other hand, the determinism of much post-Enlightenment thought.[17] He argues that Adam and Eve were historical people, and he is convinced that the fall was a historical occasion. These are, he insists, "*facts*."[18] The fact of sin is plain to see, and it can be observed in human history, in Holy Scripture (both the Old and New Testaments), and human experience.[19] Together these confirm the following facts: the general corruption of manners in all times and countries, the strength of the tendency toward evil, the very early appearance of vice within children, the conscience that convicts of evil affections and actions, and the general resistance to virtue in the human heart.[20] Such incontrovertible facts, insists Watson, can only be accounted for "by the Scriptural account of the natural and hereditary corruption of the human race, commonly called original sin."[21] Watson thus rejects not only Pelagianism but also the "Semi-Pelagianism" that he finds within some quarters of Anglicanism.[22] Instead he offers a resounding affirmation of "total depravity," for "the true Arminian, as fully as the Calvinistic, admits the doctrine of total depravity of human nature in consequence

---

15. Barry E. Bryant, "Original Sin," in *The Oxford Handbook of Methodist Studies*, ed. William J. Abraham and James E. Kirby (Oxford: Oxford University Press, 2009), 534.

16. Wesley, "Original Sin," 194.

17. Henry C. Sheldon, "Changes in Theology among American Methodists," *American Journal of Theology* 10 (1906): 32.

18. Richard Watson, *Theological Institutes: Or, a View of the Evidences, Doctrines, Morals, and Institutions of Christianity*, vol. 2 (New York: N. Bangs and J. Emory, 1826), 179.

19. Ibid., 226–39.

20. Ibid., 239.

21. Ibid., 243.

22. Ibid., 207.

of the fall of his parents; and is indeed enabled to carry through his system with greater consistency than the Calvinist himself."[23]

But what of our relation to Adam? Watson asks an important question: is Adam "to be considered as a mere individual, the consequences of whose misconduct terminated in himself, or no otherwise affected his posterity than incidentally, as the misconduct of an ordinary parent may affect the circumstances of his children; or whether he is to be regarded as a *public man,* the *head* and *representative* of the human race, who, in consequence of his fall, have fallen with him, and received direct hurt and injury in the very constitution of their bodies, and the moral state of their minds."[24] Watson is convinced that the answer to this question is "so explicit on this point, that all the attempts to evade it have been in vain": the proper understanding of Romans 5 demands the federalist position.[25] At the same time, he is careful to warn against what he sees as possible misunderstandings of federalism. Federalism must not, he insists, be understood as if Adam-plus-progeny are "one moral person"—he takes this to undercut the moral responsibility of distinct individuals and thus to be as problematic as realism. On the other hand, he is wary of both corruption-only and mediate views.[26] His solution, then, is to maintain federalism—but at the same time to insist that it be properly understood as referring to "the legal result" of Adam's evil actions.[27] Ever the apologist, Watson is concerned to demonstrate the explanatory power of the doctrine of original sin; for all of the challenges that it presents, it also helps make sense of a vast tract of human experience that would be utterly opaque without it.[28] And ever the theologian, he is exercised to demonstrate that the range of God's gracious work in Christ does not fall short of the range of Adam's sin: where sin abounded, grace abounded all the more, and prevenient grace has been bestowed upon all humanity in order to bring all humanity to justification.[29]

Thomas N. Ralston echoes much of this in his *Elements of Divinity* (1847). He insists that the record of the fall should be interpreted "literally" (by which he means that Adam and Eve were real persons with a real history).[30] The ef-

---

23. Ibid., 210. As he spells it out, the real difference between Calvinism and Arminianism concerns the extent and resistibility of grace—not sin.

24. Ibid., 215.

25. Ibid.

26. Ibid., 216.

27. Ibid., 218.

28. Ibid., 243.

29. Ibid., 222–25.

30. Thomas N. Ralston, *Elements of Divinity: A Concise and Comprehensive View of Bible Theology; Comprising the Doctrines, Evidences, Morals, and Institutions of Christianity; with Appropriate Questions Appended to Each Chapter* (New York: Abingdon, 1847), 104–5.

fects of the fall, he insists, are utterly disastrous: "where all had been holiness and love, every evil principle reigned in triumph—unbelief was there; treason, rebellion, enmity, pride, lust, murder—in a word, the root of every evil passion which Satan could instigate, or which man has ever felt, was contained in the principle which actuated man in the first transgression."[31] As the penalty for sin, the "death" that came upon all humanity is "temporal, spiritual, and eternal."[32]

Ralston rejects Pelagianism, Socinianism, and the views of Taylor and Whitby; he defends the confessional statement that "all mankind are by nature so depraved as to be totally destitute of spiritual good, and inclined only to evil continually. . . . [T]hus man is very far gone from original righteousness, and of his own nature inclined to evil, and that continually."[33] He endorses the official (Methodist, but drawn directly from the Anglican Articles) statement that "the condition of man after the fall of Adam is such that he cannot turn and prepare himself, by his own natural strength and works, to faith and calling upon God; wherefore we have no power to do good works, pleasant and acceptable to God, without the grace of God by Christ preventing us, that we may have a good will, and working with us when we have that good will."[34] Depravity is, then, rightly said to be "total."[35] He argues for this conclusion primarily from the "direct declaration of Scripture," but he also says that it is "confirmed by experience and observation."[36]

Ralston gives consideration to "the peculiar relation sustained by Adam to his posterity in the transaction of the Fall," and here he rejects both Pelagianism and realism in favor of what he holds to be the "most rational and scriptural view": this is the view that Adam "was the federal head and proper legal representative of his posterity, insomuch that they fell in him as truly, in view of the law, as he fell himself; and that the consequences of the first sin are visited upon them, as a penal infliction, for the guilt of Adam imputed to them."[37] Adam was the "federal head and public representative" of humanity.[38]

Luther Lee echoes many of these same themes. In his *Elements of Theology* (1853), he insists upon the actual historicity of the first humans and of their first sin.[39] He holds to the "universal corruption of human nature," and he

31. Ibid., 111.
32. Ibid., 114–19.
33. Ibid., 123–25.
34. Ibid., 125.
35. Ibid.
36. Ibid., 130–38.
37. Ibid., 120.
38. Ibid., 123, 127.
39. Luther Lee, *Elements of Theology: Or An Exposition of the Divine Origin, Doctrines, Morals, and Institutions of Christianity* (Syracuse: A. W. Hall, 1853), 111–14.

maintains that this depravity is so intense that the image of God is lost: "it would be absurd to suppose that the image of God, consisting in righteousness and true holiness, could be possessed by man, and he be a sinner at the same time, guilty before God, and a subject of divine punishment."[40] With respect to original sin, Lee believes that Scripture represents "*all men* as being liable to some sort of divine malediction, in consequence of Adam's sin."[41] But just how are all people liable for the sin of Adam? Here Lee offers elements of two different answers. On one hand, he endorses a federalist view; he says that "as condemnation unto death" came upon all people "before they were guilty of personal sin, and does now come upon infants, who are incapable of committing sin, it follows that this want of conformity to the law of God is an inherent defect in human nature"—one that was "caused by the sin of the first man, the Father and federal head of the human family."[42] But he asks further: "how were many made sinners by the offense of the one?" His answer moves away from federalism and toward a mediate view: "the only consistent answer to this question" is that "a corrupt state of human nature was produced by the sin of the first man, and inherited from him, by all men." Moreover, this corruption "leads to actual transgression," and "there is no other sense in which it may consistently be said, that 'by the offense of the one, many were made sinners.'"[43] So while Lee initially appears to endorse federalism, in the end he adopts a mediate view: we are guilty for the corruption we have as well as for what we do with it.

Lee offers no attempts to candy-coat the doctrine of sin. Instead, he tries to display its horror. But even when discussing sin, his hope is set upon grace:

> While the life of the Christian is a warfare, a warfare not with the world and satan only, but with the affections and passions which are attributes of his own soul, a warfare with the elements of his nature, he will carry with him an ever present evidence of the corruption of human nature; an evidence that will last until the victory is complete, and he finds himself wholly redeemed from the ruins of the fall.[44]

Samuel Wakefield follows a pattern that is similar in many respects. He insists upon the historical reality of Adam and Eve, and he is convinced that

40. Ibid., 115.
41. Ibid., 117, emphasis in original.
42. Ibid., 117–18.
43. Ibid., 118.
44. Ibid., 124.

the fall is a "matter of real history."[45] Rejecting the views of ancient Pelagians and modern Socinians alike, Wakefield insists that "original sin standeth not in the following of Adam, as the Pelagians do vainly talk, but it is the corruption of the nature of every man, that naturally is engendered of the offspring of Adam, whereby man is far gone from original righteousness, and of his own nature inclined to sin, and that continually."[46] He insists upon total depravity: we are depraved in every part, by nature we are "destitute of any thing that is morally good" and "naturally inclined to do evil."[47] He agrees fully with the position of the "Confession of Faith" of the "Church of Scotland," for that statement is a "clear and scriptural view of the doctrine of human depravity."[48] Indeed, he says, most Reformed theologians confuse "the Arminian doctrine" with the "Semi-Pelagian notions of Dr. Whitby," and the result is nothing short of "palpable misrepresentation" of genuine Arminianism.[49]

When he turns his attention to original sin, Wakefield rejects the mediate view as not going the "length of Scripture."[50] He also rejects the realist view on the grounds that it cannot account for moral responsibility, as it is "inconsistent with that individual agency which enters into the very notion of an accountable being, while it destroys the distinction between original and actual sin."[51] Wakefield defends the federal view as the one "we believe to be in accordance with the Scriptures": "the *imputation* of Adam's sin to his posterity is confined to its legal results."[52] He understands the view that Adam is the "legal head and representative of the human race" to be evidently in contrast with "the public or federal character" of Christ.[53] Wakefield compares this account to that of a man who has committed treason and "has thereby lost his estate, [and whose] crime is so imputed to his children that they, with him, are made to suffer the penalty of his offense."[54] Thus Adam's progeny, though federally related to him, are not *personally* guilty for what Adam has done. Adam's children cannot be personally guilty, for "they had

45. Samuel Wakefield, *A Complete System of Christian Theology: Or, a Concise, Comprehensive, and Systematic View of the Evidences, Doctrines, Morals, and Institutions of Christianity* (Cincinnati: Cranston and Stowe, 1858), 282.
46. Ibid., 296–97.
47. Ibid., 298.
48. Ibid., 299.
49. Ibid.
50. Ibid., 293.
51. Ibid.
52. Ibid.
53. Ibid., 292.
54. Ibid., 293.

no individual or personal existence at the time of the fall." God is omniscient and "looks upon things as they really are, [thus] he cannot regard them as being personally and actually guilty of Adam's sin." Yet Wakefield continues to insist that "it is nonetheless true, however, that they may be justly liable to all its legal consequences."[55] Adam's progeny thus are guilty, but this guilt is best understood as "liability to punishment."[56]

Wakefield believes in the universality and totality of human depravity; all are sinners, and none can even so much as come to awareness of their sin and need apart from grace. But just as the reign of sin is universal, so also, Wakefield argues, is the extent of grace: where sin abounded, grace abounded all the more. Arguing from Romans 5:18, he concludes that the "sin of Adam and the merits of Christ are pronounced to be co-extensive, the words applied to both being precisely the same."[57] This does not mean that all indeed are saved (Wakefield is no universalist), but it does mean that the prevenient grace that is necessary for salvation is made available to all by the work of Christ.[58]

The Later Nineteenth Century

By the latter part of the nineteenth century, however, we see some important shifts. Some of these are quite subtle; others are not subtle at all. Whedon's response to Edwardsian metaphysics of freedom and responsibility exercises great influence, and the freedom of the will becomes more and more prominent in the ensuing discussions.[59]

Thomas O. Summers (1888) articulates the Methodist understanding of original sin, and he explicitly defends Article VII from charges of Pelagianism and Semi-Pelagianism.[60] He largely follows Whedon's emphases,[61] but at the same time he is very concerned that various forms of "Calvinism" actually destroy the doctrine of sin. As he sees things, the determinism of traditional

55. Ibid., 300.
56. Ibid., 293.
57. Ibid., 295.
58. This also gives Wakefield the ability to argue for the salvation of infants—not on account of some supposed purity or meritorious innocence but purely on account of the fact that they have not resisted the grace that brings eternal life (see ibid., 295–96).
59. Daniel R. Whedon, *The Freedom of the Will as a Basis of Human Responsibility and Divine Government, Elucidated and Maintained in its Issue with the Necessitarian Theories of Hobbes, Edwards, the Princeton Essayists, and Other Leading Advocates* (New York: Carlton and Lanahan, 1864).
60. E.g., Thomas O. Summers, *Systematic Theology: A Complete Body of Wesleyan Arminian Divinity Consisting of Lectures on the Twenty-five Articles of Religion*, vol. 2 (Nashville: Publishing House of the Methodist Episcopal Church, South, 1888), 34–35, 62–63.
61. E.g., ibid., 38.

Calvinism (as expressed by Edwards, Hodge, and Shedd) results in the loss of moral responsibility, while the "New Divinity" waters down the biblical and traditional doctrine of sin. His focus may fairly be said to be "Christocentric," for he places heavy emphasis on the reality of Christ as the "Second Adam." Interestingly, he interprets the apparent discrepancy between Article II (which affirms Christ's sacrifice as efficacious for the guilt of original sin) and Article VII (which deletes the Anglican affirmation of original guilt) by insisting that there is no one who is damned *only* for original sin (and infants who perish are not damned at all) not because of any innate human goodness but because of the work of Christ.[62] He very clearly endorses a "mediate" account of original guilt.[63]

William Burt Pope is convinced that the doctrine of sin is vitally connected to the full range of theological loci: it is "interwoven with all the subsequent stages of theology," and "upon it is based the necessity, the possibility, the universality of the Atonement."[64] He wholeheartedly affirms the Methodist "acceptance" of the Anglican Article: "Original sin standeth not in the following of Adam (as the Pelagians do vainly talk); but it is the fault and corruption of the nature of every man, that naturally is engendered of the offspring of Adam; whereby man is very far gone from Original Righteousness, and is of his own nature inclined to evil, so that the flesh lusteth always contrary to the Spirit; and therefore in every person born into this world, it deserveth God's wrath and damnation. And this infection of nature doth remain, yea in them that are regenerated."[65]

Pope is aware of what he takes to be important literary features and symbolic elements in the Genesis account, and he thinks that recognition of such elements is important for a proper interpretation of the text. At the same time, however, he rejects a *purely* or *merely* symbolic reading of the text, and he does so on the grounds of "the clear and unclouded testimony of later Scripture" as well as the Genesis text itself.[66] As he puts it, "the purely historical character of the narrative may be maintained in perfect consistency with a full acknowledgment of the large element of symbolism in it."[67] Thus "the narrative is true, and every circumstance in it is real."[68] Adam and Eve were real people and the original sinners.

62. Ibid., 43–44.
63. E.g., ibid., 46.
64. William Burt Pope, *A Compendium of Christian Theology: Being Analytical Outlines of a Course of Theological Study, Biblical, Dogmatic, Historical*, vol. 2, 2nd ed. (New York: Hunt and Eaton, 1889), 10, 63.
65. Ibid., 80.
66. Ibid., 10.
67. Ibid.
68. Ibid.

The effect of the fall upon humanity is seen by Pope as "the universal diffusion of death as a condemnation, and of a bias of human nature towards evil."[69] This is, Pope asserts, best termed "Original Sin." Through Adam's sin, humans are both regarded as sinners and also are "made sinners" through "the inheritance of a nature of itself inclined only to evil."[70]

Pope says that the "transmission of the penalty is both direct and indirect," and he says that all humanity is "in some sense one with Adam."[71] But just *how* is original sin transmitted? What is our relation to Adam? What is the "in some sense"? While he makes statements that would seem to fit well with a mediate view (e.g., he affirms hereditary condemnation but denies that anyone other than Adam is really guilty for Adam's sinful action, and he insists that depravity and condemnation can never be separated), Pope opts for the federalist view over mediate or realist views.[72] While he denies any "so-called covenant of works," Pope resolutely affirms that Adam is the representative or legal head of humanity.[73] Original sin, he insists, "sprang from the federal constitution of the race: one in the unity of the unlimited many."[74] And he exults in the federal headship of Christ over humanity. The "many are one in the recovery as well as in sin," and Paul "invariably asserts the universality of the benefit of grace, so far as concerns the intention of God."[75] The closest we ever come to a theodicy, according to Pope, is found in the "free gift of the Second Adam."[76]

The situation changes—and does so quite drastically in some ways—with the work of John Miley.[77] Miley maintains that there were indeed original sinners: "there was a temptation and fall of primitive man, with a consequent fall of the race."[78] He insists that a doctrine of original sin is true, and he is convinced of the universal sinfulness and guiltiness of humanity.[79] But Miley also points out that the older doctrinal formulas "are human creations, and while entitled to most respectful consideration, must be open to questioning respecting the doctrines for which they stand."[80]

---

69. Ibid., 47.
70. Ibid., 48.
71. Ibid.
72. E.g., ibid., 48, 54.
73. Ibid., 13.
74. Ibid., 62.
75. Ibid., 62–63.
76. Ibid., 62. Pope thinks that we cannot push beyond this: "As to the why of this federal constitution, and the why of evil generally in the dark background, there is no solution given to man, because it is not possible to the creature" (63).
77. Miley is joined in his denial of original guilt by Randolph Sinks Foster, e.g., *Sin*, vol. 6 of *Studies in Theology* (New York: Eaton and Mains, 1899), 140–82.
78. Miley, *Systematic Theology*, 1:429.
79. Ibid., 446–61.
80. Ibid., 441.

When Miley turns his attention to the common accounts of original sin, he finds them deeply problematic. He notes that Calvinist theologians tend to promote both federalism and realism. The fact that theologians sometimes divide into the two camps, disagreeing vehemently with one another, shows that neither position is unassailable. On the other hand, Miley argues that the views are mutually exclusive, and he exclaims that those theologians who attempt to hold to both simply cannot have it both ways: "it is unscientific, mere jumbling, indeed, to hold both modes, for they are in opposition and reciprocally exclusive."[81]

Miley raises several sharp criticisms of realism. He notes that although it intends to maintain both the unity of the human race and personal moral responsibility for sin, it is able to do neither. In the first place, he claims, realism is outmoded and no longer tenable metaphysically. "Realism," he says, "is a mere assumption," one that "has long been replaced with conceptualism."[82] So while full-blown nominalism is not exactly correct either, the metaphysics demanded by realism simply is not defensible. "There are no such existences. Hence, there is no generic human nature."[83] Even if there were such a thing as a generic human nature, however, it could not commit sin—it would not be concrete enough to do so. "This generic nature, simply as such, could not sin. Adam could sin only in his personal agency, and the whole guilt of his sin was his own personal guilt."[84] Furthermore, argues Miley, the realist suggestion goes against the fact that Scripture portrays *Adam*—an individual human person—as the first sinner.[85] It is, for Miley, simply impossible for the one to individuate into the many.[86] Moreover, Miley objects, if we are morally responsible for the *first* of Adam's deeds by virtue of our presence in him, then it seems reasonable to suppose that we would be morally responsible for *all* the sins not only of Adam but indeed of all our ancestors.[87] From these arguments, Miley concludes that realism is untenable as a theory of original sin. For "guilt is a purely personal fact, and has no ground in mere nature. The guilt of Adam's sin was purely personal to himself, and could no more

81. Ibid., 467.
82. Ibid., 479.
83. Ibid.
84. Ibid., 485.
85. Ibid., 476.
86. Ibid., 480–81. Miley illustrates the problem by recourse to the illustration of a statue and the metal of which it is constituted. Whether or not Miley's objection might be bothersome to the proponent of relative identity is the subject of further exploration—and I leave it at that. On the theory of relative identity, see Harold Noonan, "Relative Identity," in *A Companion to Philosophy of Language*, ed. Bob Hale and Crispin Wright (Oxford: Blackwell, 1999), 634–52.
87. Miley, *Systematic Theology*, 481–84.

become the guilt of a generic nature in him than the hand of a murderer could share in the guilt of his crime."[88]

As Miley sees things, federalism fares no better. He is aware that many proponents of federalism draw a direct connection with the representative work of Christ, and Miley tackles this argument head-on. He raises two questions: "Is the assumed imputation of the righteousness of Christ a fact? And, if a fact, would it warrant the inference respecting the imputation of Adam's sin?"[89] His answer to the first question—and here again we see a marked departure from his theological forbears—is entirely negative. "There is, in truth, no such imputation of the righteousness of Christ as this theory maintains, and hence the argument attempted upon its assumption is utterly groundless."[90] But even if there were such an imputation of Christ's righteousness, Miley still insists that it is so different from the imputation of Adam's sin as to remove any grounds for arguments in favor of federalism. There is, he says, "a profound difference between the immediate imputation of sin as a ground of punishment and the immediate imputation of righteousness as a ground of reward," for "the representative case can say much for the latter as an outflowing of the divine grace and love; but what can it say for the former? Here no appeal can be made to the divine love. Nor can there be any appeal to the divine justice."[91] Miley quotes Shedd as saying that "the doctrine of a gratuitous justification is intelligible and rational; but the doctrine of a gratuitous damnation is unintelligible and absurd."[92] Not surprisingly, Miley concludes that the arguments for federalism are far from decisive.

Miley denies that the very idea of federal headship is biblical; the purported biblical basis for it vanishes upon closer inspection, and, since it so obviously conflicts with the moral responsibility that is unmistakably clear in Scripture, then federalism must be judged to be thoroughly *unbiblical*.[93] Even worse, he says, it posits a legal fiction:

> The immediate imputation of sin is by definition simply the accounting to all men the guilt of a sin which is confessedly not their own. They had no part in the commission of that sin. The imputed sin has no ground of demerit in them. In a merely putative mode, and without any desert in themselves, all men are accounted amenable to divine punishment.[94]

88. Ibid., 488.
89. Ibid., 500.
90. Ibid.
91. Ibid.
92. Ibid.
93. Ibid., 501–2.
94. Ibid., 504.

Federalism is, then, a fictitious and indeed dangerous doctrine of original sin for Miley, and such considerations bring him to the conclusion that federalism makes the problem of evil into a burden too great to bear. For on this model, he says, "we are born in a state of moral ruin, and the evil is very great. Hence it must be a punishment; for, otherwise, it could not be reconciled with the justice and goodness of God. But if a punishment, it must have its ground in guilt. . . . Verily, there is no theodicy in this doctrine, but only a darker problem of evil."[95]

So Miley rejects both federalism and realism.[96] But he also denies Pelagianism and Semi-Pelagianism. So what does he propose? He admits that Arminianism often has been confusing and even self-contradictory on this point, for many Arminian theologians try to hold to both the doctrine of original guilt and the principle that we are morally responsible (and thus guilty) only for what we have control over.[97] His own proposal is straightforward: the "true Arminian doctrine" is "native depravity without native demerit."[98] Original sin as original corruption, yes. Original sin as original guilt, no. "Native depravity is a part of the Arminian system, and entirely consistent with its principles; native demerit is discordant and contradictory."[99] Miley claims that the "principle of freedom" is of greatest importance for Arminianism; indeed, "there is no more fundamental principle."[100] But the doctrine of original guilt is, he insists, "openly contradictory to the deepest and most determining principle of the Arminian system."[101]

Original sin is, then, "the corruption of the nature of every man, that naturally is engendered of the offspring of Adam, whereby man is very far gone from original righteousness, and of his own nature inclined to evil, and that continually."[102] This is neither Pelagianism nor Semi-Pelagianism, for all humanity has lost original righteousness, is corrupt by nature, is guilty for actual sins, and is always dependent upon divine grace to have freedom and the power to choose the good. So Miley affirms original sin, and he is well aware of its universality and consequences. He does not deny original sin. But he critiques both historic Calvinism and earlier generations of Wesleyan theologians, and he denies that original sin includes or entails original guilt.

95. Ibid.
96. Miley also rejects a view that he associates with middle knowledge; see ibid., 470–71.
97. Ibid., 521n2, 522.
98. Ibid., 521.
99. Ibid.
100. Ibid., 522.
101. Ibid.
102. Ibid., 523.

Sin is properly understood as "disobedience to a law of God, conditioned on free moral agency and opportunity of knowing the law."[103]

The Twentieth Century . . . and Beyond

The trend away from the classical doctrine largely continues into the twentieth century. Indeed, further modifications are soon apparent. Henry C. Sheldon cautions against seeing Adam as a creature possessed of wisdom and holiness; despite the historic pedigree of such notions, this "picture was formed wholly from the colors of the speculative imagination."[104] The biblical basis for the doctrine of original sin is very slim; indeed, the Bible is "well-nigh silent on this theme."[105] Even the Pauline teaching found in Romans 5 is not obviously "literal fact" and should be read as more about potency and tendency than as something that actually happened.[106] On the other hand, Sheldon charges, it is "impossible to hold a man responsible for a deed that was committed before his birth."[107] Not surprisingly, then, he rejects both realism (on metaphysical grounds) and federalism (as legal fiction) as well as mediate views.[108] The brevity with which Sheldon can dismiss the traditional doctrine is striking indeed, and he concludes that "guilt cannot possibly be a matter of inheritance, and that consequently original sin can be affirmed of the posterity of Adam only in the sense of hereditary corruption."[109] In addition, he concludes that the term "total depravity is in any case ill-chosen" as a means of describing hereditary corruption.[110]

Olin A. Curtis takes a view that is similar in many respects. He maintains belief in the historicity of an original human pair and a historical fall. But he also rejects—and does so quite breezily—any notion of inherited guilt. "No man can inherit another man's personal bearing toward moral judgment. . . . The theological conception of 'an inherited guilt' results from a full failure to understand what personal life is, on the one hand, and what moral life is, on the other hand."[111] The term "total depravity" is "one of those unfortunate phrases with which the scholastic theologian is fond of weakening his mes-

---

103. Ibid., 528.
104. Henry C. Sheldon, *System of Christian Doctrine* (Cincinnati: Jennings & Pye, 1903), 304.
105. Ibid., 312.
106. Ibid., 314.
107. Ibid., 317.
108. Ibid., 317–19.
109. Ibid., 321.
110. Ibid.
111. Olin A. Curtis, *The Christian Faith: Personally Given in a System of Doctrine* (New York: Eaton and Mains, 1905), 199–200.

sage"; nonetheless, he insists, "there is a profound sense in which a man is, as he comes into the world, totally depraved."[112] Depravity is inherited, and it is universal.[113] This much, at least, of the traditional doctrine of original sin is true.

The tendency to dismiss major elements of the traditional doctrine becomes, in general, stronger as the twentieth century progresses. The "Boston Personalists" deny the traditional doctrine of original sin. Albert C. Knudson is representative; he says that sin and guilt "cannot be detached from the individual. They cannot be transmitted from parent to child. The idea, therefore, that all men are somehow responsible for the sin of Adam and have inherited his guilt must be regarded as a theological fiction."[114] The rise to prominence of process philosophy in Methodism drastically alters the discussion, and hamartiology more generally (not just the doctrine of original sin) takes on a different shape. For instance, Marjorie Suchocki intends nothing less than a complete "reversal of the tradition: rather than rebellion against God being the primary sin that engenders all others, I see rebellion against creation as the fundamental sin."[115] Similarly, insights from liberation, feminist, and womanist theologies exert significant influence on the doctrine of sin and lead to a focus on other issues.[116] A much smaller but determined group of theologians within the "holiness movement" hold onto significant elements of the traditional position; some work to defend a broadly federalist theory.[117] In general, however, the consistent trend in Wesleyan theology has been *away* from the traditional view—and away from any notion of original guilt in particular.

Yesterday and Today

As we move further into the twenty-first century, the range of Wesleyan views of the meaning of "sin" seems fragmented at various levels. At the same time, however, we are again seeing the rise of a Wesleyan "paleo-orthodoxy" in

112. Ibid., 200.

113. Ibid., 201.

114. Albert C. Knudson, *Present Tendencies in Religious Thought* (New York: Abingdon, 1924), 308–9.

115. Marjorie Suchocki, *The Fall to Violence: Original Sin in Relational Theology* (New York: Continuum, 1994), 13. Her panentheism has implications as well: "since God must experience the world, violence in creation also entails violence against God."

116. Significant in this respect is the work of Diane LeClerc, *Singleness of Heart: Gender, Sin, and Holiness in Historical Perspective* (Lanham, MD: Scarecrow Press, 2001).

117. E.g., J. Kenneth Grider, *A Wesleyan-Holiness Theology* (Kansas City: Beacon Hill Press, 1994), 279–86.

theology.[118] While some of the paleo-orthodox Wesleyans may wish to recover the classical Wesleyan doctrine of original sin, the challenges seem daunting. Many Wesleyans now take the criticisms made by Miley and others for granted, and discussions of the doctrine of sin have moved far afield. So how might it be possible for a Wesleyan to recover and retain the classical doctrine of original sin—while also holding to the core conviction that a person P is morally responsible only for "the obtaining of a state of affairs S only if S obtains (or obtained) and P could have prevented S from obtaining."[119]

It seems to me that there are two basic options for the Wesleyan theologian who believes that original sin includes guilt. One route forward might be to recover the mediate view that was so quickly dismissed by many (though not all) Wesleyans in the nineteenth century. As Michael C. Rea has recently argued, the mediate view—when bolstered with a Molinist account of providence—has the resources to protect *both* core convictions about moral responsibility (convictions that are characteristic of Wesleyanism) *and* the foundational belief (so common among the early Wesleyan theologians) in the guiltiness of original sin.[120] For if Molinism is successful, then it is possible both that we suffer from "transworld depravity" that "guarantees that one will fall into sin" and "that each of us has the power to prevent our suffering" from this condition.[121] Of course this option involves commitment to Molinism, and Molinism is not without detractors and critics. Nonetheless, however, it may be a way forward for the classical Wesleyan.

The other option is to combine elements of the mediate view with appropriate insights from other accounts. The proposal, which I cannot develop here in anything more than an outline, would go roughly as follows. We are corrupted by original sin. In fact, we are so corrupt that it is—apart from the radical intervention of grace—utterly impossible to refrain from sinning. We are, strictly speaking, guilty for what we do with that corruption. What we do with it—and here the view draws from federalism—is ratify what Adam did in his representation of us. According to Scripture, this is what all human moral agents (other than Christ) have done. This ratification

118. I here use the label of Thomas C. Oden, a Wesleyan and ecumenical theologian who has done much to revive and reinvigorate a theology that is both classically orthodox and authentically Wesleyan. See esp. his *After Modernity . . . What? Agenda for Theology* (Grand Rapids: Zondervan, 1990).

119. I here borrow the formulation of Michael C. Rea, "The Metaphysics of Original Sin," in *Persons: Divine and Human*, ed. Peter van Inwagen and Dean Zimmerman (Oxford: Oxford University Press, 2007), 320.

120. See ibid., 345–53. For a reliable introduction to Molinism, see Thomas P. Flint, *Divine Providence: The Molinist Account* (Ithaca, NY: Cornell University Press, 1998).

121. Rea, "Metaphysics," 347.

makes us guilty for our actions, but it also makes us guilty for our very corruption (thus intersecting with the mediate view). So are we guilty for original sin? Yes indeed, for by ratifying Adam's work we accept our corruption and are guilty for our state. Is this view consistent with the principle of moral responsibility that is so important to Wesleyan theology? Yes, for by God's prevenient grace we are enabled to respond to God. This view is also consistent with the universality of grace (as portrayed so poignantly in Rom. 5:12–21), and it is consistent as well with the Wesleyan conviction that the reception of that grace is conditional.[122] As such, this view seems to accommodate the major desiderata of historic Wesleyan doctrines of original sin.[123]

Conclusion

In this chapter I have offered an overview of the doctrine of original sin in the Wesleyan tradition. I have argued that Wesley and the early Methodist theologians believed that Adam and Eve were real persons and that they generally held to a federalist account of original sin. While Watson and those who followed in his wake modified federalism somewhat, Wesley himself defended the account given in the Westminster Confession. I have also shown that significant changes—first in emphasis and then in substance—were made in the nineteenth century.[124] A predominantly *theological* emphasis on holy love was traded for a predominantly *anthropological* emphasis on freedom of the will. This shift of emphasis is followed by major changes in the doctrine itself, with the result being that, especially following the influential work of John Miley, belief in original corruption is retained while belief in original guilt is rejected. The twentieth century is then the scene of further departures from the doctrine of original sin.

122. Richard Cross argues that there are at least seven ways in which the Christian might hold that grace is resistible while also avoiding Pelagianism (as it is defined at the Second Council of Orange in 529). He concludes that six of these ways also avoid Semi-Pelagianism. "Anti-Pelagianism and the Resistibility of Grace," *Faith and Philosophy* 22 (2005): 199–210. See also Eleonore Stump, *Aquinas* (New York: Routledge, 2003), 389–404; and Kevin Timpe, "Grace and Controlling What We Do Not Cause," *Faith and Philosophy* 24 (2007): 284–99.

123. This proposal is not without forerunners in historic Wesleyan theology; even Whedon concludes that "we need a 'sacrifice,' not only for our actual (or actional) sins, but for the antecedent guilt of the corruption from which they flow" ("Quarterly Book-Table," 367).

124. Again, we should not lose sight of the fact that this shift parallels what was taking place elsewhere in theology (especially American theology) in the nineteenth century. Further discussion would take us far beyond the frontiers of this essay, but it should not be assumed that this is a distinctively Wesleyan or Arminian development.

Whither Wesleyan theology? With its stark and uncompromising depiction of the depth and breadth of human depravity *and* its optimism about the glorious intentions and power of divine grace, perhaps historic Wesleyanism holds largely untapped resources for contemporary doctrines of sin and salvation.

8

ORIGINAL SIN AND MODERN THEOLOGY

Carl R. Trueman

To write a chapter on original sin in modern theology is no easy task. The problem is essentially one of selection: modern theology is such a diverse phenomenon that it is impossible to do justice to the range of opinions on this, or indeed any other doctrinal locus, in any kind of comprehensive way even in survey form. Indeed, modern theology, having lost its unifying foundation in a divinely inspired Bible, has become in the past fifty years little more than a function of wider identity politics. Theologians rarely produce dogmatic theology in terms of its classical structure: now we have feminist theology, queer theology, black theology, and so on. Each of these streams may well have interesting things to say, but their very existence points to the problem of how to address any single topic or how to select "representative" theologians. That which is representative to one might be a pitiful aberration to another.

Thus, in this chapter I make no claims to provide a comprehensive account of original sin in modern theology. Instead, I have chosen to survey six mainline (i.e., not conservative evangelical) theologians who have been influential on various strands of modern thought. I also consider these examples to exemplify the broad contours and emphases of approaches to original sin in a theological world that has by and large decided Adam and Eve never existed and that the fall was not an event in history that moved the created realm from a position of integrity to that of being under the curse of God. These selected theologians allow us to see what is at stake theologically in the current debates over human origins and creation.[1]

The three figures who occupy most space in the subsequent pages are Friedrich Schleiermacher, Walter Rauschenbusch, and Karl Barth. The choice of Schleiermacher really needs no justification: he is the father of modern liberalism and the classic representative of attempts to rebuild Christianity in light of the Enlightenment, and specifically Kantian, critique. Rauschenbusch may be a more surprising choice, but his theology of the social gospel surely represents the most significant application of a basically Schleiermacherian approach to original sin in the English-speaking world, and with his emphasis on the social nature of such sin, he stands in positive connection to much of subsequent liberal theology. Karl Barth, like Schleiermacher, is an obvious choice, representing the most significant dogmatic voice of the twentieth century and the most significant critical respondent to Schleiermacher who yet accepted fundamental elements of the Enlightenment critique of his great foe.

The choice of Rudolf Bultmann, Reinhold Niebuhr, and Wolfhart Pannenberg is perhaps more personal. As noted above, the last century has produced an ever more variegated crop of theologians and theologies. Yet these three men certainly represent key figures: Bultmann was to biblical scholarship what Barth was to dogmatics; Niebuhr represents a heady mix of social gospel and pessimism, which separated him from both the kind of theology espoused by Rauschenbusch and that of Barth; and Pannenberg is perhaps the latest, and maybe the last, attempt to articulate a full system of theology in the classic liberal tradition.

Friedrich Schleiermacher (1768–1834)

As with so much modern theology, the basic terms of debate were set by the great German theologian Friedrich Schleiermacher in the nineteenth century. In the wake of the Enlightenment and works such as Pierre Bayle's *Encyclopedia*,

---

1. I have also chosen only Protestant theologians. Roman Catholics have continued to address the issues of sin and original sin, but I am working on the assumption that this volume is aimed primarily at a Protestant evangelical readership and thus have focused my attention on those thinkers who are most likely to be of significance to those in that tradition. Further, I have not addressed any liberation, black, feminist, or queer theologians. This is not because such have not made significant contributions to the theological field but because they all by and large stand on the same side of the theological divide relative to the orthodox tradition on Adam and sin as those represented here.

the doctrine of original sin had become both distasteful and a matter of ridicule and consequently dropped from theological discourse.[2] Schleiermacher, however, attempted a major reconstruction of Christian doctrine that took seriously the great themes of Christian dogmatics while yet subjecting them to searching criticism and significant revision. One might summarize his project as a whole by saying that he rebuilt Christian dogmatics as an exercise in human psychology, with the notion of God-consciousness as its guiding principle.

The major text for understanding Schleiermacher on original sin is *The Christian Faith* (1830–31).[3] Central to Schleiermacher's understanding of sin is his understanding of human psychology. For Schleiermacher, human self-consciousness can be divided into two: the higher self-consciousness and the sensible self-consciousness. The latter is the human perception of the world and what we might call "feelings," or social and moral attitudes to the world around us;[4] the former is the site of Schleiermacher's famous "feeling of absolute dependence" or "God consciousness," which is the awareness that our freedom and spontaneity come from a source outside ourselves.[5] It is important to note that this higher consciousness never actually exists in the abstract but always exists in connection to the sensible self-consciousness. This is important, because it is in the relationship between these two that Schleiermacher locates the problem of sin.

He defines sin as follows:

> The evil condition can only consist in an obstruction or arrest of the vitality of the higher self-consciousness, so that there comes to be little or no union of it with the various determinations of the sensible self-consciousness, and thus little or no religious life. We may give to this condition, in its most extreme form, the name of *Godlessness*, or, better, *God-forgetfulness*.[6]

In other words, Schleiermacher is saying that it is possible for the sensible self-consciousness to become so preoccupied with the things of this world, the relationships that exist between the human subject and its various objects, that the God-consciousness can simply drop from view entirely. Men and

---

2. Of course, opposition to the notion of original sin was not an innovative contribution of the Enlightenment. Alan Jacobs aptly comments in his cultural history of the idea that no other doctrine, "not even the belief that some people are eternally damned," had generated as much hostility as original sin: *Original Sin: A Cultural History* (New York: HarperOne, 2008), xi.

3. *The Christian Faith*, trans. H. R. Mackintosh and J. S. Stewart (Edinburgh: T&T Clark, 1989), hereafter *CF*, with references to chapter and paragraph.

4. *CF* 5.1.

5. *CF* 4.3.

6. *CF* 11.2.

women can be immersed in their own lives, their own joys, sorrows, desires, and frustrations, that they lose all sense of their dependence on something greater than themselves for their freedom.

Given this, we might characterize Schleiermacher's view of sin as being something that essentially stunts the growth to psychological maturity of humans. This connects to his Christology, where Christ is the supreme example of perfect God-consciousness and therefore the basis on which Schleiermacher can defend the superiority of Christianity over other monotheistic religions. It also decisively shapes his understanding of original sin.

When he discusses Adam and Eve, Schleiermacher demonstrates an indifference to whether they were historical figures or not. In part, this is because of the rather narrow task he assigns to dogmatics, which is not to make a judgment on the interpretation of Scripture as such.[7] Yet this is not Schleiermacher's only criticism of the received confessional tradition. He sees the traditional teaching as itself incoherent. First, Adam's "sinful nature" must have preceded the first sin because of the ease with which the first pair fell. Indeed, he sees this as a problem that intensifies as one takes the narrative more literally, on the grounds that he regards the temptation as trivial and easy to avoid.[8] Second, he regards as nonsensical the notion that something was fundamentally changed in human nature by the sin of the first man: individuals can only act in accordance with their nature; if the individual appears to change the nature of a species, then either the initial definition of the species was inadequate or the individual has been wrongly classified as belonging to that species.[9] Schleiermacher allows the logical possibility that the change in human nature could have been wrought by an external agent—that is, the devil—but this he sees as plunging Christian theology into Manichaeism.[10]

If original sin is not to be understood as involving the decisive primeval act of a historical Adam that fundamentally altered human nature, then how is it to be understood? Schleiermacher sees the story of Adam and Eve as paradigmatic for subsequent generations: Eve represents the ease with which the sensuous dimension of human psychology is easily led to oppose the God-consciousness by external temptations. Adam represents how easily sin

7. "As regards the Mosaic narrative: in accordance with the limits which we have assigned to Dogmatics, that science cannot be expected to determine how the said record is to be interpreted and whether it purports to be history or allegory" (*CF* 72.5).
8. *CF* 72.2.
9. *CF* 72.3.
10. *CF* 72.3.

is assimilated by imitation even without great external pressure but simply through a forgetfulness of God.[11]

Schleiermacher's denial that human nature is fundamentally changed by the fall raises the obvious question of how sin can come to be known as sin. In earlier, orthodox theology, the pre-fall Adam had functioned as a kind of benchmark against which the post-fall human race could be measured: rather than being devoted to God and obedient to his commands, Adam (and thus his posterity) had chosen to rebel, a rebellion epitomized by the first act of disobedience in eating the forbidden fruit. For Schleiermacher, however, humanity has always shared the same basic nature and the account of the fall serves merely as a paradigm of the individual fall of every human.[12] What this does, of course, is push the theologian to look not to Adam as the benchmark for judging sin but rather to Christ who, as the supreme example of the perfect God-consciousness, becomes himself the standard by which sin can then be judged. Even if we allow that the first man had not committed an actual sin, yet the psychological preparation behind each act of sin would be enough to prevent him being a kind of benchmark for human perfection.[13] Only because the God-consciousness has been fully and perfectly revealed in Christ can we know what the depth of human imperfection is.[14]

Schleiermacher's understanding of sin is complex but its significance can be summarized very briefly. Sin is a disruption of human psychology, not primarily an offense against God; there was no golden age prior to Adam's fall (and, indeed, the historicity of Adam is itself a matter of dogmatic indifference) and thus humans were created as fallen; Adam is a paradigm of what it is to be a human, and Christ becomes the great paradigm of what it is to be a human with perfect God-consciousness, a model of that to which all should aspire. There is thus an impulse within the type of theology set forth by Schleiermacher to see the essence or outworking of Christian salvation as one defined above all by practical ethics.

Walter Rauschenbusch (1861–1918)

In the English-speaking world, Schleiermacher's understanding of original sin and its consequences received its most influential expression in the work of Walter Rauschenbusch (1861–1918). Wrestling with the social problems

11. *CF* 72.5.
12. *CF* 72.5.
13. *CF* 94.1.
14. *CF* 94.2.

created by various nineteenth-century developments—urbanization, industrialization, militarism, and so on—Rauschenbusch sought to recast Christian doctrine in a manner that would make it a dynamic force for social change. In so doing, he became the primary advocate of what has become known as the social gospel. He articulates his view of sin most clearly and concisely in *A Theology for the Social Gospel*, which he originally delivered as the Taylor Lectures at Yale in 1917.[15]

Central to Rauschenbusch's theology is the concept of the kingdom of God. This makes it clear from the outset that his concern is not with individual salvation (and thus, by inference, with individual sin) but rather with the corporate notion of society. The teaching of Christ was focused on the advent of the kingdom, of the transformation of society as a whole based on an ethic of love.[16] In so doing, he stands in the line stemming from Schleiermacher as refracted through Albrecht Ritschl.[17]

When he approaches the subject of sin, Rauschenbusch operates with the basic psychological categories that he has inherited from Schleiermacher. Ironically, from a later perspective, this allows him to criticize those social gospel advocates who try to reduce sin to a function of environment: Rauschenbusch sees this attempt as analogous to the traditional view of original sin, in its passing final responsibility for sin to something outside the individual.[18] Nevertheless, he is also concerned that an overemphasis on individual sin, manifest in the individual consciousness of sin, has led to a trivialization of what it is in which sin consists and thus in what righteousness consists. Thus, he says,

15. The lectures have been reprinted as *A Theology for the Social Gospel* (Louisville: Westminster John Knox, 1997), hereafter *TSG*.

16. Commenting on traditional "individualistic" theology, he declares, "What a spectacle, that the original teaching of our Lord has become an incongruous element in so-called evangelical theology, like a stranger with whom the other doctrines would not associate" (*TSG*, 25). In this context, he singles out Britain, which had dominated world capitalism for over a century, as having an individualistic theology that served to undergird the established order rather than to critique it (*TSG*, 29).

17. In the generation after Schleiermacher, the most significant theologian was undoubtedly Albrecht Ritschl (1822–89). Ritschl developed Schleiermacher's insights into sin and salvation and placed the kingdom of God, as anticipated in the practical ethics of Christ, as the key to Christianity; see N. P. Williams, *The Ideas of the Fall and Original Sin* (London: Longmans, Green and Co., 1927), 438–39. On Ritschl's view of sin, see Donald L. Mueller, *An Introduction to the Theology of Albrecht Ritschl* (Philadelphia: Westminster, 1969), 63–77.

18. *TSG*, 33. Nevertheless, as one recent biographer has commented, "Rauschenbusch showed no interest in confronting the possibilities that the nature of humanity was corrupted in the sense spoken of by Paul and Augustine. He believed rather that evil manifested itself 'organically,' and in biological fashion was transmitted from one group to another. Once these social evils manifested themselves collectively within society, they were nearly impossible to overcome." Christopher H. Evans, *The Kingdom Is Always but Coming: A Life of Walter Rauschenbusch* (Grand Rapids: Eerdmans, 2004), 301–2.

one minister identifies good works with church attendance, Bible reading, and financial support for public worship; another defines sin as drinking, gambling, and going to the theater; both miss the larger abuses perpetrated by the capitalist system in their home city of New York. In short, Rauschenbusch is interested in exposing structural, institutional sin.[19]

In his analysis of sin, Rauschenbusch is convinced that the significance of the fall of Adam has been massively overstated in later theology. We noted above that Schleiermacher regarded the question of Adam's historicity as of no systematic importance whatsoever. In *A Theology for the Social Gospel*, Rauschenbusch does not explicitly deny the historicity of Adam, but that would seem to be the obvious inference of his statement that the story of the fall originates in the ninth century BC as an attempt to provide a rationale for the origins not of sin but of death and evil. He also points to the fact that the fall fulfills little structural role within the theology of the Old Testament. Thus, he combines both text criticism and post-Gablerian biblical theology in his assault on the traditional doctrine of original sin.[20]

Two further things of interest emerge out of Rauschenbusch's discussion of the fall. First, it is clear that his notion of truth is, at root, profoundly pragmatic: he is not interested in what he would (no doubt) regard as speculative abstraction that makes no practical difference. The social gospel is above all things practical.

In other words, discussion of the fall as a historical event with decisive impact on all future generations is ultimately unnecessary: sin is a fact and Christians should concentrate on combating it rather than trying to explain it. There is more than a whiff of Marxist prioritizing of action over theory at this point.

Second, Rauschenbusch regards the traditional doctrine of the fall as inappropriately relativizing the sins of later generations, such as syphilis, government corruption, and imperialist wars. In this context, a fixation on a fall into sin at the start of history has actually blocked the ability of human beings to understand properly their own role, and the role of their own generation, in the perpetuation, development, and exacerbation of sin within society. In other words, the doctrine of original sin is not simply unbiblical; one might go so far as to declare it positively anti-Christian.[21]

---

19. *TSG*, 36.

20. *TSG*, 39–42. John Philipp Gabler (1753–1826) was a German biblical scholar often regarded as the founder of modern biblical theology. He made a clear distinction between dogmatic theology and biblical theology, seeing the latter as the investigation of the beliefs expressed by individual authors and books in the Bible in their historical context.

21. *TSG*, 43.

Interestingly enough, he does believe in human solidarity: one of the things which should make each generation more self-critical and careful to combat its own sinful impulses is the legacy that will be left for future generations. Indeed, the ability of humans to combat sin effectively places great responsibility on their shoulders.[22]

When Rauschenbusch comes to define sin, the influence of Schleiermacher is clear: sin is selfishness, defined as the dominance of the sensual nature over the higher, spiritual nature.[23] He is more emphatic than Schleiermacher in drawing out the social implications of this point: sin, in its most developed forms, is a conflict between the individual ego and the common good of humanity. This in turn leads him to make explicit his understanding of God: God is the common good of humanity.[24] There is no "God out there" for Rauschenbusch, at least not in any sense that is meaningful or relevant for humans and thus for their theology. God is to be identified with society as it is properly ordered in terms of its common good. The heir of Hegel and German idealism, Rauschenbusch effectively identifies God with the goal of human history.[25] In this context, he predictably demonstrates a flexible and historicist approach to the Decalogue: the first table (telling of humans' duty to God) is reduced to three commandments because Christ declared the Sabbath an ordinance made for humans; polytheism and idol worship are no longer dangers; the misuse of God's name is of little account now that sorcery is not widespread; and so the major thrust of biblical ethics is on the application of the second table—and these commands are all of social significance.[26]

This, of course, points to the fact that Rauschenbusch (like Schleiermacher and, even more so, Ritschl) regards sin as revealed not by the primeval fall of Adam but by a comparison of the world as it is with the ideal kingdom of God which is to come and which was proleptically revealed in the life and teaching of the Lord Jesus Christ. Adam is for Rauschenbusch too shadowy a figure, the details of his prelapsarian life and virtues too brief for him to provide a sound measure by which to understand sin and its impact. By contrast, the kingdom provides just such a measure.[27]

22. *TSG*, 43.
23. *TSG*, 45–46.
24. *TSG*, 47.
25. *TSG*, 49. "God is not only the spiritual representative of humanity; he is identified with it. . . . He works through humanity to realize his purposes, and our sins block and destroy the Reign of God in which he might fully reveal and realize himself. Therefore our sins against the least of our fellow-men in the last resort concern God."
26. *TSG*, 48–49.
27. *TSG*, 51.

The kingdom is marked by two characteristics: love and the commonwealth of labor.[28] In fact, of course, these two characteristics are functionally one and the same: love considered in isolation is an abstract concept that has no real positive content. For Rauschenbusch, love is the establishment and propagation of appropriate labor relations. In other words, the kingdom (and therefore God himself) looks rather like a late nineteenth-century vision of a socialist utopia, and sin looks rather like the selfish acquisition of property and capital, which should really be shared magnanimously among everyone.[29] The vertical dimension of sin as an offense against a holy God is entirely subsumed under the horizontal aspect of sin as dysfunctional social relationships with fellow humans.

Given all of this, one might have expected Rauschenbusch to have reduced the idea of the transmission of sin down to a matter of imitation. Certainly, he wishes to avoid any hint of shifting responsibility away from the individual agent and onto the action of some primeval ancestor in the garden of Eden. Yet he also wants to avoid a simplistic Pelagianism that does not take seriously the pervasive nature of sin. Thus, he emphasizes the powerful and determinative impact of social relations on the individual that cultivate and reinforce sinful behavior. Indeed, he can even use the biological metaphor for talking about the transmission of sin, but he does so in a very distinctive way, as merely an analogy with the way social structures and practices impact and mold the individual, apparently in a manner that is irresistible.[30]

Rauschenbusch's theology has had a profound and long-lasting impact on subsequent theology. Indeed, with his emphasis on what we might call structural or institutional sin, he is very much the precursor of modern theological concerns—liberal and indeed evangelical—with social justice and concepts such as institutional racism and sexism. His thought represents a popular and accessible outworking of Schleiermacher's essentially psychological understanding of the nature of sin and makes explicit the dogmatic implications of this: sin is not really a vertical problem but rather a horizontal one, a problem of not realizing one's full humanity here on earth. The note of it being a direct offense against a holy God is entirely missing. Sin is a direct offense against other humans and only indirectly, therefore, against God.

28. *TSG*, 54.
29. *TSG*, 55.
30. "The permanent vices and crimes of adults are not transmitted by heredity, but by being socialized; for instance, alcoholism and all drug evils; cruel sports, such as bull-fights and pugilism; various forms of sex perversity; voluntary deformities, such as foot-binding, corseting, piercing of ears and nose; blood-feuds in Corsica; lynching in America. Just as syphilitic corruption is forced on the helpless foetus in its mother's womb, so these hereditary social evils are forced on the individual embedded in the womb of society and drawing his ideas, moral standards, and spiritual ideals from the general life of the social body" (*TSG*, 60).

Karl Barth (1886–1968)

Karl Barth is without doubt the most significant Protestant dogmatician of the twentieth century whose work has enjoyed something of a renaissance in the past twenty years, with the advent of postmodern and narrative theologies, as well as the interest in theological interpretation. His rebellion against the kind of theology represented by Schleiermacher and Ritschl is well-known. Yet, for all of this rebellion, his thinking on sin retains certain continuities with the old liberalism.

In addressing the matter of original sin in his *Church Dogmatics*, Barth is happy to use the classical orthodox terminology.[31] Nevertheless, he is opposed to any idea that this might involve a kind of hereditary or biological defect and indeed commends later Reformed orthodoxy for arguing that the transmission of original sin is by imputation.[32] Despite this, however, Barth's construction of original sin is markedly different from that of classical Reformed orthodoxy in a number of ways.

First, there is the question of the actual historicity of Adam. Historicity in general in Barth's theology is a complicated matter. The reader of Barth is faced not only with the typical problems involved in reading a theologian whose corpus is vast and whose thought is often expressed in elliptical fashion; there is also the added complication of his famous distinction between *Historie* and *Geschichte* (loosely translated "saga"), which often gives his discussion of biblical narrative a somewhat slippery quality. This applies particularly to the biblical narrative of Eden, which Barth himself categorizes as *saga*. It is worth quoting his comments on this in full:

> Who could see and attest the coming into being of heaven and earth and especially the coming into being of Adam and his corresponding individual existence? It is not history but only saga which can tell us that he came into being in this way and existed as the one who came into being in this way—the first man. We miss the unprecedented and incomparable thing which the Genesis passages tell us of the coming into being and existence of Adam if we try to read and understand it as history, relating it either favourably or unfavourably to scientific palæontology, or to what we now know with some historical certainty concerning the oldest and

31. "There can be no objection to the Latin expression *peccatum originale* if it is not given this more exact definition. It is indeed quite adequate, telling us that we are dealing with the original and radical and therefore the comprehensive and total act of man, with the imprisonment of his existence in that circle of evil being and evil activity. In this imprisonment God speaks to him and makes Himself his liberator in Jesus Christ." Karl Barth, *Church Dogmatics*, vol. 4, *The Doctrine of Reconciliation*, part 1, trans. G. W. Bromiley and T. F. Torrance (New York: T&T Clark, 1956), 500.

32. Ibid., 511.

most primitive forms of human life. The saga as a form of historical narration is a *genre* apart. And within this *genre* biblical saga is a special instance which cannot be compared with others but has to be seen and understood in and for itself. Saga in general is the form which, using intuition and imagination, has to take up historical narration at the point where events are no longer susceptible as such of historical proof.[33]

It would appear from this that Barth is using the concept of saga, rather than straightforward history, to bring out the fact that creation and the events and actions surrounding it have a significance beyond the mere narrative, that there is something unique, not analogous to anything else, that is going on here. This might, of course, mean that Barth does regard Adam as a historical figure but simply sees his uniqueness as overriding normal categories of history. That, however, is an unlikely reading.

First, Barth sees part of the key to understanding Adam to be an acceptance of the implications of the documentary hypothesis of the Pentateuch, which for him makes it clear that the events recounted should not be taken at face value.[34] Second, Barth explicitly rejects any notion that there was ever a point in time where creation was unfallen.[35] These two points, more than the language of saga, indicate his basic rejection of the historicity of the events and actions recounted in Genesis 1–3.

If Adam's significance is not tied to his historicity or to any actual moment in time when creation was indeed unfallen, what is the significance of Adam for Barth? In brief, Adam is everyman: in him we see ourselves; in his sin, we see our sin, our dilemma, our status outside of Christ. "Adam is not a fate which God has suspended over us. Adam is the truth concerning us as it is known to God and told to us."[36]

33. Ibid., 508.
34. "In the strict exegetical sense we ought not perhaps to combine the Yahwistic text of Gen. 3 with the passage Gen. 2:2–3 which belongs to the Priestly text. Otherwise we might observe that the seventh day of creation, the first day in the life of man, in which he had nothing to do but to keep the sabbath with God Himself in peace and joy and freedom, was followed at once by the day of his pride and fall as the first day of his own will and work and activity and achievement. It is, however, not merely legitimate but necessary to combine Gen. 3 with Gen. 2:5–25, and therefore to say that man had hardly been formed of the dust of the earth and become a living soul by the breath of God, that he had hardly been put in the garden of Eden and charged to dress it and to keep it, that his creation had hardly been completed by that of the woman as an indispensable and suitable helpmeet, before he followed up and directly opposed all the good things that God had done for him by becoming disobedient to God" (ibid., 508–9).
35. Ibid., 508.
36. Ibid., 511.

This points toward Barth's understanding of Adam as the representative human as expounded by Paul in Romans 5. Here, Barth's emphasis on Christ as the revelation of God causes him to reverse the standard ordering of Adam-Christ, where Christ comes as the one who fulfills that which Adam was appointed to do but which he failed to do. In the *Church Dogmatics*, Barth states that we should not talk of an Adam-Christ but a Christ-Adam parallel. Christ, he declares, is the original, Adam merely the figure of him who was to come.[37]

This parallel receives a much fuller exposition in a separate work of Barth, *Christ and Adam*.[38] Here, Barth makes it clear that Adam is in no sense a revelation of true human nature, which then goes bad and requires rescuing via Christ. Rather, Adam is the revelation of what we are outside of Christ who is himself the archetypal man, the true and foundational revelation of humanity.[39]

This position has numerous systematic implications. First, by prioritizing Christ over Adam in Romans 5 in this way, Barth seems to be pushing in a universalist direction, as the relation of Christ to humanity must surely be as inclusive as that of Adam to humanity, even if Barth does not care to draw out explicitly what might appear to others to be the obvious soteriological conclusion.[40]

Second, this once again undercuts any need for Adam to be a historical figure or for the fall to be a historical event in the conventional sense of the term. There is no moment of "fall" within time. We are in a very real sense not simply *in* Adam but are actually Adam in that all of our lives are simply repetitions of his: "We are what Adam was and so are all our fellow men. And the one Adam is what we and all men are. Man is at once an individual and only an individual, and, at the same time, without in any way losing his individuality, he is the responsible representative of all men."[41]

Though Barth professedly breaks with the tradition of theology that stems from Schleiermacher, there are yet still points of affinity that exist between the two. The irrelevance of the historicity of Adam, the rejection of the idea that man was ever unfallen, the concern for avoiding any notion of biological heredity relative to sin, and the assumption that nothing must imply that humans are in any way to be held to account for alien guilt are all clear in Barth's

37. Ibid., 512–13.
38. Karl Barth, *Christ and Adam: Man and Humanity in Romans 5*, trans. T. A. Smail (New York: Collier, 1962).
39. Ibid., 39–41.
40. This is the argument of John Murray in his review of *Christ and Adam*. See *The Collected Writings of John Murray*, vol. 4 (Edinburgh: Banner of Truth, 1982), 316–21, 319.
41. Barth, *Christ and Adam*, 113; see also 40.

treatment of the topic. It also seems at least arguable that Barth's view of sin retains sin's fundamental character as an attitude of mind—a psychological or existential category.

Rudolf Bultmann (1884–1976)

Rudolf Bultmann was arguably the most influential New Testament scholar/ theologian of the twentieth century. His understanding of original sin is shaped both by his distinctive understanding of the intellectual roots of aspects of New Testament thought and by his appropriation of certain aspects of existentialist philosophy.

For example, in dealing with the notion of a historical fall of a pristine, innocent creation, Bultmann ascribes such a narrative concept to the influence of gnosticism on the formation of the New Testament.[42] The historicity of the fall is thus of no real significance to the theological lessons that Bultmann seeks to draw from the biblical account. In fact, the fall is part of the "mythical world picture" presented by the Bible that no longer fulfills a useful explanatory purpose in the modern day.[43] Further, he has no hesitation in saying that Paul's account of original sin is itself incoherent. On the one hand, Paul simply assumes the reality that all are indeed sinners, without positing any cause for this. On the other, he locates the cause in the sin of Adam. Here, Bultmann argues, Paul is in thrall to gnostic mythology, although Bultmann credits Paul with avoiding positing something behind the sin of Adam that might reinforce a gnostic theology.[44] The reason for this is that in Romans 5 Paul is trying to explain the universality not of sin but of death, and because he has argued that death is the punishment for Adam's sin, he is thus required to explain the universality of sin. This is further complicated by the fact that Paul also wants to make death the consequence of individual sin.[45] In this context, Bultmann understands sin as the condition of human existence whereby individuals seek to find fulfillment in themselves and for themselves.[46]

42. Rudolf Bultmann, *Theology of the New Testament*, vol. 1, trans. Kendrick Grobel (New York: Scribner's, 1951), 172–73.

43. Rudolf Bultmann, "New Testament Mythology: The Problem of Demythologizing the New Testament Proclamation," in *New Testament Mythology and Other Basic Writings*, trans. Schubert Ogden (Philadelphia: Fortress, 1984), 1–43.

44. Bultmann, *Theology of the New Testament*, 250–51. In making this comment, Bultmann surely makes an implicit contrast between Paul's account of the fall and that given in Gen. 3, where the agency of the serpent is clearly important (thus making the narrative presumably more "gnostic" on Bultmann's terms!).

45. Ibid., 252.

46. Ibid., 246–48, 253.

As with Schleiermacher, Bultmann sees no transmission of sin in the tradi-tional, Augustinian sense: sin is and always has been the condition of humanity. Behind this lies the typical modern concern for the idea of one person being considered guilty because of the failure of another.[47] Much more explicitly than Schleiermacher, however, Bultmann dismisses the historicity of the fall: it is a mythical story, a means whereby an early era was able to make sense of the universality not so much of sin as of death.

Reinhold Niebuhr (1892–1971)

Reinhold Niebuhr wrote extensively about the nature of sin, something that contributed to his image as that of a theological pessimist. His most famous discussion of original sin occurs in volume 1 of *The Nature and Destiny of Man: A Christian Interpretation*, which began as the Gifford Lectures for 1939.[48]

Niebuhr's discussion of sin draws heavily on Kierkegaard's *The Concept of Anxiety*. At the heart of the Christian doctrine lies the dilemma of inevitabil-ity and freedom: Christianity wishes to maintain both in order to underline the tragic condition of fallen humans and yet the responsibility of individuals for their sin.[49] For Niebuhr, following Kierkegaard, sinfulness is the result of the fact that humans are conscious, reflective beings who have the capacity to transcend the natural processes in which they are involved: thus they are constantly tempted to despair. In what Niebuhr calls a *quantitative* develop-ment of life, humans seek to escape their finiteness and weakness. We might characterize this as seeking to transcend their existence through finite earthly means: for example, materialism, entertainment, power, sex, and money. In fact, humans transcend themselves only through a *qualitative* development of life in their submission to the will of God.[50] Quantitative development is the sin of self-love; and the sin of self-love presupposes a prior lack of trust in God.[51]

Niebuhr does reference the sin of Adam in this context: "The sin of each individual is preceded by the sin of Adam," he comments but then completes the sentence with "but even this first sin of history is not the first sin."[52] In

47. "At the most, men sinning under the curse of Adam's sin could be regarded as guilty only in a legal sense, inasmuch as law deals only with the guilty deed; but then we would have no right to speak of guilt in the ethical sense" (ibid., 251).
48. Reinhold Niebuhr, *The Nature and Destiny of Man: A Christian Interpretation*, 2 vols. (Louisville: Westminster John Knox, 1996).
49. Ibid., 1:243.
50. Ibid., 1:251.
51. Ibid., 1:252.
52. Ibid., 1:254.

short, sin is paradoxically there in nature from the very beginning; there is no "fall" in history that would introduce evil into creation.

Niebuhr makes this explicit in his subsequent discussion of what he characterizes as "literalistic errors." While Niebuhr has no time for the moralism of Pelagian theology, which does not take seriously the tragic inevitability of sin, he regards the Augustinian notion of original sin as something inherited to be hopelessly tied to an understanding of the fall as literally historical and as fundamentally altering human nature. Niebuhr does appreciate the Augustinian motivation in this: the rejection of any ground for human pride.[53] Yet Niebuhr still regards commitment to historicity as wrong. Instead, he sets the notion of Adam as representative man in opposition to that of Adam as historical man. By this, he is not implying that Adam plays the role of a federal representative, as in the covenant theology of the seventeenth century; that would assume Adam's historical reality. Rather, he sees Adam as the archetypal representative of the way in which all humans sin. In this, it is true that his concern is not primarily with the historical difficulties of maintaining Adam's historicity but rather with the destruction of freedom that the notion of inherited sin would seem to bring with it.[54] Nevertheless, he does explicitly reject any notion that Adam was a historical figure and that the fall was a historical event.[55]

Niebuhr regards commitment to a historical fall as analogous to pagan myths about a golden age, which can then function as the criterion for judging the defection of all future epochs. Indeed, he even sees it as connecting to the nostalgic psychology of adulthood, which looks back to a mythic idyllic childhood as providing individuals with knowledge of their true, authentic natures.[56] Like Schleiermacher, he finds the idea of the fall as fundamentally changing human nature to be something that is incoherent: Catholicism attempts to avoid this by stressing the fall as the loss of a superadded gift of grace, Protestantism as loss of the image of God. Neither position does justice to the fact that sin is the corruption of humanity's true essence but not its destruction. Instead, Niebuhr points to the fall as having not chronological but vertical significance.[57] By implication, Adam is thus the paradigm, the great example of the choice that lies before all humans, and of the wrong decision made in the face of that choice.[58]

53. Ibid., 1:279.
54. Ibid., 1:26–64.
55. "Christian theology has found it difficult to refute the rationalistic rejection of the myth of the Fall without falling into the literalistic error of insisting upon the Fall as an historical event" (ibid., 1:267–68).
56. Ibid., 1:268.
57. Ibid., 1:268–69.
58. See ibid., 1:278: "Perfection before the Fall is, in other words, perfection before the act."

If Adam provides no example of humanity in a pre-fall state, the question for Niebuhr becomes where such an example of perfected humanity can be found. Where are we to look for the criterion of what it is to be a perfect human? The answer, of course, is Christ. As with Schleiermacher and his successors, it is Jesus Christ who really represents humanity as it should be. This has a threefold aspect. First, Christ provides the standard by which we know the true possibilities of life and, indeed, therefore the lost perfections of Adam.[59] Second, Christ on the cross represents the intrusion of selfless love into history, something that stands in judgment on attempts to transcend the self from within the framework of nature, and an exposé of the gap between human self-assertion and divine love.[60] Finally, it points to the fact that the kingdom will be fulfilled in history, not in some form of other-worldly mysticism.[61] For Niebuhr, this means social and political activism; though, with his emphasis on individual sin as a form of Kierkegaardian anxiety, this is clearly not set on quite the optimistic anthropological footing that we noted in Rauschenbusch.

Wolfhart Pannenberg (b. 1928)

In comparison to that of Barth and Bultmann, the theology of Wolfhart Pannenberg marks something of a return to the classic liberal concerns of Schleiermacher and Ritschl, particularly with regard to the importance of historical-critical issues.

His major treatment of original sin is in the second volume of his *Systematic Theology*.[62] For Pannenberg, the story of Adam is not a story about the origin of sin in the sense that it offers an explanation of the universality of human guilt and corruption based on the sin of one man and understood in Augustinian or federal terms. Indeed, as for Scheiermacher, the historicity of Adam seems to be for Pannenberg an issue of dogmatic indifference; his theology has no need for it. Rather, Adam stands as the great paradigm of the psychology of sinful action: Adam was deceived into thinking that he could find his fulfillment in his own finite resources, and that is the deception that reflects the psychology of all of us.[63] In this sense, Pannenberg is the heir of Schleiermacher and the nineteenth-century liberal tradition stemming therefrom.

59. Ibid., 2:76–77.
60. Ibid., 2:81–90.
61. Ibid., 2:90–95.
62. Wolfhart Pannenberg, *Systematic Theology*, trans. Geoffrey W. Bromiley (Grand Rapids: Eerdmans, 1994).
63. "We engage in sin because of the deception. Our voluntary committing of it is enough to make us guilty. There does not have to be a primal and once-for-all event of a fall for which

Pannenberg sees the connection between Adam and individual humans as one of participation by emulation: we participate in Adam's sin by sinning in the same way as him. The obvious christological implication is that humans are united to Christ by being changed into his likeness.[64] With a greater sensitivity to historical process and eschatology, Pannenberg is critical of Schleiermacher for not really giving significance to the historical actions of Christ, particularly the distinction between his pre- and postresurrection significance, and for focusing rather exclusively on Jesus's God-consciousness.[65] Pannenberg's own solution is, however, not so much a rejection of the paradigmatic nature of Christ's God-consciousness as an enriching of it: the death of Christ is a revelation to others that they no longer have to see themselves as excluded from fellowship with God. Through accepting their own finitude as Jesus did, and in fellowship with him, they now share in eternal life with the assurance that death will be overcome. Pannenberg's theology is Schleiermacher with a Hegelian/historical eschatological twist.[66]

Some Concluding Thoughts

As noted at the beginning of this essay, modern theology is a highly diverse phenomenon, and I make no claim that the theologians treated above offer a comprehensive view of modern positions on original sin. Nevertheless, the examples given are instructive because they do highlight certain axioms and emphases that pervade modern theological discussions.

All of the theologians discussed stand in continuity with certain aspects of Enlightenment critiques of classical orthodoxy. First, all of them repudiate any notion that humanity stands guilty before God because of the imputation of an alien guilt, the guilt of a historical man called Adam, to all of his descendants. By the standards of Enlightenment thought, such an imputation would be unethical. Even Barth, while seeing the language of imputation as an improvement on notions of inherited sin, does not see this imputation as built

---

Adam was guilty quite apart from all entanglement in sin. . . . In this sense the story of Adam is the story of the whole race. It is repeated in each individual. The point is not Adam's first state of innocence in contrast to that of his descendants." Pannenberg, *Systematic Theology*, 2:263. See Stanley J. Grenz, *Reason for Hope: The Systematic Theology of Wolfhart Pannenberg* (Oxford: Oxford University Press, 1990), 104–6; also E. Frank Tupper, *The Theology of Wolfhart Pannenberg* (Philadelphia: Westminster, 1973), 72–74.

64. Pannenberg, *Systematic Theology*, 2:304.

65. Ibid., 2:308.

66. Ibid., 2:434. See the discussion of sin as connecting to Christology and eschatology in Tupper, *Theology of Pannenberg*, 161–62, 182–83.

on the actions of a historical person but rather as reflecting the archetypal, paradigmatic nature of Adam's sin.

Second, all of the theologians reject the relevance of the historicity of Adam. Whether this is because it is considered of no dogmatic importance, as in Schleiermacher, or is rejected outright as in Bultmann and Pannenberg, is really of little account. All regard the idea of a creation that existed in a pristine state prior to a historical action by a human agent that caused it to fall as nonsense.

These two basic points serve to give modern treatments of original sin certain common features. First, there is no movement from innocence to guilt and condemnation in history. Creation was imperfect from the beginning. That has clear implications not only for how one understands the first chapters of Genesis (and, indeed, the trajectory of the drama of Genesis beyond chapter 3) but also for one's understanding of the doctrine of God.

Second, human nature in and of itself is always fallen, and Adam functions therefore as a paradigm to which we all conform. This is not to say that modern theology is a species of Pelagianism. The emphasis on creation as always fallen and the repudiation of any notion of a pristine world before a historical fall means that accusations of Pelagianism, with its commitment to basic moral soundness of humanity, are not appropriate. Nevertheless, the repudiation of notions of alien guilt and the rejection of any notion that sin is transmitted by heredity or biology, mean that Adam functions as the great example of the way in which we all sin, we all fall.

Third, treatments of original sin give modern theology a christological focus. If there is no primeval world by which one is able to judge the depth of humanity's fall, then that role comes to be fulfilled by Christ. Whether he functions as the great paradigm of perfect God-consciousness or as the man-before-God of Barth, Christ comes to have priority in discussions of sin.

Fourth, modern theology attenuates the nature of sin. In these modern accounts there is very little that points toward sin as being something done *against* God. In Schleiermacher, sin is a defective psychological state; in Rauschenbusch (and in modern political and feminist theologies), sin is something done by people against other people. Bultmann and Barth both employ the rhetoric about the seriousness of sin and the judgment of God but it is hard to square this with their view that creation was itself defective and fallen. In the traditional Christian orthodoxy, sin is an action that is a personal affront to a holy and righteous God, and it is that precisely because it involves a perversion of nature as he intended it to be and, indeed, as he created it to be.

Fifth, it is arguable that one of the perceived problems in orthodox dogmatics against which modern theology has reacted—the injustice of alien guilt—is not actually solved by these modern reconstructions. If there never was a time when humanity existed in a pristine state, then one wonders how these theologies are really an improvement on those that rooted the human dilemma in the sin of Adam imputed to or inherited by later generations. If it is unethical to hold me to account for the action of a primeval ancestor, then why is it morally preferable that I be held responsible for my sin if that is indeed simply the result of my status at birth, of me being merely a human creature?[67] What does it mean to say that I am responsible as an individual for my sinful state when it is actually a structural part of the original creation? And this, of course, has implications for how one understands redemption, implications that lie beyond the scope of this essay.[68] Contra Schleiermacher, the historicity of Adam is not a matter outside of the scope, or irrelevant to, the dogmatic task.[69]

In conclusion, one can perhaps summarize this survey by saying that modern theology witnesses to the fact, as clearly implied by Paul in Romans 5, that one's understanding of original sin is necessarily and decisively connected to the structure of one's theology as a whole. One's views of the historicity of Adam inevitably stand in positive connection to one's view of creation, to whether there was a fall in history or whether sin/alienation from God is part of the natural order. The nature and status of Adam are foundational to one's understanding of biblical theology. It is perhaps fitting to close with the words with which J. P. Versteeg ends his own important monograph on the theological importance of Adam to the biblical (and dogmatic) scheme:

> To be occupied with the question of how scripture speaks about Adam is thus anything but an insignificant problem of detail. As the first historical man and head of humanity, Adam is not mentioned in passing in the New Testament. The redemptive-historical correlation between Adam and Christ determines the framework in which . . . the redemptive work of Christ has its place. That work

67. See the comment of G. C. Berkouwer, aimed specifically at Schleiermacher and Ritschl, that in attempts to explain the universality of the spread of sin on the basis of man's nature, the full gravity of sin is attenuated. *Sin*, trans. Philip C. Holtrop (Grand Rapids: Eerdmans, 1971), 525–26.

68. See J. P. Versteeg, "If Adam may no longer be viewed as a historical person but in him is revealed only what is inherent in every man, so that . . . one can hardly still talk about guilt in the proper sense of the word, then the character of redemption also naturally changes." *Adam in the New Testament: Mere Teaching Model or First Historical Man*, 2nd ed., trans. Richard B. Gaffin Jr. (Phillipsburg, NJ: P&R, 2012), 65.

69. See the comment of J. van Genderen and W. H. Velema: "The abandonment of the historicity of Paradise and the fall of Adam and Eve into sin repeatedly proves to have far-reaching consequences for various aspects of the dogmatics." *Concise Reformed Dogmatics*, trans. Gerrit Bilkes and Ed M. van der Maas (Phillipsburg, NJ: P&R, 2008), 388.

of redemption can no longer be confessed according to the meaning of Scripture, if it is divorced from the framework in which it stands there. Whoever divorces the work of redemption from the framework in which it stands in Scripture no longer allows the Word to function as the norm that determines *everything*. There has been no temptation through the centuries to which theology has been more exposed than this temptation. There is no danger that theology has more to fear than this danger.[70]

70. Versteeg, *Adam in the New Testament*, 67.

PART 3

Original Sin in Theology

9

ORIGINAL SIN IN BIBLICAL THEOLOGY

James M. Hamilton

Discussions of original sin are usually regarded as exercises in systematic theology. Is it possible to consider the issue from a *biblical-theological* perspective? If so, how?

I would say that

> a biblical theology of anything seeks to describe both the storyline and the network of assumptions and presuppositions and beliefs assumed by the biblical authors as they wrote. The only access we have to what the biblical authors thought or assumed is what they wrote. When we pursue biblical theology, what we are trying to get at is the worldview reflected in the assumptions of the biblical authors, the worldview from which their statements spring, the worldview in which their statements make sense.[1]

Applying these ideas to the pursuit of a biblical theology of original sin means analyzing how the topic entered into the interpretive framework reflected in what the biblical authors wrote and what their statements indicate about

1. James M. Hamilton, "A Biblical Theology of Motherhood," *Journal of Discipleship and Family Ministry* 2.2 (2012): 6. See further my *God's Glory in Salvation through Judgment: A Biblical Theology* (Wheaton: Crossway, 2010); and *What Is Biblical Theology?* (Wheaton: Crossway, 2013).

how they understand original sin to fit into the plot of the Bible's big story. What do they take for granted about original sin, and why?

We want to allow our understanding of the issue to arise inductively so that we can understand the dynamic between original sin and other themes the biblical authors pursue. We do not merely want a catalog of words or phrases but a thick sense of how this concept fits in the story the biblical authors used to explain the world, to understand their times, and to point forward to the resolution of all things.

To pursue this understanding, this essay will take a cross-section of the statements the biblical authors make related to this issue, seeking to understand where they indicate the problem originated, what its affects and remedies are, and how it will ultimately be resolved. What we are after is clarity on this issue, specifically, how Adam's transgression fits in the backstory that informs the statements made by the biblical authors.

The cross section that I will pursue here moves across the Old Testament in canonical order—Torah, Prophets, and Writings—before continuing into the New Testament to consider the Gospels and Acts, the Epistles, and Revelation.[2] My aim is to trace out how original sin factors into the interpretive perspective of the biblical authors; special attention will therefore be given to how the later authors seem to be interpreting the earlier. I will seek to determine whether biblical authors who came before Paul interpreted Moses as Paul did, and along the way I will consider how Peter Enns responds to such evidence. Seeking to show that the Bible does not require a historical Adam, Enns writes, "Many Christians, however creative they might be willing to be about interpreting Genesis, stop dead in their tracks when they see how Paul handles Adam."[3] As they should. In his effort to show that the Bible does not require a historical Adam, Enns seeks to explain away the interpretive moves Paul makes. The claims Enns makes must be tested against the Scriptures themselves. The contention here is that Paul is not the only biblical author who interprets Genesis 3 to indicate that Adam's sin has made all his descendants moral cripples.

Removing from the biblical narrative the historical Adam and his initial transgression, with its consequences for everyone who descends from him, and replacing these realities with some other explanation of the origin of humanity

---

2. For more on this canonical structure, see my *God's Glory in Salvation through Judgment*, 59–65. I was led to this canonical structure by Stephen G. Dempster, *Dominion and Dynasty: A Biblical Theology of the Hebrew Bible*, New Studies in Biblical Theology (Downers Grove, IL: InterVarsity, 2003).

3. Peter Enns, *The Evolution of Adam: What the Bible Does and Doesn't Say about Human Origins* (Grand Rapids: Brazos, 2012), 79.

and its propensity for evil, is comparable to an attempt to make *The Hobbit* the first volume in the *Harry Potter* series rather than the setup for *The Lord of the Rings*. Try as we might to make the different stories work together, Bilbo finding the ring will not frame the plot the way the story of Harry being left on the Dursleys' doorstep after Voldemort tried to kill him does. This is the kind of move attempted when the story of Adam and original sin is replaced with an alternative account of the origin of all things.

Original Sin in the Torah

Having narrated God speaking the world into existence, Moses writes in Genesis 1:31, "And God saw everything that he had made, and behold, it was very good." When God made the world, there was no sin in it, no corruption, no malevolence, no death. What explanation does Genesis give for the origin of these terrors? Moses presents God telling the man in Genesis 2:17, "But of the tree of the knowledge of good and evil you shall not eat, for in the day that you eat of it you shall surely die." Here is a warning that transgression of God's command will introduce death into God's very good creation.

The narrative communicates more than the words say by themselves. What I mean is that Moses does not come right out and tell his audience everything that the scene he depicts shows them. Thus when he shows the aftermath of the transgression, he does not overtly say that the man and woman have experienced a spiritual death, but he shows them covering themselves (Gen. 3:7) and hiding from God (3:8). Gone is the intimacy between man and woman characterized by unashamed nakedness (2:25), and no more will they walk with their maker in undefiled innocence in the cool of the day. In fact, they will be driven out of the realm of life, the sacred space, with its trees of knowledge and life, that was to be worked and kept (2:9, 15), into the unclean realm of the dead, where the very ground is cursed (3:17–24). A cherubim with a flaming sword will prevent their reentry into Eden on their own initiative (3:24), and they shall return to the dust whence man was made (3:19).

From the very good world, untainted by sin, they go into a world now marked by transgression and laden with curses. There will be enmity between the seed of the woman and serpent, though ultimately the seed of the woman will land the more devastating blow to the head of the serpent (Gen. 3:15). There will be pain in childbearing and difficulty between man and woman (3:16). And the ground is cursed because of the man and his sin: it will no longer cooperate but malfunction, and in the end, dying he shall die (3:17–19).[4]

4. See further Hamilton, *God's Glory in Salvation through Judgment*, 75–89.

Enns writes, "What is missing from the Old Testament is any indication that Adam's disobedience is the cause of universal sin, death, and condemnation, as Paul seems to argue."[5] What Enns neglects here is the way that narratives work. The narrative immediately shows the outworking of Adam's sin: when Cain murders Abel, the reader knows that in Adam's sin the dam was breached, burst, and the water can never be put back. The flood of sin has rushed out, leaving death in its wake (Gen. 4); then the genealogy in Genesis 5 repeats again and again the awful refrain, "and he died" (5:5, 8, 11, 14, 17, 20, 26, 31; see also 9:29). So when Enns writes, "If Adam's disobedience lies at the root of universal sin and death, why does the Old Testament never once refer to Adam in this way?,"[6] my reply is simple: it does![7] The problem is not that the Old Testament does not tell the story as Paul reads it but that Enns has chosen to interpret the story in a way that diverges from Paul's reading.

No explanation needs to be offered about how Cain became someone who could murder his brother. The explanation has been given: Adam and Eve ate of the tree of the knowledge of good and evil, bringing sin and death into the world (see Rom. 5:12). Moses connects the account of Cain and Abel to the preceding narratives with key words and phrases: Adam did not "keep" the garden (Gen. 2:15), and Cain sarcastically asked if he was supposed to "keep" his brother (4:9). The villain has been introduced—the serpent, who challenged God's word and tempted the woman to eat the forbidden fruit (Gen. 3:1–5). When God spoke judgment, only the serpent heard the words, "Cursed are you" in Genesis 3:14, and when God speaks of the "seed of the serpent," he refers not to those who descend from the snake physically but to those who act like the snake. Moses makes this point by showing Yahweh repeating the words spoken over the serpent, "cursed are you," over Cain (4:11), and then showing Noah cursing Canaan, descendent of Ham (9:25). When Yahweh then tells Abram, "Him who dishonors you I will curse," the reader should conclude that God intends to curse the enemies of his people just as he has cursed the serpent.[8] This means that those who oppose what God intends to accomplish by blessing Abraham are to be identified as the seed of the serpent—they will be cursed like their father the devil. With the line of descent of those who "call on the name of the LORD" (4:26) and "walk with God" (5:24; 6:9) traced through the genealogies of Genesis 5 and 11 from Adam right down to Abram (see 12:8; 13:4), the natural conclusion is that

---

5. Enns, *Evolution of Adam*, 82.
6. Ibid.
7. See Dempster, *Dominion and Dynasty*, 66.
8. This appears to be the conclusion that Jesus drew (John 8:44–47) and that John in turn learned from Jesus (1 John 3:8–15).

those to be blessed with Abram are seed of the woman, those to be cursed with the serpent are seed of the serpent.

Moses evidently thought that no explanation was necessary for the radical evil he described in Genesis 6:5; "The Lord saw that the wickedness of man was great in the earth, and that every intention of the thoughts of his heart was only evil continually." If the reader of Genesis seeks a narratival explanation for the wickedness of man's heart, it's back in Genesis 3. This is how narratives work. The reader goes from "very good" in Genesis 1:31 to "only evil continually" in 6:5, and in between is Adam's sin in 3:1–7. Should not the reader conclude that the sin of Genesis 3 has resulted in the change from "very good" to "only evil continually"? Is the other option to leave the question of how things went from good to evil unexplored? The narrator does not have to *tell* his audience that the transition point was the sin of Adam. He has *shown* them.

The flood does not alter the sad situation, as the repetition of language similar to Genesis 6:5 in Genesis 8:21 shows; "The intention of man's heart is evil from his youth." It is no surprise, therefore, when those made in God's image to cover the dry lands with his glory (see Num. 14:21) choose rather to "make a name" for themselves by building "a tower with its top in the heavens" (11:4).

Enns protests against the natural unity of the narrative with arguments that amount to special pleading: "We do not read that Adam's disobedience is somehow causally linked to Cain's act."[9] Against this expectation for Moses to have communicated more in the style of academic prose than narrative art, Moses has not written unrelated accounts that are parceled up into modern chapter divisions, as though he intended his audience to read them as discrete entities unrelated to one another. Moses was a literary genius who gave us a narrative that is marvelously interconnected and is intended to shape how his audience understands the world.

When Moses depicts the man and woman hiding themselves from God (Gen. 3:9), the audience is to understand that they feared the consequence of their transgression already stated in the narrative (2:17). When Moses shows the man naming his wife Eve (3:20), we are to understand that the knowledge that she will have children and be "the mother of all living" has come from the announcement that her seed will bruise the head of the serpent (3:15).[10] From Eve's remarkable statement, "I have gotten a man with the help of the Lord" (4:1), the audience sees that she is looking for her offspring who will

9. Enns, *Evolution of Adam*, 85.
10. Dempster, *Dominion and Dynasty*, 68.

vanquish the serpent (3:15), and (after Cain has shown himself seed of the serpent by killing Abel) at the birth of Seth, Eve announces that God has given her "another offspring" (4:25). All these indications show a strong interconnectedness between Genesis 3 and 4, and I have not even mentioned the similarities between the wording of the curse in Genesis 3:16 and the warning to Cain in 4:7.

Is the reading Enns proposes—where Adam's sin is not "somehow causally linked to Cain's act"—a natural one? Consider the flow of the narrative. Opening scenes: very good creation, perfect innocence, creation untainted by any sin, prohibition on eating from a certain tree. Following scenes: tempter enters the pristine paradise, denies God's word, lures man and woman to transgress the prohibition; God judges them, drives man and woman out of the paradise into a world now cursed. First scenes outside paradise: children born, scenes linked to preceding narrative in thematic and linguistic ways (repeated words and phrases), and one of the sons of the original sinner murders his brother. What brought on the judgment that there would be enmity in the world? Adam's sin. What brought on the consequence that humanity would not dwell in Eden? Adam's sin. It is even arguable that the first *physical* (as opposed to spiritual) death that enters the narrative, that of Abel, is intended by Moses to be seen as the outworking of the warning that death will result from transgression in 2:17. The narrative will soon state that Adam died physically (5:5). Imagine the devastation and woe felt by a man who had lived in the garden of Eden before God in a state of moral innocence seeing one of his sons murder his other son, knowing that had he not transgressed the command it would not have happened. Enns's shallow attempt to unlink Genesis 3 and 4 is neither satisfying nor compelling.

In addition to the special pleading involved as Enns tries to parcel up the narrative, he poses a reductionistic false choice when he urges that we should read "the Adam story not as a universal story to explain human sinfulness at all but as a proto-Israel story," approaching "the Adam story as a wisdom text— a narrative version of Israel's failure to follow Proverbs' path of wisdom."[11] Enns illustrates the profound interconnectedness of the Bible's narrative and wisdom literature as he shows how what happens to Adam is what happened to Israel in the land, as narrated in Joshua–Kings, and as taught in Proverbs.[12] His reflections on these points are stimulating and thought-provoking. But he urges a false choice when he claims that since these connections exist,

11. Enns, *Evolution of Adam*, 91.
12. See also Roy E. Ciampa, "The History of Redemption," in *Central Themes in Biblical Theology: Mapping Unity in Diversity*, ed. Scott J. Hafemann and Paul R. House (Grand Rapids: Baker Academic, 2007), 256–70.

"what Genesis says about Adam and the consequences of his actions does not seem to line up with the universal picture that Paul paints in Romans and 1 Corinthians."[13] This statement can only stand if we limit the evidence to the selective sample Enns presents and make the false choice he urges.

What about the evidence in the early chapters of Genesis that points in the direction of Moses offering a universal explanation of all things? Here's a sampling:

- Genesis 1 starts, "In the beginning," and presents the creation of the heavens and the earth. Yes, there is resonance between "earth" and the "land" of Israel, but focusing the narrative such that it leads to Israel's story does not automatically exclude the universal aspects of the creation of the whole world. Genesis 1 manifestly means to narrate the creation of the whole world.

- This narrative shows that Yahweh is not some local deity whose reign is limited to the land of Israel, a conclusion that would fit with Enns's reading: Yahweh is maker of all and therefore Lord of all.

- After the narrative of the very good beginning and the entry into the world of sin and death, we read of a descendant of Cain who "was the father of those who dwell in tents and have livestock" (Gen. 4:20). This description sounds like a universal explanation of the origin of migratory ranchers. Comments like these reflect a concern broader than mere setup for the history of Israel. The world is being explained.

- The next verse tells us of "Jubal; he was the father of all those who play the lyre and pipe" (4:21). This purports to describe the beginnings of musical artistry.

- The next verse gives us Tubal-cain, who "was the forger of all instruments of bronze and iron" (4:22). Again, this seems to be a universal explanation of the origin of bronze and ironwork.

The kinds of statements we find in Genesis 4:20–22 give the impression that Moses *does* mean to tell a story that deals with universal origins. We don't have to choose between the story Moses tells being about universal origins and that story corresponding to what will happen to Israel and what will be taught in Proverbs. It is easy to imagine Moses telling this story, and the story shaping the minds of later biblical authors, who then frame their narratives such that what Moses taught is reinforced, exposited, summarized, and interpreted. Enns pushes his false choice and his reductionistic conclusions based on a selective use of the evidence because of a doctrinal commitment to the orthodoxy of

13. Enns, *Evolution of Adam*, 92.

mainstream evolution. What drives him to squeeze the narrative into categories that will not account for the evidence? He is trying to accommodate the Bible to evolution. He says he seeks a "synthesis,"[14] but this is the kind of synthesis where the Bible bows the knee to the authority of evolution.

Remarkably, Enns goes on to suggest that the presentation of Noah in Genesis 6:9 indicates that Noah has not been affected by Adam's sin:

> Notice that apparently one man, Noah, seems to have escaped this description. . . . If Adam were the cause of universal sinfulness, the description of Noah is puzzling. Further, if Adam's disobedience is the ultimate cause of this (near) universal wickedness, one can only wonder why, at this crucial juncture in the story, that is not spelled out or at least hinted at.[15]

Enns writes, "I do not think the gospel stands on whether we can read Paul's Adam in the pages of Genesis,"[16] but what Enns says about Noah makes the gospel irrelevant to Noah (and anyone else like him), for they are unaffected by Adam's sin. Paul writes, "As in Adam all die, so also in Christ shall all be made alive" (1 Cor. 15:22), but Paul's statement will not stand if there are people, like Noah, untouched by Adam's sin such that their death does not result from it.

Is Enns right about Noah? Here again the narrative does exactly what Enns says it does not do through its interconnectedness. Noah's righteousness and blamelessness are not due to his utter sinlessness, as the use of those terms and concepts elsewhere in the Old Testament demonstrates. When David, for instance, speaks of being "blameless" in Psalm 19:13, he does not refer to sinless perfection but to being "innocent of great transgression." In the previous verse David asks to be declared "innocent from hidden faults," so he is clearly not speaking of sinless perfection (Ps. 19:12). Similarly, David says that Yahweh dealt with him according to his "righteousness" in Psalm 18:20, but in view of David's clear acknowledgment of his own sin (Ps. 51), we know that David is not claiming entire perfection when he speaks of himself as righteous. Thus, the description of Noah as "a righteous man, blameless in his generation" in Genesis 6:9 does not require the conclusion that Noah knew no sin. Further, Enns has passed over Genesis 6:8, "But Noah found favor in the eyes of the LORD." That could be taken to indicate that Noah won God's favor by his righteous deeds in a merit-based way, or, in light of a text like Genesis 15:6 (to say nothing of the rest of the Bible's teaching), it could indicate that God

---

14. Ibid., 147.
15. Ibid., 86.
16. Ibid., 92.

chose to look favorably on Noah, chose to reckon him righteous because, like Abram later, he believed God. My point is that the terse statements of Genesis 6:8–9 are open to interpretation. We can interpret them in keeping with the drift of the narrative, understanding that Noah was a sinner like everyone else, and that Noah found favor in a way similar to the way that Abram later found favor, or we can interpret these verses against the current of the narrative, along the lines Enns insinuates they should be taken. I do not think what Enns implies will stand against the flow of the Pentateuch's teaching.

What of Enns's suggestion that there is no hint that Adam's disobedience is the cause of the universal wickedness at the time of the flood? The chapter that precedes Genesis 6 is punctuated by the refrain "and he died" (Gen. 5:5, 8, 11, 14, 17, 20, 26, 31). What does the narrative provide as the explanation for all this dying? Death was threatened in 2:17 and announced in 3:19. Genesis teaches that people die because Adam sinned. Does Noah somehow escape this? The end of the account of Noah in Genesis 9:28–29 reads very much like the life-summaries in Genesis 5, and like them it ends with the words "and he died" (9:29). It seems to me that when it comes to hearing the song Moses sings in Genesis, Enns is tone-deaf.

Enns claims, "What we see in the stories of Cain and Noah also holds for the Old Testament as a whole." He explains what he means when he asks, "If Adam's causal role were such a central teaching of the Old Testament, we wonder why the Old Testament writers do not return to this point again and again, given Israel's profound capacity to disobey."[17] But once an author has established what up and down are, does he need to reiterate it constantly? Once an author has established that gravity exists, does he need to point it out every time it operates?

The narrative of Genesis shows the outworking of Adam's sin in the foibles and failures of the seed of the woman—Abraham and Isaac risk their wives with the lies they tell (Gen. 12:10–20; 20:1–18; 26:6–11). These wives are the women through whom the promised seed must come. Then Jacob steals the blessing God has promised to give him (Gen. 27).[18] Again, readers of this story know what brought such impulses of fear, unbelief, and selfishness into the world. Abraham, Isaac, and Jacob are sinners because Adam sinned. Nor do we need an explanation for the flagrant sin outside the line of descent from Adam through Abraham to Jacob. We see that sin in the destruction of Sodom (Gen. 19), the idolatry of Laban (Gen. 31:30), and the rape of Dinah

17. Ibid., 86.
18. See Ciampa, "The History of Redemption," 266, "There are times, when reading through the patriarchal narratives, when one could wonder if the heirs of the promises could be any more negligent caretakers of the promises than they are."

(Gen. 34). The door was opened to all God-dishonoring, people-disregarding, creation-destroying sin when Adam transgressed the word of God.

The story of the Pentateuch shows how God set out to deal with the separation between him and man that results from man's sin. Adam was driven from the garden but not without a promise that the seed of the woman would crush the serpent's head.[19] The promises to Abram in Genesis 12:1–3 answer the curses of Genesis 3:14–19,[20] and those promises are passed to Isaac and then Jacob. In the book of Exodus, God redeems Israel as a people for his own possession. The tabernacle, the priesthood, and the sacrificial system make it possible for the holy God to live among the sinful people. The regulations for this cult continue through Leviticus down to Numbers 10, when Israel begins its march to the land of promise. When they arrive at the plains of Moab, Moses teaches the nation (in what he says to the people in Deuteronomy) that nothing short of a radical heart change will enable them to obey God. This heart change will empower them to obey, such that they will overcome the impulse to sin that infests all humanity because of Adam's fall.

Where do we see the evidence that a heart change is needed for the effects of Adam's fall to be overcome? In Deuteronomy 5, Moses gives a second account of Yahweh speaking the Ten Commandments to Israel (Exod. 20). When the people send Moses up the mountain to get the rest of Yahweh's commands lest they die from him continuing to speak to them (Deut. 5:24–27), Yahweh says that they are right in what they have spoken (v. 28), and then asks in verse 29, "Who will give them a heart like this, to fear me, to keep all my commandments always, that it may go well with them and their sons forever?" (my translation, Masoretic Text 5:26). Later, in Deuteronomy 29:4, Moses declares, "to this day the LORD has not given you a heart to understand or eyes to see or ears to hear" (my translation, Masoretic Text 29:3).

Why does Israel not have the heart they need? A clue to understanding this mystery was narrated earlier in the story, when Adam transgressed, and every indication since in the unfolding narrative has pointed to the conclusion that humans have a propensity to disobey and an inclination to transgress that they cannot by themselves overcome. In Deuteronomy 10:16 Moses urges the people of Israel to circumcise their hearts, which would address the problem of their disposition toward disobedience. As Moses describes the inevitable break-ing of the covenant and exile from the land (Deut. 28–29; see also 4:25–31),

19. James M. Hamilton, "The Skull Crushing Seed of the Woman: Inner-Biblical Interpreta-tion of Genesis 3:15," *The Southern Baptist Journal of Theology* 10.2 (2006): 30–54.

20. James M. Hamilton, "The Seed of the Woman and the Blessing of Abraham," *Tyndale Bulletin* 58 (2007): 253–73.

however, the issue is resolved with the announcement that Yahweh himself will circumcise their hearts (30:6).

Who will give them the hearts they need (Deut. 5:29, Masoretic Text 5:26)? Yahweh will, "when all these things come upon you, the blessing and the curse" (30:1, 6; see also 29:4). Moses has told Israel they will enter the land, break the covenant, be exiled, and then seek Yahweh and be restored "in the latter days" (4:25–31). So it appears that Moses is promising an eschatological resolution to the problem of original sin.[21]

To summarize the place of original sin in the story so far, we can say that Adam's transgression introduced sin into the world, and by showing that no one who descends from Adam has escaped the corruption of evil choices, Moses teaches his audience that Adam's sin results in all humanity having a sin-ward disposition. This conclusion arises naturally from the story Moses tells. Moses apparently feels no need to make it explicit because it is clear enough from the narrative. Like media bias, the views of Moses are evident, seen in the perspective reflected in the telling of the story. It would seem, then, that the devastating consequences of Adam's fall are part of the mental furniture of the mind of Moses.

The prophets who follow Moses make similar assumptions about the sinfulness of all humans, and like Moses they feel no need to offer further explanation about the origin of the problem because the explanation has been established. The burden of proof rests with anyone who wants to propose that later biblical authors disagree with Moses on the origin of sin and death. As our survey of the Prophets will show, the biblical authors who follow Moses have learned to interpret the world and Israel's place in its unfolding story from Moses, and they share the understanding of humanity's sinfulness that Moses teaches in the Torah.

Original Sin in the Prophets

Like Moses, the authors of the Former Prophets do not spell out all their presuppositions and fundamental convictions as they tell their stories. The stories, however, implicitly reflect those things their authors take for granted. Once Moses has shown the transition from innocence to sinful corruption and debility that results from the initial transgression, the evidence indicates that he himself assumed that this issue had been sufficiently established and could

---

21. For a biblical-theological discussion of regeneration and indwelling, see my *God's Indwelling Presence: The Holy Spirit in the Old and New Testaments*, NAC Studies in Bible and Theology (Nashville: Broadman & Holman, 2006).

be taken for granted in the rest of the story. If Moses did not want his audience to reach this conclusion, he would need to state that clearly or supply a demonstration of continuing human innocence. That is, to conclude that Moses did not intend to teach that Adam's sin was universal in its consequences, we would need clear evidence that there were some people somewhere unaffected by Adam's sin. Apart from an explicit statement, which we might not expect in a narrative, how could Moses show this? Simply enough, he could introduce people living in some Eden-like place naked and without shame. We never meet such people, either in Moses or in the authors who follow him, the prophets. Everyone we meet in these narratives is a sinner. If we ask how they came to be sinners, and if we let the Bible's narrative answer that question for us, the explanation is to be found in Genesis 3.

How does Joshua know that the people will not be able to serve Yahweh (Josh. 24:19)? How could things be so bad in the book of Judges? How can Eli's sons be sons of Belial (1 Sam. 2:12)? Why is Saul throwing spears at David and Jonathan (18:11; 20:33)? How could David sin so grievously (2 Sam. 11)? Why are there prostitutes in Israel (1 Kings 3:16)? Why can Solomon say in his prayer at the dedication of the temple, "There is no one who does not sin" (8:46)? How could Solomon make offerings and sacrifice to foreign gods (11:5–8)? How could the nation of Israel be divided, with the northern kingdom setting up golden calves and inventing its own religion (chap. 12)?

On and on these questions could go, but the answer will always be the same: all this wickedness is easy to explain. All humans sin because all humans have been tragically affected by Adam's fall. No humans escape the inclination to choose evil. No humans live in a world uncursed because of Adam's sin.

Paul was not the first biblical author to conclude that sin entered the world through one man, and death through sin, so that death spread to all men (Rom. 5:12). In that statement Paul articulates something that the narratives indicate was a conclusion shared by all the biblical authors since Moses. Paul *tells* what they have *shown*. The world depicted in Genesis is the world assumed in Joshua, Judges, Samuel, and Kings. This continues when we move from the Former Prophets to the Latter Prophets.

Isaiah announced a sixfold woe on the people (Isa. 5:8–23) before pronouncing the seventh woe on himself because of his own unclean lips (6:5). Jeremiah took up the metaphorical use of circumcision, seen when Moses indicated that Israel needed circumcised hearts (Deut. 10:16; 30:6), and applied it to ears. He writes,

> To whom shall I speak and give warning, that they may hear?
> Behold, their ears are uncircumcised, they cannot listen;

behold, the word of the LORD is to them an object of scorn;
they take no pleasure in it. (Jer. 6:10)

That this is not a physical problem with hearing is clear from the fact that
the people scorn and take no pleasure in the word. The problem is not that
they cannot hear the word with their ears physically; the problem is that when
they hear it, they do not like it but mock it. This is what it means to have
uncircumcised ears—to despise God's word. Jeremiah uses the Mosaic heart-
circumcision concept when he says in 9:26, "all the house of Israel are uncircumcised in heart." Jeremiah asks in 13:23, "Can the Ethiopian change his
skin or the leopard his spots? Then also you can do good who are accustomed
to do evil." He then asserts in 17:1, "The sin of Judah is written with a pen
of iron; with a point of diamond it is engraved on the tablet of their heart,"
writing a few verses later in 17:9, "The heart is deceitful above all things, and
desperately sick; who can understand it?"

Why would Israel be unable to see the goodness and truth of God's word?
Why would their confirmation in evil ways be likened to an Ethiopian being
unable to change his skin color? Jeremiah does not feel the need to detail the
origins of this state of affairs because he assumes what Moses has taught in
Genesis. This reality could be demonstrated from all the prophets, but listing
and discussing the examples would be tedious, even if there were not space
limitations.

Let us conclude our reflections on the Former and Latter Prophets by considering Hosea 6:7. Enns writes,

> Because this verse mentions Adam and the transgressing of a covenant, it is
> sometimes cited in support of an Old Testament foundation for Paul's reading
> of Adam. But that reading is impossible when we look at the larger context. . . .
> The NRSV treats Adam in verse 7 as a place name, and this is certainly correct.[22]

Note the certainty Enns feels of his own conclusion, calling a widely held
understanding of Hosea 6:7 "impossible" and saying that his view is "certainly correct."

Hosea is, however, interested in parallels between Israel's past, present,
and future. For instance, Hosea indicates that when God does the new exodus
deliverance for Israel, the people will respond to his covenant commitments
"as at the time when she came out of the land of Egypt" (Hosea 2:15).[23]

---

22. Enns, *Evolution of Adam*, 83.
23. This comes after the promise of a new exodus is hinted at as a phrase from Exod. 1:10 is
used in Hosea 1:11. Further, the mention of the "creeping things" in Hosea 2:18 indicates that

Hosea 6:7 contributes to the wider picture[24] by drawing an analogy between the history of Israel and the experience of the historical Adam. In fact, this way of looking at Hosea 6:7 fits with Enns's preferred reading of the Adam story.[25] Dealing with the locative particle "there," Derek Bass notes that "Hosea's language could have dual referents; that is, referring both to a place name as well as to the archetypical transgressor, Adam."[26] Strengthening the analogy between the exiles, Adam and Israel, is the interest Hosea shows in Jacob's departure from and return to the land (12:2–14).[27]

At the very least, reading Hosea 6:7 as a reference to the historical Adam is not "impossible." Because we know of no climactic covenant-breaking sin at a place called "Adam," I cannot agree with Enns's claim that the view that "Adam" is a place name is "certainly correct."[28] Only dogmatic concerns of the

---

just as this new exodus and return from exile will result in a new covenant like the one made at Sinai, fulfilling the promises to Abraham (see Hosea 1:10), so also this will bring about a new Adamic dominion over all created animals (Hosea 2:18; see also Gen. 1:28). The deliverance is likened to what happened at the exodus, and the redeemed state is likened to the way things were at creation prior to the fall. Dempster (*Dominion and Dynasty*, 32) describes this when he writes, "Frequently the return [from exile] is described in terms that echo the original creation and the placing of the first human pair in the Garden of Eden. Creation language often is employed to signal the return."

24. In Hosea 5:14 Yahweh is presented like a lion who will strike down the northern kingdom of Israel, personified as the individual man, Ephraim. The lion tearing the man refers to Israel being destroyed as a nation and carried off into exile. Moses prophesied that in exile Israel would seek Yahweh (Deut. 4:29), and in keeping with that prophecy, Hosea 5:15 speaks of Yahweh waiting to restore Israel until Israel seeks him. In 6:1–3 Hosea urges his audience to seek Yahweh, who will raise the man slain by the lion from the dead. That is, the new exodus and return from exile will be like resurrection from the dead (see Ezek. 37). In Hosea 6:4 Yahweh is depicted lamenting the ephemeral commitment Israel displayed toward him, then v. 5 speaks of how Yahweh's judgment has been announced by his prophets. Verse 6 explains that what Yahweh wanted was not perfunctory sacrifice but the opportunity to show mercy to sinners who repented of their sin and offered sacrifices—God wanted to show mercy not receive sacrifices from the unrepentant.

25. Adam sinned and was exiled from Eden. Israel sinned and faces exile from the land.

26. Derek Drummond Bass, "Hosea's Use of Scripture: An Analysis of His Hermeneutic" (PhD diss., Southern Baptist Theological Seminary, 2008), 185. Bass's whole discussion, 184–86, repays careful attention.

27. It would seem from Hosea 12 that Hosea views Jacob's departure from and return to the land as a type of the nation's sojourn in Egypt, followed by the exodus—note the juxtaposition of Jacob's sojourn in Aram with Israel being brought up from Egypt in vv. 12–13. This is very similar to the connection Hosea makes in 6:7 between Adam's sin and expulsion from Eden and Israel's sin and expulsion from the land. Bass and I arrived at this conclusion independently of one another. See his discussion, ibid., 186 n65, 226–41.

28. In support of the view that Hosea does mean to recall the historical Adam, Hosea uses other terms with the same consonants to evoke Jacob's name and experience (see 6:8 and 12:3). Further, the Hebrew term "there" can refer to "places" that have more to do with events than locations (see, e.g., Ps. 48:6; Masoretic Text 48:7). The adverb "there" can be used "in poetry, pointing to a spot in which a scene is localized vividly in the imagination." Francis Brown,

kind that Enns is defending—that Paul's understanding of Adam is peculiar—necessitate the categorical rejection of any reference to the historical Adam and his transgression in Hosea 6:7. If we do not allow prior commitments—such as Enns's devotion to evolution—to constrict the poetically evocative nature of Hosea's words, it is not hard to see Hosea interpreting Genesis 3 much the way that Paul does in Romans 5 and 1 Corinthians 15.

Original Sin in the Writings

Moses set the parameters for understanding the world and Scripture in the Pentateuch. The Former and Latter Prophets learned the approach to interpreting life and the Bible modeled by Moses, and the authors of the Writings carry the same perspective forward as they summarize and interpret the big story of the Bible. Space considerations permit only a sampling of the evidence in this portion of the Scriptures.

Job's awareness of the pervasive reality of sin makes him concerned not only for his own sin but also for the sins of his children (Job 1:5). As David confesses his need for God's mercy, he lays more groundwork for the conclusions Paul will articulate: "Behold, I was brought forth in iniquity, and in sin did my mother conceive me" (Ps. 51:5, my translation, Masoretic Text 51:7). Reflecting the need for a circumcised heart that Moses taught in Deuteronomy (see above), Solomon writes, "The one who commits adultery with a woman lacks a heart" (Prov. 6:32a, my translation). Similarly, in Proverbs 11:12, Solomon states, "The one who despises his neighbor lacks a heart" (my translation).[29] The curse of Genesis 3:16, where the woman's desire would be for her husband with him ruling over her, seems to be reversed as the bride is depicted saying in Song of Songs 7:10, "I am my beloved's, and his desire is for me."[30] Qohelet states plainly, "Surely there is not a righteous man on earth

---

Samuel Rolles Driver, and Charles Augustus Briggs, *Enhanced Brown-Driver-Briggs Hebrew and English Lexicon*, electronic ed. (Oak Harbor, WA: Logos Research Systems, 2000), 1027. Along these lines, Gentry writes (in Peter J. Gentry and Stephen J. Wellum, *Kingdom through Covenant: A Biblical-Theological Understanding of the Covenants* [Wheaton: Crossway, 2012], 219): "The anaphoric referent of the adverb may specify a location more indirectly by referring to circumstances."

29. My attention was drawn to these instances by Jon Akin. See his excellent work, Jonathan David Akin, "A Theology of Future Hope in the Book of Proverbs" (PhD diss., Southern Baptist Theological Seminary, 2012).

30. So also Estes, in Daniel C. Fredericks and Daniel J. Estes, *Ecclesiastes and the Song of Songs*, Apollos Old Testament Commentary (Downers Grove, IL: InterVarsity, 2010), 397–98; and Christopher W. Mitchell, *The Song of Songs*, Concordia Commentary (St. Louis: Concordia, 2003), 1112–14.

who does good and never sins" (Eccles. 7:20), and the references to the dead being dust that returns to the ground in Ecclesiastes 3:20 and 12:7 reflect the curse in Genesis 3:19.[31]

Enns does not introduce new lines of argument as he tries to fend off the implications of a text like Psalm 51:5. He ignores the way the biblical authors are assuming and operating within the world as Moses has defined it, and he continues to insist on unnecessarily explicit statements (in spite of the fact that this one is so explicit!) as he writes, "It does not support the argument, mainly because there is no indication of the main point of contention, that David's congenital condition is caused by Adam."[32] From what other cause could it come? The evidence in the Old Testament regarding the universal consequences of Adam's sin is both overwhelming and everywhere assumed by the Old Testament authors. To counter the fundamental understanding of the world set forth by Moses in Genesis 1–3, to replace that understanding with some other set of conditions, we would need an explicit statement or a description of a part of the world where the prelapsarian conditions remain in place.

It is not Paul's interpretation of Adam's sin that is out of step with the theology of the Old Testament. The interpretation of Adam that is out of step with the Old Testament is the one put forward by Peter Enns.

Original Sin in the Gospels and Acts

We have seen that Moses makes claims about how the world began—it was very good—and how that very good state came to an end—Adam sinned. We have also seen that this brought about a state of affairs where every inclination of the thoughts of a human's heart was only evil all the time. We have seen the remedy needed for this state of affairs: a circumcised heart. We have seen promises in the Old Testament of an end-time renewal that will include heart-circumcision for God's people, resulting in their desiring to obey God. This story line is assumed and developed in the Gospels and Acts. Here we can only sample the evidence from the Synoptic Gospels, John, and Acts. This evidence, however, is representative of what the biblical authors continue to assume about humanity throughout these narratives.

We see the heart condition that results from Adam's sin in Mark 7:20–23, where Mark shows Jesus listing the sins that come "out of the heart of man." Similarly, in John 2:24–25, John notes that Jesus was not entrusting himself

31. Rightly Duane A. Garrett, *Proverbs, Ecclesiastes, Song of Songs*, New American Commentary (Nashville: Broadman & Holman, 1993), 278–79.
32. Enns, *Evolution of Adam*, 157n9.

to people "because he knew all people . . . for he himself knew what was in man." These texts indicate that Jesus knows where sins come from, the heart, and he knows how people are inclined to evil. In keeping with this, describing the way that Israel rejected Joseph (Acts 7:9) and then Moses (7:35), Stephen says in Acts 7:52–53 that the pattern of rejection has been fulfilled in the generation that rejected Jesus. As he indicts the generation that rejected Jesus and compares them to previous generations of rejecters, Stephen says they are a "stiff-necked people, uncircumcised in heart and ears" who "always resist the Holy Spirit" (7:51).

So the picture seen in the Old Testament is assumed in the Gospels and Acts, but is there any evidence in these narratives that goes in the direction of what Paul says in Romans 5 and 1 Corinthians 15?

Here again we are dealing with narratives that show rather than tell, but in Luke 3–4, Luke works backward through the genealogy so that the last person mentioned is the first man, Adam, whom Luke calls "the son of God" (3:38). Immediately after this, Luke depicts the devil tempting Jesus and daring him to prove that he is "the Son of God" (4:3, see also v. 9). The juxtaposition of the genealogy's concluding reference to Adam with the temptation of Jesus, and the identification of both as "the son of God" invites readers of the narrative to compare Adam's fall with the way that Jesus resisted temptation. Adam was with his companion; Jesus was alone. Adam was in a lush garden full of food; Jesus was in a wilderness eating nothing (4:2). The serpent attacked God's word when he tempted Eve, and the devil used the same strategy against Jesus. Adam sinned. Jesus quoted Scripture to refute the devil and triumphed over temptation.[33] Luke's narrative *shows* what Paul *tells*.

Original Sin in the Epistles

Paul presents a comprehensive statement of what it means for humans to be under sin in Romans 3:10–18, and this statement consists of quotations from the Old Testament. Paul then compares and contrasts the actions of Adam and Jesus and the results of those actions in Romans 5:12–21. In the discussion of Hosea 6:7 above, I suggested that Hosea understands Adam's sin and expulsion from Eden to typify Israel's sin and expulsion from the land. Along these lines, Paul refers to Adam as a type of the one to come in Romans 5:14, and he seems to have in view the way that Adam's sin has a significance that corresponds to the obedience of Jesus. Just as Adam's sin constitutes all his

33. See esp. E. Earle Ellis, *The Gospel of Luke*, New Century Bible Commentary (Grand Rapids: Eerdmans, 1981), 92–95.

descendants sinners, so the obedience of Jesus constitutes righteous (Rom. 5:19) all who will call on his name (10:13) and "receive the abundance of grace and the free gift of righteousness" available in Christ (5:17).[34]

In 1 Corinthians 15:22, Paul writes, "For as in Adam all die, so also in Christ shall all be made alive," and then in verse 45, he writes, "Thus it is written, 'The first man Adam became a living being'; the last Adam became a life-giving spirit." Paul speaks of Adam again in 1 Timothy 2:13–14, and Jude 14 refers to "Enoch, the seventh from Adam."

Every one of these statements fits with what we have seen from the Old Testament. Each assumes that Adam was a historical person whose initial transgression had devastating consequences for all his descendants. We see from this statement by Enns that it is neither the Bible's teaching nor the history of interpretation that drives him to his novel reading of Adam. Enns writes,

> For Paul's analogy to have any force, it seems that both Adam and Jesus must be actual historical figures. Not all Christian traditions will necessarily see it that way, but this is clearly a commonly held assumption today and the root reason why Christianity and evolution are in such tension for many, in my opinion. A historical Adam has been the dominant Christian view for two thousand years. We must add, however, that the general consensus was formed before the advent of evolutionary theory. To appeal to this older consensus as a way of keeping the challenge of evolution at bay is not a viable option for readers today.[35]

It is "the advent of evolutionary theory" that pushes Enns to abandon the "older consensus." For Enns, "The problem is self-evident. Evolution demands that the special creation of the first Adam as described in the Bible is not literally historical; Paul, however, seems to require it. . . . Christians either choose Paul over Darwin or abandon their faith in favor of natural science."[36]

Enns intends to offer a synthesis and repeatedly accuses conservatives of forcing a false choice, but here Enns himself seems to be the one presenting an oversimplified false choice: (a) choose Paul over Darwin, or (b) abandon faith in favor of natural science. The "synthesis" Enns here proposes demands the rejection of the Bible's teaching on the historical Adam and the universal consequences of Adam's sin.

I wonder why evolution is so authoritative in Enns's reckoning. He never discusses the reality that there is not one agreed upon theory of evolution, that there are scientists who reject it or qualify it beyond recognition. What

34. For further discussion, see the essay on Rom. 5:12–21 by Thomas Schreiner in this volume.
35. Enns, *Evolution of Adam*, xvi.
36. Ibid.

happens when the scientific consensus shifts or continues to evolve? Enns has radically oversimplified what scientists think about evolution, but he nevertheless submits the Bible to the authority of evolution.

Against the bad logic of Enns, when we read the Bible's big story, everything coheres nicely. There is a "through-line" from Moses to the Prophets to Jesus to Paul. Adam's sin had devastating consequences for humanity, and Jesus triumphed where Adam failed.[37]

Original Sin in Revelation

What of the book of Revelation? John speaks throughout Revelation in a way that assumes the wider picture we have seen in the Bible. What I want to highlight here are the ways that John shows Jesus reversing the effects of the fall. Adam was given dominion over the beasts in Genesis 1:28. A beast usurped that dominion when the serpent tempted Adam, with the result that Paul refers to "the prince of the power of the air" (Eph. 2:2). Jesus, however, resisted the devil's offer of false dominion (e.g., Luke 4:5–8), and by his death he conquered Satan, bound the strong man, reclaimed dominion, and in Revelation 1:6 John writes that Jesus made his people "a kingdom, priests to his God and Father," ascribing to Jesus "glory and dominion forever and ever."

In Revelation 12 the conflict between the seed of the woman and the serpent is dramatically depicted, and the serpent and his seed cannot prevail over the seed of the woman. As a result of the conquest of Christ, the final state will be better than the first, and Revelation 21–22 depicts a new heaven and a new earth that are a new and better garden of Eden, indicating that the close of the canon brings the whole story to its resolution. What is lost at the beginning, the presence of God in the garden of Eden, is regained in a new and better way at the end. Everything in between is informed by the sin of Adam, and everything in between informs the obedient triumph of Jesus.

Conclusion

The Bible presents us with a coherent story. Paul exposits what Moses and the Prophets narrated, and Paul's exposition is informed by the narratives that his traveling companions, Mark and Luke, wrote about Jesus. Biblical theology is the attempt to discern the interpretive perspective that the biblical authors employed, and once we have discerned their perspective, we should

37. See Thomas R. Schreiner, *New Testament Theology: Magnifying God in Christ* (Grand Rapids: Baker Academic, 2008), 307–9.

adopt it as our own. We do this because we are followers of Jesus, because the Spirit inspired the biblical authors, and because we believe that this is our Father's world.

This chapter has demonstrated that the perspective of the biblical authors includes a first man, Adam, whose sin had ramifications for all humans. That is the way the first biblical author, Moses, depicts things at the beginning, and every biblical author after Moses shares that perspective. Jesus himself did not write any books of the New Testament, but he taught his followers how to interpret the Old Testament. From what the Gospels show us about Jesus, we can see that, like the biblical authors, he believed in a historical Adam whose sin had universal consequences. Followers of Jesus will follow him in his understanding of the world's origins, the world's problems, and the resolution to the sin of Adam in the obedience of Jesus even unto death.

Erich Auerbach writes that the intent of biblical stories

> is not to bewitch the senses, and if nevertheless they produce lively sensory effects, it is only because the moral, religious, and psychological phenomena which are their sole concern are made concrete in the sensible matter of life. But their religious intent involves an absolute claim to historical truth. . . . Without believing in Abraham's sacrifice, it is impossible to put the narrative of it to the use for which it was written. . . . The world of the Scripture stories is not satisfied with claiming to be a historically true reality—it insists that it is the only real world, is destined for autocracy . . . The Scripture stories do not, like Homer's, court our favor, they do not flatter us that they may please us and enchant us—they seek to subject us, and if we refuse to be subjected we are rebels.[38]

38. Erich Auerbach, *Mimesis: The Representation of Reality in Western Literature* (Princeton: Princeton University Press, 1953), 14–15.

10

Threads in a Seamless Garment

Original Sin in Systematic Theology

Michael Reeves and Hans Madueme

The doctrine of original sin is certainly one that generates a lot of hostility. Indeed, the very grain and alignment of modern thought, where individual autonomy is so sacred, seems to run counter to it. Quite simply, original sin looks like the enemy of liberty. Thus for many today—and not just today— original sin seems a decidedly noxious belief: stern, unjust, demotivating, and ungracious (not to mention peripheral). In this chapter we will aim to demonstrate that it is, in fact, an irremovable part of any truly Christian, truly *good* news.[1]

1. This is not to forget Eastern Orthodoxy, for while the Eastern church does have some differences with the Western over original guilt and the severity of the sinful nature we inherit from Adam, Eastern Orthodoxy *does* hold to belief in original sin. As Bishop Kallistos of Diokleia explains: "Adam's fall consisted essentially in his disobedience of the will of God. . . . As a result, a new form of existence appeared on earth—that of disease and death. . . . The consequences of Adam's disobedience extended to all his descendants . . . In virtue of this mysterious unity of the human race, not only Adam but all humankind became subject to mortality. Nor was the disintegration which followed from the fall merely physical. Cut off from God, Adam and his descendants passed under the domination of sin and the devil. Each new human being is

One of the truisms of systematic theology is that no doctrine can float freely or independently from others: pull on one and the others follow. For doctrines do not sit in the Christian faith like marbles in a jar; they are more like threads in a garment. What we shall see here is that, when the doctrine of original sin is tampered with or lost, the doctrines of God and creation, humanity, sin, and salvation are all significantly affected. And, of course, the doctrine of original sin is inextricably bound up with Adam. Now one could say that we should be prepared to examine the evidence (or lack thereof) for a historical Adam, make a decision, and let the doctrinal chips fall where they may. Certainly we must examine the evidence, as we have in chapters 1 to 3. But it would be irresponsible then not to reckon with the theological fallout of our decision there. To observe the doctrinal consequences of a denial of a historical Adam and original sin is not to employ a "thin end of the wedge" argument, scaring people into conservatism with the thought of what might be lost at the advance of any innovation. It is to be theologically circumspect. And it will be our claim in this chapter that careful consideration is most necessary here; for if we are to be theologically consistent, rejecting a historical Adam and original sin would leave us without a recognizably Christian gospel.

We will proceed in two steps: we will start by looking at the theological necessity of a historical original sin (originating sin) and the consequences of denying one; we will then move on to examine the significance of that sin being inherited (originated sin).

The Necessity of Belief in Originating Sin

Traditionally, belief in a historical sin and fall of Adam has been an essential part of Christian theodicy. That is, because Adam and Eve committed the first sin *at a particular point in time* and so fell with all the creation they had been appointed to rule, we can say that God did not create an inherently fallen world. He is not the author of evil. Rather, being *entirely* good, he created a world that was *entirely* "very good" (Gen. 1:31). The evil that we see in us and around us today is not the result of a character flaw in God, some strain of evil in him; nor is it the result of some compromise he had to make with preexistent evil or with the deficient form of matter. Evil exists because, after God had created a thoroughly and totally good world, his creatures turned away from him. If we remove a historical Adam and fall from the theological picture, then sin becomes a side effect of evolution, a part of the natural ontology

---

born into a world where sin prevails everywhere." T. Ware, *The Orthodox Church* (London: Pelican, 1963), 222–23.

of created human beings. Such a scenario is only a shade different from the Manichaean world picture that views matter as something intrinsically evil. In other words, without a fall, human sinfulness is no longer contingent but emerges from the very structure of the material world—creaturely matter is evil, not in a cosmological sense as in Manichaeism but in an evolutionary sense as in emergentist monism. The creator God is rendered ultimately responsible for sin.

N. P. Williams summarized the problem in his 1924 Bampton Lectures, arguing that "it is impossible to lift the Fall out of the time-series without falling either into Manicheism or unmoral monism"—and therefore the fall "must have been an event in time."[2] If there was no fall, we are left with only two options, dualism nor monism. In dualism, evil is an eternal principle alongside God, the two principles of good and evil existing eternally. Dualism is the doctrine of Manichaeism, the religion developed in the third century AD by Mani. In monism, God himself transcends both good and evil; all evil and good result equally from the hand of God (e.g., Hinduism). Christians are neither monists nor dualists.[3] Sin and evil are *contingent* realities within God's originally good creation. God is the thrice-holy one in whom there is no sin (Isa. 6:3). C. S. Lewis said that the fall "exists to guard against two sub-Christian theories of the origin of evil—Monism . . . and Dualism."[4] Even Paul Ricoeur, who finally could not accept the historicity of Adam's fall, understood what was at stake for Christianity. The doctrine of Adam's originating sin, he wrote, "proclaims the purely 'historical' character of that radical evil; it prevents it from being regarded as primordial evil. Sin may be 'older' than sins, but innocence is still 'older.'"[5] Christians can affirm both the absolute sovereignty of God, that he is truly the Lord and creator of all, and the absolute goodness of God, in that he is not himself the source of evil. But if there was no historical Adam and no historical entry point of evil into the world, then those are things we cannot affirm, and our very Christian confidence must be shaken to its foundations.

Things, though, are not quite as simple as that anymore. Or so it seems. In 1966, John Hick argued that there are, in fact, *two* quite different types of

2. N. P. Williams, *The Ideas of the Fall and of Original Sin: A Historical and Critical Study* (London: Longman, Green & Co., 1927), xxxiii.

3. See T. A. Noble, "Original Sin and the Fall: Definitions and a Proposal," in *Darwin, Creation and the Fall: Theological Challenges*, ed. R. J. Berry and T. A. Noble (Nottingham, UK: Apollos, 2009), 113: "Since we must exclude both of these alternatives [monism and dualism], the paradoxical doctrine of the Fall is therefore a *necessary* part of Christian theology" (emphasis added).

4. C. S. Lewis, *The Problem of Pain* (New York: Macmillan, 1962), 69.

5. Paul Ricoeur, *The Symbolism of Evil*, trans. Emerson Buchanan (Boston: Beacon Press, 1967), 251.

Christian theodicy: there is the "Augustinian" type, along the lines presented above, and then there is an "Irenaean" type, which Hick himself preferred and espoused.[6] Irenaeus of Lyons (c. 130–c. 202) sketched the basic premises for what (Hick argues) would become a more characteristic way of thinking for Greek-speaking, Eastern churches.

The essence of Irenaeus's contribution here is as follows: when God created all things he created them good *but not perfect*. Created things, precisely because they were created and are not divine, "come short of the perfect."[7] What Irenaeus meant was that Adam and Eve together in Eden were not God's end-goal in creation. God had something more glorious in mind: through Christ, humanity would have something more than it ever had with Adam; the new creation would surpass the old; humanity would be taken from the good to the perfect. Thus Irenaeus was prepared to speak of Adam and Eve as children in the garden: immature, susceptible, and at the beginning of a process of growth and development. And an important part of that good process of maturation would be the experience of evil: as humankind tasted evil, they would learn to hate and reject it.

Hick concludes: "Instead of the Augustinian view of life's trials as a divine punishment for Adam's sin, Irenaeus sees our world of mingled good and evil as a divinely appointed environment for man's development towards the perfection that represents the fulfilment of God's good purpose for him."[8] Therein lies a whole new theological opportunity: unlike how it is in the "Augustinian" scheme, death and evil *can* have been there from the beginning as part of God's "good," his grand plan to mature his creation and so bring it, at last, to final perfection where death and evil will be no more.

The idea of there being an upward movement in God's economy, a progress from Adam to Christ, from creation to new creation, is entirely sound, and it is one that has fascinated and thrilled Christian minds throughout church history. And unsurprisingly, it is an idea that has been seized on with particularly acute relish by post-Hegelian and post-Darwinian theologians. J. R. Illingworth was the first to look seriously at its potential as a means to harmonize Darwinian and biblical accounts of humanity; John Hick reawoke interest in it in the 1960s; and Christopher Southgate represents one of the most recent efforts.[9] Some of these theologians who have bid farewell to a

6. John Hick, *Evil and the God of Love* (New York: HarperCollins, 1966).

7. Irenaeus, *Against Heresies*, 4.38.1.

8. Hick, *Evil and the God of Love*, 215.

9. J. R. Illingworth, "The Incarnation and Development," in *Lux Mundi*, ed. C. Gore (London: John Murray, 1889), 181–214; Christopher Southgate, *The Groaning of Creation: God, Evolution, and the Problem of Evil* (Louisville: Westminster John Knox, 2008).

historical Adam no longer feel the burden to offer any theodicy at all. They see the entire discussion as a pseudo-problem. Others, like John Schneider, have suggested an alternative theodicy without a fall, "aesthetic supralapsarianism," which is a christological supralapsarianism with an evolutionary twist. On this understanding, the goodness of God's original creation is teleological and eschatological. What counts is not the perfection or goodness of the original state but rather its direction and ultimate goal. The presence of moral and natural evil at the dawn of history does not undermine God's holiness; it merely represents a small part of a much bigger and beautiful canvas that includes the incarnation, atonement, and resurrection. A world that begins with evolutionary evil, suffering, and death and ends with the death and resurrection of Jesus is, overall, aesthetically good. The sin and evil that emerge from the evolutionary process are, thus, "on the whole exactly what God planned from the beginning."[10]

However, Hick's so-called Irenaean theodicy actually ends up running contrary to the overall tide of Irenaeus's own theology. Irenaeus was no proto-Darwinian or proto-Marxist. Hick himself admitted that he had drawn his argument from mere inference and that "within Irenaeus's own writings there are crosscurrents and alternative suggestions that I have left aside here."[11] It might be more honest to say that Hick is building his entire argument on mere crosscurrents in Irenaeus's theology, for Irenaeus only ever made passing mention of Adam's immaturity, and yet he returns repeatedly to describe the profound severity of the fall.[12] Irenaeus would indeed argue that God uses and even appoints death and evil, but Irenaeus could not have been more emphatic that God is not the author and creator of them. Certainly he believed Adam was created childlike, as the beginning of an ongoing project of creation, but that very childlikeness implied innocence. For Irenaeus, it was vital to assert that sin, death, and evil are parasitic intrusions into God's good creation.

Of course, to say that Irenaeus himself did not go where Hick would take his theology is no argument. Irenaeus could very well set up a legitimate theological trajectory and fail to follow through on it. That is not our point at all. It is, instead, that Irenaeus had at the core of his theology something that

10. John Schneider, "Recent Genetic Science and Christian Theology on Human Origins: An 'Aesthetic Supralapsarianism,'" *Perspectives on Science and Christian Faith* 62 (2010): 208. See also his "The Fall of 'Augustinian Adam': Original Fragility and Supralapsarian Purpose," *Zygon* 47 (2012): 949–69.

11. Hick, *Evil and the God of Love*, 215.

12. The context for Irenaeus's brief depiction of Adam's immaturity (*Against Heresies* 4.37–39) is also significant, though rarely mentioned: he is specifically arguing against gnostic fatalism, seeking to show that human choices really matter.

forbade him—and that must forbid us—from accepting that sin, death, and evil were a part of God's original and "good" creation.

Irenaeus spent all we know of his theological labors in countering what we now call gnosticism, a collection of beliefs that made up what he considered to be the quintessential heresy. In gnostic thought, the physical cosmos was seen as inherently problematic, probably the consequence of a previous fall in the spiritual realm. Many gnostics saw the Creator God of the Old Testament as an inherently evil being, the author of misery. Their hope was somehow to shake off the physical and become pure spirit. For Irenaeus, this was intolerable: if death and evil are integral parts of God's creation, then in the cross and resurrection of Jesus, God is defeating his very own work. And if death is simply part of what it means to be physical, then what of the resurrection? With perfect consistency, the gnostics wished to deny a resurrection of the body, but Irenaeus's whole understanding of the economy of God was that God does not save us *from* our createdness or physicality; his salvation is precisely the *redemption* of his creation.

This is where so many of those schemes that have sought to be "Irenaean" in their theodicy fall down in their failure to appreciate the difference between Irenaeus and his gnostic opponents. Rightly seeing the upward trajectory in Irenaeus's thought, from creation to new creation, they read far too much into what that means for creation in its original state. Irenaeus himself saw that death and evil cannot be an integral part of God's creation if we are to take the cross and resurrection seriously (which the gnostics did not). Writing in the wake of the brutal persecutions of 177 in Lugdunum (Lyons), Irenaeus could not countenance synthesizing evil (something that is always easier to do when suffering and evil are viewed abstractly or from a safe distance). God in his sovereignty might and does use it, but death and evil are truly evil, and not covertly good. Thus they must be the result of sin, of a creaturely rebellion, not the direct product of a callous or malevolent God. All of which is to say that appeals to an "Irenaean" schema and theodicy do not offer a valid theological escape route from belief in a historical sin and fall of Adam.

The Necessity of Belief in Originated Sin

We now move from the significance of a historical original sin to the significance of its being inherited. We will look at five key areas of doctrine that are affected by belief in (or denial of) originated sin: the doctrines of humanity, sin, salvation, Christ, and God.

Originated Sin and the Doctrine of Humanity

Sometimes well-meaning Christians have said that Scripture and theology are only concerned with metaphysical or religious matters, those matters that are ultimate, whereas the nontheological disciplines like the natural and social sciences deal with concrete questions about how things work and how to understand various aspects of our world. The Bible answers "why" questions, while science answers "how" questions. The well-known problems with this simplistic formulation quickly emerge when we consider the doctrine of originated sin and humanity. It is impossible to understand humanity aright apart from the reality of inherited sin. Indeed, the very nexus of sin and salvation hang on the identity of Adam as the father of humanity (Acts 17:26) and our participation in his primal sin (Rom. 5:12).

Note first that this problem of inherited sin, unique to Christianity, presupposes a *common* humanity. The Nigerian woman at the market, the Chinese businessman, the Icelandic teenager—each of us, in all our glorious creaturely diversity, no matter what ethnic or cultural or geographical heritage, are ultimately children of Adam, from that same original family. This reality abolishes the very basis of racism. It destroys polygenism, the nineteenth-century view—based on our physical and cultural differences—that the various human races are different species with separate, unrelated origins (many polygenists, of course, were racist slave owners).[13] To confess that we have all inherited from Adam a morally corrupt nature is to assume monogenism, one origin to the entire human family.[14]

Inherited sin is a dark reality, but it is one with the widest silver lining. Gregory Nazianzen put it neatly when he wrote his famous maxim: "That which [Christ] has not assumed he has not healed."[15] He points to the crucial role played by the universal sinfulness we inherit from Adam. Because Adam first sinned, we all participate in that one sin, and as a result we are all in the same sinking boat, we all have the same problem. The promised Savior, the son of David, would become incarnate, *human*, like Adam, and would thus be able to save Adam and all his descendants. Since we have all inherited Adam's sin, that puts us into that single class of people who need redemption—"for as in Adam all die, so in Christ all will be made alive" (1 Cor. 15:22 NIV).

13. See G. Blair Nelson, "'Men before Adam!': American Debates over the Unity and Antiquity of Humanity," in *When Science and Christianity Meet*, ed. David Lindberg and Ronald L. Numbers (Chicago: University of Chicago Press, 2003), 161–81.

14. Granted, many monogenists were (and are) racists. Our point is simply that any theoretical basis for racism vanishes once we recognize originated sin and its assumption of common descent from Adam.

15. Gregory of Nazianzus, *Epistle 101, Nicene and Post-Nicene Fathers*, series 2, vol. 7, 438.

In the wisdom of God, Jesus became incarnate as a *physical* descendant of Adam (Luke 3:23–38); he did not become incarnate as an angel, or a dog, or a dinosaur, or an orangutan. He became a human being, a man, precisely so that he could save humanity. But if we are not all descended from Adam, and if our moral depravity is not in substantive continuity with Adam, then salvation becomes a risky, disturbing thing. For how will I know for sure that Christ assumed *my* "human" nature? How will I know for sure that he became incarnate and died for a creature like me?

One might think that Darwin has the answer. After all, Darwin was a convinced monogenist and hailed from a family of dyed-in-the-wool abolitionists.[16] One often reads of how his argument for common descent dealt a deathblow to polygenism, establishing monogenism as the new scientific orthodoxy. It is true that, on one level, evolutionary theory does give us a common origin and a unified humanity. Darwinian common descent avoids the racist assumptions of polygenist theory. In spite of these gains, however, the *theological* problems with historical polygenism still lie nascent within Darwin's evolutionary biology. According to the standard account, there was never a time in our history when our ancestor population was less than thousands of individuals.[17] That rules out Adam and Eve as the progenitors of the entire human race. Darwin secured the idea that all living creatures descended from a common source, not that all human beings descended from Adam and Eve. Common descent here does not entail monogenesis. All human beings today, according to accepted evolutionary theory, do *not* share a common human ancestor. And so Darwin has not escaped the basic problem posed by the nature of sin and salvation. Only a robust notion of *Adamic* common descent, entailed in the reality that we have inherited a sinful nature, resolves the problem.

But perhaps there is another way out? In his commentary on Genesis, Derek Kidner speculated that there may be an interpretation of Genesis 3 that is compatible with polygenesis. The problem with the scientific picture is that, if true, Adam had many humanlike contemporaries who were physiologically similar to him though not descended from him. That seems in blatant contradiction to the biblical teaching that Adam was the first true man who unites all of humanity. Kidner's hypothetical response relied on the concept of "federal headship," acting not merely temporally but also geographically. In his own oft-cited words, "God may have now conferred His image on Adam's

16. Peter J. Bowler, *Darwin Deleted: Imagining a World without Darwin* (Chicago: University of Chicago Press, 2013), 260.

17. See Francisco J. Ayala, "The Myth of Eve: Molecular Biology and Human Origins," *Science* 270 (1995): 1930–36.

collaterals, to bring them into the same realm of being. Adam's 'federal' headship of humanity extended, if that was the case, outwards to his contemporaries as well as onwards to his offspring, and his disobedience disinherited both alike."[18] One might object that such an account strains the meaning of *headship* since these "collaterals" are neither biologically nor ontologically connected to Adam. Here Kidner suggests that solidarity, not heredity, is the key biblical image of our connection with Adam, and he thinks this fits rather well with his expanded notion of federal headship.[19]

A number of respected evangelicals are sympathetic to this proposal (including John Stott, Denis Alexander, and Tim Keller). And only a fool would doubt the warm evangelical piety that permeates Kidner's scholarly work. In his efforts to find concordance with the scientific picture, it is refreshing that he never loses sight of Adam's role as the head of all humanity. The federal headship theory is far better than a world without a trace of Adam. But the model surely strains the biblical text! One looks in vain for any indication in Genesis 2–3 that there were any humans, or humanlike beings, other than Adam and Eve. God's words prior to Eve's creation are difficult to reconcile with polygenesis ("It is not good for man to be alone," Gen. 2:18 NLV).

The theological implications are just as troubling.[20] According to Kidner, Adam's federal headship has no connection to his natural headship. In other words, Adam's imputed sin has no *ontological* basis. If only Africans and Asians, let us say, are true physical descendants of Adam, God will still impute Adam's sin to Britons and Americans since Adam was also the federal head of all his contemporaries (among whom would have been their ancestors). This divine decree seems unfair and arbitrary since it is not grounded in an antecedent natural reality. It is the divine fiat that makes it so. The fact is that headship always has ontological roots. Our union with Christ in the New Testament is not based on a legal fiction or divine whim. A true Christian is righteous because the Spirit has brought him or her into a living, ontological union with Christ. If that is true, the symmetry between the roles of Adam and Christ in Romans 5:12–21 suggests that our union with Adam is likewise not a legal fiction. The inheritance of sin remains one of the most poignant reminders that each one of us, regardless of culture, ethnicity, and gender, is a physical descendant of Adam.

18. Derek Kidner, *Genesis: An Introduction and Commentary* (London: Tyndale Press, 1967), 29.

19. Ibid., 30.

20. This paragraph draws on Michael Reeves, "Adam and Eve," in *Should Christians Embrace Evolution? Biblical and Scientific Responses*, ed. Norman Nevin (Nottingham, UK: Inter-Varsity, 2009), 43–56.

Originated Sin and the Doctrine of Sin

A key question that every responsible theologian must deal with at some point is this: how deep does sin go in us? The answer we give to that question will determine much of how we think the gospel works, and what the very nature of salvation is. Indeed, in his debate with Erasmus over precisely this issue, Martin Luther called this "the real issue [of the Reformation], the essence of the matter in dispute . . . the question on which everything hinges . . . the vital spot."[21] To be clear, the question is not about the extremity of our sin: no theologian claims that we are all utterly depraved and as evil as we could possibly be. Rather, it is this: Is sin a superficial aberration? Deep down, is there a core to us that remains unscathed by sin, that remains unsullied, neutral, or pure? Or is sin something that is now in the very roots of a sinner, in the heart, affecting the very grain of our being?

When Pelagius denied that we inherit Adam's original sin and affirmed instead that we are born innocent and untainted by sin, an immediate consequence was that sin became, for him, a mere matter of imitation. If, after all, we are each born without sin, the only way we can start sinning is by copying the sin committed by our forebears and contemporaries. Thus sin, for Pelagius, becomes a decidedly superficial matter of our free will choosing badly: it is not a problem we are born with and that affects and shapes us through and through; it is something we freely opt into. Denying that we inherit Adam's original sin meant denying that sin has any real depth in us.

Of course, that all instinctively appeals. We like the idea of our core identity being somehow above and beyond our sin and that we have an absolute liberty to determine our own destinies. But there are a number of unsightly problems with such thinking. First and foremost, if sin is something superficial, something I simply opt into, then my need for grace is equally superficial. Such a view assumes that my will and my choice stand before all things, both sin and grace. And thus my own choosing becomes the essential basis for determining my destiny: I am under sin or under grace simply because of my own decision to be there. Yet both Scripture and experience show that I do not make my choices in such a detached and neutral way. My choices are motivated by something deeper in me: by my inclinations, my internal dispositions—by who I am (James 1:14–15). Why then do I sin? Not because I have chosen to "opt in," as if that were truly possible, but because my deepest inclinations are sinful. I sin because I am a sinner. A good tree bears good fruit and a bad tree bears bad fruit, said Jesus (Matt. 7:17). In other words, my choices and so

---

21. Martin Luther, "The Bondage of the Will," in *Luther's Works*, ed. P. S. Watson, vol. 33 (Philadelphia: Fortress, 1972), 294.

my actions are the fruit of who I already am. They do not so much *determine* what we are as *show* what we are. At root, then, sin is not actually something we choose; it is the deep tendency that shapes our sinful choices.

What of Adam, though? If Adam and Eve could choose sin from a position of innocence, surely sin *is* just a matter of choices? Here we should probably note that Adam and Eve were something of a special case. They were created with an ability not to sin, a moral innocence, that none of us have this side of Eden. But in some ways, that is beside the point because even in Eden, the act of sin arose from something much deeper down, a heartfelt desire. The woman's desire prompted her action (Gen. 3:6). Even in Eden, sin is a profound thing, the shaper of choices and not just the choice itself. *Why* the hearts of Adam and Eve should have turned to sin is of course a mystery. There we seem to be dealing with the impenetrable obscurity of darkness, the illogicality of evil.[22] But there is actually less difficulty to deal with overall if there is such a thing as originated sin. We all must deal with the mystery of Adam's primal sin, but if all subsequent sin is by imitation only, then *all* postlapsarian sinning becomes as mysterious as that first sin. In that sense, the Pelagian account of sin actually multiplies exponentially the number of impenetrable mysteries and is therefore considerably more difficult than the Augustinian. Under the Pelagian account, one would expect to see at least a few individuals in the history of humanity not opting for sin and so not requiring grace.

Perhaps the real difficulty with any idea of originated sin is how scandalous it is to modern sensibilities about autonomy, at which point we must note that being at odds with modernity is not in and of itself problematic. We would argue that the deep understanding of sin that originated sin gives is instead prophetic; instead of leaving us desperately trying to construct our destinies by our own weak choices, originated sin suggests that our identity is something that is essentially constructed outside ourselves, and for us. Thus we come to despair of our own efforts and choices, and long instead for a rebirth into a new identity. Sin, we have argued, is not a superficial matter of imitation, of "opting in" to a particular way of life from a basic position of neutrality. It is a profound thing, affecting us all the way down and thus forcing us to look outside ourselves for hope. To maintain such a *deep* view of sin is, of course, what it means to confess an *originated* sin.

What we are saying, in essence, is that originated sin is a daily reminder of our need for divine grace. But there is more. To reject the reality of Adam

22. See Donald Fairbairn's *Life in the Trinity* (Downers Grove, IL: InterVarsity, 2009), chap. 5, which draws on bk. 14 of Augustine's *City of God* to show how Eve's heartfelt desire could arise where no sinful inclination was previously present.

and originated sin is, in fact, to suffocate our very understanding of the *nature* of God's grace. Again and again in the pages of Scripture we see men and women coming to realize the deep heart-level wickedness that separates them from communion with God. It is God who gives them a glimpse of that horrible blight on their souls, allowing them to open up to the boundless joy of experiencing God's grace and forgiveness (see Isa. 6:5). Think of Naaman, the Aramean commander afflicted by an incurable skin condition—what a compelling metaphor for our own sinful condition! God heals him, and his skin became "like that of a young boy" (2 Kings 5:14 NIV). His reaction is that of one who cannot believe the illimitable grace of God (v. 15). Or consider the Samaritan woman, beset by her own sin, without God and without salvation (John 4:22), who then encounters God's grace. Her experience of God is so transformative that she instantly turns evangelist with an astonishing message to tell (v. 39). The same King David who knew he was born in sin (Ps. 51:5) also came to realize, after his darkest hour, that words cannot capture the exhilarating experience of God's grace in forgiveness (32:1–2).

It is one of the reasons Augustine was always spoiling for a fight with the Pelagians. This was not mere rhetorical gamesmanship—he saw clearly that the very nature of grace hung in the balance. If Julian of Eclanum was right, that original sin has not corrupted us to the very core, then "grace" is actually a form of law. It is something we must choose or opt into—for our own good, and by our own power. But such a view, Augustine saw, had simply terrifying pastoral consequences. If Julian was right, a good shepherd would not, like Jesus, be filled with compassion at how "harassed and helpless" his people were (Matt. 9:36); he could simply rail at their failings, for their problem is solvable by themselves. On this account, sinners are not helpless addicts in need of outside rescue; they are more like spiritual slobs who need to be told to buck up. For Augustine, on the other hand, our disease is incurable, which is precisely why we need Someone to heal us, "the Spirit of grace [who] freely brings aid."[23]

This deep view of sin as something that corrupts all the way down may initially sound gloomy (hence its unpopularity), but historically it has been the motor behind spiritual awakening and revival. Like a sounding gong, it is repeated endlessly throughout church history, whether by the Protestant Reformers or the Wesleyan revivals. Luther's realization of his moral inability unlocked the door of justification by faith. As Richard Lovelace has shown, this assumption guided the Reformers, the Puritans, and the Pietists. It was the reason that the world was turned upside down during the first Great

---

23. Augustine, *A Treatise Against Two Letters of the Pelagians* III, 9, 25, *Nicene and Post-Nicene Fathers*, series 1, vol. 5, 415.

Awakening when it heard thundering sermons from men like John Wesley and Jonathan Edwards.[24] These preachers saw that the moral reform championed by others as the solution to our woes is insufficient, and they saw it because of their radical view of the human problem. For them, our sin goes so deep that our very hearts must be renewed, and that not by our own efforts, but by the Spirit of life himself. For them, belief in originated sin was not a dour and graceless theological nicety; it was the very thing that made them proclaim our need for a heart-renewing experience of the Spirit.

Originated Sin and Soteriology

We have already hinted at the fact that the nature of sin and the nature of salvation are inextricably bound together as correlatives. It is not just a matter of a few Pauline texts, such as Romans 5:12–21 and 1 Corinthians 15:20–23; what one says about Adam and sin unavoidably affects how one thinks of Christ and salvation. Thus, for example, Augustine felt able to reason from one to the other: if Christ is the Savior of all, he argued, then all need to be saved and cannot save themselves. (Or, to put it another way, precisely because salvation is a gift, we must all lack the ability to save ourselves.) Similarly, Martin Luther saw clearly that the issues he fought for in his *Bondage of the Will* were "the real issue" undergirding the gospel he encapsulated in his *Freedom of the Christian*. In modern times Karl Barth equally saw the bond between sin and salvation as "obvious": "The man who is saved in the person of another, and can be saved only in that way, is obviously in himself a lost man."[25]

So what must happen to our soteriology if we deny a historical Adam and so any idea that we inherit his sin? We have seen that such a view inevitably trivializes sin, treating it as a merely *functional* problem of basically neutral people choosing badly. It is unable to account for—or see—sin as a deeply *ontological* matter, channelling and driving the very wills that make our choices. In such a view, I may avoid sin simply by choosing better—something that I am quite capable of doing. By the summoning up of my own internal resources, I may choose righteousness and life. Thus, just as sin is construed as a simple matter of imitation, of opting in to evil, so salvation becomes (in various degrees) a matter of imitation, of helping ourselves. If death comes ultimately by copying Adam, so life comes ultimately by copying Christ. Salvation need not entail a supernatural regeneration of my heart and very being, for I have no such need or incapacity.

24. Richard F. Lovelace, *Dynamics of Spiritual Life: An Evangelical Theology of Renewal* (Downers Grove, IL: InterVarsity, 1979), 82–89.
25. Karl Barth, *Church Dogmatics* (Edinburgh: T&T Clark, 1956), IV/1, 413.

It all cuts against the grain, both of what we see in Scripture and what we know by experience. We go through life and we shape all our choices according to what seems preferable to us. We do not have an Olympian detachment, enabling us to make our choices with pure logic and total self-disregard. We act according to what Scripture calls our "heart," that deepest internal seat of our desires, loves, hates, and inclinations. Deep down in our hearts is where the problem of our sin lies, and so salvation must entail a new birth into a new life by the Spirit giving us new hearts (Ezek. 36:26; John 3:3–8). Salvation, then, is not about *imitation* on the part of the basically neutral; it entails the *regeneration* of those who, in themselves, would otherwise be utterly incapable of choosing true life.

Belief in an originated sin that leaves us entirely affected and spiritually incapacitated is the direct corollary of belief in an entirely gracious salvation. One simply cannot have one without the other, imagining that our salvation is all of grace and yet that deep down we can choose life without the need for such grace. Ian McFarland puts it like this:

> In summary, the Augustinian doctrine of original sin insists on the pervasiveness of sin both extensively across the human species and intensively within each human being. Its point is to affirm the absolutely free and gracious character of human salvation in Christ. Were the reign of sin any less complete, Christ's role would be correspondingly less ultimate; at best, he would be but one factor among others in determining a person's ultimate destiny, and that would render him something less than Lord.[26]

Originated Sin and Christology

The Catechism of the Catholic Church is equally explicit in seeing original sin and the gospel of salvation as inseparable correlatives:

> The doctrine of original sin is, so to speak, the "reverse side" of the Good News that Jesus is the Savior of all men, that all need salvation and that salvation is offered to all through Christ. The Church, which has the mind of Christ, knows very well that we cannot tamper with the revelation of original sin without undermining the mystery of Christ.[27]

26. Ian McFarland, "The Fall and Sin," in J. B. Webster, K. Tanner, and I. Torrance, eds., *The Oxford Handbook of Systematic Theology* (Oxford: Oxford University Press, 2007), 149. Although elsewhere McFarland has argued that modern science forces us to reject a historical Adam, his intuitions here fit much better with the traditional account. Cf. *In Adam's Fall: A Meditation on the Christian Doctrine of Original Sin* (Malden, MA: Wiley-Blackwell, 2010), 169n67.
27. *Catechism of the Catholic Church*, 1.2.1, para. 7, 389.

It adds something, though, that we have not observed yet: that tampering with original sin undermines the very "mystery of Christ," not just soteriology as such. The doctrine of original sin directly affects what it means to say that Jesus is Savior.

The incarnation, death, and resurrection of Jesus prove a number of things about the sinful state we find ourselves in. First, they prove that the state of sin is not one from which we can rescue ourselves. There is no possibility of humanity evolving or advancing itself into righteousness and eternal life: help must come from outside; God the Son must come down from heaven. The cross especially becomes something deeply problematic if it is not necessary. What would that say about the God who ordained it? Second, the incarnation, death, and resurrection prove that sin is not a superficial, functional problem in us. Sin is clearly such a deep, ontological problem that nothing less will do for our salvation than that *every aspect of our humanity* be assumed by the Son, and then that *every aspect of our humanity* be destroyed in death so that *every aspect of our humanity* can be remade anew in the resurrection.

Gregory Nazianzen's maxim (cited earlier) encapsulated the truth that, because the entirety of our humanity needs healing from sin, Christ assumed an entire human nature in his incarnation. Had his humanity been lacking something, that something in humanity could not be healed by him. That is the common witness of the early church: that there is no humanity—not a single individual or any part of us—that is not in need of redemption. Sin, therefore, must have entirely corrupted us, meaning that none are born innocent and none have simply "opted in" to sin. The more, then, that original sin is denied, the more Christ becomes an example or a teacher instead of a savior. If there is no radical problem with our very humanity, if we are as able to choose for God as easily as we choose sin, then Christ could simply have called for us to repent and follow him. No incarnation, death, and resurrection would actually have been needed. Thus, indirectly but unavoidably, a denial of Adam's original sin, inherited by us all, strikes at the very heart of the Christian faith.

Originated Sin and the Doctrine of God

In the end, each and every doctrinal claim makes a statement about God. What sort of creator, what sort of savior, what sort of God is God? When it comes to salvation, the more eternal life is achieved through our own ability instead of God's grace, the less kind God is shown to be. And that is the grand irony with denials of original sin. They are normally associated with disgust at the immediate ugliness of original sin, but their effect is to strip God himself of the beauty of his love and mercy. If salvation is God's call to the spiritually neutral to function correctly, then God is a God who places a cruel burden of responsibility on individuals who in practice seem hopelessly confused, weak, and addicted to sin. In that case, salvation is really law and not gospel.

Of course, while that describes raw Pelagianism well, few who seek to reinterpret original sin today would advocate such a view of salvation. And yet the more they do dismiss original sin, the more the overall consistency of their theology must be questioned. The gracious God is the one who redeems the truly lost, granting new life to the dead, not simply by demanding or even enabling right choices, but by winning and turning their very hearts.

Conclusion

Holding out for the importance of the doctrine of original sin is, understandably, going to make us look like narrow and prickly reactionaries in the eyes of many. What we have tried to demonstrate briefly here, though, is that a gospel that omits Adam and original sin is actually far less good news, if good news at all. We are not holding out for traditional orthodoxy simply because we are scared of what might happen should we ever let ourselves think freely; instead, we happily embrace these old doctrines for how kind and good they show God to be and what good news is therefore offered to the weak and helpless sinner.

Believing in a historical, originating sin we can confidently affirm that God is not the author of evil, that the suffering and evil in the world is not covertly good, and that God is a God who is faithful to his creation and who redeems it (instead of redeeming us *from* it). Believing in consequential, originated sin we can know that Christ is truly for us, having taken our united humanity to himself; that he is truly a Savior and not just an example. We can know a salvation that is entirely gracious, the gift of a most generous God to men and women otherwise enslaved to their sin. They may not look it at first, but these are truths that accentuate grace and glorify Christ; it is no wonder that they have been integral to the most life-changing, influential preachers in Christian history.[28]

28. Thanks to Professor Donald Fairbairn for his comments on an earlier draft of this chapter.

11

"The Most Vulnerable Part of the Whole Christian Account"

Original Sin and Modern Science

Hans Madueme

In 1930, a philosopher lamented the absence of any serious treatment of sin and wickedness in the philosophical literature. He blamed the doctrine of original sin, calling it "the most vulnerable part of the whole Christian account of the relations of God and man."[1] Augustine's idea of original sin was bedeviled by too many moral and logical difficulties, he wrote, so that it was in desperate need of "reconstruction in light of philosophy and history."[2] The quotation reminds us that science is not the only reason people are dissatisfied with the received doctrine of original sin. It is a mistake to demonize science

---

1. A. E. Taylor, *The Faith of a Moralist* (London: Macmillan, 1930), 165. Since those words were penned, philosophers have been filling this gap. E.g., see Robert Merrihew Adams, "Original Sin: A Study in the Interaction of Philosophy and Theology," in *The Question of Christian Philosophy Today*, ed. Francis J. Ambrosio (New York: Fordham University Press, 1999), 80–110; Michael C. Rea, "The Metaphysics of Original Sin," in *Persons: Human and Divine*, ed. Peter van Inwagen and Dean Zimmerman (Oxford: Clarendon, 2007), 319–56; and Oliver Crisp, *Original Sin Redux* (Oxford: Oxford University Press, forthcoming).

2. Taylor, *Faith of a Moralist*, 165.

as the sole reason for the modern eclipse of Adam. Darwin's theory was only the most recent extrabiblical claim that was in tension with Adamic doctrine. There were earlier claims, such as the discovery of the New World and Native Americans, that raised questions about Adam as father of all humanity.[3] In fact, ever since Pelagius and long before the birth of modern science, people have questioned the rationality of an imputed guilt from Adam. Nonetheless, in our day natural science does shape Western intuitions and plausibility structures, helping to explain the growing consensus in academic theology that we should abandon or, at least, radically revise the doctrine of original sin.

But the chapters in this volume resist this consensus. What should we make of this? Are these essays merely reactionary, the dying gasps of a hopelessly outdated theology? Are we simply unwilling, or perhaps intellectually unable, to read the handwriting on the wall? These concerns are legitimate, especially in light of the seemingly wide-ranging scientific evidence against the Augustinian hamartiology. Evidence for human evolution comes primarily from the data in paleoanthropology (see the chapter in this volume by William Stone). More recently, molecular genetics seems to confirm this picture of human-ape common ancestry. Population genetics also suggests that the human population in our evolutionary history has never fallen below tens of thousands of individuals—a bottleneck that rules out one couple as the source of all humanity.[4] The doctrine of original sin proper is also contradicted by current interpretations of the evidence from neuroscience, evolutionary psychology, and behavioral genetics.

Studies in neuroscience suggest that damage to areas like the ventral prefrontal cortex, amygdala, and angular gyrus can cause impaired emotional functioning and decision making as well as psychopathic and antisocial behavior.[5] Evolutionary psychology describes human behaviors as genetic adaptations, the product of natural selection. Thus rape, war, genocide, and other forms of aggression—human sin?—evolved by natural selection.[6] Researchers in behavioral genetics investigate genes for specific behavioral traits and tell us that

3. Other extrabiblical notions in tension with Adam's traditional role included pagan chronologies vastly older than accepted biblical estimates; Isaac La Peyrère's pre-Adamite thesis (the proposal that Adam was not the first human being and other humans existed before him); and geology. See David Livingstone, *Adam's Ancestors: Race, Religion, and the Politics of Human Origins* (Baltimore: Johns Hopkins University Press, 2009).

4. See Dennis Venema, "Genesis and the Genome: Genomics Evidence for Human-Ape Common Ancestry and Ancestral Hominid Population Sizes," *Perspectives on Science and Christian Faith* 62 (2010): 166–78.

5. E.g., Adrian Raine, *The Anatomy of Violence: The Biological Roots of Crime* (New York: Pantheon Books, 2013).

6. For background, see David J. Buller, *Adapting Minds: Evolutionary Psychology and the Persistent Quest for Human Nature* (Cambridge, MA: MIT Press, 2005).

human behavior is a complex synthesis of genes *and* environment. A striking example of the genetic factor is Brunner syndrome, the case of a Dutch family in which eight of the men were affected by a mutation in the monoamine oxidase gene. All the men displayed borderline mental retardation, extreme antisocial behavior, and abnormal levels of criminal activity (e.g., voyeurism, exhibitionism, arson, sudden groping of female relatives),[7] behaviors that are prime candidates for what Christians call "sin." Such scientific data have the cumulative effect of casting doubt on traditional formulations of original sin.

The central question is this: Should modern scientific knowledge compel Christians to abandon or radically revise the doctrine of original sin—and if so, how?[8] This chapter tries to answer that question in four steps. First, I show how most Christians after Darwin recognized deep conflict between the doctrine of original sin and emerging scientific developments. I then examine the nest of problems theologians have created as they have tried to handle this conflict between science and original sin. Third, moving from description to prescription, I offer a methodological proposal for how to begin resolving these problems in dialogue with Scripture and tradition. I conclude with some concrete suggestions for how to understand the relationship between original sin and science.

The Conflict between Science and Original Sin

This chapter has a chief assumption, as does this whole book, that there are deep tensions between a Christian doctrine of sin and the mainstream interpretations of data from evolutionary biology and related disciplines. Such a position might appear suspect given the recent arguments of historians of science and scholars in science-and-theology. They have argued that "conflict" is an obtuse, unhelpful, and downright inaccurate way to depict the relation between science and faith. John Hedley Brooke shows persuasively that science has interacted with religion in many complex ways. "To portray the relations between science and religion as a continuous retreat from theological dogma before a cumulative and infallible science," warns Brooke, "is to overlook the fine structure of scientific controversy, in which religious interests intruded, but often in subtle rather than overtly obstructive ways."[9] He amasses historical

---

7. H. G. Brunner et al., "X-Linked Borderline Mental Retardation with Prominent Behavioral Disturbance: Phenotype, Genetic Localization, and Evidence for Disturbed Monoamine Metabolism," *American Journal of Human Genetics* 52 (1993): 1032–39.

8. See Eva-Lotta Grantén, "How Scientific Knowledge Changes Theology: A Case Study from Original Sin," in *How Do We Know? Understanding in Science and Theology*, ed. Dirk Evers, Antje Jackelén, and Taede Smedes (New York: T&T Clark, 2010), 95–104.

9. John Hedley Brooke, *Science and Religion: Some Historical Perspectives* (Cambridge: Cambridge University Press, 1991), 6.

case studies to demonstrate how science and theology have often intermingled in rich and varied ways (dubbed the "complexity thesis").

To think as we do that an irresolvable conflict exists between original sin and evolutionary science will thus appear naïve or misguided. Some may even infer that we are flouting recent scholarship by promoting the old canard of science and theology perpetually at war. But there is a basic confusion here. One can accept the insights of the complexity thesis and still acknowledge genuine, *particular* instances of conflict between science and theology. Conflict is a temporary, episodic feature in the science and theology relationship—not an essential one.[10] That the doctrine of original sin invited such conflict with science was widely assumed in the years following Darwin's *Origin of Species* (1859).

Many Christian thinkers at the time rejected Adam's fall because it contradicted human evolution. Among those who rejected the historicity of the fall was one Minot Judson Savage, a Congregationalist minister in the late nineteenth century and a severe critic of orthodoxy. In an essay on the atonement, he concluded from evolution that the fall "is proved, absolutely proved, to have been untrue. . . . Humanity has never fallen."[11] He declaimed later that "modern science has demonstrated the antiquity of man and his derivation from lower forms of life," facts "demonstrated as conclusively, and in precisely the same way, as is the rotation of the earth on its axis or its revolution about the sun."[12] Savage and his allies saw conflict between the two interpretive schemes of evolution and the fall, so they ditched the latter.

Others rejected *human* evolution because of the biblical attestation to the fall. The conflict was insurmountable. Herman Bavinck, like his colleague Abraham Kuyper, was open to a teleological, organic evolution guided by divine providence. But for dogmatic reasons Bavinck rejected any evolution of human beings.[13] He described the fall as "the silent hypothesis of the whole [biblical] doctrine of sin and redemption,"[14] and he faulted the evolutionary

10. See the helpful corrective in Geoffrey Cantor, "What Shall We Do with the 'Conflict Thesis'?," in *Science and Religion: New Historical Perspectives*, ed. Thomas Dixon, Geoffrey Cantor, and Stephen Pumfrey (Cambridge: Cambridge University Press, 2010), 283–98.

11. Minot Savage, *The Religion of Evolution* (Boston: Lockwood, Brooks, & Company, 1881), 205.

12. Minot Savage, "The Inevitable Surrender of Orthodoxy," *North American Review* 148 (1889): 724. He continues: "but for theological bias, no competent intelligence on earth to-day would think of disputing it."

13. Rob Visser, "Dutch Calvinists and Darwinism, 1900–1960," in *Nature and Scripture in the Abrahamic Religions: 1700–Present*, ed. Jitse M. van der Meer and Scott Mandelbrote (Leiden: Brill, 2008), 296.

14. Herman Bavinck, "The Fall," in *International Standard Bible Encyclopedia*, ed. G. W. Bromiley (Grand Rapids: Eerdmans, 1979–88), 2:1092.

account for "setting to one side the objective standard of sin."[15] James Orr, the Scottish theologian, also rejected evolution when applied to humanity because it rendered sin a "natural necessity; whereas, on the Biblical view, it is clearly not man's misfortune only, but his fault—a deep and terrible evil for which he is responsible."[16] A similar story emerges from the Old Princetonians, most of whom were theistic evolutionists. B. B. Warfield, for instance, argued that the fall contradicts "thoroughgoing evolutionism."[17] The overriding concern was that to accept human evolution was to recast the entire doctrine of sin.

Even for the small minority that tried to show compatibility between the fall and human evolution, their strategies at reconciliation were (in retrospect) far more creative than compelling.[18] The fact was that most Christians after Darwin perceived significant conflict between original sin and the emerging science. Perhaps they were wrong to do so. Perhaps in retrospect their claims were mistaken, time bound, or impetuous—but that is something one would need to argue, not simply assume. Far from being idiosyncratic or reactionary, this chapter and this book stand in the same tradition as these early responses to evolution.

Attempts to Resolve the Conflict

The two primary areas of conflict with mainstream scientific theories are the doctrine of the fall (originating sin) and the doctrine of original sin proper (originated sin). Both are evident in the first major attempt by F. R. Tennant at a full integration of hamartiology and evolution in his Hulsean Lectures of 1901–2.[19] Denying a historical fall, he argued that we inherit a capacity to sin from biology. Evolution offers the ingredients or "material" of sin (e.g., fear, anger, emotion, appetite), but these are morally neutral as they are part of common human nature. They *become* sin when our individual free will acts on that inert material (notice that sin is merely voluntaristic for Tennant). Since Tennant's groundbreaking work, three main attempts at resolving the conflict can be discerned: (1) modern theologians who agree with Tennant have devised different strategies for a theology without the fall; (2) with the

15. Ibid., 1093. Similar claims are made in Bavinck's *Reformed Dogmatics*.

16. James Orr, *The Christian View of God and the World* (Grand Rapids: Eerdmans, 1954), 174.

17. B. B. Warfield, "Evolution or Development," in *Evolution, Science, and Scripture*, ed. Mark Noll and David Livingstone (original from 1888; Grand Rapids: Baker, 2000), 128.

18. See Jon Roberts, *Darwinism and the Divine in America* (Madison: University of Wisconsin Press, 1988), 107–10, 192–97.

19. F. R. Tennant, *The Origin and Propagation of Sin*, 2nd ed. (Cambridge: Cambridge University Press, 1906).

help of biology such moves in turn generate broad revisions of originated sin; and (3) a number of theologians, rejecting Tennant's way forward, try instead to locate Adam and the fall within the paleoanthropological record. A review of these three approaches follows.

Removing the Fall

Once the fall is rejected, something must fill the void. There are plenty of candidates. Some theistic evolutionists use the concepts of *nature and nurture* to do the theological work. On this understanding of human nature, sin and guilt originate from the tension between genes (nature) and culture (nurture). As one scholar put it, "We share a transtemporal and universal biological and cultural heritage that predisposes us to sin."[20] Another concept that is often employed is *human freedom*. The Adamic narrative on this view is a premodern symbol for the evolutionary and psychological complexity of humans. "Falling" is "an inevitable consequence of human freedom."[21] The Eden story evokes human freedom and moral responsibility; since Adam is everyman, we can legitimately talk of a "fall" without appealing to a *historical* fall.[22] Others point to *entropy* as the real meaning of the fall. Our moral capacities for evil (and for good) emerge from analogous capacities within precursor animals, and these in turn originated from the physical processes of the world. As the measure of disorder, entropy is the "background, predisposition, or precursor to what emerges in us as sin."[23] We can therefore trace the origin of sin to the microphysical infrastructure of the universe. Finally, *relationality* has also been identified as the proper background to our sinful condition. Ian Barbour, who seeks to take the fall seriously but not historically, sees its main lesson as "a violation of relatedness."[24] Fallenness, then, "needs to be explored in light of a relationalist model for apprehending the interconnectedness of the living and nonliving domains."[25]

These are all creative attempts to demythologize originating sin. They become even more compelling when joined to three further motifs that recur in this literature. First, there is a shift in emphasis away from an originating sin

---

20. Daniel Harlow, "After Adam: Reading Genesis in an Age of Evolutionary Science," *Perspectives on Science and Christian Faith* 62 (2010): 191.

21. Gregory R. Peterson, *Minding God: Theology and the Cognitive Sciences* (Minneapolis: Fortress, 2003), 179.

22. Philip Clayton, *God and Contemporary Science* (Grand Rapids: Eerdmans, 1997), 40.

23. Robert J. Russell, *Cosmology, Evolution, and Resurrection Hope* (Kitchener, ON: Pandora, 2006), 32.

24. Ian Barbour, *Religion and Science: Historical and Contemporary Issues* (San Francisco: HarperSanFrancisco, 1997), 270.

25. Ted Peters, *Anticipating Omega: Science, Faith, and Our Ultimate Future* (Göttingen: Vandenhoeck & Ruprecht, 2006), 23–24.

to Christology and soteriology. Who needs a historical fall if you can invoke humanity's need for salvation, the deeper reality to which the Adamic story points? At one level this move makes sense, for it is hard to see how science can ever falsify the reality of the resurrection or salvation. "The paradise story and the concept of inherited sin," Lutheran theologian Ted Peters explains, "are the dressing for the otherwise naked proposition that God and God alone is responsible for establishing a divine-human relationship that is *salvific*."[26] Conor Cunningham suggests, "It is folly to interpret the Fall or the existence of Adam in either positivistic terms or strictly historical terms, in the sense that there is no Fall before Christ"—Christ is "the *only* Adam."[27] Adam is swallowed up by Christology and soteriology.

The second motif is a shift from protology (the origin of the created order) to eschatology. Neil Messer informs us that "there is no past golden age to which we can look back with longing"; our transformation is grounded in the future, "to the ultimate fulfillment of God's purposes for humans and the whole created order."[28] Peters weighs in here too when he suggests that the myth of the fall stimulates us to strive "toward the good . . . toward individual and collective betterment, toward perfection."[29] Instead of looking to a mythical past for clues to our predicament, we can instead look *forward* to the eschaton. Again we see that this move strategically safeguards theology, for science seems unable to falsify such eschatological promises.

The last motif is Irenaeus's interpretation of Genesis 3, preferred over Augustine's because it is more compatible with human evolution.[30]

What is interesting is that, without recourse to Adam's fall as a grounding narrative, these theological moves must still explain the human experience of sin and the need for salvation. Original sin traditionally implies both *originating* and *originated* sin, but once you strip original sin of the notion of an *originating* sin, the center of gravity shifts almost entirely to *originated* sin. George Murphy thinks this is a good thing because, in his mind, soteriology does not need an originating sin. It needs only originated sin: "The Christian claim is that a Savior is needed because all people are sinners. It is that simple.

---

26. Ted Peters, *Playing God? Genetic Determinism and Human Freedom*, 2nd ed. (London: Routledge, 2003), 90.

27. Conor Cunningham, *Darwin's Pious Idea* (Grand Rapids: Eerdmans, 2010), 378.

28. Neil Messer, *Selfish Genes and Christian Ethics* (London: SCM, 2007), 203.

29. Ted Peters, *Sin: Radical Evil in Soul and Society* (Grand Rapids: Eerdmans, 1994), 32.

30. For more on Irenaeus, see the chapter by Reeves and Madueme in this volume. See also Douglas Farrow, "St. Irenaeus of Lyons: The Church and the World," *Pro Ecclesia* 4 (1995): 333–55; and Andrew M. McCoy, "Becoming Who We Are Supposed to Be: An Evaluation of Schneider's Use of Christian Theology in Conversation with Recent Genetic Science," *Calvin Theological Journal* 49 (2014): 63–84 (the helpful material on Irenaeus is on pp. 66–74).

Why all people are sinners is an important question but an answer to it is not required in order to recognize the need for salvation."[31] As other authors in this volume have argued, however, such attempts to eradicate the fall present a massive problem for theodicy. Sin's origin in the world must be traceable to an earlier free choice of one of God's creatures. Otherwise good and evil are eternal coprinciples (dualism), or God is *both* good and evil (monism)—that is, God is the author of sin. Surely the cure is far worse than the disease.[32]

Incorporating Biology

If evolution replaces the fall as the story of sin's beginning, then originated sin necessarily must change. Some have thus argued that originated sin is an innate, evolved, inherited biological selfishness (e.g., Patricia Williams, Daryl Domning).[33] This view might be called "strong biologism," where human sinfulness is largely, or entirely, biological because sin arises from genetic, creaturely reality. Human violence and aggression are a normal part of human nature. In that sense, humans are no different from primates and other social animals who also display violence, physical abuse, murder, self-centeredness, and other vices, and who manifest virtuous traits like sympathy, honesty, care, and love. Sinful actions are no different experientially from the nonsinful actions of our animal ancestors. The human inclination to sin, we might say, "arose out of our animal nature itself."[34] My concern with this kind of strong biologism is that, in translating originated sin into a biological idiom, it effectively naturalizes it. This move loses the idea of originated sin as a *sinful* condition that is deeply internal to us, something morally awry at the very depths of our being, its guilt attributable to each of us in a just way. In the biblical witness, murder, adultery, sexual immorality, evil thoughts, and the like, arise from the moral center of our lives (the "heart"). They are not natural in a merely biological sense but are rather reflective of a more sinister, pervasive wickedness that consumes the core of our human identity (see Matt. 15:17–20; Jer. 17:9).

Others have argued that originated sin is significantly but not exhaustively biological—there is room for nonbiological factors. This more moderate

31. George Murphy, "Roads to Paradise and Perdition: Christ, Evolution, and Original Sin," *Perspectives on Science and Christian Faith* 58 (2006): 110.

32. I develop this argument in the article "Adam the Linchpin: Evil and Evolution," Union (website), http://www.uniontheology.org/resources/doctrine/sin-and-evil/adam-the-linchpin -evil-evolution.

33. Patricia Williams, *Doing without Adam and Eve: Sociobiology and Original Sin* (Minneapolis: Fortress, 2001); Daryl Domning and Monika Hellwig, *Original Selfishness: Original Sin and Evil in the Light of Evolution* (Burlington, VT: Ashgate, 2006).

34. Domning and Hellwig, *Original Selfishness*, 108.

position is a "weak biologism." Here originated sin is simply another way to talk about how genes and cultural environment constrain human behavior.[35] We inherit a human nature from the genome, which then conditions our moral predispositions and proclivities—all of this, they claim, is consistent with traditional notions of responsibility and moral agency. This position suffers from fewer problems and is therefore more attractive than strong biologism. But a lingering question is what actually *grounds* moral responsibility or human freedom. Theistic evolutionists who defend weak biologism tend to be anthropological monists or materialists, but it is far from clear how a monistic framework can make sense of moral responsibility, the minimal requirement for any viable notion of sin.[36]

A third approach—call it suprabiologism—endorses evolutionary biology but conceives of originated sin as exclusively nonbiological.[37] Denis Edwards, who defends this position, claims that human beings are the symbiosis of genes and culture. We are subjects of genetic and cultural forces that are often impulsive and disorderly. But this experience is not sinful. "This experience is *intrinsic* to being an evolutionary human," he insists, "but it is *not* sin."[38] Edwards is borrowing a distinction made by Karl Rahner (and rooted in the medievals), namely, sinful versus nonsinful concupiscence. Sinful concupiscence is original sin, the history of our rejection of God that conditions our lives and our free decisions. But there is a separate, morally neutral, nonsinful concupiscence "which is not the result of sin but which is intrinsic to being a spiritual creature who is at the same time radically bodily and limited."[39] Genes

35. E.g., see Ted Peters, "The Genesis and Genetics of Sin," in *Sin and Salvation*, ed. Duncan Reid and Mark Worthing (Adelaide: Australian Theological Forum, 2003), 89–112 and "The Evolution of Evil," in *The Evolution of Evil*, ed. Gaymon Bennett et al. (Göttingen: Vandenhoeck & Ruprecht, 2008), 19–52; Ronald Cole-Turner, "The Genetics of Moral Agency," in *The Genetic Frontier*, ed. Mark Frankel and Albert Teich (Washington, DC: American Association for the Advancement of Science, 1994), 161–74.

36. There have been interesting attempts by theistic evolutionists to preserve moral responsibility within a monistic anthropology. E.g., see works by Philip Clayton, Nancey Murphy, Joel Green, Malcolm Jeeves, and many others.

37. This is the view of John Haught—he acknowledges that we inherit aggressive and violent instincts from our evolutionary ancestors, but we should not attribute this fact to original sin. Why? Originated sin is emphatically nonbiological; it is "the *culturally* and *environmentally* inherited deposit of humanity's violence and injustice that burdens and threatens to corrupt each of us born into this world." *God after Darwin: A Theology of Evolution*, 2nd ed. (Boulder, CO: Westview, 2000), 139, emphasis added.

38. Denis Edwards, *The God of Evolution: A Trinitarian Theology* (Mahwah, NJ: Paulist, 1999), 65.

39. Denis Edwards, "Original Sin and Saving Grace in Evolutionary Context," in *Evolutionary and Molecular Biology: Scientific Perspectives on Divine Action*, ed. Robert J. Russell, William R. Stoeger, and Francisco Ayala (Notre Dame: University of Notre Dame Press, 1998), 384. Cf.

and culture are, therefore, nonsinful concupiscence, a part of our finitude and thus part of God's *good* creation.[40]

According to Edwards, culture tells a long story of inherited sinfulness, countless personal and communal sins that are taken up into our inner selves to become part of our own moral story. "Original sin," he explains, "involves the inner effect on a person of the history of human rejection of God and of our creaturely status before God."[41] We should note that Edwards is only using the language of "original sin" loosely. This "inherited sinfulness" that results from the sins of others is *not yet sin*, for sin itself is "personal and actual; it is the free and deliberate rejection of God. It is only for this kind of personal sin that we are morally responsible."[42] Only when we personally *choose* to disobey God can we speak of genuine sin. For Edwards, our inherited tendencies "are simply part of being a bodily, finite, and fallible creature."[43]

The shadow of Tennant looms large. Edwards, like Tennant, has naturalized originated sin so that our inherited tendencies to sin are no longer sinful. According to Tennant, the property of *sinfulness* only applies to the free human will. Evolutionary biology leaves all human beings with "perfectly non-moral antecedents of sin," and those antecedents form the material out of which the human will then freely chooses to sin.[44] Both Tennant and Edwards argue that "originated sin" is an ill-conceived concept for if it is truly originated then it can hardly be sinful. This sounds like Pelagianism in a biological key. Edwards is right to distance the doctrine of original sin from the reductive grasp of evolutionary biology. But one worries that he has developed a reactionary, overinflated concept of free will that is obscuring the fact that our sinfulness is a deep and pervasive sinfulness antecedent to all our choices and actions.

In the background of these discussions are wider cultural assumptions about the role of nature versus nurture in human behavior. Evolutionary psychology and behavioral genetics have shifted the emphasis to nature over nurture, and that is part of the context within which theistic evolutionists are now reframing the doctrine of originated sin. All of this invites us to ask some formal (normative) and material (substantive) questions. We have already seen the formal question, the issue of authority: Given that the doctrine of originated sin was formulated by the church long before Darwin, on what basis could

---

Karl Rahner, "The Theological Concept of Concupiscentia," *Theological Investigations*, trans. Cornelius Ernst (Baltimore: Helicon, 1961), 1:347–82.

40. Patricia Williams makes the same appeal to concupiscence (see above).

41. Edwards, "Original Sin and Saving Grace," 385.

42. Edwards, *God of Evolution*, 67.

43. Denis Edwards, *How God Acts: Creation, Redemption, and Special Divine Action* (Minneapolis: Fortress, 2010), 135.

44. Tennant, *Origin and Propagation of Sin*, 172–73.

an extrabiblical theory, such as evolution or behavioral genetics, warrant a significant revision in this doctrine? (At this stage in the argument, the question can be put from the other direction: Given scientific disclosure, on what basis could biblical teachings to the contrary be intellectually credible?) The material question is whether the actual content of a biological doctrine of originated sin can do the work required of it.

We have three options: originated sin is exhausted by biological forces; it transcends biological forces; or it involves a combination of both biological and nonbiological forces (in the latter case, one would need to clarify how biological and nonbiological forces in original sin relate to each other). What is at stake in these choices? In the first place, a naturalistic evolutionary conception of originated sin collapses the distinction between "natural" and "moral" evil. Our free will is only an illusion because there is a more fundamental biological nature driving our thoughts and our actions.[45] More radically, it is meaningless to even talk about "sin" as such (for that assumes responsibility and guilt, which are moot concepts if biological determinism holds). In the second place, if fallenness is indeed a precritical way to talk about predisposing genetic realities, then evolutionary psychology and behavioral genetics offer scientific *confirmation* of original sin.[46] Michael Ruse entertains just this possibility when he identifies original sin with the self-interested Darwinian struggle for existence. "Original sin is part of the biological package," he claims; "It comes with being human. . . . With respect to original sin, sociobiological *Homo sapiens* is nigh identical to Christian *Homo sapiens*."[47] According to this picture, the moral experience of animals and humans has a degree of hamartiological continuity that sheds light on otherwise perplexing discussions about whether animals can (or cannot) sin against God.[48]

In spite of these considerations, the move to assimilate sin into a biological matrix faces daunting challenges. Christian biologism transforms human sin into a problem of biology.[49] But that places us on the horns of a christological dilemma: either Christ was fully human—that is, participated fully in human biology—and therefore sinful; or, if Christ was not sinful, he lacked a nature in common with the rest of humanity (docetism). If Christian biologism en-

45. Peters, "Evolution of Evil," 21.
46. See John Mullen, "Can Evolutionary Psychology *Confirm* Original Sin?," *Faith and Philosophy* 24 (2007): 268–83.
47. Michael Ruse, *Can a Darwinian Be a Christian?* (Cambridge: Cambridge University Press, 2001), 210.
48. E.g., see Michael Northcott, "Do Dolphins Carry the Cross? Biological Moral Realism and Theological Ethics," *New Blackfriars* (2003): 540–53.
49. "Christian biologism" is my umbrella term for the three common evolutionary revisions of originated sin: strong biologism, weak biologism, and suprabiologism.

tails a loss of Christ's impeccability, we face a serious problem indeed. Similar misgivings extend to soteriology. Justification by grace through faith is the "solution" to the "plight" of human sin, but if the solution is nonbiological, one would expect the plight to be nonbiological too (nor does any serious Christian suggest that the solution to sin is biological).[50] A biologized hamartiology, at its core, is simply unable to capture the true essence of sin. Furthermore, a doctrine of sin is impossible without a viable notion of moral responsibility. And yet the status of moral responsibility is problematic for an evolutionary doctrine of sin. If our behavior has ultimate genetic causes, then we lose any real notion of freedom that can ground responsibility.

Retaining the Fall

An easy way to avoid all these difficulties is to identify Adam (and the fall) within the paleoanthropological record. Theologically conservative Christians have offered "pre-Adamite" hypotheses, the most common of these falling under three heads: creationist, evolutionary, and federal headship. *Creationist pre-Adamism* is popular with North American evangelicals. This family of views, sometimes referred to as "progressive" or "old-earth" creationism, accepts varying degrees of the evolutionary narrative. The key point is that it *rejects any evolutionary development of human beings*. Representatives are Millard Erickson, John Bloom, Robert Newman, and Hugh Ross and his colleagues at Reasons to Believe.[51]

Evolutionary pre-Adamism goes one step further by including humans within the evolutionary process. Proponents of this view say that Adam evolved from an earlier hominin[52] and then became, with Eve, the father of all his descendants (i.e., true humanity)—notable exponents are John Jefferson Davis and Henri Blocher.[53] *Federal headship pre-Adamism* is the idea that

50. See the relevant discussion in Ted Peters, "Holy Therapy: Can a Drug Do the Work of the Spirit?," *Christian Century* 120 (August 9, 2003): 23–26.

51. Millard Erickson, *Christian Theology*, 3rd ed. (Grand Rapids: Baker Academic, 2013), 446–47; John Bloom, "On Human Origins: A Survey," *Christian Scholar's Review* 27 (1997): 200; Robert Newman, "Progressive Creationism," in *Three Views on Creation and Evolution*, ed. J. P. Moreland and John Mark Reynolds (Grand Rapids: Zondervan, 1999), 105–33; Fazale Rana with Hugh Ross, *Who Was Adam? A Creation Model Approach to the Origin of Man* (Colorado Springs: NavPress, 2005).

52. Older studies classified humans and their evolutionary ancestors as hominids (i.e., part of the family Hominidae) to distinguish them from the great apes and their family lineage (Pongidae). But more recent studies classify humans and chimps within the hominin family (Hominini). For further detail, see the chapter by William Stone in this volume.

53. John Jefferson Davis, "Is 'Progressive Creation' Still a Helpful Concept?," *Perspectives on Science and Christian Faith* 50 (1998): 254, and "Genesis, Inerrancy, and the Antiquity of Man," in *Inerrancy and Common Sense*, ed. Roger Nicole and J. Ramsey Michaels (Grand

Adam evolved from a hominin and had many hominin neighbors—when Adam fell, he acted as the federal head of both his descendants *and* his contemporaries.[54] Derek Kidner suggested this picture over forty years ago, and it has been picked up by the likes of John Stott, R. J. Berry, Denis Alexander, and Tim Keller.[55]

These pre-Adamite proposals embrace a more or less realist understanding of the fall—Adam's fall happened in our space-time history. One weakness, however, is the potential of an Adam-of-the-gaps fallacy. Paleontology, paleoanthropology, and associated disciplines are judged basically reliable as sources of truth and they provide the main story; the task of the theologian is then to find a way to identify the historical Adam *within* that story. Thus Adam and the fall are held hostage to the fortunes of science (e.g., many of the pre-Adamite scenarios surveyed earlier are already meaningless in light of current paleoanthropology).

Consider Henri Blocher. He originally dated Adam at around 40,000 BC, but as new evidence came in, he was forced to reject that thesis and retreat to a date earlier than 100,000 BC.[56] He is searching for Adam within the gaps of the paleoanthropological record. Among Roman Catholics, Karl Rahner was on a similar hunt. In his early work, he insisted that monogenism is non-negotiable for orthodoxy.[57] But later, as pressure from the sciences grew, he found polygenism consistent with original sin. In one of his scenarios, "Adam" was one man among other co-Adamites, his fall affecting the entire group; in another scenario, "Adam" was a community of hominids that fell as one and thus affected all their descendants.[58] A potential way to resolve this Adam-of-the-gaps tension is to accept some form of human evolution on scientific grounds and maintain the historicity of Adam on theological grounds; thus

Rapids: Baker, 1980), 137–59; Henri Blocher, *Original Sin: Illuminating the Riddle* (1997; Grand Rapids: Eerdmans, 1999), 40.

54. Derek Kidner, *Genesis* (Downers Grove, IL: InterVarsity, 1967), 29.

55. John Stott, *Romans* (Leicester, UK: Inter-Varsity, 1994), 164–65; R. J. Berry, "Did Darwin Dethrone Humankind?," in *Darwin, Creation and the Fall: Theological Challenges*, ed. R. J. Berry and T. A. Noble (Nottingham, UK: Apollos, 2009), 55–63; Denis Alexander, *Creation or Evolution: Do We Have to Choose?* (Oxford: Monarch, 2008), 214–43; and Tim Keller, "Creation, Evolution, and Christian Laypeople," The BioLogos Foundation, http://biologos.org/uploads/projects/Keller_white_paper.pdf, accessed January 4, 2014.

56. See his "The Theology of the Fall and the Origins of Evil," in *Darwin, Creation and the Fall*, 171–72.

57. Karl Rahner, "Theological Reflexions on Monogenism," in *Theological Investigations*, vol. 1, trans. Cornelius Ernst (Baltimore: Helicon, 1961), 229–96.

58. Karl Rahner, "Evolution and Original Sin," in *The Evolving World and Theology*, trans. Theodore L. Westow (New York: Paulist, 1967), 61–73; and "Erbsünde und Monogenismus," in *Theologie der Erbsünde*, ed. Karl Weger (Freiburg: Herder, 1970), 176–223.

Adam fits in there somewhere but, because the scientific scenarios keep changing, one remains agnostic about where.

These matters give us a window into vexing methodological questions on
how to relate science and theology. For over 1,700 years the catholic tradition
confessed a real, historical fall of Adam and Eve based on texts like Genesis
3; Romans 5:12–19; and 1 Corinthians 15:21–22. Furthermore, the doctrine
of original sin lies at the heart of our understanding of God, Christology,
soteriology, hamartiology, and theodicy. On what grounds then can extrabiblical, natural science change, or overturn, a doctrine authorized by God's
Word? Some will find the question grating, especially if well-grounded scientific claims are de facto judged more secure epistemologically than Christian
dogma. But as we shall see, this question is the hinge on which our discussion
turns. The Scripture question lies behind the different pre-Adamite scenarios.
The advocates are wrestling with the scientific implications of the biblical
material. There is a trade-off between what is biblically plausible and what
is scientifically plausible. To the degree that the doctrine of the fall reflects the
biblical story, to the same degree is it inversely faithful to the evolutionary story.

The pattern that emerged repeatedly with the rise of the modern world
is that the natural sciences often triggered the theological shifts, and herme-
neutical justifications came after the fact. Is this an ominous pattern? Not
necessarily. The qualification we should make is that God may use science
providentially to bring to light genuine realities about our world, which then
alert us to faulty readings of Scripture.[59] Even if science *was* the genuine trig-
ger for shifts in theology, that fact in itself does not automatically disqualify
theological change. Sometimes theological change is necessary in order better
to align our thinking with God's Word and with the world God created.

Privileging Revealed Dogma

That brings us to the jackpot: So how *should* we relate science and theology
methodologically? Ian Barbour gave the classic statement for how science and
theology relate. He says there are four ways to view the relationship between
science and theology: independence, dialogue, integration, and conflict.[60] The
independence approach is often adopted by Christians who reject the historicity
of Adam's fall. The mantra is that original sin and evolutionary biology are

59. A point made forcefully in Francis Watson, "Genesis before Darwin: Why Scripture
Needed Liberating from Science," in *Reading Genesis after Darwin*, ed. Stephen C. Barton and
David Wilkinson (New York: Oxford University Press, 2009), 23–37.

60. Ian Barbour, *Religion in an Age of Science* (San Francisco: Harper & Row, 1990), 3–30.

complementary not contradictory (the Bible answers "why" questions; science answers "how" questions). No one denies the element of truth here, but taken as a full account this approach comes at the expense of the biblical narrative. Adam's fall, like Christ's resurrection, was an event within our space-time universe and impinges inescapably on the evolutionary story ("why?" and "how?" are not neatly separable).

Others reject Adam's fall to promote *dialogue* or *integration* between science and theology—but, as I shall argue, such proposals fail to satisfy. That leaves the *conflict* position, classically embodied in "concordism" (e.g., as seen in Christian pre-Adamism), the view, roughly, that there should be harmony between the claims of science and the teachings of Scripture. These two domains can be in conflict, but when all the facts are known any conflict dissipates.

The weakness of concordism was brought to light in a trenchant essay by Charles Goodwin in the controversial 1860 *Essays and Reviews*.[61] Goodwin saw nineteenth-century geology as the analogue to Copernicus in the seventeenth century. The two disciplines forced Christians to revise their understanding of divine revelation. Prior to the rise of modern geology, he argued, the opening chapter of Genesis was thought to teach that the earth was created in six days and is a few thousand years old.[62] By the nineteenth century, it was clear to "geologists of all religious creeds . . . that the earth has existed for an immense series of years,—to be counted by millions rather than by thousands."[63] Theologians initially reacted by rejecting geology but, once they saw the handwriting on the wall, they regrouped to show how Scripture could be reconciled with the new data (e.g., the gap theory and the day-age theory).

Goodwin complained that these reconciliation attempts "divest the Mosaic narrative of real accordance with fact." Their interpretations only seem plausible given a prior commitment to the geological story. They obliterate the clear meaning of Genesis, introducing "obscurity into one of the simplest stories ever told, for the sake of making it accord with the complex system of the universe which modern science has unfolded."[64] Goodwin's own solution was to appeal to divine accommodation.[65] Scripture is a book of "religious instruction," not "physical science," since God has already given us the faculties to discover scientific facts on our own. God used imperfect men to

---

61. Charles W. Goodwin, "On the Mosaic Cosmogony," in *Essays and Reviews*, 2nd ed. (London: John W. Parker & Son, 1860), 207–53.

62. Ibid., 210.

63. Ibid., 209.

64. Ibid., 249.

65. But note that the original Reformation doctrine of accommodation denied any attribution of error to Scripture. Cf. Martin Klauber and Glenn Sunshine, "Jean-Alphonse Turrettini on Biblical Accommodation: Calvinist or Socinian?," *Calvin Theological Journal* 25 (1990): 7–27.

communicate his message, so we should not be surprised that the Bible contains errors that reflect the primitive mind.[66] John Hedley Brooke arrives at the same conclusion of the failure of the harmonization project, "partly because of dissonance between the harmonizers, but also because the more successful the harmonization, the more trouble it caused when the science moved on."[67] Theology married to science in one generation will be widowed in the next.

These problems have led a growing number of evangelicals to defend the independence model and a limited inerrancy position.[68] God on this view has inerrantly accommodated himself to us in Scripture through the fallible assumptions of the biblical authors. The distinction is made between the theological message that God communicated through the biblical writers and their extraneous, marginal beliefs on history, cosmology, geography, and the like (reminiscent of Goodwin's earlier thesis).[69] So Denis Lamoureux concludes that "Adam never actually existed" and the fall was not an event in history.[70] In response, we can agree that the Bible is not a handbook of science and yet, as Henri Blocher notes,

> that does not mean it will have *nothing* to say which touches the realm of the scientist. The fact that the primary purpose of Genesis is not to instruct us in geology does not exclude the possibility that it says something of relevance to the subject. In the last analysis one cannot make an absolute distinction between physics and metaphysics, and religion has to do with everything, precisely because all realms are created by God and continue to depend on him.[71]

Scriptural Realism

Is there a way forward? The proposal I want to unpack briefly is *scriptural realism* and it draws on classical themes within the Reformational traditions.[72] It is designed to answer our key question—on what grounds can extrabiblical,

66. Goodwin, "Mosaic Cosmogony," 250–51.

67. John Hedley Brooke, "Genesis and the Scientists: Dissonance among the Harmonizers," in *Reading Genesis after Darwin*, 106.

68. E.g., see Denis Lamoureux, *Evolutionary Creation* (Eugene, OR: Wipf & Stock, 2008), 174.

69. Thus Peter Enns argues that Paul's views on the historical Adam were wrong *historically* but correct *theologically*. *The Evolution of Adam* (Grand Rapids: Baker Academic, 2012), 119–35.

70. Lamoureux, *Evolutionary Creation*, 202–6, quotation from 319.

71. Henri Blocher, *In the Beginning: The Opening Chapters of Genesis*, trans. David Preston (1979; Downers Grove, IL: InterVarsity, 1984), 24.

72. I am also obviously indebted to Alvin Plantinga, especially his *Warranted Christian Belief* (Oxford: Oxford University Press, 2000), 258–66. See also his "Games Scientists Play," in *The Believing Primate*, ed. Jeffrey Schloss and Michael Murray (Oxford: Oxford University Press, 2009), 159–67.

natural science change, or even overturn, a doctrine that is authorized by God's Word in Scripture? I will sketch out my proposal in three moves.

The first move—or rather, commitment—is to affirm *biblical inerrancy*. Since God cannot err or deceive, Scripture as his self-expression cannot err or deceive (e.g., 1 John 3:20; Titus 1:2; Heb. 6:18). God is holy and faithful. Scripture is truthful in all that it affirms, so that "when all the facts are known, the Scriptures in their original autographs and properly interpreted will be shown to be wholly true in everything that they affirm, whether that has to do with doctrine or morality or with the social, physical, or life sciences."[73] This conviction functions inescapably as a premise shaping our understanding of the relationship between science and theology. In the modern mind, beliefs derived from Scripture belong to the realm of opinion and probability, whereas the claims of science, at least in some cases, belong to the realm of justifiable certainty and knowledge. But this misunderstands or ignores a key implication of biblical authority; there are indeed other legitimate windows into reality (e.g., history, science, archaeology, etc.), but Scripture stands on an entirely different plane as the Word of God.

The second move invokes a *pneumatic certainty*. John Calvin acknowledges the objective dimension of Scripture's authority, what he calls the "firm proofs" that help establish the credibility of Scripture. But Calvin goes on to argue that far greater than any such external proof is the internal proof that God himself speaks in the Scriptures. The assurance of biblical authority, he says, comes from "a higher place than human reasons, judgments, or conjectures, that is, in the secret testimony of the Spirit."[74] Christians know that Scripture is authoritative with a theological certainty: "the testimony of the Spirit," Calvin says, "is more excellent than all reason."[75]

This internal testimony of the Holy Spirit induces in believers a theological certainty of the divinity of Scripture. In the seventeenth century, Francis Turretin classified three kinds of certainty: mathematical, moral, and theological.[76]

73. Paul Feinberg, "The Meaning of Inerrancy," in *Inerrancy*, ed. Norman Geisler (Grand Rapids: Zondervan, 1980), 294.
74. John Calvin, *Institutes of the Christian Religion*, 1.7.4. See also 3.1.3, 3.2.15, 3.2.33–36.
75. Ibid., 1.7.4, 79.
76. Mathematical certainty comes from demonstrable truth, first principles guaranteed by logic. Moral certainty derives from highly probable, though not self-evident, truths that almost all educated people will assent to. But Christians receive from Scripture something entirely different: "The Scriptures do not possess metaphysical certainty; otherwise the assent which we give to them would bespeak knowledge, not faith. Neither do they possess simply a moral or probable certainty; otherwise our faith would not be more certain than any historical assent given to human writings. *But they have a theological and infallible certainty, which cannot possibly deceive the true believer illuminated by the Spirit of God.*" Francis Turretin, *Institutes of*

Appropriating the latter, we can call this a *pneumatic certainty*, by which we mean that autonomous human reason does not have final authority over faith. Our sinfulness ensures that reason must sometimes be instructed by faith as it is supernaturally mediated by the Spirit through the Word of God. Such a pneumatic certainty has implications for how we understand Christian doctrine in relation to science. Taking our cue from Martin Chemnitz, believers should firmly accept doctrines that "are not set forth in so many letters and syllables in Scripture but are brought together from clear testimonies of Scripture by way of good, certain, firm, and clear reasoning."[77] Dogmas and confessions, Carl Braaten observes, "are binding norms because (*quia*) and not merely insofar as (*quatenus*) they are a perfectly true distillation of Scripture's witness to God's saving revelation in Jesus Christ."[78] The authority of the biblical canon implies that doctrine has a "derivative" authority. To be sure, special revelation must be distinguished from our interpretations enshrined in doctrine (Protestants can exhale). "Yet too much can be made of this point," cautions Paul Helm,

> for presumably the special revelation has what status it does have in the believing community because that community believes that at least some of its interpretations admit of no real debate. To suppose that all interpretations of the special revelation might be overturned would call into question the whole status of the special revelation in the community of believers, for it has this status because the community holds that at least some of the expressions of the special revelation express certain propositions.[79]

The biblical canon is divinely authorized, and doctrine shares derivatively in that authority. This implies that it is possible for some doctrines to be held with a measure of theological certainty. This kind of theological certainty, though necessary, is of course not sufficient for a healthy church. After all, at the height of the Reformation era, opposing groups all claimed theological certainty for their side (shedding much blood in the process). Sometimes humility is far more important than "certainty"!

The concept of dogmatic rank can help at just this point. Some doctrines are more central to the biblical witness and others more peripheral, less certain.

Elenctic Theology, vol. 1, ed. James T. Dennison, trans. George Musgrave Giger (Phillipsburg, NJ: P&R, 1992), 69, emphasis added.

77. *Examination of the Council of Trent, Part I*, trans. Fred Kramer (St. Louis: Concordia, 1971), 249.

78. Carl Braaten, "The Problem of Authority in the Church," in *The Catholicity of the Reformation*, ed. Carl Braaten and Robert Jenson (Grand Rapids: Eerdmans, 1996), 62.

79. Paul Helm, *Divine Revelation* (Westchester, IL: Crossway, 1982), 113.

Central doctrines are more clearly attested and more vital to the very structure of faith, so that they shape the lives of believers at much deeper levels. These beliefs have a high depth of ingression (perhaps even a maximal depth of ingression). They are not on the periphery but at the very center of my noetic (intellectual) structure. As J. P. Moreland has remarked,

> One can think of a noetic structure as a web of beliefs. The more depth of ingression a belief has in one's noetic structure, the more it exhibits two important features. First, it is more closely and complexly interrelated with other beliefs in my noetic structure. It is less independent than a belief on the periphery. Second, it is an epistemically important belief in my noetic structure. It provides mutual support for other important beliefs deeply ingressed, and it provides epistemic support for a number of beliefs closer to the periphery.[80]

Throughout this web of belief, some of our convictions will be more implicit than explicit—there may be large tracts of the biblical witness that have not yet been fully worked out intellectually. Even some convictions that are central may not be as worked out as others that are central (or even as some that are peripheral). That is all to say that our finitude and sinfulness prompt us to recognize that not all of our theological convictions are equally central to the Bible or equally honed intellectually. Some are more flexible and less certain. In truth, even our central theological convictions must be put to the test of Scripture. So the pneumatic certainty must be a *qualified* pneumatic certainty.

The third move is to adopt an *eclectic approach* to scientific theories. Scholars in science-and-theology, influenced by Barbour, almost always recommend integration or dialogue as the best way to relate science and theology. Most dismiss the independence approach. Conflict is the ultimate heresy; it is the pariah that threatens all interdisciplinary dialogue. My question is: why should we choose sides? Theology should be *eclectic* in how it engages with science.[81] Christians should engage scientific theories on a case-by-case basis. Different theories will invite different attitudes and responses (sometimes dialogue, sometimes conflict, sometimes independence, and so on).

This kind of eclecticism is committed to a "soft" rather than "hard" concordism. Science and theology will *ultimately* harmonize—when Christ comes back—but in the meantime attempts to harmonize them are often premature.

---

80. J. P. Moreland, "The Rationality of Belief in Inerrancy," *Trinity Journal* 7 (1986): 81. The depth of ingression idea is originally from W. V. O. Quine. E.g., see his "The Two Dogmas of Empiricism," in *From a Logical Point of View* (Cambridge, MA: Harvard University Press, 1953), 20–46.

81. Theology *must* be eclectic if it is true to itself; the contours of modern thought force it to be so.

This is partly because Scripture does not usually answer our scientific questions and partly because scientific claims are by nature revisable. Reading Scripture responsibly involves paying attention to literary genre and the distinct claims the text is making (without illicitly imposing our own concerns). That said, the Bible *does* address material issues that bear directly on the claims of science. Scripture is not merely about religious or "spiritual" truths that, like fairies and fantasies, float free of historical, physical, or cosmological realities. That would be gnosticism.

The upshot of all this is that there will at times be real conflict between science and theology (or better, between widely accepted scientific *theories* and Christian doctrine). Sometimes a major doctrine will thus be in tension with the scientific consensus. How should one proceed in such a situation? Recall that the ultimate harmonization of scientific theorizing with our doctrinal conceptions is an *eschatological* claim. The reality explored by science is most truly, though not exhaustively, disclosed to us in Scripture; since our world is fallen, scientific theory and practice are fully enmeshed in the noetic effects of sin. In this life east of Eden we will therefore not always be able to reconcile science and theology—to think that we will, or to assume too quickly that we have successfully done so, will tend to betray an over realized eschatology. During those episodes of genuine conflict between science and theology there will be times that scientific consensus will simply need to be rejected by Christians.

Scriptural realism is a three-stranded cord of biblical inerrancy, (qualified) pneumatic certainty, and an eclectic approach to scientific theories. Scripture's affirmations are epistemologically ultimate, but because of the noetic effects of sin we often fail to discern the divinely intended meaning. If we take all of these factors into account, we can offer a *minimal* criterion for the epistemic force of doctrine in its encounter with a scientific theory.[82] Let us say that when our doctrinal convictions are clearly attested to in Holy Scripture, when they are central—not peripheral—to the redemptive-historical narrative, and when they are taught universally in the catholic church, then those convictions are deeply, even maximally, ingressed in our noetic structure. They are confirmed supernaturally by the internal witness of the Holy Spirit and we are thus convinced of their divinity. They are theologically certain. They are warranted on the sole authority of God and his word in Scripture and they need no warrant or evidential support from modern science or any other area

---

82. By "minimal," I mean that there is much more that can and should be said about science and Christian doctrine, but I am limiting myself to what is *sufficient* for the questions before us (hence "minimal").

of human learning. They effectively serve as theological lenses with which we then apprehend the rest of reality.

For Protestants, *sola scriptura* still applies so that it is possible for further, genuine exegesis to overturn these theological lenses—but in the case of central doctrines, this is relatively unlikely if the catholic consensus has judged them to be a true distillation of the biblical witness. It is also possible that these central doctrinal beliefs may be overturned by a future scientific finding, but, practically speaking, the threshold for such defeasibility is very high. As theology engages various scientific theories, it should do so eclectically—sometimes fully, sometimes partially endorsing them. But theology will usually reject any well-attested scientific theory that conflicts with a central Christian doctrine.

Original Sin and Science: Between Conflict and Dialogue

Methodological reflections are always in danger of appearing too abstract, hence the value of concrete examples. I suggest that scriptural realism should engage with science eclectically. This last section will defend two claims that exemplify this eclecticism: (1) theology should reject the scientific consensus when it *conflicts* with the doctrine of originating sin, and (2) aspects of this science present an opportunity for *dialogue* with the doctrine of originated sin.

Doctrine of Originating Sin—Conflict with Science

The doctrine of Adam's fall is a central, not peripheral, doctrine. It is warranted by Holy Scripture (*norma normans*) and the catholic tradition (*norma normata*). Adam and Eve were historical people. They were the head of the human race, and they fell from God's goodness and grace. This doctrine is essential for our knowledge of sin and our experience of redemption. It is warranted by God's Word in Scripture and therefore theologically certain. Given this antecedent truth of Adam's fall, Christian dogmatics calmly rejects any evidential claim from scientific theories that conflict with it (e.g., recent Darwinian theories of evolution or current interpretations of population genetics).

True enough we may have misread Scripture, but the threshold for abandoning, or significantly revising, the doctrine of the fall is very high. Now the questions come fast and furious: How high is "very high"? When does a scientific theory legitimately reach the "threshold"? At what point *is* theology obliged to revise or abandon a central doctrine? When does dogmatic commitment to the traditional doctrine of the fall become just silly? At the back of these queries is a more basic and fundamental question: how *intrinsically compelling* is the scientific evidence against Adam's fall?[83] This is where Christians disagree strongly.

Scientific evidence that is overwhelmingly persuasive *can* therefore overturn a central doctrine like the fall. We would then have to revise our understanding of Scripture without a historical Adam or fall. But such a decisive judgment should never be made by one or even many individuals; like earlier conciliar or creedal decrees, it would be an ecclesial decision superintended by God's Spirit and involving church leaders from across the globe. Such a scenario is logically possible yet extremely unlikely. The biblical evidence for the fall has an *intrinsic* warrant that is far greater than any current evidence for paleoanthropology and evolutionary biology. Moreover, the fall is an essential thread tying together key doctrines in the seamless garment of systematic theology; pull it loose and the whole thing unravels. Some of the pre-Adamite proposals are, on this point, more plausible than others—different church traditions will assess them using their own internal theological standards—but none fully persuade (they leave too many questions unanswered).[84] Individuals may hold these proposals as nondogmatic, *tentative* hypotheses that are not binding on the church.

Doctrine of Originated Sin—Dialogue with Science

Concerning originated sin, we have already seen areas of significant conflict with current scientific theories. But conflict is not the only note to sound. A number of clinical cases actually prompt some conceptual clarification in hamartiology—here there is opportunity for dialogue between science and theology. For example, patients with a neuropsychiatric disorder called Tourette's syndrome sometimes manifest the rare symptom of sudden, inappropriate swearing and profusion of obscenities. In one case report, the individual had no control over these outbursts and shouted obscenities at a frequency of fifty words per minute, including racial slurs and inappropriate words—only to apologize immediately after.[85] Take another example: orbitofrontal tumor causing pornography addiction. In a famous case, a man had developed an insatiable appetite for sex and pedophilia; a chronic headache prompted an

83. For a helpful way to adjudicate possible scientific defeaters of Christian belief, see Plantinga, "Games Scientists Play."

84. The proposal by William Stone in chap. 3 is a much more rigorous engagement of current paleoanthropological evidence. His account is a happy ally to my own concerns here, although he is more optimistic perhaps than I am about the *theological* significance of the relevant fossil evidence.

85. Mouna Ben Djebara et al., "Aripiprazole: A Treatment for Severe Coprolalia in 'Refractory' Gilles de la Tourette Syndrome," *Movement Disorders* 23 (2008): 438–40.

MRI, which led to the discovery of a tumor mass. The mass was removed and his symptoms vanished completely.[86]

What is going on in such cases? An apparent result of the fall is that people may suffer *biological* conditions that present themselves as outwardly *sinful behaviors*. Here originated sin has failed reliably to express itself in actual sins—the "sinful" behaviors are not genuinely sinful. That is because we are morally responsible for desires and beliefs, and actions or inactions motivated by them, if they are produced in us when we are properly functioning. I have genuine moral agency when my moral states and actions are properly functioning, that is, they are produced in me in a way that reliably discloses the heart—"for *out of the heart* come evil thoughts, murder, adultery, sexual immorality, theft, false testimony, slander" (Matt. 15:19 NIV). If they are produced by a more basic, overriding biological condition, then they do not reliably disclose my heart.[87] We can speculate that here the intimate union between soul and body is disrupted. Such rare physical conditions induce a lack of proper function causing apparently "sinful" behaviors that fail to disclose the heart. Our sins arise from "the overflow of the heart" (Matt. 12:34 NIV 1984)—the "heart" is what most fully discloses *me* (see also Gen. 6:5; Ps. 14; 58:3; Rom. 3:9–20; Mark 7:21; etc.).

Jesse Couenhoven has argued that we are culpable for those things for which we are "deeply responsible," those things that truly disclose our hearts. Deep responsibility, he explains, "is not so much self-making as self-disclosure."[88] It is a compatibilist (self-disclosure), not voluntarist (self-making) notion. It would be wrong to blame a person "for evils that are not evils of the heart; leprosy, cancer, and the like do not disclose a person's beliefs and desires," Couenhoven explains, "and so they are not things for which a person can be considered culpable."[89] Sin is not biological for we are not deeply responsible for biological facts that are true of us. Biological realities do not disclose the heart in any meaningful way.

We should notice what is happening here. Science is offering us data for theological reflection. At the same time, the data have not provoked us to revise our understanding of sin scientifically. The tail is not wagging the dog. Our hamartiology is searching for greater conceptual and theological clarity

---

86. Jeffrey Burns and Russell Swerdlow, "Right Orbitofrontal Tumor with Pedophilia Symptom and Constructional Apraxia Sign," *Archives of Neurology* 60 (2003): 437–40.
87. Jesse Couenhoven, "What Sin Is: A Differential Analysis," *Modern Theology* 25 (2009): 580. I am indebted to Couenhoven's development of proper function as a helpful concept here.
88. Ibid., 577.
89. Ibid., 578. Couenhoven has developed these themes at greater length in his *Stricken by Sin, Cured by Christ: Agency, Necessity, and Culpability in Augustinian Theology* (Oxford: Oxford University Press, 2013).

in the face of compelling scientific findings. These physical conditions appear to be poignant examples of a rare effect of Adam's fall, namely the severance of the natural bond between originated sin and actual sinful behaviors.[90] If this is correct, then I have given one specific example of how a theology that is informed by scriptural realism can engage in genuine dialogue with science.

Conclusion

Science can be a thorn in the flesh of theology. Original sin is a case in point where we have a classic tension between the doctrines of creation and revelation. The sphere of science, at least in principle, is an aspect of God's general revelation. Science at its best is the patient investigation of God's good creation and the processes that he governs providentially. And yet there is a sting in the tail, for the most widely embraced theories in many of the scientific disciplines are incompatible with the traditional doctrine of original sin, a doctrine the church has long interpreted as a sure deliverance of revelation. This Augustinian hamartiology is dying on the vine, no longer plausible for a growing number of Christians—it is outdated, a strike against the credibility of the faith. So we are told. There is a grain of truth here. Whether we like it or not, our functional beliefs are shaped by the natural sciences. It is in the food we eat and the water we drink. The ancient understanding of sin sounds to some like a tall tale. The soteriological and pastoral functions of the doctrine of sin are losing existential traction. Precisely to rectify this abysmal situation, a number of theologians have abandoned or radically revised the doctrine of original sin.

While I sympathize with these motivations, this chapter has not been optimistic about such efforts. When there is conflict between a widely attested scientific claim and a Christian doctrine, the best option is not necessarily to change or abandon the doctrine. Christianity is after all a revelatory faith. If those words mean anything, then it is in the nature of divine revelation that some doctrines, especially those doctrines central to the faith, will always resist change. Original sin, as I have argued, is one of those doctrines.

Have we simply offered another recipe for sloppy, antiscientific railings that only bring ridicule to the faith? The danger for abuse is there, but we should not allow the fear of worn-out stereotypes to hijack a more responsible conception

---

90. This analysis is schematized since lack of proper function likely comes in degrees. One can imagine cases in which a person's beliefs, desires, and (in)actions motivated by them, will be both sinful *and* sick. For a stimulating secular analysis, see Mike Martin, *From Morality to Mental Health: Virtue and Vice in a Therapeutic Culture* (New York: Oxford University Press, 2006).

of the relationship between science and theology. The blessed apostles delivered to us a realistic and humble faith, one that realizes that the effects of sin extend—how could they not?—into the very practices of science (in the interests of fair play, the same applies to theology!). Science and theology will ultimately harmonize; indeed they will *certainly* harmonize. But for now this is a promise, something to be taken on faith, because full harmonization will likely continue to elude our grasp pending the eschaton. Until then, original sin and similar doctrines will happily engage the claims of science eclectically. There will sometimes be dialogue, and there will sometimes be conflict (with everything in between). This may appear arbitrary or ad hoc, but that is only a surface appearance. Such tensions are unavoidable, subtle clues to a deeper reality, as faith seeks understanding in a world awash in scientific opinions.[91]

91. Thanks to Phillip Anderas, Bill Davis, Paul Helm, Jonathan King, Tim Morris, Ryan Peterson, Mike Reeves, Doug Sweeney, Kevin Vanhoozer, and Stephen Williams for their comments on an earlier draft.

12

ORIGINAL SIN IN PASTORAL THEOLOGY

Daniel Doriani

Original Sin and the Pastoral Call

The doctrine of original sin, understood in the classic Christian sense, runs contrary to core Western convictions about human nature. People are still willing to use the term but in ways that misconstrue and minimize its force. Many think that "original sin" refers to Adam, Eve, and forbidden fruit. Our metaphorical uses of the term reduce it to nothing more than a prevailing error. So slavery is called "America's original sin." And Oscar Wilde says, "Humanity takes itself too seriously. It is the world's original sin."[1] Such misconceptions have driven the theological concept of original sin underground. The Belgic Confession's word on original sin can stand as our definition and description:

> By the disobedience of Adam and Eve, original sin has been spread through the whole human race. It is a corruption of all human nature—an inherited depravity. . . . Sin constantly boils forth as though from a contaminated spring. Nevertheless, it is not imputed to God's children for their condemnation but is forgiven by his grace and mercy. . . . The awareness of this corruption might make believers groan [to be] free from the body of this death.[2]

The Belgic Confession captures the orthodox Protestant conviction that original sin or depravity is the constant source of particular sins. Scripture

1. Alan Jacobs, *Original Sin: A Cultural History* (New York: HarperOne, 2008), x.
2. Belgic Confession, Article 15: The Doctrine of Original Sin.

teaches that after the fall, humans are continually inclined to commit sins and to form sinful habits because sinfulness has contaminated our nature (Gen. 6:5; Rom. 8:5–8). The doctrine of original sin asserts that humanity in its fallen condition continually tends toward sin and self-ruin. The fallen will is in bondage to sin, rebellion, and self-deception so that it does not and cannot choose the right and is blind to its plight.

The doctrine of original sin is essential to a proper concept of the pastoral calling. To be sure, the work has its glories. Pastors are *paid* to study and proclaim God's truth, to evangelize the lost, to counsel wanderers, to comfort the grieving, and to guide God's energetic servants. On the other hand, pastors are surrounded by congenital sinners. We are the target of an enemy who will use those sinners to thwart God's work at every turn. Pastors must expect that listeners will misrepresent their words, that counselees will misrepresent their problems and misuse pastoral counsel. Christians will unduly exalt pastors one day and denigrate them the next. They will offer love, generosity, sacrifice, patience, and loyalty one day, but envy, criticism, gossip, and even betrayal the next.

Meanwhile, the wise pastor will remember that false religion is, with materialism and oppression, Satan's great ally in his battle against Christ and his people. Revelation warns about opposition from false religion as often it warns against the seduction of Babylon and the oppression of the corrupt state (Rev. 11:8). False religion murders the prophets and the apostles because it hates and kills their master (Rev. 11:1–10; Matt. 10:24–25). The false prophet lies and deceives on behalf of the dragon and the fallen state (Rev. 13:11–18; 16:13; 19:20; 20:10). So false religion opposes the church and its leaders.

The wise pastor will expect such opposition from outside and from inside as well. Most of the unregenerate want no part of the church. But some, in the thrall of the false prophet, are drawn to the church, which they perceive as the locus of religious activities: sacred art and music, feelings of transcendence, spirituality, and acts of love. The doctrine of original sin teaches church leaders to expect disruption and malice even within the church.

Yet before we consider additional implications of original sin, we need to consider the pervasive rejection of this essential biblical doctrine.

The Pastor's Challenge: Pervasive Rejection of the Doctrine of Original Sin

The rejection of original sin takes several forms. Humanism necessarily rejects it. Naturalism construes selfishness as a necessary effect of the instincts of survival and propagation. Sadly, an entire class of contemporary theologians deny that humans are born with a disposition toward evil and therefore with an absolute need of a Savior. Some blame Augustine for creating the doctrine of original sin, despite its prior articulation in Tertullian and Cyprian, and the independence of the anti-Pelagian councils (not to mention Paul).[3] And certain post-evangelicals mock and distort the doctrine of original sin, claiming that "Jesus believed in original goodness."[4] Important as post-evangelical deviations from orthodoxy may be, they are essentially a capitulation to the culture's prevailing view of humanity, whether we ascribe it to Enlightenment philosophy or the contemporary culture of self-help literature.

In 1762, Rousseau opened his *Social Contract* with the immortal but indefensible line, "Man is born free, and everywhere he is in chains." Rousseau affirmed "the natural goodness of man," maintaining that human vices come from the outside, from the arts, sciences, government, and defective education. To his detriment, he never plausibly explained how decent people consistently create indecent communities. Like many others, including Pelagius, he cited the power of bad examples and corrupt and perverse institutions. But even if Kant, Voltaire, and the rest had subtler appraisals of human nature, the Enlightenment project demanded that human reason and volition remain fundamentally intact, free to discern what is right and good and to act on it. The Enlightenment insists that the informed and rational mind *can* choose well. It is no surprise that Ernst Cassirer, the great analyst and advocate of Enlightenment thought, declares, "The concept of original sin is the common opponent against which all the different trends of the philosophy of the Enlightenment join forces."[5]

No doubt, there are vestigial concepts of sin in our society, even if the words "sin" and "sinner" are typically used in jest. Popular Western culture has an Enlightenment mentality. It has forgotten about sinfulness and inability. People may say that tyrants, criminals, and "haters" are evil, but most public discourse has no place for original sin in the sense of pervasive human inability. Society believes that ordinary people are essentially good. With proper education and mindfulness, anyone can make the right decisions on most occasions. Mainstream popular ethics assumes that people want to do the right thing and will generally choose the right, if someone should be kind enough to point out the right path.

3. Jacobs, *Original Sin*, 32. See also Elaine Pagels, *Adam, Eve and the Serpent* (New York: Random House, 1988) and the chapter by Peter Sanlon in this volume.
4. Steve Chalke and Alan Mann, *The Lost Message of Jesus* (Grand Rapids: Zondervan, 2003), 126; see also Doug Pagitt, *A Christianity Worth Believing* (San Francisco: Jossey Bass, 2008).
5. Ernst Cassirer, *The Philosophy of the Enlightenment* (Princeton: Princeton University Press, 1951), 141, cf. 139–48.

For example, Bruce Weinstein is a public ethicist who regularly appears in high-profile media outlets. His books' titles suggest his convictions: *What Should I Do? Four Simple Steps to Making Better Decisions in Everyday Life* and *Ethical Intelligence: Five Principles for Untangling Your Toughest Problems at Work and Beyond*. The latter book presents five classic principles: do no harm; make things better; respect others; be fair; and be loving. He then applies his principles to realistic cases. Weinstein's popular work is bent on clarity and simplicity more than analysis of presuppositions. He wants his ethically intelligent readers to make good ethical decisions; he ignores the possibility that his readers might *see* the right course and deliberately choose the wrong.

Weinstein entertains a double question, "Why don't more people do the right thing? What gets in the way?" He names three principal causes of ethically unintelligent behavior: fear, focus on short-term benefits, and foul moods. First, he says *fear* arises from the ability to foresee negative consequences of the right action. Second, people make bad personal decisions (eating harmful foods) and foolish business decisions (seeking profit in corrosive ways) because they can't see past the *short-term benefits*. Third, *foul moods*, caused by sleep deprivation or relational problems, impede mindfulness and rational thought.[6] In short, Weinstein has no point of contact with Christian concepts of original or innate sin. He is aware of human flaws but construes them as weakness, not sinfulness. He admits that "it's sometimes challenging" to live ethically. "But if you're aware of the things that are likely to trip you up, you can be on guard against them and improve the odds of making ethically intelligent choices." He believes people have the capacity to be intelligent and therefore can do "intelligent things . . . more often than not."[7]

Weinstein knows people can be lazy, undisciplined, short-sighted, bossy, critical, and selfish. He admits that his five ethical principles are "tremendously difficult to live by."[8] Yet, like Kant, he believes humans ought to learn, and can learn, to treat other humans as ends in themselves.[9]

Orthodox Christians can agree with certain elements of humanistic or Enlightenment ethics. People do *choose* to violate ethical principles, whether from ignorance, bad models, addiction, or the quest for personal gain. We agree that people violate ethical rules because violations proffer short-term benefits. Business professionals trade on inside information because it promises financial

---

6. Bruce Weinstein, *Ethical Intelligence: Five Principles for Untangling Your Toughest Problems at Work and Beyond* (Novato, CA: New World Library, 2011), 50–52.
7. Ibid., 52, 57.
8. Ibid., 6.
9. Ibid., 199.

gain and athletes take performance-enhancing drugs because they promise a competitive advantage—or at least a level playing field. But Christianity and the Enlightenment differ on the *final* cause or root of ethical infractions.

The Enlightenment essentially ignores human sinfulness. It believes humanity's primary ethical principles are logically necessary and universally binding. No society can flourish without rules that forbid murder, theft, and treachery. Rational people should see that it is best for all if everyone is good. Further, ordinary people can attain substantial goodness, both in good actions and in the capacity to choose the good, if they are mindful, know the rules, and heed germane counsel.

Weinstein is a successful public ethicist because he is capable and because he aligns with society's prevailing ethical perspective. His view of human nature is manifest throughout popular literature. The best recent works on organizational management and leadership reveal a similarly optimistic view of human nature. *The Leadership Challenge*, by James Kouzes and Barry Posner, is a respected and popular work. It is well-researched, well-written, and its wisdom generally coheres with biblical principles. Nonetheless, the authors presuppose that leaders *want to do* what is right and that, with proper guidance, they *will do so*. Readers can appreciate the authors' central points by scanning chapter subheadings: Create a Climate of Trust . . . Expect the Best . . . Create a Spirit of Community . . . Be Personally Involved . . . Moral Leadership Calls Us to Higher Purposes . . . Humility Is the Antidote to Hubris.[10]

This is excellent advice, grounded in extensive research. We could probably slap a proof text onto most of their points. But Kouzes and Posner virtually ignore the nettlesome truth that some leaders have scant interest in their principles. They stuff themselves with hubris and like it that way. They sow rivalry and distrust in their offices because they think it makes people work harder. A book like *The Leadership Challenge* makes perfect sense line by line and paragraph by paragraph. For example, an upbeat section titled "Expect the Best" urges leaders to "believe in the abilities of their constituents," to "expect them to succeed," and to challenge them to do so. Leaders will find that "high expectations lead to high performance," which, when recognized, builds community and generates further successes.[11] The authors ignore the hard truth that some leaders want to suppress talent and take perverse pleasure in expecting the worst. So it seems that Kouzes and Posner have no functional concept of human sinfulness.

10. James Kouzes and Barry Posner, *The Leadership Challenge*, 4th ed. (San Francisco: Jossey Bass, 2007).
11. Ibid., 282–86.

Weinstein, Kouzes, and Posner sell millions of books to readers who most likely share their convictions or worldview. Otherwise, their advice makes little sense and invites rejection. Such thinkers share something in common with successful advice columnists. An effective advice columnist is a bold and witty polymath with insight into human behavior. He or she must reflect mainstream views even while advancing and clarifying them. Consider Emily Yoffe, known as "Dear Prudence" at the online journal *Slate*. Like our other authors, Yoffe assumes that her readers can and will follow her counsel, although her optimism about humanity is tempered both by a harrowing personal history of abuse at the hands of a congressman who was also a priest and by the miserable letters from her readers. She seems to have no concept of human sinfulness, although she does believe certain people are evil and beyond reform. For example, a 2012 letter describes an uncle who mistreats his nephews by pushing them, taking toys from them, and mocking one who has a speech impediment. Yoffe calls the uncle "a cruel, disturbed person" and commands, "Don't let this bully ruin your holiday, harm your boys, or attack you." She judges that he will not be open to reason and proposes decisive action to control his behavior.[12]

As long as the memory of Hitler, Stalin, and Mao remains, the category of "evil people" will remain. And as long as public figures ruin themselves through pointless infidelity and corruption, we will call some people fools. But mainstream Western society prefers to think that *certain people* are evil or foolish and to deny that sin corrupts the race as a whole.

One genre, the literature of addiction, takes a more sober view and admits that evil can gain a terrible grip on anyone. It acknowledges that people destroy themselves through a compulsion to take drugs, drink alcohol, and seek sexual thrills. Yet addiction literature typically describes the addict as a victim, stricken by a disease, rather than a sinner (let alone someone governed by a sinful nature).

Sadly, mainstream popular Christian literature appears to adopt the prevailing culture's perspective. I once reviewed dozens of popular Christian monographs on the family life and gender roles. The literature did mention sin, the work of Christ, and the need for repentance, but all too often it was a mere aside. The bulk of the works relentlessly pressed the need to live better, according to the author's advice. These authors love how-to lists: five steps for edifying friendship, six ways to handle conflict, seven for loving leadership in the home, eight for effective parenting.

12. Emily Yoffe, "Dear Prudence," *Slate* (website), November 21, 2012, http://www.slate.com/articles/life/dear_prudence/2012/11/dear_prudence_i_m_incredibly_attracted_to_much_older_men.html.

This library denounced the woes afflicting our culture, then charged godly men and women to reverse the spiral. One book told the negligent man to confess his sins to God and then, "Recommit yourself to your spiritual priorities. Get back on your feet, dust yourself off, and 'go and sin no more.'" The literature assumed that believers can and should promptly do what is good, according to the plans in this book. A true disciple will commit to God 100 percent, pray faithfully, shun temptation, guard the eyes and heart, find an accountability partner, and so stay on the right path. In short, the view of human capacity was remarkably similar to that of the secular literature: anyone can do what is right if they have the appetite for it.

But the doctrine of original sin lets us see that many believers refuse the steps outlined in self-help literature because they want no part of such steps. Believers are double-minded, embracing God's authority one hour and resisting it the next. We avoid accountability because we prefer to answer to ourselves alone. We don't want to guard the mind and or the eye; too often we want to indulge the eye's lusts or the mind's fantasies of dominance or wealth.

These books often invoke the example of Jesus but rarely discuss the regeneration and renewal of the Spirit or the loving grace of Jesus that draws us to faith and obedience. The absence of a doctrine of sin has consequences. I once happened to read a self-help book for women as my wife sat nearby. The author told women how to act so their husbands would long for their company. They must never nag or greet their beleaguered heroes with a litany of the day's woes. Rather, they must ever be welcoming, gentle, thankful, complimentary. Never criticize, complain, or get angry, the author said. Then your husband will love your very presence.

As the obligations heaped up, I wondered what my wife might think of them. I selected the lead thought in twenty sections, then invited her response. "It's good advice," she said thoughtfully, "but I felt overwhelmed and defeated after the first five ideas—and there were a dozen more." Exactly. In essence, the book told wives their husbands will love them if they are flawless. Clearly, the author lacked a concept of sin and inability.

So orthodox pastors must recognize that their concept of sin is alien to our secular culture and to much popular Christian thinking. Even if few explicitly reject the doctrine, many misunderstand or minimize it.

Turning now to the direct pastoral implications of the doctrine of original sin, we will briefly consider its role in evangelism, the pastor's self-regard, church leadership, and implications of the doctrine of original sin for the practice of pastoral care. In the final sections we will consider the effect of original sin on the interior life of the redeemed. We will reflect on the human capacity—our capacity—to do good and be good. We will also consider the pervasive effects of original sin, focusing briefly on its impact on our minds and emotions.

Original Sin and Evangelism

The doctrine of original sin clarifies the task of evangelism. As Jonathan Edwards says, humankind is in a state of ruin, both from the afflictions to which we are exposed and from the moral evil that issues from us; since moral evil is the source of human affliction, we must hope in deliverance through the gospel, not social reform.[13] It is alleged that Calvinism, including its concept of human sinfulness, suppresses evangelism, yet both Edwards and George Whitefield were mighty and Calvinistic evangelists. Both held that a proper doctrine of sin is essential to evangelism. Whitefield maintained that the Spirit "generally convinces the sinner of his actual sin first, yet it leads him to see and bewail his original sin, the fountain from which all these polluted streams do flow."[14] The rationale is plain. An awareness of sin *and inability* drives the sinner to Christ for healing. When we confess that there is no health in our bones, that we are dead in our sin, we should turn to Christ alone for salvation (Ps. 38:1–22; Eph. 2:1–10).

The doctrine must remain at the center of the church's preaching, especially its evangelism. If not for original sin, we would need no incarnation, no atonement, no gospel.[15] Clear instruction, good examples, timely mentoring, and fiery exhortations would be enough to reform humanity and lead to eternal life. But Scripture teaches not simply that humans sin, but that we cannot stop, we cannot reform ourselves, so that we must hope in Christ alone.

Original Sin and the Pastor

It would be foolish to address the needs of the church and omit the problem of original sin within pastors and theologians themselves. Pastors are cardiologists who have heart disease, diagnosticians who detect deadly disease in themselves. We who oppose sin commit the sins we describe. The vain preach humility. The temperamental promote calm. Gluttons, drunkards, and obsessive exercisers urge self-control. We hold the gospel in soiled hands.

---

13. Jonathan Edwards, "The Great Christian Doctrine of Original Sin Defended, Author's Preface," in *The Complete Works of Jonathan Edwards* (Carlisle, PA: Banner of Truth, 1995), 1:145.

14. Quoted in Jacobs, *Original Sin*, 132–35.

15. For elaboration of these points, see the chapter by Reeves and Madueme in this volume.

Consider, for example, our preference for people like ourselves—educated, witty, professional. At worst, pastors want friendships that approximate mutual admiration societies. It is a tendency that can lead us to avoid the wounded, the awkward, and the critical.

Sin also taints our exegesis, preaching, and teaching. We miss some biblical truth due to ignorance and imperfect training, but our sinfulness makes us lazy scholars. We also miss some points due to blindness, willful or otherwise. We lack insight because it would be too painful to humble ourselves and repent. Or we may see something perfectly well and let fear silence us, since we know the point will not be welcomed. A gifted pastor once told me, "I don't want to think about that topic because I'm afraid of what I might conclude."

Pastors need the courage to see the world as it is, to hear the biblical message, and to declare the difference between the two. Too often we foresee the cost of candor and fall silent. If the subject is marriage, we should say cohabitation is sinful and destructive, but we are tempted to censor ourselves, knowing that some might walk out, causing a drop in attendance or giving, or an increase in criticism. So then, the sins of pastors weaken and corrupt their work. Our meditation on original sin must include that.

Original Sin and Church Leadership

Sin pervades the church, which is, after all, inhabited exclusively by sinners. Our doctrine of sin should shape our church government. I advocate church government through a plurality of elders, believing both that it is close to New Testament patterns and that it can rein in the abuse of power. But whether one believes in the congregational, episcopal, or presbyterian form of government, we must recognize that sinners will abuse power. Congregationalists can concentrate power in the hands of the persuasive or influential few. Presbyterians can fall in behind a senior pastor or powerful elder. And in episcopal systems, the people can find it impossible to question or resist a leader officially invested with higher authority. The doctrine of sin teaches us to resist the concentration of power.

The doctrine of sin also teaches pastors what to expect in their calling. Young pastors are shocked when the church first treats them badly. On Monday a committee misunderstands and criticizes. On Tuesday, what seemed like a minor disagreement between church leaders blossoms into distrust, even enmity. On Wednesday someone befriends the new pastor, but it is soon clear that the "friend" was only searching for an ally for a cause, so that when no alliance occurs, the relationship quickly ends.

Pastors have a right to feel hurt, but they should not be surprised at mistreatment. In many churches, membership vows include this: "I am a sinner in God's sight and without hope for salvation except in His sovereign mercy. I believe in Jesus Christ, the Savior of sinners, and depend upon Him alone for my salvation." One must sincerely *say* "I am a sinner" to join the church, and all too often our professed sinners act the part. The people flatter and demand, encourage and enrage because they are sinners. They sin against us, and we sin against them too.

Sin creates all of the church's problems. Pastors endure opposition from self-appointed watchdogs, envy from those who feel power slipping, rivalry from one whose vision was not adopted, anger over perceived favoritism or snubs. The doctrine of original sin teaches us to govern our hopes, to curb our optimism. Other doctrines forbid despair, so that we have sound expectations. But the doctrine of sin shapes more than the *pastor's* expectations; it speaks to everyone.

Original Sin and Pastoral Care

A wise pastor will check in on newlyweds a few months after the wedding. A candid couple is likely to say something like this: "We heard that marriage is hard, but we didn't believe it. We thought *we would be different*. We're happy and we love each other, but it's true: marriage is hard. We ignored the warnings, but now we're glad people told us. At least we know our struggles are typical." It's no surprise that marriage is difficult, given that it unites two sinners who live in close quarters, not merely as roommates, but as partners trying to chart a common course on an array of matters large and small. If newlyweds imagine that *their* marriage will be easy, it's because they underestimate their sinfulness.

When a pastor tells an engaged couple that their sinfulness will make marriage hard, he applies the doctrine of original sin, not to rob the new couple of joy but to protect them, so they can steel themselves for their battle with sin. Ideally, they will then seek God's Spirit and the Christian community as their allies in the struggle. The doctrine of sin teaches believers to shun self-reliance and to seek grace and assurance in Christ.

It is sad but predictable that original sin taints every aspect of pastoral work, even our worship. The people who intend to come to worship God have selfishness so bound in their hearts that they cannot help but complain about whatever displeases them. Prayers are too long (or short). Confessions of faith are too old (or new). Sermons are too dry, too complex, too shallow. Corporate confessions of sin are too vague or too specific (leading some people to ask, "How can I confess sins I don't commit?"). Sin so pervades our soul that even when we gather to worship God, "Do I like it?" becomes more important than "Does it please God? Does it help my fellow believers?"

Responses to sermons can be astonishing in many ways, but the most painful is when sinful desires lead listeners to distort the message. People think they hear their pastor affirm things the pastor explicitly denies: "Pastor, I'm glad you favor the legalization of marijuana and its moderate use." Or, "I'm so glad I came today. I've just realized I'm never going to flourish if I'm married to a man who can't keep up with me. You've liberated me to move on." The pastor is baffled, but the doctrine of original sin explains why the "ignorant and unstable twist" Scripture (2 Pet. 3:16). If they cannot find teachers "that suit their own likings" (RSV) and tickle their ears, they will distort the sound teaching that they seem to hear (2 Tim. 4:3). They may not intend to distort Scripture, but sin is deep and deceitful (Jer. 17:9).

Pastors, elders, and deacons are the servants of the church; the great majority of the time their service is remarkable for its wisdom, humility, and sacrifice, but sin tempts the best leaders too. They preserve and assert their power and push their agenda, too confident that their plans are God's. They declare where they will and will not serve, who they do and do not want on their teams. Indeed, the effect of sin is so pervasive that the officers' vow to serve Christ out of pure motives includes the warning "so far as you know your own heart."

We can approach this from another angle. Christine Pohl has written an excellent book, *Living into Community*, that describes the practices that sustain Christian community. She identifies and explores four principal values that foster community: embracing gratitude, making and keeping promises, living truthfully, and practicing hospitality. In each section she wisely devotes a chapter to "complications" in gratitude, promising, or truthfulness. Instead of embracing gratitude, we grumble and complain about whatever is displeasing. Instead of giving thanks for the blessings God grants others, we become jealous or envious. We make and keep foolish promises and break sound but inconvenient ones. We substitute entertainment and reciprocity for true hospitality, and when we do see a clear need, we often recoil out of a selfish desire to preserve our property or ease. We spin the truth, hide the truth, and dole out the truth in self-serving packages. Worst of all, we speak falsely to others because we already have deceived ourselves. This is why counseling is so difficult. Original sin wants to hide itself. How often do pastors or counselors sense that we are talking to someone who is hiding something? We probe, but they insist we know the whole story. Sometimes it's a lie, but sometimes deception has burrowed so deep that the speaker thinks he is honest. All of this is the fruit of original sin.

Pelagius and Moral Expectations Revisited

Wise pastors watch themselves, and teach their people to do the same, because Scripture teaches us to expect a gap between our goals and our achievements. We aim for moral probity since God is morally perfect and has stated his standards. He has described the acts and dispositions that please him and commands all, but especially his people, to keep those standards. Moses summoned Israel to "walk in all his ways" (Deut. 11:22). Paul says Christians should "walk in the footsteps of the faith of our father Abraham" (Rom. 4:12). The life of faith is a journey on the right path, but even the most devout believer will battle inborn sin till the day of death.

Pastors must distinguish between the operation of original sin in the believer and its work in the unbeliever. If we tell atheists, "Store up for yourselves treasures in heaven," they *cannot obey* (unless they first repent and believe) for the command is nonsense to them. Why would a person store up treasures in heaven if the person believes there is no heaven? We might as well command a drowning person to swim. The drowning person *does* need to swim, but the problem, precisely, is that he or she cannot. So too the atheist's unbelief and sinfulness make full obedience to God, external and internal, impossible.

Original sin plays out differently in believers. Imagine that a mother and daughter have a tense relationship. If the daughter despises her mother, the command "Respect your mother" seems impossible. How can the girl show respect if she has none? She may obey her mother—grudgingly, with rolling eyes and slouching shoulders. Yet, however sinfulness manifests itself in mother and daughter, if a relationship exists, there is potential for repentance and healing over time. Because we have a relationship with God, however much we sin, there is hope for obedience and reconciliation. Yet we must rightly appraise our hope.

Expecting to Be Good

The Roman Empire was declining in the day of Augustine and Pelagius. The great city of Rome crumbled physically and retained too many of the moral failings of its pagan past. The empire was officially Christian and some emperors cared deeply for the church, but many leaders were corrupt and the common people typically lived in material misery and moral decay. The ultraviolent gladiatorial games remained an immensely popular entertainment and vice was rampant, to the dismay of Pelagius, who thought an allegedly Christian city and an ostensibly believing people could and should behave far better.

Two theologians, Augustine and Pelagius, appraised the problem, seeking the root of Rome's corruption and of human corruption in general. Whatever Pelagius's precise beliefs, his followers said that humans can fulfill God's law and that he expects us to do so. Since we sin due to bad examples, sinful habits, and laziness, we can resolve to obey God's laws. The very fact that God *commands* proves that he expects us to obey. Why would God command what we cannot do? Pelagius rightly decried bad habits and corrosive examples, but he seemed to assume that human nature is essentially unhindered by the fall. He believed humans retain the power of will, the capacity for self-determination that puts obedience within reach. Adam set a bad example, but Pelagius denied that his sin corrupted human nature itself. Since we chose to sin, we can choose to stop if we discipline ourselves and follow Jesus's example. Corruption and reform are both chosen.

Pelagianism appeals to the proud will and ego, but every branch of Christianity has labeled this view heresy because it denies the need for the renewing grace of the Holy Spirit.

The doctrine of original sin, joined with the doctrine of creation in God's image, explains why we act as we do. Walter Isaacson's magisterial 2011 biography of Steve Jobs captures the tension as it manifested itself in that life.[16] Jobs had a transcendent talent for design, for translating grand dreams into pocket-sized realities, for communicating his vision to others, for enlisting talent and pushing talented people to do things beyond their self-imposed limits. But Jobs routinely insulted, humiliated, and manipulated his friends and co-workers. When he did not get his way, he pouted and cried (literally) like a child. He abandoned his friends and even, for a while, his first child. Yet arguably he made the world a better place, and most people who worked for him were, in the end, glad they did. On a grand scale, Jobs shows that everyman is a glory and ruin, a king and a wretch.

Original sin shapes and explains so much of daily life. Work is hard because of sin. The people around us are funny but self-absorbed, encouraging but unfair, generous but demanding, because of their sin. They sin against us, and we sin against them. Marriage is hard for the same reason. We never love so much and never sin so much as we do at home, with our family.

Sin even pollutes the way we address our sin. As Kevin DeYoung says, in our hypertherapeutic culture, our very grasp of our sin, pain, and authentic

16. Walter Isaacson, *Steve Jobs* (New York: Simon & Schuster, 2011).

struggles can become forms of "narcissism and self-absorption rather than maturity." Further, we would rather take a pill to make the pain go away than toil to stop sinning.[17] At a minimum, we should brace ourselves to see sin and its toxic effects at any time, should repent quickly when we see sin in ourselves, and should pray for endurance when we suffer sin.

But the doctrine of original sin, rightly taught, does not turn downcast believers inward. It leads us away from ourselves and upward to Christ. It brings pastoral comfort as we learn to rely on the Lord, not ourselves. When we recognize that our many sins spread from our sinfulness, we give up on vain efforts at self-improvement. We stop looking at our obedience, our achievement. We stop trying to prove ourselves, whether to outside observers or to the internal eye, and look instead to the work of Jesus on the cross.

The doctrine of original sin gives us a healthy dose of realism. We see our condition as it is, as God sees it. It silences the vain thought that we can perfect ourselves and teaches us to seek justification by faith now and perfection upon his return. It bars one of the broad roads to ruin, the notion that we can be good enough to please God or merit his favor, and sends us to the gospel of grace. The doctrine cuts off the hopeless quest for perfection, and urges us onto the path of growth in holiness by the work of the Spirit.

In this age, anyone who leads feels pressure from twin forces—the spirit of criticism, which allows anyone to say anything to anyone, and the spirit of meritocracy, which says perform or step aside. The doctrine of original sin lets us resist these two potential enemies of the soul. It teaches us to ignore the critics a bit and to doubt the meritocratic imperative. We already know our failures. More important, the Lord knows them. He does not insist that we "make amends" or "try harder" in order to be accepted. Rather, when we ask forgiveness, he grants it freely. And while he certainly expects us to do battle with sin, sin's power will lead to so many defeats that we must find our peace in Jesus's finished work, not our incomplete and imperfect efforts.

The Pervasive Effects of Original Sin

Pastors must also teach their people that sin and the fall corrupt every human faculty—mind, body, emotions, and will. Because people use terms like heart, mind, and emotions in different ways, let me define my terms. First, I take the "heart" to be the core or essence of a person. The heart is the center of a person's emotional, intellectual, and moral activity. This use of heart appears in Proverbs 4:23: "Above all else, guard your heart, for it is the wellspring of

---

17. Kevin DeYoung and Ted Kluck, *Why We Love the Church* (Chicago: Moody, 2009), 221.

life." And Jesus says, "Out of the overflow of the heart the mouth speaks" (Matt. 12:34; see also 1 Sam. 16:7; Jer. 18:10; Rom. 10:9). If the heart is the core of a person, then the mind, will, emotions, conscience, as well as the hands and mouth are faculties the heart—the whole person—uses to express his or her core commitments and convictions. Faculties such as the mind, will, and emotions are, from one perspective, functions of the heart. From another perspective our faculties are the tools the heart uses to accomplish its goals and serve its loves or masters. The hands, emotions, and will both serve and reveal the heart. A fallen mind rationalizes wicked acts and refuses to accept unwelcome truths. A fallen body has disorderly desires. The fallen will countermands or indulges those desires, according to its deepest loves. The mind justifies its choices, providing a rationale for the heart to do what it wants. The will rejects authority because the heart bristles at external control. It chooses good or evil according to the heart's affection. In fact, each fallen faculty has the capacity to lead other faculties astray. My youngest child once told me, "I wish I weren't so smart. If I had less ability, I wouldn't have to work so hard in all these AP classes." I replied, "That's true, but if you were less intelligent, regular classes would *seem* just as hard as AP classes." What inspired her odd wish? A spell of laziness led her to foolish thoughts and hopes.

Original Sin and the Mind

The mind is not a neutral thinking machine; it takes direction from the heart. And since the heart, the whole person, is fallen, the mind, like every other faculty, is fallen too. Indeed, the mind suppresses the truth and needs gospel renewal.

In Romans 1, Paul said that godless people "suppress the truth by their wickedness." Creation declares God's existence and power, but the godless do not want to see. They know but do not want to know. "For although they knew God, they neither glorified him as God nor gave thanks to him, but their thinking became futile and their foolish hearts were darkened. Although they claimed to be wise, they became fools." They worshiped idols that they had devised (vv. 18, 21–22 NIV). More, although God wrote his law on every heart, we ignore it and follow our desires. Paul concludes, "Although they know God's righteous decree . . . they not only continue to do these very things but also approve of those who practice them" (v. 32 NIV). As a result, the conscience loses its capacity to commend good and condemn evil (2:14–15).

Elsewhere, Paul says the fallen mind is futile (or vain) since it is devoted to things unworthy of supreme devotion. Further, the understanding is darkened, creating an ignorance that further alienates people from God. Darkened hearts refuse the light and become calloused, even depraved (Eph. 4:17–19; 1 Tim. 6:5). If we work with loud machines without protecting our ears, hearing falters. Likewise, if we ignore God's Word long enough, we eventually cannot hear its warnings about rebellion and sin.

In popular culture, it is axiomatic that the movie's hero or song's singer will prosper if he or she but finds the courage to follow his heart or pursue her dreams. Scripture disagrees. Judges says that Israel descended into moral and spiritual chaos when "everyone did what was right in his own eyes" (Judg. 17:6; 21:25). Similarly, Jude warns against people who rely on their dreams. "These dreamers pollute their own bodies [and] reject authority." They speak "against whatever they do not understand." They trust their misguided instincts and follow sinful appetites or passions (1:7–10, 16–19 NIV). Jude compares dreamers to Korah, who judged himself Moses's equal and concluded that he should lead Israel. Dreamers refuse God's order and reject authority. They stuff themselves at the church's love feasts because they are their own guides. They are "shepherds feeding themselves" (1:12). "They shepherd themselves" (as the Greek literally reads). That is, no one shepherds them, for they tolerate no authority. If an outsider or even their own conscience should accuse them, they justify themselves. Thus the mind serves the fallen heart's purposes. In his acclaimed composition "In the Light," Charlie Peacock sings, "I am the king of excuses. I've got one for every selfish thing I do."

The doctrine of original sin has vital implications. First, pastors should teach their people to test their dreams as they test themselves. Second, it teaches us that we need accountability and authority over us. Even the wisest believer is capable of playing the fool. Thus in rigorous self-examination and in many counselors "there is safety" (Prov. 11:14).

Original Sin and the Emotions

In 2000, novelist and travel writer Paul Theroux traveled overland from Cairo to Cape Town. In Kenya, he intersected a scene of mob violence. A known thief, he learned, had been caught. The panicked man ran wildly but ineffectually as a jubilant mob pursued him, "the toughest men swaggering at the front, the older men cheering them on, the women ululating" as the small children jumped up and down. The man fell, and the laughing crowd surged toward him, swinging sticks, giddy with the thrill of impending mayhem, moments before they beat him to death. It is tempting to despise such reckless or primitive emotions, forgetting that the West judged public hangings to be thrilling entertainment until the early twentieth century.

Contrary to popular opinion, scenes of mob violence and rage do not prove that emotions are irrational and uncontrollable. According to Scripture, healthy emotions are God's gift, and emotions are as fallen, flawed, and sinful as any other faculty. Scripture often commands our emotions, which necessarily implies that they are not irrational and that we are responsible for them. For example, Paul orders, "Love one another with brotherly affection. . . . Rejoice with those who rejoice, weep with those who weep" (Rom. 12:10, 15). And Solomon says, "For everything there is a season, . . . a time to weep, and a time to laugh; a time to mourn, and a time to dance" (Eccles. 3:1, 4).

Robert Roberts wisely calls emotions "concern-based construals."[18] That is, we "get emotional" when we care, perhaps passionately, about something or someone. Proverbs 4:23 (NIV) says, "Above all else, guard your heart, for everything you do flows from it." Our emotions come over us, but they don't *simply* come over us; they flow from the heart. Suppose your team loses a big game. Whether the team is one you cheer for or play for, if you are devastated, you should ask why. Most likely, the team takes up too much space in your heart. You could ask, "Are the right things in the center of my life?" Roberts explains:

> The emotional person . . . is weak not because he has emotions, but because he has such poor ones, or such a limited repertoire. The concerns his emotions go back to are momentary, primitive, immature, badly ordered. He lacks personal integration and depth not because he feels strongly, but because his feelings are erratic and chaotic, or because he feels strongly about the wrong things.[19]

Jesus says evil emotions, like evil desires, come from an evil heart. When the Pharisees slandered Jesus, he explained, "Out of the abundance of the heart the mouth speaks." Their hatred of Jesus led to slander and murder (Matt. 12:34). So emotions are a window to the soul. The character of the emotion hinges on our appraisal of the way events affect the objects of our concern. Emotions are heart-driven responses to events, words, or deeds that feel important to us. They rouse the whole person and offer a window to the spirit. They express "the inner workings of our soul."[20] Emotions sweep over us, but we have the capacity to question, resist, and redirect our emotions. They arise from our core values and *reflect* our heart condition. They reveal what matters to us. That is why feelings cannot change at once or at will. Like

18. Robert Roberts, *Spiritual Emotions: A Psychology of Christian Virtues* (Grand Rapids: Eerdmans, 2007), 11–26.

19. Roberts, *Emotions*, 16.

20. Dan Allender, *Cry of the Soul* (Colorado Springs: NavPress, 1994), 14–17.

our words, our emotions flow from the heart. And since our hearts are fallen, we misconstrue things, and our emotions go astray. Thus a proper concern for justice—thievery should be punished—becomes bloodlust. A proper concern for our name becomes defensiveness. A valid interest in avoiding danger becomes fearfulness, and so on.

As I said, original sin corrupts every human faculty—mind, body, will, and emotions. It would be tedious to explore the fallenness of every faculty, but we may tolerate a word on original sin and the body. Because of the fall, we forfeit our right to life and health. James asks, "What is your life? You are a mist that appears for a little while and then vanishes" (4:14). We are frail, as wispy and fleeting as the morning mist on a lake. We cannot guarantee our existence for a single day.

Psalm 90 says God is eternal. He is "our dwelling place," but he also sees our iniquities and secret sins. Therefore, "the length of our days is seventy years—or eighty, if we have the strength; yet their span is but trouble and sorrow, for they quickly pass, and we fly away" (Ps. 90:1, 10 NIV 1984). Let pastors therefore teach God's people to expect trouble—illness, pain, disease, disappointment, and sorrow—and to give thanks for every day that we are healthy and whole.

Of course, we must place the doctrine of original sin in the context of all biblical theology. Romans 7 is, after all, bracketed by Romans 6 and 8, which assure us that believers are no longer slaves of sin. We are not subject to condemnation, and we are free from the law of sin and death. We can, therefore, make incremental progress against sin, even in this life. Nonetheless, the sobering doctrine of original sin prepares for a life of hardship and tribulation, as Jesus said (John 16:33).

Today, the doctrine of original sin is misunderstood, rejected, mocked, and ignored. Even within the visible church, some argue that the doctrine is unbiblical and oppressive. Rightly understood, however, it does not turn the downcast inward in self-condemnation and misery; it leads upward to Christ. It teaches us to rest in Jesus as he is offered in the gospel. It precludes preening self-reliance based on achievements and urges quiet repentance and faith. It instructs believers, who are simultaneously sinners and saints, to find assurance in Christ. It teaches pastors that a robust doctrine of sin is central to gospel preaching and discipleship because it insists that we place our hope, our trust, in Jesus alone.

PART 4

Adam and the Fall in Dispute

13

ORIGINAL SIN AND ORIGINAL DEATH

Romans 5:12–19

Thomas R. Schreiner

Whether Scripture teaches what is traditionally called "original sin" depends significantly on the exegesis of Romans 5:12–19. Since the days of Augustine, the interpretation of this text functions as the basis for denying or affirming original sin.[1] I will argue in this chapter that the most plausible reading of Romans 5:12–19, both exegetically and theologically, supports the doctrine of original sin and original death. Romans 5:12–19 forms part of Paul's larger argument in chapters 5–8, where the central theme is hope for those who are justified by faith. These particular verses contribute to this theme by emphasizing the astonishing grace of Jesus Christ, for life and righteousness now reign through him in contrast to the death and condemnation inflicted on the world through Adam.[2] Since grace has triumphed over Adam's sin,

---

1. For a brief history of interpretation, see Mark Reasoner, *Romans in Full Circle: A History of Interpretation* (Louisville: Westminster John Knox, 2005), 43–54.
2. Clearly Paul believes Adam is a historical figure. Rightly Frank Matera, *Romans*, Paideia: Commentaries on the New Testament (Grand Rapids: Baker Academic, 2010), 137; Otfried Hofius, "The Adam-Christ Antithesis and the Law: Reflections on Romans 5:12–21," in *Paul and*

believers should be full of hope, for if the sin and death inducted into the world through Adam have been defeated, nothing can separate believers from the love of Christ.

Romans 5:12–14

5:12ab

The interpretation of 5:12 plunges us into a thicket of difficulties, but the first part of the verse is clear, setting the stage for all that follows. Paul begins by asserting that "through one man sin entered the world and death through sin."[3] The one man is Adam, and hence Paul reflects on Genesis 3 where Adam and Eve transgressed the Lord's command not to eat from the tree of the knowledge of good and evil. Adam's sin, just as the Lord threatened, had death as its consequence (Gen. 2:17).[4] The universal consequences of Adam's sin are emphasized, for his sin did not just affect himself; it introduced both sin and death into the world.[5] Death must not be restricted to physical death here, for both physical and spiritual death are intended.[6] The narrator in Genesis doesn't explicitly say that all human beings shared in Adam's sin, but the narrative supports such a reading, for paradise has certainly been left far behind beginning with chapter 4, which relays the murder of Abel. And death (notwithstanding the story of Enoch) punctuates the roll call in chapter 5. Paul reflects on Genesis in concluding that sin and death invaded the world through *one man*. The sin and death of Adam were not confined to him. All human beings since Adam have entered the world as sinners and are spiritually dead.

The grammar here is quite interesting. Most scholars maintain that Paul breaks off his comparison in midsentence and doesn't complete it until 5:18,

---

the *Mosaic Law*, ed. James D. G. Dunn (Grand Rapids: Eerdmans, 2001), 181. See the chapter in this volume by Robert Yarbrough.

3. All translations are mine unless noted otherwise.

4. Some interpreters object that Adam did not die on the day he sinned. Such an objection, though superficially attractive, fails to see the point of the narrative. Both Adam and Eve when they sinned died spiritually in that they were separated from God.

5. The word κόσμον here refers specifically to human beings.

6. Contra John Murray, *The Epistle to the Romans: The English Text with Introduction, Exposition and Notes,* vol. 1, *Chapters 1–8*, New International Commentary on the New Testament (Grand Rapids: Eerdmans, 1959), 181–82; J. A. Ziesler, *Paul's Letter to the Romans*, TPI New Testament Commentaries (Philadelphia: Trinity Press International, 1989), 145. Rightly Johan Christiaan Beker, *Paul the Apostle: The Triumph of God in Life and Thought* (Philadelphia: Fortress, 1980), 224. This is not to say, of course, that spiritual and physical death occurred at the same moment.

since Paul uses the phrase καὶ οὕτως instead of οὕτως καί.[7] It is more likely, however, that the order of the words in the phrase should not be pressed, so that the comparison is completed in 5:12cd.[8] We could paraphrase the verse this way: "since sin and death entered the world through one man, so also death spread to all people since all sinned." The logic of the verse is that all people sin and die because Adam introduced sin and death into the world. Sin and death as evil powers, as twin towers, rule over all people by virtue of Adam's sin.

5:12cd–14

What Paul says in 5:12cd is fiercely contested and difficult to understand. Indeed, I have changed my mind on what 5:12cd means since writing my Romans commentary, though the change does not affect the truth that Adam is the covenant head of all human beings, so that all enter the world condemned and dead because of Adam's sin.

Perhaps it is best to begin with the interpretation I argued for in my Romans commentary. I argued there the words ἐφ' ᾧ should be translated as a result clause or be rendered "on the basis of which."[9] Joseph Fitzmyer has demonstrated in an important article that ἐφ' ᾧ often introduces a result clause.[10] Taking up Fitzmyer's reading, I suggested that 5:12cd should be translated, "and so death spread to all people, and on the basis of this death all sinned."[11] According to this reading all people sin individually because they enter the

---

7. E.g., C. E. B. Cranfield, *A Critical and Exegetical Commentary on the Epistle to the Romans: Introduction and Commentary on Romans I–VIII*, International Critical Commentary (Edinburgh: T&T Clark), 272.

8. So Richard J. Erickson, "The Damned and the Justified in Romans 5:12–21: An Analysis of Semantic Structure," in *Discourse Analysis and the New Testament: Approaches and Results*, eds. Stanley E. Porter and Jeffrey T. Reed, Journal of the Study of the New Testament: Supplement Series 170 (Sheffield, UK: Sheffield Academic Press, 1999), 290; Arland J. Hultgren, *Paul's Letter to the Romans: A Commentary* (Grand Rapids: Eerdmans, 2011), 223–24; John T. Kirby, "The Syntax of Romans 5.12: A Rhetorical Approach," *New Testament Studies* 33 (1987): 283–86.

9. Thomas R. Schreiner, *Romans*, Baker Exegetical Commentary on the New Testament (Grand Rapids: Baker Academic, 1998), 273–77. For a similar interpretation, see Brian Vickers, "Grammar and Theology in the Interpretation of Rom 5:12," *Trinity Journal* 27 (2006): 271–88. Other interpretations proposed are quite implausible. For instance, that ᾧ refers to νόμος, Frederick W. Danker, "Romans V.12: Sin Under Law," *New Testament Studies* 14 (1967–68): 424–39; or to θάνατος, Ethelbert Stauffer, *New Testament Theology*, trans. J. Marsh (London: SCM, 1955), 270; or that it refers to κόσμον, Robert Jewett, *Romans: A Commentary*, Hermeneia (Minneapolis: Fortress, 2007), 369, 376.

10. Joseph A. Fitzmyer, "The Consecutive Meaning of ἐφ' ᾧ in Romans 5.12," *New Testament Studies* 39 (1993): 321–39.

11. Schreiner, *Romans*, 270. See also Brian Vickers, *Jesus' Blood and Righteousness: Paul's Theology of Imputation* (Wheaton: Crossway, 2006), 124, 136–41.

world spiritually dead on the basis of their union with Adam. Since all human beings, as a result of Adam's sin, are spiritually dead, they express their spiritual death by their sin.

I still believe this interpretation fits theologically with what Romans 5:12–19 teaches and is a possible reading of the text. For reasons that will be explained in due course, my theological reading of the text has not changed. Still, this particular reading of 5:12cd seems less likely to me for two reasons. First and most important, though it is theologically true that spiritual death leads to sin (see Eph. 2:1–3), in Romans 5 and 6 Paul emphasizes that sin leads to death.[12] That sin leads to death is the specific point in 5:12ab, and it is reiterated in verses 13–14, 15, and 17, and is confirmed in 6:23, "for the wages of sin is death." It is possible, of course, that Paul teaches both truths in these verses, that is, sin leads to death and spiritual death leads to sin. But the latter notion is not articulated clearly elsewhere in chapters 5–6, whereas Paul repeatedly affirms that death is the result of sin. Hence, it seems more plausible to think that 5:12cd teaches that death spread to all because all sinned.

That brings us to the second and subordinate reason, though it is related to the first argument, for rejecting the interpretation noted above. Fitzmyer has clearly shown that ἐφ' ᾧ can designate result. Indeed, it is apparent from several biblical texts (the Septuagint and the New Testament) that the phrase is not invariably causal (Gen. 38:30; Josh. 5:15; 2 Kings 19:10; Prov. 21:22; Isa. 25:9; 37:10; 62:8; Jer. 7:14; Acts 7:33). But we need to be careful, for Pauline usage elsewhere demonstrates that the phrase may have a causal sense.[13] Indeed, a causal reading seems preferable for the meaning of ἐφ' ᾧ on the three other occasions in which Paul uses the phrase (2 Cor. 5:4; Phil. 3:12; 4:10). Therefore, whether ἐφ' ᾧ denotes result or cause must be discerned from context. And that brings us to what was argued above. Since Paul regularly argues in Romans 5 and 6 that sin begets death, context supports the interpretation, "and so death spread to all men because all sinned" (5:12).

---

12. Rightly N. T. Wright, "The Letter to the Romans: Introduction, Commentary, and Reflections," in *The New Interpreter's Bible*, vol. 10 (Nashville: Abingdon, 2002), 527; John Piper, *Counted Righteous in Christ: Should We Abandon the Imputation of Christ's Righteousness?* (Wheaton: Crossway, 2002), 91n37.

13. Cf. here C. F. D. Moule, *An Idiom Book of New Testament Greek*, 2nd ed. (Cambridge: Cambridge University Press, 1959), 50; Murray J. Harris, "Prepositions and Theology in the Greek New Testament," *New International Dictionary of New Testament Theology*, ed. C. Brown, 4 vols. (Grand Rapids: Zondervan, 1975–1985), 3:1194–95; Ulrich Wilckens, *Der Brief an die Römer*, Teilband 1: *Röm 1–5*, Evangelisch-katholischer Kommentar zum Neuen Testament (Zürich: Neukirchener, 1978), 316; Hofius, "The Adam-Christ Antithesis and the Law," 172n27; Hultgren, *Romans*, 222; Erickson, "The Damned and the Justified," 291n12. Contra Vickers, *Jesus' Blood and Righteousness*, 124–27.

I set aside, then, the interpretation which reads ἐφ’ ᾧ as a result clause. Let's consider several interpretations where ἐφ’ ᾧ designates the cause. The text could be construed to say that death spread to all because all without exception sinned individually. Such a reading fits well with a Pelagian reading of the text where death is only the result of individual sin. I will argue shortly that Paul indeed teaches here that individuals die because of personal sin, but such an interpretation should not be used, given the whole context, to buttress a Pelagian perspective.[14] Indeed, the Pelagian reading fails on exegetical grounds, for 5:12 begins with sin and death invading the world through the one man, Adam. The death and sin of individuals in the latter part of 5:12 cannot be neatly sundered from the devastation Adam inflicted on the world, that is, on human beings.[15] Furthermore, Paul emphasizes five times in verses 15–19 that death and condemnation are the portion of all human beings because of Adam's one sin. It simply won't work exegetically to limit death to personal and individual sin, when Paul communicates repeatedly and forcefully that human beings experience death and judgment because of Adam's sin.

According to Charles Cranfield, the text means that human beings sin because they inherited a corrupt nature from Adam.[16] But the word "sinned" (ἥμαρτον) does not mean "became corrupted" in one's nature. It refers to the act of sinning, and hence Cranfield strays from the wording of the text.[17]

Henri Blocher, who is in the Augustinian camp, has written an incisive defense of original sin,[18] where he attempts to defend a variation of the federal headship view. Blocher doesn't simply repristinate the federal view, for he maintains that Adam's guilt is not imputed to all. Still, he attempts to explain why we are condemned both for Adam's sin and for our own.[19] The sin of Adam, says Blocher, is the fountainhead for the condemnation of all human beings.[20] God views all human beings in Adam, and thus their personal and individual

14. According to Pelagius, human beings sin by imitating Adam's example. See Theodore de Bruyn, *Pelagius's Commentary on St. Paul's Epistle to the Romans: Translated with Introduction and Notes*, Oxford Early Christian Studies (Oxford: Clarendon, 1993), 92, 95.

15. See the decisive arguments of Hultgren, *Romans*, 223–24. Cf. also Erickson, who rightly says that Paul teaches here that all die because of Adam's sin and their own sin ("The Damned and the Justified," 303).

16. Cranfield, *Romans I–VIII*, 278–79.

17. Rightly S. Lewis Johnson Jr., "Romans 5:12—An Exercise in Exegesis and Theology," in *New Dimensions in New Testament Study*, ed. Richard N. Longenecker and Merrill C. Tenney (Grand Rapids: Zondervan, 1974), 311.

18. Henri Blocher, *Original Sin: Illuminating the Riddle*, New Studies in Biblical Theology 5 (Downers Grove, IL: InterVarsity, 1997).

19. Particular thanks are due to Steve Wellum, who helped me enormously to understand the particulars of Blocher's position. Any defects are my own.

20. Blocher, *Original Sin*, 77.

sin is "grafted on to Adam's sin in Eden."[21] According to Blocher, the sin of each human being is linked to the sin of Adam since he is the covenant head. The "community" is "stricken" through Adam's sin, and yet Adam's guilt is not imputed to them.[22] Adam's headship makes *"possible the imputation, the judicial treatment, of human sins."*[23] Human beings are guilty because Adam's paradigmatic sin is repristinated or recommitted, so to speak, when individuals sin. At the same time Blocher insists that the sin of human beings is not separable from Adamic headship.[24]

Blocher is more sympathetic toward a federal over a realist view of imputation.[25] Still, he finds tensions in the federal view. He doesn't think it squares with God's justice for God to impute alien guilt to human beings.[26] He maintains, therefore, that Adam is our federal head, but the guilt of Adam is not imputed to the account of human beings.[27] Human beings are "deprived and depraved" because of Adam's sin and their union with him, but are not counted as guilty on the basis of Adam's sin.[28] Entering the world as sinners is not a "penalty" but "a *fact* for human beings since Adam."[29] Blocher thinks his view explains God's justice in a more satisfactory way than alien guilt being imputed to all. Skeptics will wonder why we enter the world depraved and deprived because of Adam's sin. Blocher's answer is rather simple. Adam is our head.[30] That is just the way the world is, for the human race is in solidarity with Adam.

Blocher certainly deserves credit for creativity and for being willing to rethink the text exegetically and theologically. Still, his solution must be assessed as unconvincing for several reasons. Remarkably, he scarcely comments on Romans 5:15–19, attending mainly to verses 12–14. The omission is significant and damaging to his case, for five times in verses 15–19 judgment and death are attributed to Adam's one sin.[31] There is no conception here in verses 15–19 that the sins of individuals somehow mirror Adam's sin. Instead, human beings enter into the world condemned and spiritually dead because of Adam's one sin. As I will argue below, verses 15–19 clearly teach that Adam's guilt is imputed to all human beings.

21. Ibid.
22. Ibid., 75, 130.
23. Ibid., 77, emphasis in original.
24. Ibid., 76–79.
25. Ibid., 114–22.
26. Ibid., 121.
27. Ibid., 128.
28. Ibid.
29. Ibid., 129, emphasis in original.
30. Ibid., 129–30.
31. I will explain this text further below.

Blocher's case depends on his reading of verse 12, but his interpretation seems strained, for to say that all sinned individually relative to the prohibition given to Adam flies in the face of the most natural reading of the text. Blocher links the personal sin of individuals to the sin of Adam, but Paul severs that link. They did not sin "in the likeness of Adam's transgression" (v. 14). Their "sin" was "not reckoned" (οὐκ ἐλλογεῖται) against them (v. 13). Blocher thinks all people "sinned" (v. 12) by violating, in a sense, the Adamic prohibition. But Paul says precisely the opposite. Adam's sin was unique and paradigmatic in contrast to the sins of those who followed him. Furthermore, Adam transgressed a command that was revealed specifically, and those who lived in the time between Adam and Moses did not violate an articulated command. Blocher's interpretation, then, should be rejected, for it supplies a notion to the text (human sin repristinates Adam's sin) that Paul does not state and amounts to a denial of what Paul actually says (the sin of human beings must be distinguished from Adam's sin).

Blocher acknowledges that Romans 2:12 could be adduced against his view, but he understands it along the same lines as 5:12.[32] Violating the law written on the heart describes in a complementary way the transgression of the covenant made with Adam. Blocher's explanation here, though possible, does not constitute a likely reading of 2:12, for the text emphasizes sinning *without the law* and does not naturally point to the relationship of sinners to Adam.

Blocher's position is difficult to untangle because he wants to uphold a federal view, but his explanation, historically, seems to fit with a mediate imputation view, even though he rejects the latter view as unsatisfactory.[33] He inclines to a federal view, but its federalism is called seriously into question by his rejection of imputed guilt, for what he emphasizes is the depraved nature that human beings inherited through Adam. It seems that they are counted as guilty when they act on that depraved nature, imitating, so to speak, Adam's sin. Blocher rejects the imputation of Adam's guilt to his descendants on the basis of God's justice. But how does his solution really solve the problem? Human beings in solidarity with Adam have a depraved nature that will inevitably lead to sin and death. It is difficult to see how anyone who struggles with God's justice in the matter of Adamic headship will find Blocher's solution much of an improvement over the theory of an imputed guilt.

John Murray, in his book *The Imputation of Adam's Sin*, proposes an interpretation that fits with a Reformed and Augustinian reading of the text.[34]

32. Blocher, *Original Sin*, 80–81.
33. Ibid., 66–67.
34. John Murray, *The Imputation of Adam's Sin* (reprint; Nutley, NJ: P&R, 1977). See also Johnson, "Romans 5:12," 306–7, 312–13; Herman N. Ridderbos, *Paul: An Outline of His*

Augustine, working from the Latin, understood the text to say that all people sinned in Adam (*in quo* in Latin). Few scholars today think that the anteced-ent of ἐφ' ᾧ is Adam. Murray argues that the words ἐφ' ᾧ should be rendered "because," supporting the Augustinian case on different grounds grammatically and exegetically. Taking ἐφ' ᾧ as causal, he understands Paul to say that "death spread to all because all sinned" (5:12cd). The words "all sinned," however, should not be understood to say that all sinned personally and individually. When Paul says "all sinned," he means that *all sinned in Adam*. Death spread to all people without exception because everyone sinned in Adam. Adam's sin was their sin, and Adam is their covenantal and federal head.[35]

How does Murray defend the idea that Paul refers to sinning in Adam rather than personal sin in 5:12? The parenthetical explanation in verses 13–14 is crucial to Murray's case. According to verse 13, sin was not reckoned to anyone's account in the interval between Adam and Moses since there was no law. Nevertheless, we find in verse 14 that those who lived in this time period still died, even though they did not violate a law that was specifically revealed as Adam did. Here Murray proposes a brilliant solution. Why did they die if their sins were not reckoned to them? They died, says Murray, because of Adam's sin, not their own. If their sin was not counted against them, then their death cannot be based on their own sin. They had to die for another reason. And the reason that is given is Adam's sin. The parenthesis in verses 13–14, then, unpacks the meaning of "all sinned" at the end of verse 12, clarifying that the sin that led to death was Adam's. It cannot be the sin of Adam's de-scendants since Paul says their sin was *not counted* against them. The genius of this solution is that it matches remarkably well with the fivefold description of the impact of Adam's sin in verses 15–19. Human beings enter the world condemned and spiritually dead because they sinned in Adam.

Murray's reading of the text is profound and theologically rich. Indeed, I will explain in due course why I think he is right in seeing Adam as our cov-enant head, with the result that all human beings are condemned before God because of Adam's one sin. But we must distinguish between Murray's theo-logical judgment about the text as a whole and his interpretation of verses 12–14. I think the former is on target, but the latter veers away from Paul's argument in these particular verses. It should be said that Murray's reading of these verses is a *possible* interpretation, which he defends with great skill. His argument makes sense of the flow of the argument in verses 12–14, but it

---

Theology, trans. J. R. de Witt (Grand Rapids: Eerdmans, 1975), 96–97; Piper, *Counted Righ-teous in Christ*, 91–94.

35. I am using the terms covenantal and federal synonymously. See Vickers, *Jesus' Blood and Righteousness*, 149–50.

should be rejected because it does not square as easily with what we find in the Old Testament and what Paul teaches elsewhere.

The fundamental weakness of Murray's interpretation of verses 12–14 needs to be unpacked. His interpretation rests on the premise that the sins of those who lived between Adam and Moses were not counted against them (v. 13). They died because of Adam's sin, not their own. Such a reading does not fit, however, the narrative in Genesis (6–9). The prime example is the generation of the flood. Clearly, the flood generation existed in the interval of time between Adam and Moses. The entire generation, apart from Noah and his family, perished in the flood that inundated the world. Those destroyed by the flood were judged, condemned, and died for their own sin. We have no indication that the sin assessed against them was Adam's sin.[36] Apparently, their sin, which led to the destructive deluge, was reckoned against them, even though they did not violate commands revealed to them by God. The same point could be made about the judgment at Babel (Gen. 11:1–9). Those constructing (what was probably) a ziggurat were judged by God for their arrogance and refusal to honor God's name. Such a judgment was inflicted on them, even though they lived before the era of the law and thus did not violate laws or commands published by God. Those judged and condemned at Babel were held accountable for their sin, even though they lived in the interval between Adam and Moses and did not live under the law. It should also be noted that the framework of Adam to Moses indicates that any reference to infants, which are commonly brought up in the Reformed tradition,[37] are not within Paul's purview.[38]

I am not suggesting that Paul misread the Old Testament here. Rather, the judgment at the flood and at Babel indicates that Murray's interpretation of Romans 5:12–14 is flawed.[39] Those who lived in the era between Adam and Moses were accountable for their sin, so that they were condemned because they violated God's moral norms. Their sin was counted against them and thus they were judged. Paul himself teaches the same truth in 2:12, when he claims that "all those who sinned without the law will also perish without

36. I am not denying that when we consider all of biblical revelation they were also condemned because of Adam's sin. The point I am making is that the reason stated in Genesis for their judgment is their own sin, not the sin of Adam.

37. See esp. Piper, *Counted Righteous in Christ*, 95–100.

38. Rightly Vickers, *Jesus' Blood and Righteousness*, 143n118 and 144n119. If the focus were on infants, there is no need to refer to the time period between Adam and Moses, for infants are always without the law. The focus on the time between Adam and Moses indicates that Paul confines himself to a definite period in salvation history.

39. Cf. here Timo Laato, *Paulus und das Judentum: Anthropologische Erwägungen* (Åbo: Åbo Academi Press, 1991), 134.

the law." The word "perish" (ἀπολοῦνται) denotes, as is typically the case in Paul, final judgment and destruction. Gentiles who did not know or possess the Mosaic law were judged for violating the law inscribed on their hearts (2:14–15). What Paul claims here fits with the judgments inflicted on the flood generation and at Babel. Gentiles did not have the Mosaic law, but they were judged for violating the unwritten law—the law inscribed on their hearts. Romans 2:12 is of paramount importance, for it prevents us from adopting a mistaken view of 5:12–14. Paul does not mean, when he says that sin is not counted against those who have no law (v. 13), that those who do not have the law are only judged on the basis of Adam's sin. For he clearly says in 2:12 that those without the law perish because they violate the law written on their hearts. Paul does not argue in chapter 2 that Adam's sin is the basis for their judgment.[40] They perished because they contravened God's moral norms.

To sum up, Murray's interpretation of Romans 5:12–14 does not cohere with what Paul says elsewhere (2:12) or with the judgments poured out during the time between Adam and Moses (the flood, Babel, Cain's judgment, etc.). Against Murray, sin was counted against those who did not possess the law, and human beings without the law were judged and condemned for violating moral norms.

I have argued that Murray's interpretation does not fit with what Paul teaches elsewhere or with what we find in the Old Testament. I propose that Paul speaks of individual sin here, without buying into a Pelagian interpretation. To paraphrase: "death spread to all people because all sinned individually." Paul does not deny in this text that the sin of individuals lead to death. What he affirms, however, contra the Pelagian reading, is that individuals come into the world condemned and spiritually dead because of Adam's sin. The latter part of 5:12 must not be separated from the first part of the verse. Sin and death entered into the world through Adam, and hence people sin and die both because of Adam's sin and their own sin, though the sin of Adam is fundamental and foundational.

What role do verses 13–14 play in the argument if verse 12cd says that death extended to the entire world because of individual sin? Paul explains in verses 13–14 that the sins of those who lived between the time of Adam and Moses must be distinguished from Adam's sin. Adam transgressed a specifically revealed commandment (v. 14) so that sin and death entered the world through him (v. 12). As the first human being he occupies a typological role in the same way as Jesus Christ (v. 14). The subsequent verses (vv. 15–19) clarify that one

---

40. Again, I am not denying here that Adam's sin played a role in their judgment. The point I am making is that this is not Paul's *specific argument* in Rom. 2:12.

is either in Adam or in Christ. Hence, the sins of those who lived in the era between Adam and Moses cannot be assigned the same import or function as Adam's sin. It was Adam's first sin that brought havoc into the world, so that all human beings are under the reign of both sin and death.[41]

The unique role of Adam does not mean that sin did not exist in the interval in which there was no law. As 5:13 says, "sin was in the world" during this time, which is evident to anyone who has read the stories about Cain, Lamech, the flood generation, and Babel. But then how can Paul say that "sin is not reckoned [οὐκ ἐλλογεῖται] when there is no law" (v. 13)? That seems patently false on first glance since the flood generation and those at Babel were judged and condemned for their sin, even if they did not violate a specifically revealed command.

Paul's point in 5:13–14 must be discerned by attending to what he says in verse 14. Those who sinned without violating a specifically revealed command, as Adam did, still died. Death reigned and ruled over them. As N. T. Wright says, Paul's "explanation is simple; sin must be there (5:13a) because death was there ruling like a king (5:14a)."[42] So, when Paul says that their sins were not reckoned or counted against them, he is not teaching that their sins were not counted against them in any sense. They were punished for their sins, for they experienced the reign of death because of their sins. Paul's point is that their sins, though still punishable by death, were not technically counted against them in the same way as sin was counted against Adam.[43] Yes, they died because of their personal and individual sin. But their sin did not have the same typological and fundamental role as Adam's sin, for Adam's sin was of such a nature that sin and death encompassed the whole world because of his transgression of God's revealed command.[44] Therefore, Paul considers in 5:12–14 both the sin of Adam and the sin of those who lived between the time of Adam and Moses. In both cases, sin led to death, but Adam played a fundamental and typological role that those who followed him did not play, and hence Adam's sin and death are the fountainhead for the sin and death that ensued. As Arland Hultgren says, Adam is "positioned as the head of humanity."[45] Adam and Christ are the typological heads, and their fundamental role is explicated in the following verses.

41. Jewett rightly says that ruling is a key theme in the text. *Romans*, 370.

42. Wright, "Romans," 527.

43. So Cranfield, *Romans I–VIII*, 282–83; Günther Bornkamm, *Das Ende des Gesetzes: Paulusstudien*, Beiträge zur evangelischen Theologie 16 (Munich: Chr. Kaiser, 1952), 84.

44. See Stephen Westerholm, *Israel's Law and the Church's Faith: Paul and His Recent Interpreters* (Grand Rapids: Eerdmans, 1988), 183–84.

45. Hultgren, *Romans*, 226. See also 227.

Romans 5:15–19

Five times in 5:15–19 Paul contrasts Adam and Christ. A person belongs to either Adam or Christ, but the impact of these two is remarkably different, for Adam brought death and judgment into the world, whereas Jesus Christ brought grace and life and righteousness. Since Paul reiterates the same truth, it is exceedingly important for his argument, and hence it is quite remarkable that many focus on verses 12–14 and say little about verses 15–19. I will proceed verse by verse in summarizing the contrasts between Adam and Christ and then reflect on the text theologically, particularly insofar as it relates to Adam's sin.

5:15

Paul begins by contrasting Adam and Christ, asserting that "the gift is not like the trespass."[46] There is continuity between the two in that history has been shaped by Adam and Christ, but there is discontinuity in that Adam brought devastation to the world and Christ brought grace. What has Adam wrought? Paul answers, "By the trespass of the one the many died." The trespass, of course, was Adam's violation in Genesis 3 of the prohibition against eating from the tree of the knowledge of good and evil (Gen. 2:17). Since Paul reflects on Genesis, we might expect him to say that Adam died when he sinned, but Paul reaches far beyond that, claiming that "many died" through Adam's trespass. The word "many" (πολλοί) here certainly means "all," as subsequent verses attest. No room is allowed for exceptions. All of humanity, apart from the Christ, died because Adam sinned.

Does Paul refer to physical death or spiritual death? It would be a mistake to drive a wedge between these two conceptions, for the one is inextricably tied to the other. Physical death is the consequence of spiritual death, so that the former serves as the emblem and concrete instantiation of the latter. We saw in 5:12 that human beings die because of individual sin, but here Paul returns to the thought of verse 12ab and expands on it. There is something prior to individual sin, something that undergirds and explains it, that is, human beings enter the world spiritually dead (and physical death will follow in due

---

46. The first clause of 5:15 (so also 5:16) is not to be rendered as a question. Contra Chrys C. Caragounis, "Romans 5:15–16 in the Context of 5:12–21: Contrast or Comparison?," *New Testament Studies* 31 (1985): 144–45; Stanley E. Porter, "The Pauline Concept of Original Sin, in Light of Rabbinic Background," *Tyndale Bulletin* 41 (1990): 27–28; Don B. Garlington, *Faith, Obedience, and Perseverance: Aspects of Paul's Letter to the Romans*, Wissenschaftliche Untersuchungen zum Neuen Testament 79 (Tübingen: Mohr Siebeck, 1994), 98. Rightly Hultgren, *Romans*, 218.

course) because of Adam's sin. Human beings do not enter into the world in a neutral state. They are "dead upon arrival" because of Adam's sin!

Conversely, Paul marvels over the grace of Christ, piling up terms to communicate its richness and extent. Paul is moved to astonishment when he considers the freedom and extent of his grace. He does not wonder why human beings are held accountable for Adam's sin. He marvels that God's grace in Christ liberates those worthy of death.

5:16

The contrast between Adam and Christ is again pursued: "the gift is not like the one man's sin." The sin affected all as did the gift, but the effects were profoundly different. "For the judgment from the one sin resulted in condemnation, but the gift after many trespasses resulted in justification." The one sin here is clearly Adam's. Because of his sin, he was judged and condemned in the garden, which is apparent on reading Genesis 3. What is striking and perhaps even shocking is that the condemnation (κατάκριμα) here is not limited to Adam. The surrounding context (vv. 15–19) demonstrates that the condemnation extends to all people because of Adam's one sin.[47] The scandal of original sin stands out in all its starkness. The text does not say that human beings are condemned because of their own sin, though such a thought is clearly true. But something different, something deeper and more profound about the origin of human sin, is communicated here. All human beings enter the world condemned before God because of Adam's sin. Paul does not defend or apologize for such a notion. He simply asserts it. Nor does Paul explain here how or why human beings are condemned because of Adam's one sin, though I will return to this issue at the close of the chapter.

Paul is struck by the astonishing generosity of the gift granted to human beings, confirming that forgiveness of sins is undeserved, that the condemnation meted out because of Adam's one sin is right and just. The depth and breadth of God's grace is featured, for he covered "many transgressions." The one sin of Adam unleashed a torrent of transgressions into the world, but the river of sin finds its source in Adam's one sin in the garden. Sin, though it seems small in the beginning, wreaks untold devastation in the world in that one sin leads to an unending cascade of sin. Jesus did not only forgive the multitude of transgressions and give people a clean slate. Wright says, "Christ has not only restored that which Adam lost, but has gone far beyond. . . . God's action in the Messiah did not start where Adam's started, and, as it

---

47. The word denotes eschatological condemnation. So Hofius, "The Adam-Christ Antithesis and the Law," 182.

were, merely get it right this time. God's action in the Messiah began at the point where Adam's ended—with many sins and many sinners."[48] Those who belong to Christ are also justified. They are not merely forgiven but also stand in the right before God.

5:17

Death reigns as a power over those who are in Adam, for death is not merely an event that occurs but a state in which human beings live as a result of Adam's sin. As noted above, death can't be limited to spiritual or physical death, for both realities are designated by the word "death." Interpreters who focus on one reality apart from the other miss the intention of the text here, for physical death stands as the culmination point for the spiritual death that dominated human beings during their earthly lives.

Death reigns (ἐβασίλευσεν) over all through the *one* (ἑνὸς) transgression of the *one* (ἑνὸς) man. Human beings certainly die because of their own sin (5:12cd), but here Paul considers the origin of sin and death in the world. He reaches further back, contemplating why it is that all people sin. Death has invaded their lives because of the one transgression of the one man, Adam. Paul assumes here that the human race is a unity, rejecting any notion that people are separate from Adam. They enter the world spiritually dead and destined for physical death because of Adam's one sin. Clearly, Adam is the fountainhead for sin and death in the world (see v. 12ab). Incidentally, some object that the unity of the human race with Adam means that all of Adam's sins must be imputed to his descendants, but note that Paul limits death to Adam's one sin. The infection, so to speak, has spread through the body at the first incidence of the disease. Hence, Adam's subsequent sins are irrelevant to the argument made here.

Paul continues to marvel at the grace of God in Jesus Christ. Adam's transgression introduced death as the king of human beings, but the grace of God brooks no rivals, conquering both sin and death. Hence, the recipients of God's grace now enjoy "the gift of righteousness" (τῆς δωρεᾶς τῆς δικαιοσύνης).[49] Their righteousness is not in themselves but in the second Adam, Jesus Christ. They are counted as righteous in Christ. Through the one man (διὰ τοῦ ἑνὸς), Jesus Christ, they now reign in life (ἐν ζωῇ βασιλεύσουσιν). History hangs on the work of two men. Either a person is in Adam where sin and death reign, or a person is in Christ where one reigns in life and enjoys the gift of righ-

48. Wright, "Romans," 528.
49. The word δικαιοσύνης is appositional here, denoting the gift that is righteousness (Wilckens, *Röm* 1–5, 325).

teousness. The future tense of βασιλεύσουσιν is not just a logical future but refers to the eschaton. Still, the eschaton has penetrated the present evil age through the death and resurrection of Jesus Christ. Believers enjoy even now the life of the age to come; they have begun to reign, but their reign will come into full flower when Jesus Christ returns.[50]

5:18

Verse 18 draws an inference from 5:15–17, as is indicated by the words "therefore then" (Ἄρα οὖν). "Just as condemnation came to all people through the trespass of the one, so also the justification that leads to life came to all people through the righteous act of the one." It is instructive that "condemnation" (κατάκριμα) is contrasted with "justification" (δικαίωσιν). Justification means that one is declared to be right before God, and conversely "condemnation" refers to those upon whom a sentence of judgment has been passed. Paul unequivocally says here that all people without exception are condemned before God because of the one transgression of Adam. If they are condemned before God because of Adam's sin, then they are guilty for Adam's sin. They can hardly be condemned for Adam's sin if they are not guilty for the sin he committed. Paul offers no apologetic here, nor does he defend the justice of what God has done. He asserts the facts of the case, claiming that Adam's sin spells our condemnation.

On the other hand, Jesus's "righteous act" (δικαιώματος) results in the justification that leads to life for all those who belong to him. The word "life" in the phrase "justification of life" (δικαίωσιν ζωῆς) should be understood as a genitive of result. The consequence of justification is eschatological life. The work of Christ does not merely return human beings to the state of Adam prior to his sin. Those in Christ now enjoy the righteousness of another, a righteousness that is not their own. By virtue of their union with Christ, they are reckoned to be righteous before God and enjoy the life of the age to come. When Paul speaks of the "righteous act of the one" (δι᾽ ἑνὸς δικαιώματος) as the means by which justification is given to all, the work of Christ on the cross is in view. Forgiveness and justification are secured through the sin-bearing and atoning work of Christ.

5:19

Paul wraps up his argument regarding Adam and Christ in 5:19. He provides the grounds for the argument in 5:18 here (supported by "for," γάρ). The

---

50. See Douglas J. Moo, *The Epistle to the Romans*, New International Commentary on the New Testament (Grand Rapids: Eerdmans, 1996), 340.

reason all are condemned in Adam and justified in Christ (v. 18) is that human beings are counted as sinners in Adam and righteous in Christ (v. 19). In verse 19 we read that "for just as the many were constituted as sinners through the disobedience of the one man, so also the many were constituted as righteous through the obedience of the one man." The word "many" (οἱ πολλοί) refers to all people here, and should not be limited to some. Scholars particularly debate the meaning of the word "constituted" (two uses of καθίστημι). Is the term forensic, meaning that human beings are *counted as sinners* by virtue of Adam's disobedience and *counted righteous* by virtue of Christ's obedience?[51] Or, is Paul saying that human beings are *truly sinners* (made sinners) because of Adam's disobedience and *truly righteous* (made righteous) because of Christ's obedience?[52] Evidence can be adduced for both views (for the meaning "count" or "appoint," see Matt. 24:45, 47; 25:21, 23; Luke 12:14; Acts 6:3; 7:10, 27, 35; Titus 1:5; Heb. 5:1; 7:28; 8:3; for the meaning "made," see James 4:4; 2 Pet. 1:8). Given the emphasis on Adam and Christ in the surrounding context and the insistence that both death and life and condemnation and justification stem from them, it seems that the forensic meaning is more likely. Still, the forensic cannot be separated from what is actual. Those who are constituted as sinners in Adam become sinners in practice, and those who are counted righteous in Christ live righteously.

The main point is that all human beings are constituted as sinners by virtue of Adam's disobedience. His sin is reckoned to them. Conversely, all those who belong to Christ are counted as righteous by virtue of his obedience.[53] Whether one is a sinner or righteous depends on whether one belongs to Adam or Christ. One's relationship to Adam and Christ is the fundamental reality. Human beings certainly do not enter into the world in a neutral state. By virtue of Adam's disobedience they commence life from its inception as sinners. Their sin is not merely individualistic, though they do sin individually, but their sin finds its root in Adam's sin; and they are counted as sinners because of Adam's disobedience. Still, their actually *becoming* sinners or righteous is the consequence or result of their being *counted* as sinners in Adam or as righteous in Christ.

---

51. Vickers, *Jesus' Blood and Righteousness*, 116–22, 155–56; Wright, "Romans," 529; Ridderbos, *Paul*, 98; Porter, "Pauline Concept of Original Sin," 29; Murray, *Romans 1–8*, 205–6; Moo, *Romans*, 345; Piper, *Counted Righteous in Christ*, 108–10.

52. Wilckens, *Röm 1–5*, 328; Dunn, *Romans 1–8*, 284; Albrecht Oepke, "καθίστημι," *Theological Dictionary of the New Testament*, ed. G. Kittel and G. Friedrich, trans. G. W. Bromiley, 10 vols. (Grand Rapids: Eerdmans, 1964–1976), 3:445.

53. The same debate crops up here: Is Jesus's obedience limited to the cross? Once again, the focus is on the cross, but Jesus's obedience on the cross cannot be separated from the sinless life he lived.

Theological Reflection

Other chapters in this volume work out the theological ramifications of what Paul teaches here in more detail. Some brief comments must suffice at this juncture. Paul clearly teaches in Romans 5:12–19 that human beings die because of personal sin and Adam's sin. An either-or is not posited here. Adam's typological and foundational role, however, is emphasized. Sin and death came into the world through him, and personal and individual sin find their roots in Adam's sin. All human beings are sinners, dead, and condemned before God because of Adam's one sin.

Believers have attempted to sort through the theological significance of what Paul asserts here for all of Christian history. I have already argued that the Pelagian view does not do justice to the text, for human beings do not simply imitate Adam's sin. They enter the world as sinners, spiritually dead, and condemned before God because of Adam's one sin.

I have also devoted some attention to Blocher's view since he offers, in a scintillating and learned way, a variation on the view that Adam functions as the head of the human race. Blocher rejects alien guilt, and ends up arguing that Adam as our head transmits a depraved and corrupt nature to human beings. Hence, the individual sin of human beings mirrors the sin of Adam. The upshot of Blocher's view is that human beings become guilty when they sin personally since they are not charged with guilt because of Adam's sin. I argued that Blocher's argument fails at two levels. First, his claim that the sin of human beings mirrors Adam's sin veers away from what Paul actually teaches in Romans 5:12–19, for Paul specifically and emphatically distinguishes the sin of those who live in the era between Adam and Moses from Adam's sin. Second, the text does not share Blocher's squeamishness about alien guilt, for it teaches that human beings are sinners and condemned (and hence guilty!) because of Adam's one sin. Just as human beings are righteous because of what Christ has done, so too they are guilty because of what Adam has done.

Seeing Adam as our covenant head accords with what I have argued above in the interpretation of 5:12–19. Sin, death, and condemnation are the portion of all people because of Adam's one sin. Human beings do not enter the world neutral or inclined toward what is good. They enter the world as sinners since they are sons and daughters of Adam. Paul explicitly teaches that human beings are condemned and dead because of Adam's sin. Identifying Adam as our covenant head also makes sense of the other side of the equation as well. For Christ is the covenant head of those who belong to him (1 Cor. 15:23), that is, of those who receive the gift of righteousness (Rom. 5:17). We receive alien guilt in Adam but alien righteousness in Christ.

It must be added immediately that the Scriptures do not treat the matter of Adam's headship abstractly, for as sons and daughters of Adam we also sin personally and are destined for death (5:12cd). Paul does not contemplate the sin of Adam apart from our sin. Hence, there is no discussion of infants or those who lack the mental capacities to make choices. What Paul focuses on is the fact that all enter the world as the descendants of Adam and therefore as sinners, spiritually dead, and condemned. Human beings die because of Adam's sin and their own sin, but Adam's sin and death have a fundamental and typological role.

Original sin and original death are taught in the Scriptures and are evident from human experience. The Scriptures do not attempt to give a complete rationale for the doctrine. I argued above that it makes sense for the human race to function as an organic whole. The doctrine of original sin is not irrational, but it is an offense to human reason. It is fitting that the final words belong to Blaise Pascal, who reflected deeply on original sin:

> Without doubt nothing is more shocking to our reason than to say that the sin of the first man has implicated in its guilt [men and women] so far from the original sin that they seem incapable of sharing it. This flow of guilt does not seem merely impossible to us, but indeed most unjust. . . . Certainly nothing jolts us more rudely than this doctrine, and yet, but for this mystery, the most incomprehensible of all, we remain incomprehensible to ourselves.[54]

---

54. Blaise Pascal, *Pensées*, trans. A. J. Krailsheimer (New York: Penguin, 1966), 65.

THE FALL AND GENESIS 3

Noel Weeks

Preliminary Considerations

The Bible introduces Adam as the first man. If, however, it is denied that Adam was the first man, then a search for the "pre-Adamites" results. Suspicion that Genesis 3 is actually a reconfiguration of earlier texts or sources will also be a likely consequence of denying that Adam was the first man. I will deal with the difficulties of the latter search before turning to what the text itself says. In terms of the text itself, I will try to deal with some of the crucial exegetical puzzles before then making sense of the sequential narrative.

Attempts to find the source of the ideas in the text outside Israel are influenced by what is seen as the main theme of the text. If one sees the concern as human sin, then the best parallel sources are Egyptian. There are two Egyptian texts that make a claim of human rebellion. *The Instructions of Merikare* comes to us in the form of advice from a ruler of the First Intermediate Period (approximately the turn of the third millennium and early second millennium BC).[1] The statement about human rebellion gives no details of the event or its consequences. A possibly similar story occurs in *The Book of the Heavenly Cow*,[2] found in

1. For translation see Miriam Lichtheim, *Ancient Egyptian Literature: A Book of Readings* (Berkeley: University of California, 1973), 1, 97–109.
2. Erik Hornung, *Der ägyptische Mythos von der Himmelskuh: Eine Ätiologie des Unvollkommen* (Freiburg: Universitätsverlag, 1982). For translation see ibid., 2, 197–99.

a number of royal graves of the eighteenth and nineteenth dynasties (late second millennium BC). There are no details given of the rebellion, and the consequences are not long-term.

Focusing on Mesopotamia as the source changes the way we read Genesis because the Mesopotamian "parallels" are concerned with human immortality.[3] The theme of the late form of *The Gilgamesh Epic* is Gilgamesh's vain search for immortality.[4] The presence of a form of the Babylonian flood story brings this narrative to the attention of biblical scholars. Gilgamesh's companion, Enkidu, is introduced into the story as a hairy, animal-like creature. He eats, drinks, and consorts with the animals. After seduction by a prostitute, he is alienated from the animals and adopts human ways, including clothing. The "civilizing" of Enkidu forms a parallel for interpretations that see the Genesis story as about the ascent of humanity from naïveté to maturity.[5] For others who see the story as reflecting humanity's quest for immortality, the major theme of the *Gilgamesh Epic* is also a parallel to Genesis.[6]

Yet, though Enkidu's death through conflict with the gods is the stimulus for Gilgamesh's quest to avoid death, in his search for immortality Gilgamesh is not in conflict with the gods. The moral of the story is that it is a vain quest: when the gods created man, they reserved immortality for themselves. Thus the story fits into the general Mesopotamian tendency to regard death, toil, and other human miseries as the imposition of the gods. Certainly one can see parallels with Genesis: life and death are at issue in both. However, two different treatments of fundamental questions of human existence do not become interdependent just because they deal with the same issues. Regarding the Genesis story as based on the Babylonian story reflects the tendency to make the Bible inferior and derivative. Note also that humanity does not stem from Gilgamesh or Enkidu. Gilgamesh may be an early king, but he is not the original one, and his search is for his own immortality, not that of all humanity.

Another Mesopotamian "parallel" is the story of Adapa, a priest of the god Ea.[7] Adapa was summoned before the supreme god Anu for a crime. He

3. Works that see Mesopotamia as the crucial source include Hermann Gunkel, *Schöpfung und Chaos in Urzeit und Endzeit: Eine religionsgeschichtliche Untersuchung über Gen 1 und Ap Joh 12* (Göttingen: Vandenhoeck und Ruprecht, 1895); E. A. Speiser, *Genesis* (Garden City, NY: Doubleday, 1964); Claus Westermann, *Genesis 1–11*, trans. John J. Scullion (London: SPCK, 1984).

4. A. R. George, *The Babylonian Gilgamesh Epic: Introduction, Critical Edition and Cuneiform Texts* (Oxford: Oxford University Press, 2003). There are many other translations.

5. Speiser, *Genesis*, 26–27.

6. Tryggve N. D. Mettinger, *The Eden Narrative: A Literary and Religio-historical Study of Genesis 2–3* (Winona Lake, IN: Eisenbrauns, 2007), 109–22.

7. S. Izre'el, *Adapa and the South Wind: Language Has the Power of Life and Death* (Winona Lake, IN: Eisenbrauns, 2001).

was advised by Ea to reject any food or drink he was offered because he would be given the food and drink of death. Hence he rejected the offered food and drink, not realizing he was being given the food and drink of life.

The point of this story has been much debated, and the debate is not aided by the obscure conclusion to the story. Adapa is not represented as an original human. Once again his actions are for his own immortality.[8]

In summary, there were Egyptian allusions to rebellions against the gods but no evidence of the Mesopotamian belief that immortality was reserved to the gods. Perhaps the Egyptian funerary cult points to a different way of thinking in Egypt. In Mesopotamia the issues of life, death, and immortality are certainly present but are treated in terms of the gods' decision not to grant immortality. There is no collective human rebellion or guilt.[9]

Some scholars attempt to relate the biblical story to a supposedly common conception of the nature of chaos and evil. There are myths of various sorts of a god who dies or who disappears, leading to a loss of fertility. The reappearance of that god was then seen as reversing the previous decline. The death or disappearance of the god was variously explained in the ancient texts, but modern discussion fastened on cases where the cause was a conflict. Scholars connected this to cosmogonic myths where the world was created out of unformed matter. It was asserted that this unformed matter was seen as still residually present and periodically threatening the existing order, particularly in the form of a reptilian adversary of the main god, who was in turn the dying and rising god. It was postulated that the resurrection of the god was an annual event celebrated and actualized at the New Year festival where the myth of the conflict was dramatized in mimetic rites. The reptilian form of the chaos was connected to the serpent of Genesis 3.[10]

Significantly, the theory is synthetic, taking bits from different cultures and creating a hybrid. Of the many problems two are crucial. A major plank of the theory is the late Babylonian New Year festival, but Marduk, the god celebrated in

8. In the wider tradition, Adapa was one of the sages who brought wisdom to humans, but he does not play a representative role—he was not portrayed as acting in a way that would have consequences for the human race as a whole; see E. Reiner, "The Etiological Myth of the Seven Sages," *Orientalia* 30 (1961): 1–11.

9. For rebellions by the gods, see *Atrahasis* in W. G. Lambert and A. R. Millard, *Atra-hasis: The Babylonian Story of the Flood* (Oxford: Oxford University Press, 1969) and *Enuma Elish* (often referred to as The Babylonian Creation Epic). There are many translations and studies of the latter, e.g., Benjamin Foster, *Before the Muses: An Anthology of Akkadian Literature* (Bethesda, MD: CDL, 1993, 1996); and W. G. Lambert, "Mesopotamian Creation Stories," in *Imaging Creation*, ed. M. J. Geller and M. Schipper (Leiden: Brill, 2008), 15–59.

10. Mettinger, *The Eden Narrative*, 80–84; Jon D. Levenson, *Creation and the Persistence of Evil: The Jewish Drama of Divine Omnipotence* (Princeton: Princeton University Press, 1988).

that festival, was not seen as a dying and rising god,[11] and while *Enuma Elish*[12] was recited at the New Year festival, the further ritual of the New Year festival does not make specific connection to *Enuma Elish*.[13] In general, the attempt to connect myth and ritual is flawed. Myths of disappearing gods do not uniformly connect the death/disappearance of the god to a conflict with a reptilian monster.[14] The theory that the adversary of a god is primal chaos returned to threaten the world is not supported by the ancient Near Eastern myths themselves.

Hence one may claim that in a particular context somebody imagined a primordial situation, but we have no knowledge, independent of the biblical text, of what that context was. Rather than conjectures, we have to go to the text itself to know what it means. Belief in the divine inspiration of Scripture would lead us to that approach anyway. In doing this I am not adopting the canonical approach of Brevard Childs, for that method presupposes an earlier chaotic history for the text but ignores that history because it leads into a chaos of conjecture from which no meaningful interpretation can emerge. I believe there are cogent arguments against the source-critical treatment of the text,[15] but that is not the focus of this exercise.

The fact that the Bible begins with a primordial situation and frequently uses earlier situations and images in later descriptions and prophecies raises an issue. When we meet "Edenic" language and images in a later text, may we take these as informative about the original Eden, or is the original Eden being used to describe something related but different?[16] Checking to see whether

---

11. Wolfram von Soden, "Gibt es ein Zeugnis dafür, dass die Babylonier an die Wiederauferstehung Marduks geglaubt haben?," *Zeitschrift für Assyriologie* 51 (1955): 130–66.

12. See note 9.

13. Since the myth was read before Marduk in his temple, it does not seem that a public performance was involved. Some of the helpers of Marduk's foe, Tiamat, were reptilian, but Tiamat herself is of uncertain form. This story may form a sort of "foundation legend" for Marduk's temple in Babylon. For the ritual see Beate Pongratz-Leisten, Ina Šulmi Īrub: *Die kulttopographische und ideologische Programmatik der akītu-Prozession in Babylonien und Assyrien im 1. Jahrtausend v. Chr.* (Mainz: Philipp von Zabern, 1994).

14. Thus the Hittite god Telipinu becomes angry and leaves, William W. Hallo and K. Lawson Younger Jr., eds. and trans., *The Context of Scripture* (Leiden: Brill, 1997), 1, 151–53; the Ugaritic god Baal yields to Mot ("Death") without a fight (ibid., 264–69); and the Sumerian Dumuzi is carried off to the underworld as a replacement for the goddess Inanna, Thorkild Jacobsen, trans., *The Harps that Once . . . : Sumerian Poetry in Translation* (New Haven: Yale University Press, 1987), 205–37. The one reptilian enemy of the gods who constantly reappears is Apopis, who threatens the Egyptian sun god every day. However, he is always repulsed, and there is no ritual of a dying god connected with this myth. See Jan Assmann, *Egyptian Solar Religion in the New Kingdom: Re, Amun and the Crisis of Polytheism*, trans. Anthony Alcock (London: Kegan Paul International, 1995), 51–57.

15. See my *Sources and Authors* (Piscataway, NJ: Gorgias, 2011), 50–53.

16. An example is use of Ezek. 28:13–14, a condemnation of the ruler of Tyre, as a description of the original garden of Eden, e.g., Meredith G. Kline, *Kingdom Prologue: Genesis Foundations for*

what we think we see in early Genesis is consistent with the rest of the Bible is one thing. Taking back what we find in the later narrative into Genesis, without evidence in the original narrative, is something different.

While I do not want to examine source-critical issues here, it has to be pointed out that there are certain emphases in chapter 2 that are strengthened when chapter 2 is read along with chapter 1. God provides what the man needs for life in the world. In chapter 2, that is illustrated by the provision of water for the ground, the planting of the garden, and the gift of the woman to the man. In chapter 1 the same message comes through in the way the stages of creation are arranged so that the earlier days furnish a prepared environment for the later creatures.

A second common element is that humanity consists of male and female. In 1:26–27 we are told that the image of a God, who speaks here (and only here in chap. 1) in the plural, has the diversity of male and female. In chapter 2 God's provision for the needs of his creatures includes the woman for the man.

Chapter 1 has an obvious structure, and there is also a less obvious structuring of the text in terms of significant numbers of words and elements.[17] Hence in interpretation of Genesis 1, structure needs to be taken very seriously. Chapters 2 and 3 also have structural elements, maybe not as obvious but definitely present. In both chapters 1 and 2 we have man placed over the animals; once by divine decree and once by illustration in the naming exercise. Further, woman was created as a help to man. Thus we see an order of the man, the woman, and the animal. Chapter 3 shows us that that order is reversed in the temptation and sin. There the initiative flows from the animal to the woman to the man. God's order of interrogation goes from the man to the woman. The order of judgment is from the animal to the woman to the man. Those judgments contain elements clearly intended to reassert the original order of relationships, though including elements of conflict.

It has been suggested that elements of the narrative, leading up to the crucial transgression, are mirrored in the subsequent narrative but in reverse order. Thus if we imagine the elements of the narrative as laid out in a line, which

---

a Covenantal Worldview (Eugene, OR: Wipf & Stock, 2006), 48; Mettinger, *The Eden Narrative*, 85–98. The fact that the way into the garden was to the east (Gen. 3:24) has been connected with the fact that the tabernacle and the temple opened to the east: Gordon J. Wenham, "Sanctuary Symbolism in the Garden of Eden Story," *Proceedings of the 9th World Congress of Jewish Studies*, div. A (Jerusalem: World Union of Jewish Studies, 1986), 20. Hence it has been asserted that Eden was being depicted as a sanctuary. It is equally plausible that tabernacle and temple open to the east because they have the "Edenic" character of bringing man into association with God. We would then read temple and tabernacle in terms of the earlier Eden and not vice versa.

17. U. Cassuto, *A Commentary on the Book of Genesis*, part 1 (Jerusalem: Magnes, 1961), 12–15.

is then bent in a U with the turning point at the point of sin, the result would be that the two arms of the U would place the equivalent elements opposite each other.[18] This is not as convincing a structure because the elements are not exactly matched, and one of the pair may be described much more succinctly than the other. Nevertheless there is a structure whereby the things that are in place before the transgression are seen to be lost after the transgression. (See further below.) The effect of pairing what was in place before with what was lost afterward is to stress the importance of the change point. Thus the structure directs our attention to what is crucial in the story.

The Exegetical Enigmas

There are several basic interpretive puzzles in the text. God threatens death as a consequence of eating the forbidden fruit, yet Adam and Eve do not die. What do the trees represent or signify? They have names, but how do those names correlate with events? It has been argued, because of the lack of involvement of the tree of life in the crucial events, that it is peripheral to the story and did not belong to it in its original form.[19] Another discussion concerns the exact meaning of the "knowledge of good and evil." Perhaps as important for the interpretation of the story is why this fruit was seen as having such significant effects. Does fruit with nonphysical effects point to myth, magic, symbolism, allegory, or what?

The threat of 2:17 is expressed by means of a Hebrew infinitive absolute so that it reads literally "dying you shall die." This construction is usually a way of adding emphasis and seriousness to a statement. Yet the immediate consequence of the eating appears to be shame and fear rather than literal death. Attempts to resolve this contradiction often reflect the exegete's view of the point of the story. Those who see the story as about humanity's coming to maturity and assertion of independence believe that God had no other choice but to accept the reality of the new situation, if there was to be any continuance of the human race. James Barr, seeing the story as a rise, or in his version a potential rise, rather than a fall, suggested that God simply set aside his previous threat.[20] Thus the prospect of human accomplishment, rather than human transgression, is the focus. With humanity's potential accomplishment

---

18. Jerome T. Walsh, "Genesis 2:4b–3:24: A Synchronic Approach," *Journal of Biblical Literature* 96 (1977): 161–77.

19. For a history of this theory, see Mettinger, *The Eden Narrative*, 6–10.

20. James Barr, *The Garden of Eden and the Hope of Immortality: The Read Tuckwell Lectures for 1990* (London: SCM, 1992); "The Authority of Scripture: The Book of Genesis and the Origin of Evil in Jewish and Christian Tradition," in *Christian Authority: Essays in*

rather than the divine-human relationship at the center, the contradiction between threat and result seems less bothersome. Further, Barr argues that the text does not use the word "sin," and the transgression is mild compared with the later sins in Genesis.[21]

This interpretation treats the divine threat too lightly and does not place sufficient emphasis on the fact that the consequences are depicted in catastrophic terms. Walter Moberly objected that Barr's explanation made God a liar. His own solution was that "death" had to be seen metaphorically so that it amounted to a change in the quality of life rather than to literal death.[22] Barr countered that Moberly was himself making God a liar because the human couple would naturally take God's words literally rather than metaphorically.[23] Moberly's defense is that the story is told with attention to the reader's perspective rather than that of the participants. The reader sees the discrepancy and is naturally driven to the metaphorical explanation.[24] Neither explanation seems convincing.[25] Certainly there are heinous sins in the following chapter, but one of the themes of what follows is the spread of sin. The lack of the word "sin" is a weak argument because many biblical transgressions are narrated without the use of that specific word.

Each participant in the debate considers the other common explanation: that God "repented" of his intention to bring death. They cogently argue that there is no word of this in the text, and the considerations that bring about such "repentance" elsewhere, such as intercession or contrition, are not present here.

In 3:22 God expresses concern "lest he [the man] stretch out his hand, and take *also* from the tree of life, and eat, and live forever" (NASB, emphasis mine). The "also" seems to imply that the human pair had not already eaten from that tree.[26] Once again, the eating of a particular fruit is seen as having momentous consequences.

Honour of Henry Chadwick, ed. G. R. Evans (Oxford: Clarendon, 1988), 59–75. Similarly, John Skinner, *A Critical and Exegetical Commentary on Genesis* (Edinburgh: T&T Clark, 1910), 67.

21. Barr, "Authority of Scripture," 62.

22. R. W. L. Moberly, "Did the Serpent Get It Right?," *Journal of Theological Studies* 39 (1988): 1–27; "Review of James Barr, *The Garden of Eden and the Hope of Immortality*," *Journal of Theological Studies* 45 (1992): 172–75.

23. James Barr, "Is God a Liar? (Genesis 2–3) and Related Matters," *Journal of Theological Studies* 37 (2006): 14–15.

24. R. W. L. Moberly, "Did the Interpreters Get It Right? Genesis 2–3 Reconsidered," *Journal of Theological Studies* 59 (2008): 35–36.

25. For a summary that leans to Moberly's side, see Robert Gordon, "The Ethics of Eden: Truth Telling in Genesis 2–3," in *Ethical and Unethical in the Old Testament: God and Humans in Dialogue*, ed. K. J. Dell (New York: T&T Clark, 2010), 11–33.

26. Cassuto, *Commentary on the Book of Genesis*, 124; Mettinger, *The Eden Narrative*, 20.

In the background of academic Old Testament studies, as we have inherited them, lies an assumption that we are dealing with authors who lack our sophistication. The result must be clumsy connection of sources, lack of realization of contradictions, traces of development of different approaches, and so on.[27] A further consequence is that we do not expect a nuanced and sophisticated text in which the author has deliberately excluded extraneous material to focus on the significant. Yet we are now realizing the use of complex literary structure in the composition. Surely that should lead us to reconsider whether there is also sophistication in the message conveyed.

Going back to 3:22, note that it says "stretch out his hand and take." Life was as easy and available as that simple exercise. The simplicity of narration and action emphasizes what was lost. Let us take that simplicity to the story of what did happen after they ate the forbidden fruit. It would follow that we are to take the text to say what it says: death will follow eating, and therefore death did follow eating. The point of the text is to present death as a process: a process that began after the eating and is signified first by the separation of the human pair from each other and second by their separation from God. The divine judgments explicate further how that dying process will proceed, especially in the work that consumes the man, in the double sense of engaging him and eating him up until he returns to the dust. Perhaps there is a deliberate counter to the common perception that death comes only with the last breath. Already we are dead in our trespasses and sins, in our alienation, and in our pain and misery.

Death may be a process, but the entry or beginning point is punctiliar. It is the narrated consequences that give significance to the entry point. Barr points out that, after the transgression, God continues to speak to them and to do things for them, seeing this as indication that this transgression was not as serious as some that came later.[28] We can agree on the facts but not on the interpretation. Before and after the eating, God engages with humanity, but repeated judgment characterizes the later interaction. The subsequent expulsion shows that God has not yielded possession of his garden to sinners. Rather, as a number of authors have noted, one of the themes of the following chapters is the spread of sin.[29]

Does seeing death as a process give a clue as to how we should see life in this passage? From the fact that man is described as becoming a "living being" in 2:7 (NASB), let alone from the description of human activity, we are justified

27. See my *Sources and Authors*, 186–208.
28. Barr, "Is God a Liar?," 3–4.
29. D. J. A. Clines, "Theme in Genesis 1–11," *Catholic Biblical Quarterly* 38 (1976): 490–99.

in saying that humankind is alive. Yet what is then the meaning of 3:22 and the implied boon there? Conceivably it means that life is not a once-and-for-all endowment but something that is somehow augmented or supplemented. Life in that sense is also a process.

It is at this point that I think it is justifiable to ask whether the interpretation, reached to satisfy the demands of the passage itself, accords with the rest of Scripture. There are quite a number of Old Testament passages that speak of life as "a way." By analogy we might add those passages where the way of death is contrasted with the way of life.[30] New Testament usage is clear. Consider the passages: "in him we live and move and exist" (Acts 17:28 NASB); "reign in life" (Rom. 5:17 NASB); "walk in newness of life" (Rom. 6:4 NASB); "allow the dead to bury their dead" (Matt. 8:22 NASB); "dead in your trespasses and sins" (Eph. 2:1 NASB); "dead even while she lives" (1 Tim. 5:6 NASB). These passages have a clearly durative sense of life and death.

Am I imposing an exclusively New Testament sense on an Old Testament passage? In defense I would argue that seeing both life and death as states, each with a particular terminus, makes sense of the passage and other interpretations have considerable deficiencies. "Life" is clearly durative in the Old Testament, and "death" may be also. Therefore, as in many other cases, the New Testament is making explicit something implicit in the Old Testament.

Some commentators have seen the meaning of the tree of the knowledge of good and evil as knowledge in the abstract and thus tend to turn the story into exploration of the human quest for enlightenment.[31] That interpretation brings the story closer to the assumed Mesopotamian parallels, where "wisdom" in the general sense is the issue. Appeal is further made to the fact that "good and evil" can be a way of saying "everything." Yet in the passages cited by Gerhard von Rad,[32] the general meaning of "everything" is possible for some,[33] but in others the distinction between good and evil is the crucial point.[34] Thus an interpretation that sees that distinction as crucial is not excluded by usage elsewhere.

Any interpretation must accept that something happened as the result of eating. Adam and Eve were enlightened, but the enlightenment had an unexpected result: shame at nakedness, which forms a contrast with the lack of shame immediately preceding the eating. Further, our interpretation must

30. E.g., Deut. 30:15, 19; Jer. 21:8.
31. Westermann, *Genesis 1–11*, 242–52; Gerhard von Rad, *Genesis*, trans. John H. Marks (London: SCM, 1961), 79; Mettinger, *The Eden Narrative*, 63.
32. Gen. 24:50; 31:24; Num. 24:13; 2 Sam. 13:22; 14:17; 19:36 (English 35); 1 Kings 3:9.
33. Gen. 24:50; 31:24; 2 Sam. 13:22.
34. This is particularly the case in 1 Kings 3:9 and would also fit 2 Sam. 19:36 (English 35).

accommodate God's admission (3:22) that there was an element of truth in what the serpent said.

A satisfactory interpretation is one that puts good in contrast to evil. Both have to be present, but they are experienced in their contradiction.[35] The repeated emphasis on the structure of relationships is deliberately drawing our attention to the created order. Humankind has listened to the serpent and not to God. That was a violation of the created order and also meant the experience of evil in contrast to good. The woman led the man into sin and he followed: another upsetting of the created order as male and female stepped out of their ordained roles. However, male and female are not just relationship roles; they are sexual types as 2:24 reminds us. With the failure of male and female roles comes shame at the distinctiveness of male and female bodies.[36]

To make sense of God's statement in 3:22, we have to see an irony and a contrast. Experientially, and yet in a totally different way, God also knows good and evil. For he always rejects evil and knows only good. If this interpretation of the knowledge of good and evil is accepted, it adds a further irony. If Adam and Eve had resisted the temptation, they would have also known good and evil but in a way that was actually more like God.

One issue remains: why trees? I suggested above that we are meant to note the easy availability with which the fruit, both permitted and forbidden, hangs before Adam and Eve. Perhaps there is an intentional contrast with the new order of toil to produce food out of the plant of the field (3:17–19). God's gifts were easily available in the world before sin.

The fact that in the present world the fruit of trees is not so readily available and not of such effect should not constrain our understanding of what existed in a former age. The Scriptures mention a number of physical objects that have surprising effects: Moses's bronze serpent (Num. 21:8–9); the waters of the Jordan (2 Kings 5:14); Elisha's stick (2 Kings 6); and so on. In spite of our concern about encouragements to magical thinking, the Scripture does not

---

35. C. F. Keil and F. Delitzsch, *Biblical Commentary on the Old Testament*, trans. James Martin (Grand Rapids: Eerdmans, n.d.), 1, 84–86; Edward J. Young, *Genesis 3* (London: Banner of Truth, 1966), 40–42. Note also David Clines's argument that there is a connection between the terms in which the law is praised in Ps. 19 and this tree. It strengthens the argument that the issue in the context of the Old Testament is obedience rather than intellectual wisdom. See Clines, "The Tree of Knowledge and the Law of Yahweh (Psalm XIX)," *Vetus Testamentum* 24 (1974): 8–14.

36. Note that the divine plural appears again in 3:22. I think Paul in 1 Cor. 11:3 is giving a trinitarian interpretation to the divine plural in 1:26–27, which is related to humanity's diversity as male and female. It would suit an ironic interpretation of 3:22 if the reappearance of the divine plural was intended to set God's unity in diversity over against human disunity.

shun all ascription of effects to physical objects. Of course we are justified in doubting that the effect exists apart from the particular circumstance and the divine purpose in those circumstances. Hezekiah's destruction of the bronze serpent (2 Kings 18:4) and Jeremiah's rebuke of false trust in the temple (Jer. 7) are examples of the rejection of incorrect inferences from physical objects.

Given the role of physical objects elsewhere in the Scriptures, we should not assume that the trees have to be symbolic and nonliteral, thus giving grounds for seeing the whole narrative as nonhistorical.[37] Things outside of our experience in a pre-sin world no more threaten the historicity of the account than do miracles in the Gospels.

Drawing Threads Together

The crucial thing told us about the serpent is that it belongs among the beasts of the field. As mentioned above, this is key to the relational structures being emphasized, and hence there is no concern with who else may be involved or with the enigma of a speaking serpent. The Bible regularly shuns discursive explanations that may satisfy our curiosity but obscure the point being made. Yet there is some explanation for the skill of the serpent in the subsequent dialogue. The Hebrew word, given translations such as "crafty," has both positive and negative connotations. It also allows the writer, by a play on words, to make a subsequent point (see below).

The implication of the serpent's opening remark is that God has withheld something. Both chapters 1 and 2 show God's provision for human needs, so the serpent insinuates against the logic of the text. The narrator uses "YHWH God," but the serpent and the woman following him use only "God." Since in chapter 1 the word used was simply "God," this cannot be seen as wrong, yet in a text of carefully chosen words, one wonders if there is something significant there. In chapter 1 God is transcendent, supreme, one who merely speaks and it comes to pass. True, what comes to pass is for the benefit of man, but the transcendence is real. In chapter 2, YHWH God is depicted as far more immanent and personal. That raises the possibility that the change of name is part of the serpent's strategy.

Commentators, on the justifiable premise that the state of the heart determines the action, probe the woman's formal answer for evidence that

37. Henri Blocher takes items such as the trees as symbolic. He then struggles with the fact that the rest of Scripture sees Adam and his sin as a real historical event. In the end he seems reduced to saying that he is certain something happened but that translating from the symbolic to the actual is beyond us. See *In the Beginning: The Opening Chapters of Genesis*, trans. David G. Preston (Leicester, UK: Inter-Varsity, 1984).

the acid of doubt is already at work. Yet note the characteristic of the text, indeed of so much of the biblical text, in allowing the deeds to speak for what is in the heart.

The biblical portrayal of the father of lies shows hims to be a plausible liar.[38] If my explanation is correct that the threat is one of entering into the *state* of death rather than immediate cessation of existence, and given that their eyes were opened, and given God's ironic concession that the human was now like "us," what the serpent says is indeed a plausible lie. Yet on each point the result is far different from the expectation created. Plausibility does not eliminate the reality of the lie, as humankind continues to learn, to its cost, to this day.

James Barr claims that the woman's motivation does not include a desire to usurp God's throne.[39] He therefore questions the traditional interpretation of this act as sinful rebellion. I think that misses the crucial fact that the woman was "deceived," as the text clearly says. By not justifying the divine prohibition, the text has set "bare" divine Word in contrast to the attractiveness of disobedience to the naïve. The consequence will show the foolishness of acting on appearance and desire.

The woman's action is given detailed explanation and motivation. The description of Adam's act is set in deliberate contrast as bare of all motivation. It is that characteristic of the text that Paul picks up in 1 Timothy 2:14. In that context Paul applies it to the situation of women, but we should not miss the implication for the man in the Genesis text. The woman has something of an excuse in that she was deceived. The man has no such excuse. If we understand what Paul saw in the text, we will be less inclined to accuse him of misogyny. We should also see that, if the text implies that women are liable to being deceived, it also implies that males are liable to be "missing in action."[40]

The sequel is multilayered. It fulfills the promise that their eyes would be opened and that they would know good and evil. However, their eyes are opened to behold themselves in the shame of nakedness that is appropriate to those who have failed in their distinctive male and female roles. Despite the bravado of later humans, to see oneself in the nakedness of evil is to be ashamed and fearful.

38. E.g., "Does Job fear God for nothing?" (Job 1:9 NASB); "Joshua . . . and Satan standing . . . to accuse him. . . . Joshua was clothed in filthy garments" (Zech. 3:1, 3 NASB).
39. Barr, "Authority of Scripture," 65.
40. While I am not persuaded by Phyllis Trible's contention that the man was originally created a sexless being before the creation of the woman, she explicates well the text's contrast between the active female and the passive male. *God and the Rhetoric of Sexuality* (Philadelphia: Fortress, 1978), 80, 113.

It also allows the author to begin to describe the unravelling that the crucial act of sin brings. The verse immediately before the story of temptation and sin spoke of the lack of shame at nakedness, whereas the verse following the sin starts the great reversal that shall take place, step by step, until they are out of the garden. The similarity in sound between "naked" (*'ārôm*) and "crafty" (*'rûm*), used to describe the serpent, allows the author to make a point. Rather than being like God, they are like the serpent.

The second separation follows: that of humankind from God.[41] Adam and Eve's separation from each other took the form of a realization about their physical state. Their separation from God took the form of fear.[42]

The earlier part of the chapter placed the woman in the leading position; now the order changes. When the serpent spoke to the woman he used the second person plural, implying that he was addressing the man as well. Yet when God calls to the man and speaks to him, he addresses him alone. This shows that though the action had placed the woman in the leading role, this is clearly not the view of the text as to the primary site of responsibility.

Under interrogation both spoke the truth and yet tried to transfer blame. The man's excuse has an extra edge, which, read in connection with the economy of words that characterizes the whole text, accuses rather than excuses him, whatever his intention. He tried to transfer blame to the woman that God gave to be "with him," which alerts the reader to the fact that during the previous transgression he was shown as being, apparently passively, "with her."

The order of God's judgments follows the order of initiatives. With each there is a part that is a form of punishment and a part that may involve a punishment but also has a crucial relationship component. With the serpent the punishment is a curse, which not only shows that the serpent belongs in the world of the animals but also places it in the most degraded position among those animals. The relationship the serpent had established of influence on the woman is not allowed to continue. Enmity must replace naïve credence. There is an element of prophecy involved with the culminating stage of that enmity, and that makes translation difficult. "Seed" in the sense of descendants is a plural concept. An enmity established between the descendants of the woman and the serpent might be expected to be played out with many on each side. Yet the text reverts to the singular for the finale. It is "he" against "thee"

41. The text uses the hithpaʿel of *hālak* ("to go") for what God was doing. This has been used in the thesis that Eden was depicted as a sanctuary. However, because the cited proof text (Deut. 23:15) speaks of God's activity in the camp of Israel and not in the sanctuary, I suspect it means simply to move about and has no necessary sacral connotation.

42. Alan Jon Hauser, "Genesis 2–3: The Theme of Intimacy and Alienation," in *Art and Meaning: Rhetoric in Biblical Literature*, ed. David J. A. Clines et al. (Sheffield: JSOT, 1982), 20–36.

and "thou" against "him." While the exact meaning will become clear in the future, in that future a single representative of the woman's seed will come into conflict with the serpent. The mechanics of how that will happen are not revealed here. There is a question about the meaning of the crucial verb in the last part of the prophecy.[43] The problem is that while "crush" seems an appropriate image for what happens to the serpent's head, it does not seem an appropriate image for what a serpent does to a heel.[44] That problem is overcome if we realize that both injuries are delivered at the same time. The underlying picture is of a man delivering a mortal blow by stamping on the head of a snake. The very act causes a reciprocal injury, though since it is to the heel, not a mortal one. To maintain the sense of reciprocal injury, "crush" is an appropriate term. The amiability of the original creation will be no more, replaced by currents of hostility, which are just a symptom of the great change, and yet the prophecy contains a source of hope because the initiating point of the problem, the one who seemed to speak out of concern for man, but really to his ruin, will be dealt with.

In the case of the woman, the punishment, as with the man, focuses on the special role of the woman and hence her glory. Failure to play one part of the role intended for the woman is recompensed with pain and difficulty in another part of her intended role. The part of the sentence that deals with relationships depends, once more, on a crucial word. How are we meant to understand the woman's "desire"? Is it to be seen with reference to the previous judgment so that, irrespective of the pain childbirth entails, her desire for her husband will prevent her avoiding the role of wife and mother? In that case "desire" has a positive connotation, a connotation supported by its use in Song of Songs 7:10.[45] Or is our understanding to be informed by the only other biblical use of this particular word (Gen. 4:7), so that it has the negative connotation of a desire to master and overcome?[46] In that case we would be reminded of the woman's role in the temptation, perhaps magnified, and the following statement would indicate that God would not allow that to prevail, so that the counterclause contains connotations of domination. While advocates may be found on either side, it would not be surprising if a word, with a basic meaning of "desire," had both positive and negative connotations depending on context. In that case context must decide,

43. Cassuto, *Commentary on the Book of Genesis*, 161, suggests two different verbs. This seems unlikely given the similarity of form and the parallelism of the statement.
44. Skinner, *A Critical and Exegetical Commentary*, 80.
45. Von Rad, *Genesis*, 90.
46. Susan H. Foh, "What Is the Woman's Desire?," *Westminster Theological Journal* 37 (1974/75): 376–83; Bruce K. Waltke, *Genesis* (Grand Rapids: Zondervan, 2001), 94.

but which context, preceding or following? The following statement seems syntactically more closely bound to the statement in question and therefore should have preference. Even that does not decide the case, because if the woman's desire is a positive thing, then the role ascribed to the man would just become more reprehensible, a taking advantage of the woman's need so that he can be more dominant. Judgments do involve negative consequences so we cannot exclude this interpretation on the grounds that it is not what we would like. If it is a negative desire, then the description of the male response fits God's intent of making relationships closer to their intended function, and yet here is another indication that the peace of the garden and its relationships has been shattered. The choice is not easy, but the fact that the negative usage occurs in close proximity in the very next chapter inclines me to the second alternative.

The negatives, the very real painful negatives, in this judgment should not obscure the positive. There will be pain and conflict, but childbirth and the male-female bond will endure. Therein is hope! A long dying allows other life to come into being. And the enemy will be destroyed by the seed of the woman.

With the man, the punishment once more strikes at an essential function: the role of worker. Pain and toil in labor is the male equivalent of difficult childbearing. In these punishments it is not the man and the woman, but rather the serpent and now the ground, which are cursed. Cursing the serpent is understandable . . . but the ground? Perhaps there is here an element of corporate responsibility: if the governor sins, the territory under his control must experience some of the consequences. Whatever the cause, the ground will now act differently with respect to the man. As the man acted against the one over him, so the ground acts against the one over it. However prolonged the contest, the ground will ultimately win. Yet once again the slow dying gives hope. That is reinforced by the immediately following naming of Eve, the mother of all living. The hope is further reinforced by the act of God in clothing them. It is an anticipation of the fact that, in the midst of the slow dying, merciful providence will be experienced.

Revelation 22:2 introduces a tree in the new Jerusalem of the remade universe that has leaves for the "healing of the nations" (NASB). Why is such needed where sorrow and sickness are no more? May I suggest that once more life is a durative experience: there is enduring pain-free life because everything is in place to make it so. I suggest we need to read Genesis 3:22 the same way. Among all the life-sustaining provisions of the garden, the tree of life had a crucial role. The sentence of death bars it to humankind. The expulsion and the guard make that clear. Humanity continues its life unto death, until the seed comes.

Conclusion

That the biblical text begins with a primordial earth unlike anything known to subsequent humanity has important consequences. We do not do justice to the whole biblical narrative if we ignore the scene-setting. It is not just that it stands at the beginning of the Bible; the text clearly sets out to depict a different situation and to explain some of the steps from that situation to ours. Crucial things changed.

Those changes are shown by the narrative and especially by the structure of the narrative, with its before and after parallels, to be a consequence of human transgression of the explicit command of God. The fact that death is depicted as a process does not diminish the focus on the crucial act. That is where the dying began. We are also repeatedly reminded of the importance of the relative relationships of God, Adam, Eve, and the animals. The sin involved changes the original order of those relationships and hence led to continuing turmoil in those relationships. The man was first in the order of creation and first in the order of responsibility. God's dealing with the transgression involved both an element of judgment and an element of restoration. In the short term the restorative element concentrated on reestablishing the created order of relationships, but that was to take place in an environment in which conflict replaced some of the harmony of the original order. In the longer term the restoration was connected to a decisive dealing with the serpent. Between the short and long term, the fact that dying is a process placed man under the continuing supervision of God.

The text conveys a message to the reader or hearer who lives in a world in which shame is connected with nakedness. That world is also a world of pain in childbirth, unending toil, and disrupted relationships. The text shows that the shame and misery of humanity outside the garden flows from the sin of Adam. It does this in the typical biblical way in which factors and facts extraneous to the points the text wishes to convey are simply ignored. Nevertheless, a connection is created between the original pair and their later descendants that is just as real as the connection created by the later genealogies. Just as the shame, pain, and misery are real historical experiences, so their cause is traced to real events. Perhaps the example of one of the silences of the text will make that clearer. Any mention of influences behind the serpent is suppressed in order for the fact that the serpent is a created beast to be more prominent. Sin involved a disruption in the orderly array of created relationships and lines of authority. How would it have been possible for a perfect created order to come into the disarray and confusion we now experience without some form of transgression of that order being involved in the vital change? Original order, change, and present disorder form such a connected series that denial of any one makes the others problematic, if not totally incomprehensible.

The trees represent another crucial part of that original order: the given and permitted, in distinction from the available but not permitted. Relationship to God is connected to that crucial distinction. The terms by which that distinction will be experienced may change, but that distinction will remain part of the created order.

Thus the biblical text presents an explanation of crucial elements of the world in which we live. The changes were a result of actions by people who existed in a set of relationships that define us with respect to God, to each other, and to animals. I have not dealt with interpretations that see the story as "symbolic" in some nonhistorical form because such readings are pure arbitrary imposition unless they are anchored in something within the text itself. Clearly the text aims to show us that the present conditions of our life have an origin. Just as the genealogies show that we descend from the original pair, so the story shows that our situation is explicable in terms of original events. Unlike the Mesopotamian viewpoint, which would trace human misery to factors other than the humans themselves, a position with many imitators today, the biblical text says human misery comes from real historical humans and that those humans were the first pair.

15

ADAM, HISTORY, AND THEODICY

William Edgar

—For, said he, all this is for the best, since if there is a volcano at Lisbon, it cannot be somewhere else, since it is unthinkable that things should not be where they are, since everything is well.

A little man in black, an officer of the Inquisition, who was sitting beside him, politely took up the question, and said:—It would seem that the gentleman does not believe in original sin, since if everything is for the best, man has not fallen and is not liable to eternal punishment.

—I most humbly beg pardon of your excellency, Pangloss answered, even more politely, but the fall of man and the curse of original sin entered necessarily into the best of all possible worlds.

—Then you do not believe in free will? said the officer.

—Your excellency must excuse me, said Pangloss; free will agrees very well with absolute necessity, for it was necessary that we should be free, since a will that is determined . . .

—Pangloss was in the middle of his sentence, when the officer nodded significantly to the attendant who was pouring him a glass of port, or Oporto wine.[1]

Voltaire's critique of the philosophy of "optimism" was made more devastating by his use of a "philosophical novel," *Candide*.[2] The protagonist in the

1. Voltaire, *Candide or Optimism*, 2nd ed., ed. and trans. Robert M. Adams (New York: W. W. Norton, 1991), 11.
2. The name is from the Latin *candidus*, meaning "white." By the eighteenth century it meant "uncorrupted," "fair-minded," and we rightly could infer Voltaire's sarcasm, depicting a man who is earnest, even naïve.

story is the young man, Candide, who loses everything and witnesses every tragedy, including, here, the dreadful earthquake in Lisbon (which really did occur in 1755, provoking a huge international debate over the problem of evil). His interlocutor is Master Pangloss, who represents the philosopher Gottfried Leibniz (1646–1716), a major proponent of the popular Enlightenment philosophy of optimism, according to which we are in the best of all possible worlds. Leibniz, who coined the term "theodicy," believed that if there is evil in the world, it is a necessary part of the larger tapestry of God's creation since God could not make anything second best. Pangloss always renders pat answers to the honest Candide, or, as here, to the officer from the Inquisition. Voltaire, though always the skeptic, rightly understands the relation of a historical fall (original sin) to human responsibility.

The Heart of the Issue

Was there a historical fall? Were Adam and Eve real people? Many today, including theologians, would no doubt wonder at anyone even raising serious questions about the historicity of Adam and Eve. Rather, they would scorn it as obscure at best, harmful at worst, to worry about such things. Nor, certainly, would they imagine that the historicity of our first parents has any bearing on the problem of evil. Indeed, they might say, what could sound more unfair than to blame the fall of the entire human race, with such dire consequences, on the choice of a single man in a garden so many centuries ago?[3]

This is a place where even the most reverent tend to stumble. We can admit responsibility for things over which we have some control. We can even accept the fact that we are partly shaped by our circumstances, our families, our times, but the idea that our evil inclinations are in us simply by birth, how could that be just? One of the articles of faith in Mormon religion is this: "We believe that man will be punished for his own sins, and not for Adam's transgression."[4] The historic Christian religion does subscribe to the idea of "original sin," that through the transgression of Adam the entire human race was somehow affected. But behind the particular issue of Adam and Eve is the underlying question of God's role in allowing evil: how could a good God create a world that he will govern that would fall into sin and misery?

3. There is, at the same time, a long tradition up to the present that equates human depravity with the warriorlike nature of our primate ancestors. See, for example, David Livingstone Smith, *The Most Dangerous Animal: Human Nature and the Origins of War* (New York: St. Martin's Griffin, 2009).

4. See "Articles of Faith," The Church of Jesus Christ of Latter-Day Saints (website), http://mormon.org/articles-of-faith, accessed December 31, 2013.

If we state the problem of "theodicy" in the form put by the Enlightenment philosopher David Hume, it is hard to see what difference it would make if Adam and Eve were actual human beings or not. In his famous formulation, Hume thought he could not reconcile two of God's attributes with the existence of evil: "Is He willing to prevent evil, but not able? Then He is impotent. Is He able, but not willing? Then He is malevolent. Is He both able and willing? Whence then is evil?"[5] We do not know exactly what Hume might have thought about the existence of Adam and Eve.[6] But on the surface, it does not appear materially to affect his argument, or, rather, his question about God's power and goodness. But is Hume putting the matter correctly here? The existence of a first couple may be of more relevance than he thought.

We want to raise the question here because we think the role of Adam really does affect the matter of theodicy. If the Bible is right about Adam's role, it affects the issue of theodicy decisively. How does the Bible itself reason about the place of Adam? We want to look at the structure of biblical theology in hopes of answering Hume's dilemma. We will not here be dealing with the important discoveries in paleoanthropology since those have been featured in other chapters in the present volume.

Some think there is no relation of the historicity of our first parents to the theological purposes they serve in the Bible. C. H. Dodd stated many years ago that "Paul's argument of Christ as the 'second Adam' is not so bound up with the story of the fall happening as a literal happening that it ceases to have meaning when we no longer accept the story as such."[7] Some even argue that while Paul believed it, we do not need to do so in order to apply his theological reasoning. Is that the case? Often it is argued that asking whether or not Paul believed in a historical Adam is to ask the wrong question, a sort of Enlightenment or positivist concern with measurable history and facticity, rather than a biblical one.

Yet even to the amateur reader it is clear that the apostle Paul, among others, argues forcefully that sin entered the world through Adam. There is virtually no doubt that Paul believed that such a person had to have existed in order to have introduced sin into history. We cannot address all of the issues here, but it is our purpose to show on at least two grounds why there must be an original couple if we are going to have a sound view of the problem of evil and its resolution.

---

5. David Hume, *Dialogues Concerning Natural Religion* (New York: Oxford University Press, 2009), 198.

6. In Hume's *Enquiry concerning Human Understanding*, he makes several allusions to the belief in Adam but makes no commitments himself to his existence.

7. C. H. Dodd, *The Epistle of Paul to the Romans* (New York: Harper Brothers, 1932), 80.

If we deny the historicity of Adam, how can we explain the introduction of evil into the world in history? Leibniz's attempt to make evil a part of the ideal system that God created is rightly opposed by Voltaire, who, though he did not offer a Christian response—far from it—helped steer us away from *optimism*, which simply did not square with reality. The fall occurred not because of a flaw built into the creation. Because Leibniz did not separate creation from fall, he then was forced to justify evil as properly belonging to the creation. By this he thought to get God off the hook. But if there was a flaw in the creation, then it is hard to see how God would not be to blame for the entrance of sin into the world. The role of Adam becomes crucially important here.

Why the Events in the Garden?

A not unimportant parenthesis can be introduced at this point. Those who might think there was a flaw in the creation because the evil one was present in the garden in the form of a talking serpent should be careful not to confuse the *presence* of a tempter with the *creation* of fallen angelic beings. There is mystery here, but if the creation, the heavens and the earth, are "good and very good," that cannot exclude the invisible world (Gen. 1:31). Whatever may have happened between finished creation and the introduction of the talking serpent into the garden of Eden, we dare not say God was putting a fly in the ointment. Then he could no longer be called the Father of lights who cannot be tempted nor can he tempt (James 1:13, 17). Instead, it is best to say, while God is incapable of creating evil ("neither is he the author of sin"), once evil is introduced into the world, he can use it for his good purposes.[8] One might speculate that there must have been a fall in the angelic world, although we just do not know. The Bible refers to elect angels (1 Tim. 5:21), which presumes there were nonelect angels as well. There are hints of a fall in the angelic world in passages such as 2 Peter 2:4 and Jude 6. However things may have happened, we simply must not suggest that God built a flaw into the creation, whether the visible portion or the invisible portion.

Once evil was in the world, how would God then use it? Here, Reformed theology often refers to the *probation* (test). Adam was created upright but put to a test, one that was meant to lead to consummate bliss and immortality. Had he obeyed, resisting the serpent who suggested it was a good thing to partake of the fruit of the tree of the knowledge of good and evil, he could have led humanity into eternal life. Geerhardus Vos surmises that such a brush

8. Westminster Confession of Faith, 3.1.

with evil without succumbing to evil is the way humanity would have matured. While upright, Adam could not have lived forever without moving forward into a state of confirmed righteousness.[9] As it was, Adam transgressed and led humanity into sin, condemnation, and death. Then God, in his mercy, promised judgment on the serpent's descendants and grace to the people of a new covenant head, Jesus Christ, who would successfully pass a far more difficult probation than the one our first parents faced. The tree of life and healing would now be opened to those who put their trust in the one who obeyed unto death and was rewarded with resurrection and fellowship with the people God gave him (Rev. 22:2; John 17:2; Rom. 8:11; Heb. 2:10–18).

As we close the parenthesis, we must admit we cannot fully know why God allowed evil in the world. It is safe to say (though it does not get us very far) that he did so for his greater glory. The Bible rarely alludes to this question. It does talk about God ordaining some to judgment, but that is always in view of the fall, never of innocent creatures. Romans 9:21 discusses God's right to make some of the clay into vessels for "dishonorable use." Clay in the Bible is not a picture of the original, good creation, but of humankind in its fallenness. While it is a demanding chapter, Romans 9 never suggests that God condemns innocent people.[10] Anyone who desires to confuse God's mysterious foreordination with determinism is on very shaky ground. At any rate, a God who would orchestrate the condemnation of sinful people without regard to their responsibility would be a cruel god, not the just and loving God presented in the Bible. He certainly would not be the same God who went to such an astonishing and costly extent as the sacrifice of his own Son.

An Alternative Reading

We should not be surprised to discover that a number of Christian scholars who have been convinced that the data from Darwinian or neo-Darwinian views are essentially sound have attempted salvaging, or in some cases radically revising, the biblical narrative in order to conform it to the evolutionary

9. Geerhardus Vos, *Biblical Theology: Old and New Testaments* (Grand Rapids: Eerdmans, 1948), 31–32.

10. Again the Westminster Confession of Faith talks about God "withholding mercy" and "passing by some," but never of setting out to visit evil on the innocent (3.7). My own position leans toward what is called "infralapsarianism," although neither it, nor its rival, "supralapsarianism," answer all the questions. Infralapsarianism teaches that in God's eternal decrees, the decision to elect some to grace was made *after* the decree to permit the fall, thus making it an act of mercy in Christ. The supralapsarian position places the decision to elect some *before* the resolution to permit the fall.

approach, all the while trying to defend a good and powerful God in the face of evil. Two of these theodicies are particularly persuasive, though, I believe, ultimately flawed.

One is that of Christopher Southgate. His book, *The Groaning of Creation*, is an attempt at a theodicy in view of the problem of animal suffering.[11] He argues that evolution (for him a given), in order to produce complexity, beauty, and diversity, also needed to produce predation, suffering, and selfish behavior. The evidence for violence in the animal world having existed millions of years before Adam (or the first human creatures) is persuasive for him. It must follow, then, that the standard account of a pre-fallen world followed by a historical fall, which issued in an accursed world, is erroneous (Paul himself got it wrong).[12] God, he asserts, was at work during this beauty-plus-suffering process; indeed, it was the only option available to him in order to arrive at the good features in creation, including freely-choosing conscious creatures.

Further, God's purposes include a final state in which animals will be relieved of their suffering. That liberty is guaranteed by the death and resurrection of Christ, which inaugurates not only the redemption of human beings but of the nonhuman world as well.[13] Southgate interacts with the theory of *kenosis*, according to which God "emptied himself" (Phil. 2:7) in order to empower the creation. He does not quite accept the classical free-will defense as it came down to us through Augustine, Thomas Aquinas, and then the Arminian theologians.[14] Rather, he suggests there is a sort of self-denying love within the Trinity itself, which then explains the extent to which God is willing to sacrifice in order to bring the creation from its present "ambiguity" (cruelty alongside goodness) to its final liberation.[15] In the end Southgate invites the reader actively and energetically to participate in this love and to exercise the kind of care of the creation that promotes less violence and the elimination of unnecessary extinctions.

The appeal of Southgate's theodicy is that it appears to conform the Christian worldview to the data of evolution. However, the price for such a solution is high indeed. Several issues should give pause for anyone believing the Bible to be infallible. First, try as he might, his rereading of the early chapters of Genesis renders the narrative nearly unrecognizable. Quoting Patricia A.

11. Christopher Southgate, *The Groaning of Creation: God, Evolution and the Problem of Evil* (Louisville: Westminster John Knox, 2008).

12. Ibid., 29.

13. Ibid., 76.

14. For a helpful review of this position, see Henri Blocher, *Evil and the Cross* (Downers Grove, IL: InterVarsity, 1994), 36–64.

15. Blocher considers that this view, represented by Hans Urs von Balthasar, downplays divine omnipotence. See ibid., 131n2.

Williams, he tells us that to derive from those chapters a "catastrophe" from which "the Christ-event is our 'rescue'" is unacceptable. Genesis 3:11–19 has little purpose other than to describe a troubled world from the beginning. This view claims that a shift from a pre-fall to a fallen world has no biblical warrant.

However, not only does the text of Genesis itself declare clearly that human death is the consequence of disobedience, and that the ground has become accursed because of that transgression, but numerous other places in Scripture confirm the same view (Gen. 5:29; Hosea 6:7; Rom. 5:12). Actually, the major premise of all of Scripture is that death is an abnormal state connected with human moral guilt and not connected to an evolutionary past (Pss. 6:5; 30:9; 55:15; Prov. 5:5; 7:27; 12:28; Isa. 28:15; Jer. 21:8; 1 Cor. 15:43; Rev. 21:8). Southgate has no problem calling suffering and death abnormal, but he does not associate them altogether with human choice, let alone the disobedience of our first parents.

A second difficulty is with the manner in which Southgate puts God into relationship with the creation. To begin with, he believes God is somehow involved in guiding the world through a Darwinian process and that he will somehow bring it all to a happy end. He seeks to affirm both God's involvement in the development of life on earth and also the relative autonomy of that life. He is "both the origin of all things and the universe's ultimate hope," but yet the creation itself has a Darwinian mind of its own.[16] God's work of creation is trinitarian, with each person of the Godhead having a role. The Logos tends to inform the world, giving it certain patterns to follow. Somehow, the work of the Spirit in creation means a guaranty for both the particularity and the self-transcendence of the creature. This means the creature will "explore" new possibilities in the attempt to be fit and survive. We have a kind of "survival" of those who best "fit" the divine pattern.[17]

I find elements of this attractive, but on the whole it is highly speculative. It is more reminiscent of Leibniz's theodicy, wherein evil is a necessary underside of the good.[18] Southgate offers little scriptural support for his arguments. Beside some fleeting references to the psalms, there is almost no significant biblical theology involved. Yet the Bible tells us a great deal about how God brought the world about, although not in ways that answer many of our modern scientific questions. Still, there is a good deal about the Lord's ways with the creation. The Bible teaches uniformly that God is utterly sovereign

---

16. Southgate, *Groaning of Creation*, 22.

17. Ibid., 62.

18. See Gottfried W. Leibniz, *Theodicy*, ed. Austin Farrer, trans. E. M. Huggard (New Haven: Yale University Press, 1952). This is the very philosophy, known as "optimism," that Voltaire was attacking in his *Candide*.

and that his council from all eternity determines everything that comes to pass (Isa. 40:12–28; Acts 17:24–26; Col. 1:17). Genesis 1 tells us he spoke the different parts of the world into existence. After finishing with the heavens and earth and their hosts, we are told that God rested from all the work that he had done. Psalm 104 tells us how he created and continues to interact with the creation. Albeit with poetic language, it tells us that he makes each part of the creation one of his servants. He "rebuked" the waters so that the dry land could appear (v. 7). He appointed the places where mountains and valleys were formed (vv. 8–9). He abundantly provided for the fauna (vv. 10–18). None of this is mentioned in Southgate's book. Perhaps Southgate would call Psalm 104 poetic and therefore not factual—a dichotomy the biblical writers would not have accepted.

What Southgate offers us instead is the idea that God's involvement with creation is seen through the lens of *kenosis*. According to this view, God gave up some of his power in order to supply the creation with significance. The Scripture text most often used to justify the theory is Philippians 2:6–7, which states, among other things, that Christ "emptied himself" (*ekenosen*, from which we derive *kenosis*) in order to become incarnate and thus die and be raised for our salvation. Yet kenotic theory is in serious dissonance with the historic Christian position on the incarnation. Orthodox Chalcedonian Christology states that Christ is one person with two natures, divine and human, joined together in hypostatic union, yet without confusion, change, division, or separation.[19] If we follow Chalcedon, the Second Person of the Trinity could remain God yet become fully human, subject to every aspect of our condition (yet without sin) only if he *adds* humanity to himself, not by subtracting any divinity. Thus, when Paul tells the Philippians that Christ "did not count equality with God a thing to be grasped," he is not suggesting that the Second Person left off being divine. God who is less than God is simply not God. Rather, Paul is telling the reader that the Second Person did not "regard the advantage of his deity as grounds to avoid the incarnation."[20] The word *ekenosen* has the sense of self-renunciation.[21]

Southgate's case is not advanced if God becomes less than God. If God "gives up" any of his ontological qualities, such as his omnipotence, he cannot properly be identified as God, nor can he guide the creation process providentially. How do we know the creation, in its Darwinian character, could not become self-determining? For that matter, how could we be sure the "evil"

19. Philip Schaff, *Creeds of Christendom*, 6th ed., vol. 2, 62–63.
20. Moisés Silva, *Philippians*, 2nd ed. (Grand Rapids: Baker Academic, 2005), 99.
21. See Roy W. Hoover, "The Harpagmos Enigma: A Philological Solution," *Harvard Theological Review* 64 (October 1971): 95–119.

aspects of creation could not somehow triumph over the "good" ones? If God is not fully sovereign, there is no such guaranty. The answer to this dilemma is not to tone down God's power but to tone it up! God is so powerful that he can create a world with extraordinary significance. The human choice to become disobedient is real, not manipulated by God. Not only the responsibility for wrong decisions is on humanity, but the decisions themselves are self-directed. Of course, we are dealing with one of the central mysteries of the Christian faith. How can God be God and yet the world have such real meaning? We do not know, but it does not help to downplay God's utter sovereignty.

Southgate's solution ultimately cannot find a way for God to remain good as well as powerful. By accommodating the violence of creation gone wrong, God somehow must lower his own standards. And thus, when he declares, "None righteous, no, not one" (Rom. 3:10), he has to be a part of the problem since he helped generate a world of sin and evil. Again, the way out is not to downplay his goodness in the face of evil but to defend it. A God less than fully good is no god at all, a position that Southgate would never suggest; however, the implications of his arguments lead in that direction. Of course, goodness will have to be defined in such a way as being able, at least for a time, to coexist with a world gone wrong. Again, there is mystery here. But it is imperative that we argue for God's ability to act into the world (to condescend, as theologians sometimes put it) without giving up any of the fullness of his attributes.

A problem with Southgate's approach is that it does not explain with any kind of satisfaction how it is that at the end of the creation week (however long it might have been) God declared what he had made to be good or "very good" (Gen. 1:31). The Hebrew word *tov*, which is used twelve times in the first two chapters of Genesis, has a rich complex of meanings: ethically good, beautiful, appropriate, pleasant, beneficial. Southgate rather cheerily dismisses any claims to a pre-fallen world in which there was no evil. His proof? Animal violence. He compares the "peaceable kingdom" imagery of a paradise in which all the animals get along and death is a foreign concept to the very unpeaceable world in both the fossil evidence and the present natural world. But are we sure that the *tov* world of the finished creation can tolerate no violence or no death whatsoever? The question is legitimate, especially when we are promised that in the resurrection the wolf will dwell with the lamb and the small child will play with the adder's den (Isa. 11:6–8).

Many of us who are evangelicals have no difficulty believing that the process of creation could have involved taming the pre-fallen world of its chaotic elements, which include primordial waters, darkness, the abyss, raging oceans, and the like. The Lord thus "stilled the sea; by his understanding he shattered

Rahab. By his wind the heavens were made fair" (Job 26:12–13). He "broke the heads of the sea monsters on the waters" and claimed both the day and the night (Ps. 74:13–16). God's rebuke of Job in the final chapters of the book that bears his name is a recitation of the many ways God wrestled down the untamed creation (Job 38–41). In such an atmosphere, the death of animals is not the great challenge to theodicy that Southgate avers. Certainly, before the fall of humankind, there is every reason to believe that death and violence in the animal world could have been a part of the natural order.

How much of this untamed world was domesticated by the time of the end of the sixth day of creation? We do not rightly know. But apparently the idea of *tov* does not have to carry with it the total absence of death. Certainly the death of human beings is precluded. Human death is the consequence of transgression, as Genesis 2:17 clearly states. And how much did the world change because of the fall of humankind? Again, we do not know altogether. A curse was put on the ground that had not been there before (Gen. 3:17). Relations with animals became very problematic (Gen. 9:2). But we do not know altogether what stayed constant and simply *became* a problem and what actually changed because God subjected it to futility (Rom. 8:20). Parallels between animal death and human death are of limited validity. To be sure, many Christians will disagree with that conclusion, but in my judgment there is no sound biblical reason to think that every kind of death is a manifestation of the problem of evil. The death of an animal, particularly by a violent predator, may disturb our modern sensibilities. Southgate turns it into evidence for God's working with a less-than-perfect world in order finally one day to release it from its bondage. But the Bible does not consider all acts of animal predators to be evil. Often they are simply examples of the way creation reflects the power of God (see Job 4:11; 9:26; 28:7, 17; 38:39–41; Ps. 104:21; Isa. 5:29; 46:11; etc.). Thus, Southgate's re-reading of the Scripture without the transition from a pre-fallen to a fallen world in order to defend Darwin is rather an unnecessary effort. It resembles Hegel's idea, developed by Paul Tillich, that the fall was "upward."[22]

A Second Alternative Approach

A second attempt at theodicy in the context of an ancient earth is even more imaginative. William Dembski has set forth a way to deal with what he believes is evil before the fall. Similar to Southgate, he accepts an older date for the beginning of the world. Unlike Southgate, however, Dembski is less committed

---

22. Paul Tillich, *Systematic Theology*, vol. 1 (Chicago: University of Chicago Press, 1951), 255.

to Darwinian evolution. He believes in *intelligent design* but not necessarily through a Darwinian evolutionary process. His book, *The End of Christianity*, explains how he deals with the problem of theodicy.[23]

His basic argument is as follows.[24] Evil did enter the world through the personal choice of the first true human beings, the first bearers of the divine image. Similarly, the cross of Christ in history is the answer to the problem of evil. It is also the ultimate demonstration of the goodness (or benevolence, as he prefers) of God in creation. Though God allows natural evil, things like earthquakes and volcanoes as well as animal death result from his curse in response to the fall of humankind. Although we do not know all of the reasons God could allow natural evil in relation to human sin, the basic one, he maintains, is "to get our attention."[25] That is, the presence of evil in the world underscores the gravity of sin, so that we will be all the more aware of the cost of Christ's work for our salvation.

The problem is that the earth and its evils existed millions of years before Adam and Eve. How can our first parents be a cause, in any meaningful sense, of the evils in a world that they did not inhabit? How could the fall affect not only the future but also the past? Dembski's answer comes by being able to distinguish between two concepts of time: *kairos* as opposed to *chronos*. The first is something like "purposeful time," whereas the latter is chronological time. While *chronos* is operative in the visible world, the world of observable history, *kairos* is at work in the invisible world where God orders reality for his own purposes.[26] God, being above time, acts, as it were, by anticipation of events not yet occurring in human history. To put it simply, God can cause the effects of the fall before the fall actually occurs. In Dembski's scheme, then, causality is an "infinite dialectic" whereby God anticipates novel events by divine action in the realm of *kairos*, which is not time bound, and interacts with human agency, which is not predetermined but free. Accordingly, Genesis 1 does not record chronological time but purposeful, or *kairological*, time.[27]

This way, God remains good and powerful, even though human beings have freely chosen to go astray. And he remains good, despite the existence of evil early on in the creation. Indeed, Dembski argues that we live in a "double creation," whereby all things are created in two steps. First, there is the concept,

---

23. William A. Dembski, *The End of Christianity: Finding a Good God in an Evil World* (Nashville: B&H Academic; Milton Keynes, UK: Paternoster, 2009).

24. Some of the following material I have already published in a review of the book that appeared in *Themelios* 35.1 (April 2010): 137–41. It has been amplified and reworked in the present volume.

25. Dembski, *End of Christianity*, 45.

26. Ibid., 125.

27. Ibid., 140.

and then the realization. Using the analogy of the playwright and the actors, God has a general plan, but then the actors must perform with their gifts and choices. Unfortunately in this theater the actors performed badly. Still, there can be a happy end because God can still "rewrite history" in order to save us. "God can rewrite our story while it is being performed and even change the entire backdrop against which it is performed—that includes past, present and future." Not only can he thus make the effects of the fall retroactive, but he can (indeed, he must) act to undo the damage. And he manages to do this without violating the freedom of the actors.[28]

The argument is intriguing. And the book is quite brilliant, full of learned references to both science and literature, to theology as well as history and mathematics. It is an unusual and creative apologetic. Yet it is deeply flawed, in my judgment.

Despite the colorful use of a dialectical causality, God emerges as far less than sovereign. Dembski's argument is similar to the classical Arminian version of the "free-will" defense, mentioned above. Put succinctly, God creates humankind upright but with freedom to choose the wrong as well as the right. God, as it were, took a risk, and sadly things did not go well. Still, he is not responsible for evil, and he is also free to intervene with a solution. To obtain true human freedom God had to give up some of his own power, or, as Dembski puts it, God's power must be "tempered" with wisdom, or it would "rip the fabric of creation."[29] The argument is similar to Southgate's kenotic understanding but more philosophically based.

Salvation is a gift of God through Jesus Christ. Dembski goes on to argue that just as Adam's action could be applied to the past, so, through the incarnation, Christ lives on both sides of the time abyss, kairological and chronological. That is what allows his work of redemption to be applied forward as well as backward. He can take on the sins of the whole world because his passion, though short in chronological time, was a "window" into a deeper reality of divine suffering. That way, all of human suffering is somehow funneled into the "mere six hours" of Jesus's hanging on the cross.[30]

However, is chronological time so unreal that it can be manipulated by kairological gestures? The Bible presents history as real and moving in one direction. This is the case not despite but because of God's sovereignty. As we argued above, while God is utterly sovereign and ordains all things, yet he has endowed the creation with significance and responsibility. These are not

28. Ibid., 110–11.
29. Ibid., 140.
30. Ibid., 21.

contradicted by his sovereignty but upheld by it. Furthermore, while God ordains everything that comes to pass, even the darker aspects of history, yet he is not responsible (or accountable) for evil. There is great mystery here. But if we attempt to weaken either side—God's power or human responsibility—we lose both. The Westminster Confession of Faith puts the relationship this way: "God from all eternity did, by the most wise and holy counsel of his own will, freely and unchangeably ordain whatsoever comes to pass: yet so, as thereby neither is God the author of sin, nor is violence offered to the will of the creatures, nor is the liberty or contingency of second causes taken away, but rather established."[31]

It seems to me that Dembski tries to retain the power of God at the expense of the significance of history. But does he even salvage God's power? Certainly God can and does change human history. But he does so by respecting its contours, not by reversing its direction. To do that he never has to give up his power, as the free-will defense suggests. He can maintain a real relationship to the creation, not because he exists in some sort of kairological time but because of his divine condescension (as the theologians put it). Thus, while God does not (and cannot) change *ontologically*, nor does he modify his eternal decrees, yet he does change with respect to his covenant relationship with his creation. So, when the Bible tells us that in view of the people's repentance, God relented of the disaster he had planned to send on Ninevah, we can say he really did relent. Certainly, all of that was planned from eternity, but that does not remove the reality of the event or of the people's decision. He does not pretend to change his mind, anymore than he pretends to answer our prayers. Again, we are dealing with a mystery here, but it is equally dangerous to try and downplay either the sovereignty of God or the reality of history.

In the end Dembski's suggestion that God acts backward in time detracts from the significance of creation. It makes the world malleable, with no established second causes. At times this picture resembles gnosticism more than historic Christianity. Bolstering the argument, as he does, by saying God is above time does not help. Although God is indeed eternal, he has *decided* to honor his creation by entering into time for its sake. He will not violate earthly sequential history simply to apply judgments or blessings anachronistically. And using, as he does, the case of Israel being saved before the historical event of the atonement is not convincing either. Again, classical theology recognizes the people of the Old Testament were favored by God in anticipation of the atonement, but yet their salvation was not actualized until the cross and the

31. Westminster Confession of Faith, 3.1.

resurrection. And it will not be fully realized, for them or for us, until the resurrection.

As to Dembski's need to explain the presence of evil before the fall, the same answer used in the case of Southgate's proposal is applicable here. While we might love the idea of a "peaceable kingdom" without conflict or tension, that is not a necessary implication from the biblical data. Neither plant death nor animal death carry the same moral freight as human death. There is no inherent incompatibility between animal predators or erupting volcanoes and a creation declared to be "very good" (Gen. 1:31).

Conclusion

Putting into question the historical covenant head, Adam, while on the surface seeming to harmonize with various data from paleoanthropology, leads to very serious obstacles in front of believing in a good and all-powerful God.[32] For those who accept the Bible as the very Word of God, the exegetical basis for the historicity of Adam is sufficient to establish the view that our first parents were created specially and that they and their progeny share the image of God, even as they now share the sin of Adam. Without such a conviction it is difficult to see how God would not be liable for the introduction of evil into the world.

Much as we may be drawn to David Hume's way of formulating the problem of evil, how God could be both good and powerful if there is evil, we need to acknowledge that his assumed definitions of goodness and power are rather narrow. There is no intrinsic reason why divine goodness could not allow evil to appear in the world, as long as it will one day be eradicated. Nor is there a reason why the divine power of a good God could not allow evil to appear in the world, as long as he is not the accountable cause for it. Believing that Adam is the first man, and that his relation to the rest of humanity is one of covenant headship, while perhaps not answering all questions about God's relation to evil, nevertheless is a far better option than attempting to answer Hume on his own terms.

And it is a far better option than that of Leibniz, who thought evil to be a necessary component of the best of all possible worlds. Voltaire was right to mock such a view. However, mockery is not a complete answer. At the very end of *Candide*, there was nothing better to say than, "we must each cultivate

---

32. It has not been our purpose to evaluate the various approaches to the origins of human-kind from a scientific point of view, something this author lacks the competence to do. There are a number of defenders of the historical identity of the first man who can harmonize that view with the known scientific data, whether from paleontology or genetics.

our garden."[33] Instead, a robust understanding of a God who is truly good, in the full biblical sense, and truly omnipotent, while it does not answer all the questions, yet sets the atmosphere within which a nonskeptical answer can be given. And believing in a historical Adam is a crucial piece for such a theodicy.

33. Voltaire, *Candide*, 75.

Postscript

Michael Reeves and Hans Madueme

In this collection of essays we have sought to demonstrate that a historical Adam and original sin are essential, irremovable, relevant, and credible elements of the Christian faith. Eschewing narrow partisanship, we the editors deliberately assembled an array of respected scholars from different traditions and standpoints to articulate in harmony our common agreement that the traditional doctrine of Adam's fall and original sin is the most theologically mature and cogent option in today's debate. It is not that those who have contributed have always believed this and find it just too challenging to consider any alternative; nor is it that we are simply theologically trigger-happy and spoil for a fight with anything that looks novel. Rather, it is that we find the Old and New Testaments do not finally support a mythological or purely figurative reading of Adam and Eve. Nor does the scientific evidence, such as it is, demand it. Biblical theology has a coherent story and systematic theology a coherent framework only with a historical Adam. We should not think that the latest scientific consensus on these matters gives us an opportunity for creative doctrinal tinkering and readjustment; the threads of Adam and original sin run throughout the cloth of the faith: remove them and the cloth must be wholly reconstructed.

Historically, this has long been recognized, and so belief in a historical Adam and original sin has long been championed as theologically and pastorally vital. That is exactly why we devoted an entire section of the book to historical theology—not because we are exclusively governed by tradition (though it should at the very least concern us—beware theological mavericks!—if we find ourselves going against the ecumenical consensus of the church through the ages) but because of how these doctrines have been tested and proven down through the centuries. In other words, we have not simply been appealing to tradition as the authority that will settle the matter; we have wanted to hear the wisdom of the church, both past and present, as it impinges on this modern debate. Historical theology gives us a wealth of insightful resources and the opportunity to approach the key questions along multiple parallels, shedding more light on what is at stake.

Of course, we do not imagine for a moment that this extended argument will persuade everyone. Where one stands in this dispute depends in large part on theological prolegomena and what is accorded supreme epistemological authority. But into a situation where traditionally core doctrines have often quite breezily been jettisoned, forgotten, or transmogrified, we hope this argument will at least sound a strong note of caution. It is not just the doctrine of original sin, with all its explanatory power, that is affected by the Adam question. The kindness, goodness, and generosity of God; the coherence of the Scriptures; glad tidings for those who are helplessly enslaved to sin; the salvation of the incarnate Christ: none of these precious and beautiful truths, on which the vitality of the church is built, can remain unscathed by the mythologizing of Adam.

Contributor Biographies

C. John Collins (PhD, University of Liverpool) is professor of Old Testament at Covenant Theological Seminary in St. Louis, Missouri. Chair of the Old Testament translation committee for the English Standard Version of the Bible, he is the author of *Genesis 1–4: A Linguistic, Literary, and Theological Commentary*; *The God of Miracles: An Exegetical Examination of God's Action in the World*; *Science and Faith: Friends or Foes?*; and *Did Adam and Eve Really Exist? Who They Were and Why You Should Care.*

Daniel Doriani (PhD, Westminster Theological Seminary) is professor of theology and vice president of strategic academic projects at Covenant Theological Seminary in St. Louis, Missouri, where he has also been dean of faculty. He also served ten years as senior pastor of Central Presbyterian Church in St. Louis, Missouri. He is the author of several books, including *Putting the Truth to Work* and commentaries on Matthew and James.

William Edgar (D. Théol., University of Geneva) is professor of apologetics at Westminster Theological Seminary in Philadelphia. Previously he was professeur d'apologétique at the Faculté Jean Calvin in Aix-en-Provence, France. He has written a number of books, including *The Face of Truth*, *Reasons of the Heart*, *You Asked?*, and *Francis Schaeffer on the Christian Life.*

James M. Hamilton (PhD, Southern Baptist Theological Seminary) is associate professor of biblical theology at Southern Baptist Theological Seminary and preaching pastor at Kenwood Baptist Church in Louisville, Kentucky. His books include *God's Glory in Salvation through Judgment: A Biblical Theology*, *The Bible's Big Story: Salvation History for Kids*, and *What Is Biblical Theology?*

Robert Kolb (PhD, University of Wisconsin) is missions professor of systematic theology at Concordia Seminary in St. Louis, Missouri (now emeritus). Previously he was professor of religion and history at Concordia College in St. Paul, Minnesota. He is the author of several books, including *Luther and the Stories of God*, *The Genius of Luther's Theology* (with Charles Arand), and *The Book of Concord* (co-edited with Timothy Wengert).

Donald Macleod (DD, Westminster Theological Seminary) recently retired as professor of systematic theology at the Free Church of Scotland College, Edinburgh, 1978–2012. He graduated with his MA from the University of Glasgow in 1958 and was awarded an honorary DD from Westminster Theological Seminary, Philadelphia, in 2008. He has written numerous articles and books, including *A Faith to Live By* and *The Person of Christ*.

Hans Madueme (PhD, Trinity Evangelical Divinity School) is assistant professor of theological studies at Covenant College in Lookout Mountain, Georgia. He is the author of several articles, and his dissertation explored recent attempts to revise the doctrine of sin in light of modern science.

Thomas H. McCall (PhD, Calvin Theological Seminary) is associate professor of biblical and systematic theology and director of the Carl F. H. Henry Center for Theological Understanding at Trinity Evangelical Divinity School in Deerfield, Illinois. He is the author, co-author, or co-editor of several books in systematic and historical theology, including *Which Trinity? Whose Monotheism? Systematic and Philosophical Theologians on the Metaphysics of Trinitarian Theology* and *Jacob Arminius: Theologian of Grace*.

Michael Reeves (PhD, King's College, University of London) is Director of Union and Senior Lecturer at Wales Evangelical School of Theology. He is the author of several books, including *Delighting in the Trinity: An Introduction to the Christian Faith* and *The Unquenchable Flame: Discovering the Heart of the Reformation*.

Peter Sanlon (PhD, University of Cambridge) is vicar of St. Mark's Church, Royal Tunbridge Wells. Prior to ordination he was a speechwriter for a member of the House of Lords. He is distance tutor in systematic theology for St. John's College, Nottingham. His research on Augustine's preaching will be published by Fortress Press.

Thomas R. Schreiner (PhD, Fuller Theological Seminary) is the James Buchanan Harrison Professor of New Testament Interpretation at Southern

Baptist Theological Seminary in Louisville, Kentucky. He has also taught New Testament at Azusa Pacific University and Bethel Theological Seminary. He has written numerous commentaries, a theology of the apostle Paul, a New Testament theology, and a theology of the entire Bible.

Carl R. Trueman (PhD, University of Aberdeen) is Paul Woolley Professor of Church History at Westminster Theological Seminary. He previously served on faculty at the Universities of Nottingham and Aberdeen. He is the author of numerous books on the history of Reformed theology and is currently working on a Reformed-Lutheran dialogue volume with Luther scholar Robert Kolb.

Noel Weeks (PhD, Brandeis University) is an honorary senior lecturer in the department of classics and ancient history at the University of Sydney, having taught ancient Near Eastern history and Akkadian at that university. His primary interests are Old Testament historiography and comparative studies of ancient Near Eastern cultures. He is the author of books on ancient Near Eastern treaties and biblical narrative.

Robert W. Yarbrough (PhD, University of Aberdeen) is professor of New Testament at Covenant Theological Seminary in St. Louis, Missouri. He taught previously at Trinity Evangelical Divinity School, Wheaton College, and Liberty University. He has been involved in theological education and pastoral training in Eastern Europe and Africa. Among his numerous publications are *1–3 John* and *The Salvation-Historical Fallacy?*

Scripture Index

Subject Index

Abel, 192–93
Abraham, 6–7, 16–17, 24
Abrahamic covenant, 131–32
Adam
  historical consequences of, 21–22, 105–6, 151–52, 178–79
  historicity and the fossil record, 54–81
  and imputation of sin, 139–44, 155, 183–84, 276
  in the New Testament, 33–52
  primal disobedience of, 4, 26–27, 146, 192–93
  as representative human, 14–18, 25, 137–39
  in Second Temple Jewish literature, 27–31
addiction, 256
adoption, 45
Albo, Joseph, 37
Ambrose, 87
Ames, William, 131, 134, 136, 139
ancient Near Eastern myths, 7–9
Anderson, G., 37–38
Apocrypha, 28
apologetics, xi
Ashley, J. Matthew, 4n5
Atrahasis Epic, 8
Auerbach, Erich, 208
Augsburg Confession, 118
Augustine, 38, 85–107, 220–21
australopithecines, 59–60, 67–69, 76–77

Babylonian Epic of Creation, 8
Baier, Johann Wilhelm, 125
Barbour, Ian, 230, 237–38
Barr, James, 3–4, 11–12, 15, 19n50, 27n73, 294–95, 300
Barth, Karl, 176–79, 221
Bass, Derek, 202
Bavinck, Herman, 95, 228

Beale, Gregory, 24
Bechtel, Lyn, 23n61
Belgic Confession, 251
Bellarmine, Robert, 124
Ben Sira, 29–30
biblical inerrancy, 241
BioLogos, viii
bipedalism, 60n26, 65, 68–69
Blocher, Henri, 237, 240, 275–86, 299n37
Book of the Heavenly Cow, 289–90
"Boston Personalists," 163
Braaten, Carl, 242
brain size, 69–70, 74–75
Brooke, John Hedley, 227–28, 240
Brunner, Emil, vii
Bryant, Barry, 151
Bultmann, Rudolf, 179–80
Bunta, S., 36–37

Caelestius, 86–87
Cain, 10, 192–93
Callender, D., 38
Calvin, John, 130–31, 135, 142
Calvinism, 156–57, 159
Cassuto, Umberto, 16
Chemnitz, Martin, 121–22, 242
Chiles, Robert, 147–48
church tradition, xi
Collins, Francis, vii–viii
concordism, 239–40
concupiscence, 103–4
consubstantiation, 111
conversion, 112
Couenhoven, Jesse, 247
Council of Carthage, 91
Council of Trent, 118, 122
covenant of works, 131–36